# A
# PERSPECTIVE OF
# WAGES AND PRICES

# A
# PERSPECTIVE OF
# WAGES AND PRICES

*

Henry Phelps Brown

*and*

Sheila V. Hopkins

Methuen: London and New York

1981

First published in 1981 by
Methuen & Co. Ltd
11 New Fetter Lane, London EC4P 4EE
Published in the USA by
Methuen & Co.
in association with Methuen, Inc.
733 Third Avenue, New York, NY 10017

Printed in Great Britain at the
University Press, Cambridge

*British Library Cataloguing in Publication Data*
Phelps Brown, Henry
A Perspective of Wages and Prices.
1. Europe—Economic conditions—History
I. Title      II. Hopkins, Sheila V.
339.5094      HC240

ISBN 0-416-31950-5

# Contents

22237677

# Acknowledgements

The authors and publishers of this volume gratefully acknowledge their indebtedness for the consent to the reproduction of these papers that has been kindly given by the editors and publishers of the journals in which the papers originally appeared and by Her Majesty's Stationery Office. The original publications were as follows:

ch. 1    Seven Centuries of Building Wages. *Economica*, 22, 87, August 1955.

ch. 2    Seven Centuries of the Prices of Consumables, compared with Builders' Wage-rates. *Economica*, 23, 92, November 1956.

ch. 3    Wage-rates and Prices: Evidence for Population Pressure in the Sixteenth Century. *Economica*, 24, 97, November 1957.

ch. 4    Builders' Wage-rates, Prices and Population: Some Further Evidence. *Economica*, 26, 101, February 1959.

ch. 5    Seven Centuries of Wages and Prices: Some Earlier Estimates. *Economica*, 28, 109, February 1961.

ch. 6    The Share of Wages in National Income. *Economic Journal*, 62, 246, June 1952.

ch. 7    The Climacteric of the 1890's: A Study in the Expanding Economy. *Oxford Economic Papers (NS)* IV, 3, October 1952.

ch. 8    Economic Growth and the Price Level. *Economic Journal*, 65, 257, March 1955.

ch. 9    The Economic Consequences of Collective Bargaining. Minutes of Evidence before the Royal Commission on Trade Unions and Employers' Associations, 38, 24 May 1966.

# List of figures

## List of figures

# List of tables

Page

# Introduction

One day early in the 1950s I was looking through a copy of the *Economic History of England: a study in social development* by H.O. Meredith, Professor of Economic History in The Queen's University of Belfast,[1] among the accessions to the Library of the London School of Economics. In a pull-out at the back were two graphs. One struck me by the great span of years over which it displayed the course of wage-rates: it showed the daily wages of a carpenter and an agricultural labourer in England, by decennial averages from the 1270s to the 1880s. The other was even more remarkable, for it showed the equivalent of each wage-rate over the same span in terms of the amount of wheat that it would buy at the prices of the day and, as Meredith remarked, a glance at it showed that the real wages so measured 'were greater for both skilled and unskilled labour between 1440 and 1490 than at any subsequent period until the last half century'. This challenged investigation.

But first, honour where honour is due. Meredith acknowledged his indebtedness to the Swedish scholar Gustaf Fredrik Steffen, from whose work he had reproduced those graphs. Steffen had displayed them originally in lectures he gave in the summer of 1892 in University Hall (the University Extension Settlement) in London, under the Presidency of P.H. Wicksteed. He published them in his *Studies of the History of the Wage System in England* (in Swedish) in 1895–9.[2] A German translation, on which Meredith drew, appeared in 1901–5.[3] But before Steffen, and above all, honour is due to Thorold Rogers,[4] on whose work Steffen drew. It was Thorold Rogers's laborious researches, many of them in the accounts in the muniment rooms of the Oxford colleges, that brought together the main series of wages and prices down to 1600. For a long time the tradition persisted that these

---

[1] This work, first published in 1908, went through six editions, the last in 1958.

[2] *Studier öfver lönsystemets historia i England* (Lorénska Stiftelse Skrifter, Nos 11 & 16, Stockholm, 1895–9, 3 vols).

[3] *Studien zur Geschichte der englischen Lohnarbeiter, mit besonderer Berücksichtigung der Veränderungen ihrer Lebenshaltungen* (Stuttgart, 1901–1905, 3 vols).

[4] J.E. Thorold Rogers, 1823–90. MA Oxon. 1849, and curate of St. Paul's, Oxford. Left the Church and became first Tooke Professor of Statistics and Economic Science at King's College London, 1859–90. Meanwhile he held the Drummond Chair of Political Economy in Oxford, 1862–7, and was a Member of Parliament 1880–6. He was re-elected to the Drummond Chair in 1888. His great work, the *History of Agriculture and Prices*, was published in six volumes 1866–87.

findings were to be disregarded as unreliable. The disparagement may have owed something to disapproval of Thorold Rogers himself—a curate who had left the Church and thrown himself into radical politics: from his statistics, moreover, he had drawn inferences painful to the authorities in Church and State. But perhaps also his critics genuinely failed to distinguish between dispersion and confusion: lacking the training of a later generation in statistical methods, they did not see how central tendencies could be derived from distributions, or scattered data be tested for consistency. Today we pay our tribute to a great pioneer.

In his original work Steffen did not confine himself to units of wheat. He also had a diagram showing what percentage of the daily wage of the carpenter and of the agricultural labourer was required from time to time to buy 6lb 14oz of wheat, 1lb 8oz of meat and the two together, these being taken as the daily requirement for the average family. This was a first step towards forming an index number of the cost of living based upon a pattern of outlay. The papers reprinted in this volume go further in that direction, by drawing on some evidence available at certain points down the centuries to specify a 'basket of consumables' that would be representative, in contents and proportions, of the pattern of wage-earners' outlay from time to time. The task was then to find series of prices for the commodities comprised.

This was a formidable inquiry. It came in any case only after a prior task had been completed, that of taking out the predominant or representative wage-rate from the range of Thorold Rogers's quotations year by year, and continuing the series from other sources when his quotations petered out in the seventeenth century. Both tasks were undertaken with zest, and performed with equal skill and success, by Sheila Hopkins (Mrs L.S. Pressnell). The range of the materials she drew upon for prices is shown by the close-packed detail of Appendix A of the second paper (see pp. 23-7), though this does not include all those materials included in her reconnaissance but later discarded as unhelpful. One entry set deep in that Appendix runs: '(15) *Potatoes 1832–45*: 1832–36, middlings and middling whites from Borough and Spitalfields markets; 1837–45 Yorkshire Reds... at Southwark Waterside. Averages of weekly quotations for October in each year, given in *The Christian Advocate* and *Mark Lane Express*.' The entry still stirs lively memories of the outstanding obstinacy of a gap in the price series at that time, and the triumph of filling it at last from a Wesleyan journal which served commerce if not Mammon as well as God.

The resultant studies of wages and prices have continued to attract an attention that has seemed to justify bringing them together for republication, and making available the separate components of the price index, hitherto unpublished. The interest that the indexes have aroused lies partly in the very long period over which the change in the purchasing power of money is traced. This continuity is an asset which maintains their value despite the availability of studies providing further accounts of particular periods. Outstanding among these periods is the Great Inflation of the sixteenth century. The salience of inflation among contemporary problems has stimulated retrospect to past periods of rapid change in the purchasing power of money and to the periods of comparative stability, as also to the implied course of change and stability in the purchasing power of gold: hence a sustained interest, and in the United States a fresh interest, in the long perspective that these studies afford. Their evidence for the movement of 'the equivalent of the wage-rate expressed in a composite physical unit of consumables' has likewise been subject to amplification by later studies. This has been so particularly in the debate concerning standards of living in the Industrial Revolution: the series presented here, not without change as time goes on but always with an eye to continuity, do much less than justice to the data available from the late eighteenth century onwards, but have their place in that debate.

However, much of the interest of the estimates of the real purchasing power of wage-rates lies in the inferences drawn from price history about the causes of changes in it. The argument will be found in the third and fourth chapters (see pp. 60 and 78). It is that, in an economy where agricultural methods are changing little and do not allow for the absorption of additional manpower on the land, so as to increase the output of food proportionally, an increase in the labour force must be employed mainly in manufactures, so that the output of these rises and their prices are depressed relative to the output and prices of foodstuffs. The essence is a shift in relative prices—those of foodstuffs rising relatively to cloth, nails, timber and bricks when the population is growing, and falling relatively when plague or devastation brings the population down. Whether there is an upward or downward movement in the general level of prices, taking foodstuffs and manufactures together, will depend on other factors and not directly on population pressure.

The five papers on 'wages down the ages' that I published jointly with Sheila Hopkins (Mrs L.S. Pressnell) are only part of the work I was enabled to do during my tenure of the Chair of the Economics of Labour at the London School of Economics, with funds provided by the School, and the collaboration of assistants whose great ability has been shown by their later careers. Of those who worked with me to produce the three other papers reproduced here from the journals, Peter Hart is now Professor of Economics in the University of Reading, Stephen Handfield-Jones is Assistant Deputy Minister in the Department of Finance in Ottawa, and Andrew Ozga, who died in 1978, became Reader in Economics in the London School of Economics.

The paper written with Peter Hart, on 'The Share of Wages in National Income', has been much cited. It deals with the problem of distribution in the form in which that problem was commonly presented, and helps to show that this presentation was misleading. Under the guidance of marginal productivity analysis, economists thought of the national product as being distributed between the factors of production, and they naturally asked of the statisticians what were the actual shares of land, labour and capital, and how they had changed. When, moreover, it was found that, after all the upheavals during and after the First World War, the share of wages was virtually the same as it had been in the pre-war economy, observers wondered if they had not come upon a natural law. The purpose of this paper was to examine that conjecture. It brought out the elementary but basic point, which it drove home by its diagrams, that the share of income accruing to any group depends not only on their relative pay but also on their relative numbers. During this period the relative number of wage-earners had changed substantially. Stability in the share of wage-earners alone could arise from offsetting movements of pay and numbers; but if we took the share of earned incomes as a whole, there was no evidence of inherent stability. In these ways the paper applied to the study of distribution the fuller statistics of national income which became available from the Second World War onwards. In so doing it removed some misapprehensions and cleared the way for later work.

One intriguing feature of curves of the commodity equivalent of the wage-rate prompted an inquiry that was carried out with Stephen Handfield-Jones and is reported in the paper, 'The Climacteric of the 1890's: A Study in the Expanding Economy'. The rise in the commodity equivalent that persisted through the Great Victorian Depression was cut off quite sharply in the 1890s, and from then down to 1914 there was on balance no rise at all. This break in the trend we called 'the climacteric', and the term went into currency in the discussion that the paper initiated. This ranged ever more widely, tracing the decline in real wages to a decline in productivity whose beginnings could be discerned already in the 1870s, and examining the changing position of the British economy in the international market. The paper thus has its place in the literature of economic history; but its discussion of the constraints on the British economy, and the internal causes of its shortcomings, remains unhappily of contemporary significance.

There is much in common with these themes in the last of the papers from the journals, that written with Andrew Ozga on 'Economic Growth and the Price Level'. It deals with the rate of rise of productivity, and one especial element in the international position of the British economy, namely the terms of trade. But it also suggests the connection between these and the movement of the general level of prices, offering thereby a solution of the Gibson paradox—why it was that for more than a hundred years down to 1914 the long-term rate of interest and the wholesale price level progressively rose and fell together. This gives the paper contemporary relevance. It deals with the part played by the terms of trade not only in the standard of living of the British people but in the movement of the general level of prices. It considers the quantity of money as an effect as well as a possible cause of price movements, shows it as responsive to demand, and gives historical grounds for rejecting the form of monetarism that treats changes in the stock of money as uniquely determining subsequent changes in prices and/or output.

The last document in this volume is the written evidence that I submitted in 1966 to the Royal Commission on Trade Unions and Employers' Associations—the Donovan Commission. This again is concerned with wages and productivity. There is a general belief that trade union pressure has been the source of the great advances in real wages achieved by their members, and certainly these advances have largely been realized in agreements negotiated by the unions. The statistical record, on the other hand, shows that the rise in real wages has generally proceeded in close agreement with the rise in productivity, that is, in output per occupied person. This relation has held fairly steadily in several countries, in periods of trade union weakness as well as in those of vigour. How the belief and the record can be reconciled, if at all, and what distinct impact remains to be assigned to the unions, are the questions that I took up in this document. It proved to lie outside the interests of the Commission. Though its terms of reference did direct it to consider, among other things, 'the role of trade unions...in promoting the interests of their members and in accelerating the social and economic advance of the nation', it did not ask how much they had brought their members that productivity would not have brought them in any case, and what part they had played in economic progress. It was these questions that I tried to answer to the best of my ability at the time, and I trust that what I wrote is worth lifting from the mass of the Commission's published papers, to be made more accessible here.

Henry Phelps Brown
October 1980

# 1

# Seven Centuries of Building Wages[1]

The secondary sources exist from which to construct a fairly continuous record of the money wage-rates of building craftsmen and labourers in southern England, typically in Oxford, from the later thirteenth century to the present day. Some apology is due for piecing
and patching with secondary sources, when the primary materials are
probably there for more detailed and solid work; but the magnitudes
and epochs of the main movements are not in doubt, and the results
which can be won from what is immediately accessible seem worth setting out for the sake of their grand perspective.

The changes of seven centuries can be surveyed together in Fig. 1,
and are set out period by period in Fig. 2. The data are in Table I.

## I

We must say something first about the sources[2] and how we have
used them.

Until 1700 we have depended on Thorold Rogers. He drew
chiefly on the college and estate accounts in the muniment rooms of
some of the Oxford and Cambridge colleges, and the farm bailiffs'
rolls and monastic accounts in the Public Record Office. Of his
builders' wages, some 40 or 50 per cent. come from Oxford itself, down
to 1620; the other main region of origin is the southern counties, of
which fourteen provide entries, the most represented being Bucks,
Hants, Sussex, and Kent. Cambridge contributes substantially
throughout, and when the entries from Oxford fall off after 1620 it is
Cambridge, and Eton, that take up the running. For the most part,
the entries for craftsmen come at the rate of fifteen or more a year;
but except for 1580–1620, those for building labourers are much
fewer—more like three a year. There is a great falling off in entries of
all kinds after 1660.

---

[1] Mr. B. D. Nomvete carried out the first survey down to 1700. We are indebted
to Professors T. S. Ashton, E. M. Carus-Wilson and F. J. Fisher for reading our
script and giving us much judicious encouragement and restraint in this gallop
across their fields.

[2] J. E. Thorold Rogers: *A History of Agriculture and Prices in England.* Elizabeth
W. Gilboy: *Wages in Eighteenth Century England* (Harvard Economic Studies,
1934). A. L. Bowley: " The Statistics of Wages in the U.K. during the last Hundred
Years (Part VIII). Wages in the Building Trades—concluded " (*Journal of the
Royal Statistical Society*, LXIV, March, 1901). *Standard Time Rates of Wages and
Hours of Labour in the U.K.*, published by the Labour Department of the Board of
Trade, later the Ministry of Labour, in 1894 and later years. Articles on " Changes
in Rates of Wages and Hours of Labour " in the *Labour Gazette* of the Board of
Trade, later the *Ministry of Labour Gazette*, monthly from May 1893.

When he had assembled his quotations for each occupation in each year, Thorold Rogers sometimes took out the average of them all, but often selected the highest. Both methods have the advantage of drawing, in some measure, on the whole range of evidence available each year, but both may be affected by changes between one year and another in the places from which the quotations came—we know that regional differentials were sometimes wide; they also altered a good deal in the course of time.[1] The apparent movement between one year and another may also be influenced by the cropping up of high rates paid to specially skilled men, or low rates paid when part of the wage was in kind, or reduced rates for the shorter winter day.

For these reasons we avoided any mechanical treatment of the series for the various crafts and their labourers, but graphed them: then, amid the year-to-year movements, we looked for rates which we could regard as representative because they were recurrent. When the labour market was settled, such rates usually did appear clearly, especially for the carpenter: there might be, for instance, a higher and a lower rate, a penny apart, appearing in rough alternation for a number of years together; or, as in the fifteenth century, a powerful concentration upon a single rate. In such periods we assumed that the prevailing rate, or bracket of rates, was unchanged. When the labour market was moving, however, the picture was far less clear; what usually happened then is illustrated by Fig. 3. It is what we should expect in a market of individual contracts: when the demand for labour rose, certain new engagements took place at higher rates; this marginal demand price took time to spread to other engagements, which at first continued at the customary rates, but as the proportion of new engagements rose, or some of the men in old engagements got sympathetic rises, a market formerly concentrated upon one rate now came to show a bracket of two; and then perhaps a third, yet higher rate would appear, and the general rise in the market would be brought about by the gradual cessation of engagements at the original rate while those at this latest rate increased. In such times of transition we could not take any one rate as representative, and the data are not numerous or similar enough to make an average reliable: so the most we could do was to set bounds to the movement. Even these bounds are somewhat indefinite: signs of the stirring of demand may appear before the first date we give for movement, and some dispersion persist after we regard a new rate as established.

[1] Thorold Rogers gives a regional array of rates for threshing in the 14th century, with Norfolk highest and the west lowest (*A History of Agriculture and Prices*, Vol. I, p. 263). But of the 15th century he says, " I detect but little difference in the wages of the husbandman, wherever he was hired, from the extreme east to the farthest west of England, from the north to the south ", except in and around London, and this differential too " almost disappears " in the later part of the 16th century, (*op. cit.*, Vol. IV, p. 490). Of 1583–1702 he says " the wages paid in the Midland and Eastern are fully 50 per cent. higher than the Northern rates, and such a difference appears to be regularly maintained " (*op. cit.*, Vol. V, p. 632). Dr. Gilboy (*op. cit.*, p. 220), has brought out the great relative rise of wages in the North in the eighteenth century.

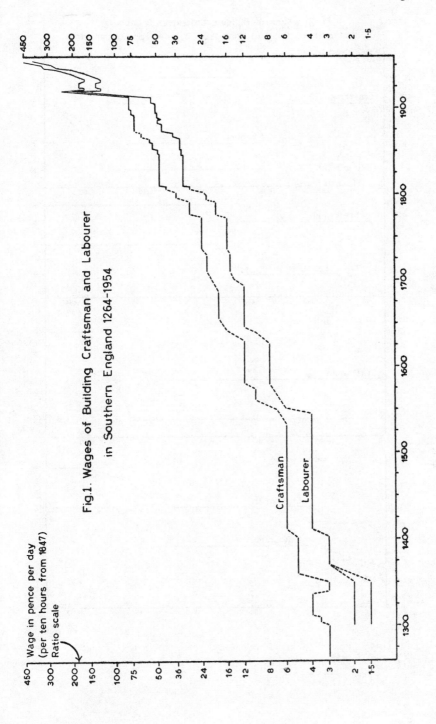

450 ─ Wage in pence per day
300 ─ (per ten hours from 1847)
200 ─ Ratio scale

Fig.1. Wages of Building Craftsman and Labourer
in Southern England 1264-1954

Craftsman

Labourer

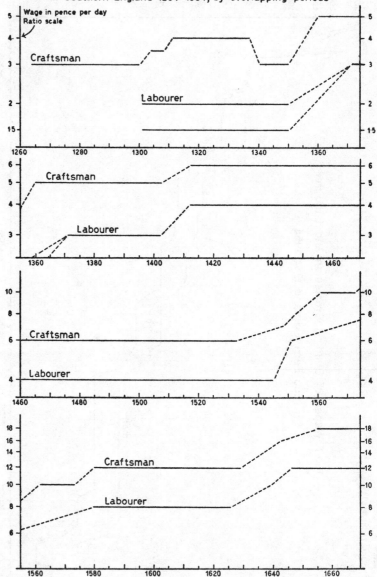

Fig.2: Wages of Building Craftsman & Labourer in Southern England 1264-1954, by overlapping periods

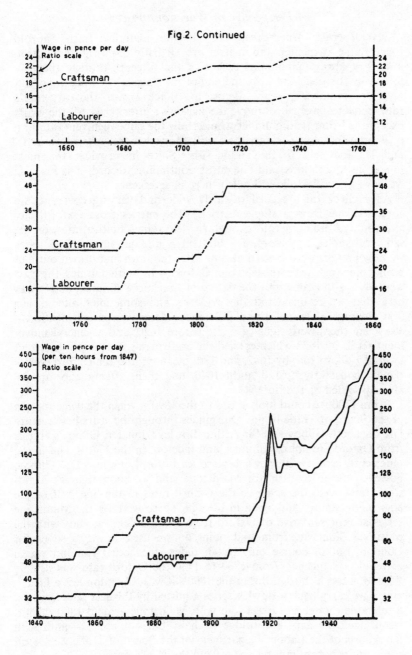

Fig.2. Continued

Several crafts are represented.  In our materials from Thorold
Rogers, the carpenter and mason are virtually alone at the outset,
and they always predominate, but in the fifteenth century they are
joined by the tiler, and near the end of the sixteenth century the brick-
layer and plumber appear.  Before the Black Death, the carpenter's
rate seems to have ruled above the mason's; afterwards, all the crafts
except the better paid plumber would show the same recurrent rate in a
settled market, but the carpenter still showed more upward variants,
and led the field in the Tudor rise.  Since he provides the most
numerous quotations and the most continuous record, it is his rate
we have generally followed when there is divergence.

As a check on a record of fairly wide and varying coverage, we
compiled one from a single district.  The entries from Oxford, city
and county,[1] are numerous enough to yield representative rates, on the
same principles as before, for craftsman and labourer.  The series
we now present were arrived at only after the rates first drawn out had
been compared with those from Oxford.  In settled times the two
were always the same, but the dating of transitions differed, and it was
here that we reconsidered the evidence and sometimes altered our
first findings.  One of these differences deserves special mention—
elsewhere there were signs of a rise before 1620, and a general movement set in by 1628 which carried the craftsman's rate, from its settled
level of 12d., to 16d. by 1642, and 18d. by 1655; but the Oxford entries
remain constantly at 12d. until 1640, and then, after a gap, appear
already settled at 18d. in 1644.

From 1700 we could look ahead to the 1890's, when the wage reports
of the Board of Trade begin.  Our guides through the years between are
Dr. Elizabeth Gilboy and Sir Arthur Bowley: but Dr. Gilboy's entries
from Oxford are not continuous, and fade out in the 1770's, and in the
nineteenth century Bowley's best series is for London.  Dr. Gilboy,
however, has a long run for Maidstone, and we know that the Maidstone rates were the same as the Oxford rates in the first half of the
eighteenth century and again in the 1890's: so we took the Maidstone
series as representative of Oxford from the 1730's till it ends with the
century.  Similarly, from that point on we used Bowley's series for
London, but of course only as an index, the actual London wages
being always higher; from 1700 to 1780 the Oxford rate was usually
" London less a third ", but in the 1890's it was " London less a fifth ",
and if we carry back a Bowley series adjusted by this last figure, we get
a tolerable though not exact join with Maidstone around 1800.  Thus
we bridged the gap—the bridge is shaky but not useless—until with
the reports of the Labour Department of the Board of Trade we are on
comparatively firm ground again from the 1890's onward.

Our rate for the labourer was reached in the same way as the craftsman's rate, except that since Thorold Rogers does not tabulate a

---

[1] The county entries are relatively few, and virtually cease after 1542.  Surpris-
ingly, perhaps, they show no systematic difference from the city.

labourer's rate before 1402, we had to do the best we could there with the not very numerous original entries. But in 1801–60 we have had to rely solely on Bowley's observation that " labourers' wages were in general almost exactly two-thirds of artisans' wages throughout the century, but in times of change show a tendency to lag behind for a year or two ".[1]

The modern shortening of the working week began in our field about 1847. We have assumed that the day which was the unit until then was one of ten hours (though the winter day was shorter), and to maintain continuity from 1847 onwards we have quoted the pay for ten hours.

At the last, how much reliance can we place on the results ? The years for which evidence is thinnest are from about 1660 to 1891, and for most of this time we depend on the assumption that the course of change was the same in Oxford as in Maidstone or London. Outside those years, our line is reasonably continuous for Oxford, but its wider application is limited by the fact that regional differentials were considerable and changed from time to time. In times of transition there was a dispersion of rates in any one place, and we have not been able to do more than set bounds to the movement and sometimes indicate the level reached at some stage within it. But when there was a settled rate, prevailing for some years together, we can hardly have failed to get hold of it.

## II

Some features of the broad view these results afford may interest the economist. But since they have been reached in a particular way, from series of a particular kind, in a particular industry, the question how far they are representative must always be borne in mind.

(1) There is, first, the extraordinary absence of falls. On the face of it our record shows only three for the craftsman—in the 1330's, in 1921–23, and in 1930–33; with falls for the labourer in these last two depressions and once earlier, in 1887. Certainly, our method of taking a representative rate is biased towards stability: in an unorganised market, with individual engagements, the average might rise or fall while one and the same rate remained predominant, and in ignoring variants which arose from special conditions of the job we may well have neglected not a few which marked an actual movement of the market.[2] It is likely, moreover, that there were fewer actual falls among our kind of wage-payments than elsewhere, since for most of our period these payments were made not by employers to wage-earners but by customers to craftsmen working on their own account, and these customers were generally institutions and not private

---

[1] *J.R.S.S.*, March, 1901, p. 104.
[2] cf. Beveridge's evidence for a fall in builders' rates within the first decade of the 14th century: " Wages in the Winchester Manors ", *Economic History Review*, VII, 1, Nov. 1936, p. 30, n.1.

persons who had to put their hands into their own pockets. In later years, again, the recognised or negotiated rates we follow will have been secretly cut, in not a few engagements, when trade was slack. In the eighteenth century Ashton has found that " the inelasticity of rates of pay in the building trades was not representative of wages in industry as a whole ".[1] But after due allowance for these things, the absence of *sustained* falls and of falling *trends* remains remarkable. It has been called the elbow-joint or ratchet effect.

(2) Subject to the qualifications just suggested, the record substantiates Adam Smith's remarks that " in many places the money price of labour remains uniformly the same sometimes for half a century together "[2]; and that wages did not vary from year to year with the price of provisions.[3] The great case is the persistence of the craftsman's rate of 6d. a day without apparent variations for a hundred and twenty years, from around Agincourt until the Reformation[4]; but of the whole span until 1914 it can be said that rises in the rate were interspersed with periods of no change, persisting for as much as thirty and sometimes more than forty years together. In all, there seems to have been no change, of the sustained kind we record, in about 500 years out of 690. It is unlikely that supply and demand remained exactly balanced at the ruling price; rather it must have been that their movements were not wide enough to overcome the inertia of convention. That inertia may have been strong enough to resist considerable pressure—especially, as we have suggested, pressure downwards. But the market forces may none the less have changed the effective terms of engagement from time to time, by altering, for instance, the output expected, or what nowadays we call the fringe benefits, without the quoted rate being changed.

(3) The same strength of convention may be seen in the remarkable stability of the differential between the rates of the craftsman and his labourer. Our figures bear out the decline in that differential noted by Beveridge[5] and Postan[6] in the hundred years down to about 1410; but after that there was no sustained change until the First World War. In the fifteenth century the craftsman got half as much again as the labourer, 6d. a day to his 4d.; in the 1890's he got half as much again, 7½d. an hour to his 5d.; he got half as much again, or within a halfpenny of it, in every settled period in between. Here as before, we cannot believe that market forces always worked to keep the equilibrium prices of the two grades of labour in so constant a relation: the most that

[1] T. S. Ashton: *An Economic History of England: the 18th Century*, pp. 224–226.
[2] *Wealth of Nations*, Bk. 1, c. VIII.
[3] *Op. cit.*, Bk. I, c. V.
[4] But of eight Winchester manors in our region, five show definitely higher rates for carpenters after 1439 than before : Beveridge, *op. cit.*
[5] *Op. cit.*
[6] M. M. Postan, " Some Economic Evidence of Declining Population in the Later Middle Ages ", *Economic History Review*, N.S. II, 3, 1950. See also Johan Schreiner, " Wages and Prices in England in the Later Middle Ages ", *Scandinavian Economic History Review*, II, 2, 1954.

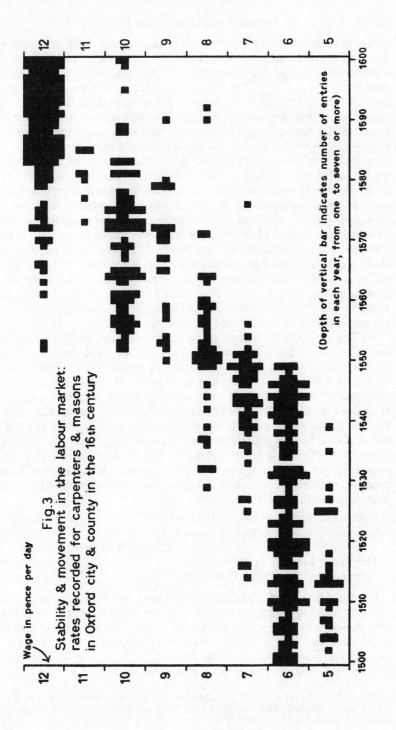

Wage in pence per day

Fig.3
Stability & movement in the labour market:
rates recorded for carpenters & masons
in Oxford city & county in the 16th century

(Depth of vertical bar indicates number of entries
in each year, from one to seven or more)

seems probable is that they did not make for any wide divergence, until in the twentieth century the effects of more widespread education, together with inflation, became apparent in a general reduction of the differential for skill—by 1954 the craftsman's rate was less than 15 per cent. above the labourer's. In times of rising rates the differential was disturbed; there are indications that the labourer's rate sometimes began to rise later than the craftsman's, and then rose faster so as to narrow the gap for a while; but the dispersal of quoted rates at these times is generally too great for any definite relation to be established. So far as the five hundred years' recurrence of the one simple differential was due to convention, we may wonder whether it worked to hold the craftsman's rate back to that which ruled for general labour, or to give those general labourers who entered the building trade the benefit of a fixed proportion of the rate the craftsman could command. The convention that related the labourer's rate to the craftsman's as two to three made for a narrower differential than is recorded in 1880–1900 for some other employments: in engineering then the labourer was getting about three-fifths of the fitter's rate, in shipbuilding the labourer got about half the shipwright's rate, on the railways the goods porter got about half the engine driver's rate.[1]

(4) The most salient feature of all is the extent of the rise: for the craftsman, from 3d. a day under Henry III, to 445d. for 10 hours' work under Elizabeth II—multiplication by nearly 150. There is one sense in which the rise does not appear so great; if it had gone on at the same rate all the way through, an annual rise of less than three-quarters of one per cent. would have sufficed to cumulate it. But we have seen that out of 690 years, only about 190 seem to have been years in which the craftsman's rate underwent a sustained change, and within these alone the total rise is equivalent to an annual rise of nearly two and two-thirds per cent., compounded. It is instructive to compare four epochs: the average annually compounded rates of rise, taking all years together in each epoch, are:—

Reformation to Restoration (1532–1660):　　..　　0·86 per cent.
Industrial Revolution to First World War
　　　　　　　　　　　　(1760–1913): 0·79 per cent.
The Tudor Inflation (1532–1580):　　..　　..　　1·46 per cent.
Epoch of the Two Great Wars (1914–54):　　..　　4·24 per cent.

It is for a detailed study of each period to show how far the observed rises can be attributed to one or more of the possible causes—changes of demand and supply in the market for building labour; the initiative of combinations in that market; and changes in the flow of aggregate monetary demand throughout the economy. But it can be said here that the vast change which has come about from end to end is the

---

[1] K. G. J. C. Knowles and D. J. Robertson, " Differences between the Wages of Skilled and Unskilled Workers, 1880–1950 ". *Bulletin of the Oxford University Institute of Statistics*, 13, 4, April, 1951.

product of rises which themselves did not need to be very great from one year to another, in a system whose ratchet prevented the rises of some years being offset by falls in others, and so caused the rises to cumulate.

In a later article we hope to compare these movements of money wage-rates with contemporary changes in the prices of some basic consumables.

TABLE 1

MONEY WAGE-RATES OF BUILDING CRAFTSMAN AND LABOURER, IN SOUTHERN ENGLAND 1264–1954. PENCE PER DAY THROUGH 1846; FROM 1847, PENCE PER 10 HOURS. CALENDAR YEARS.

| | Craftsman | | Labourer | |
|---|---|---|---|---|
| | | *d.* | | *d.* |
| 1264–1300 | | 3 | | |
| 1300–04 | From | 3 to 3½ | | |
| 1304–08 | | 3½ | | |
| 1308–11 | From | 3½ to 4 | 1301–50 | 1½ or 2 |
| 1311–37 | | 4 | | |
| 1337–40 | From | 4 to 3 | | |
| 1340–50 | | 3 | | |
| 1350–60 | From | 3 to 5 | 1350–71 | From 1½ or 2 to 3 |
| 1360–1402 | | 5 | 1371–1402 | 3 |
| 1402–12 | From | 5 to 6 | 1402–12 | From 3 to 4 |
| 1412–1532 | | 6 | 1412–1545 | 4 |
| 1532–48 | From | 6 to 7 | | |
| 1548–52 | From | 7 to 8 | 1545–51 | From 4 to 6 |
| 1552–61 | From | 8 to 10 | | |
| 1561–73 | | 10 | 1551–80 | From 6 to 8 |
| 1573–80 | From | 10 to 12 | | |
| 1580–1629 | | 12 | 1580–1626 | 8 |
| 1629–42 | From | 12 to 16 | 1626–39 | From 8 to 10 |
| 1642–55 | From | 16 to 18 | 1639–46 | From 10 to 12 |
| 1655–87 | | 18 | 1646–93 | 12 |
| 1687–1701 | From | 18 to 20 | 1693–1701 | From 12 to 14 |
| 1701–10 | From | 20 to 22 | 1701–10 | From 14 to 15 |
| 1710–30 | | 22 | 1710–30 | 15 |
| 1730–36 | From | 22 to 24 | 1730–36 | From 15 to 16 |
| 1736–73 | | 24 | 1736–73 | 16 |
| 1773–76 | From | 24 to 29 | 1773–76 | From 16 to 19 |
| 1776–91 | | 29 | 1776–91 | 19 |
| 1791–96 | From | 29 to 36 | 1791–93 | From 19 to 22 |
| 1796–1802 | | 36 | 1793–98 | 22 |
| | | | 1799–1802 | 23 |
| 1802–06 | From | 36 to 43 | 1802–06 | From 23 to 29 |
| 1806–09 | | 43 | 1806–09 | 29 |
| 1810–46 | | 48 | 1810–46 | 32 |
| 1847–52 | | 49 | 1847–52 | 33 |
| 1853–60 | | 54 | 1853–65 | 34 |
| 1861–64 | | 56 | | |
| 1864–66 | From | 56 to 64 | 1866 | 36 |
| 1866–71 | | 64 | 1867–71 | 38 |
| 1871–73 | From | 64 to 72 | 1872 | 42 |
| 1873–92 | | 72 | 1873–82 | 46 |

| Craftsman | | Labourer | |
|---|---|---|---|
| | d. | | d. |
| | | 1883–86 | 48 |
| | | 1887 | 46 |
| | | 1888–93 | 48 |
| 1893–98 | 75 | 1894–1905 | 50 |
| 1899–1913 | 80 | 1906–12 | 55 |
| 1914 | 85 | 1913–14 | 60 |
| 1915 | 90 | 1915 | 65 |
| 1916 | 93 | 1916 | 73 |
| 1917 | 103 | 1917 | 83 |
| 1918 | 120 | 1918 | 95 |
| 1919 | 170 | 1919 | 140 |
| 1920 | 240 | 1920 | 210 |
| 1921 | 205 | 1921 | 165 |
| 1922–23 | 165 | 1922–23 | 125 |
| 1924–29 | 180 | 1924–29 | 138 |
| 1930 | 175 | 1930 | 133 |
| 1931–32 | 170 | 1931–32 | 128 |
| 1933–34 | 165 | 1933–34 | 125 |
| 1935 | 175 | 1935 | 133 |
| 1936 | 180 | 1936 | 135 |
| 1937 | 185 | 1937 | 140 |
| 1938 | 190 | 1938 | 143 |
| 1939 | 195 | 1939 | 148 |
| 1940 | 210 | 1940 | 163 |
| 1941 | 220 | 1941 | 173 |
| 1942 | 225 | 1942 | 178 |
| 1943 | 235 | 1943 | 185 |
| 1944 | 245 | 1944 | 193 |
| 1945 | 255 | 1945 | 205 |
| 1946 | 295 | 1946 | 238 |
| 1947 | 325 | 1947 | 260 |
| 1948 | 330 | 1948 | 265 |
| 1949 | 335 | 1949 | 275 |
| 1950 | 340 | 1950 | 285 |
| 1951 | 370 | 1951 | 315 |
| 1952 | 400 | 1952 | 345 |
| 1953 | 420 | 1953 | 365 |
| 1954 | 445 | 1954 | 390 |

# 2

# Seven Centuries of the Prices of Consumables compared with Builders' Wage-rates[1]

In an earlier paper[2] we gave an account of builders' wages in southern England from 1264 to 1954, and now we shall try to relate these to the prices of some of the main articles of consumption. In 1901 Steffen[3] displayed the movements of two wage-rates in comparison with those of the prices of wheat and meat through the preceding six centuries and more: it was his Tafel II that first displayed the striking evidence for a great rise and fall in the real income of the wage-earner between 1300 and 1600, the level reached in 1450–1500 apparently not being regained until after 1860. We shall test these indications by bringing a wider range of prices to bear.

## I

Nowadays, real wages are commonly estimated by comparing money earnings with an index of the cost of living, but there are several reasons why we cannot do that here. On the side of income, all we have is the rate of pay for a day, and we do not know how many days' work the builder was getting in the year from time to time, nor what other resources he had. On the side of outlay, we know little or nothing about some important costs, notably rent, and the prices we do have are more wholesale than retail. These things apart, we still could not attach much meaning to " the cost of maintaining a constant standard of living " through seven centuries of social change.

So we have not tried to construct any measure of real wages in the modern sense. Yet when we find the craftsmen who have been building Nuffield College in Oxford in our own day earning a hundred and fifty pennies in the time it took their forbears building Merton to earn one, the impulse to break through the veil of money becomes powerful: we are bound to ask, what sort of command over the things builders buy did these pennies give from time to time? It is this question we try to answer here.

Our answer takes the form of an aggregate price year by year for a composite commodity, made up always of the same amounts of some of the main heads of consumption : we can think of it as a package

[1] We owe to Mr. S. Ahmed, Dr. Gethyn Davies and Mr. J. Veverka much valued help in computing, and are further indebted to our colleagues Professors Carus-Wilson and Fisher and Dr. A. H. John for commenting on our work in galley.

[2] " Seven Centuries of Building Wages ", *Economica*, XXII, 87 (August 1955).

[3] G. F. Steffen, *Studien zur Geschichte der englischen Lohnarbeiter*, vol. I (Stuttgart, 1901), esp. Tafel I and II, at p. 112. Most of the materials of these two graphs are reproduced in Appx. I of H. O. Meredith, *Economic History of England*, 5th ed. 1949.

always containing the same sized bagfuls of bread-stuffs, meat, cloth, and so on. The contents of each bag have been made up variously from time to time: in our bread-stuffs, for instance, we give a greater place to wheat, and correspondingly less to rye and barley, as the eighteenth century wears on. But we have kept the bags themselves of the same size throughout, so that the package they make up should provide what is in the main a common composite physical unit, in which to express the purchasing powers of sums of money at different dates throughout our long period. Whenever the costs of the bagfuls move differently from one another, the changes in the cost of our composite unit will indicate those of the wage-earner's cost of living only to the extent that the make-up of our unit resembles that of his actual basketful. But this will certainly have varied from time to time, particularly when his purchasing power changed as much as this inquiry proves to suggest it did; and the evidence by which we chose the make-up of our unit is in any case fragmentary.

This evidence is set out in Table 1. William Savernak's account book[1] records seven years of the weekly expenditure of a small household—two priests and a servant—at Bridport in Dorset, in the 1450's:

TABLE 1

DISTRIBUTION OF OUTLAY BETWEEN CERTAIN HEADS OF
HOUSEHOLD EXPENDITURE

|  | W. Savernak 1453–60 | Davies & Eden 1790's | Board of Trade 1904–13 | Weights taken here |
|---|---|---|---|---|
|  | % | % | % | % |
| 1. Farinaceous | 20 | 53 | 16 | 20 |
| 2. Meat, fish | 35 | 12 | 21½ | 25 |
| 3. Butter, cheese | 2 | 7 | 16 | 12½ |
| 4. Drink (malt, hops, sugar, tea) | 23 | 9 | 24 | 22½ |
| *Subtotal*, Food | 80 | 81 | 77½ | 80 |
| 5. Fuel and light | 7½ | 7½ | 9 | 7½ |
| 6. Textiles | n.a. | 11½ | 13½ | 12½ |
| *Total* | 87½ | 100 | 100 | 100 |

within our scope here fall the entries for thirteen articles of food, and for candles and fuel, to the amount of some forty pence a week, or getting on for seven days' pay of a building craftsman at that time. But there is no sufficient record of outlay on clothes, and in showing the distribution of the outlay included in Table 1 over its first five heads, we have allowed them only the 87½ percentage points in all that they

[1] K. L. Wood-Legh, *A Small Household of the Fifteenth Century* (Manchester University Press, 1956).

get in the last column. The second column summarises the accounts of nearly sixty households in the villages or small towns of southern England, that two students of poverty recorded in the 1790's.[1] The third column rests on the estimate made, when the old Cost of Living Index was set up during the First World War, of the distribution of " average pre-war working-class expenditure ", and so its detail for food derives mainly from the " 1,944 urban working-class budgets collected by the Board of Trade in 1904 ",[2] but we have raised the weight of the fourth head and of food as a whole by adding outlay on beer, which we took to be a slightly greater part of all outlay in 1904–13 than in 1938.[3]

The most striking feature of the Table is the similarity between Savernak's budget and that of the wage-earners four-and-a-half centuries later: Savernak, it is true, spent much more on meat and fish and less on butter and cheese, but the combined weight of these two heads is almost the same in both columns. Davies and Eden portray poor people in hard times, and it is not surprising that they show so great a part of the outlay on food as spent on bread-stuffs: what again is striking is that the distribution of the recorded outlay over food and the two remaining heads should differ so little from the budgets of 1904–13. So it seemed not unreasonable at the outset to adopt the figures of the last column as weights with which to combine the price-indexes of the six heads, all through the centuries: though since this amounts to following the total cost of a package of unchanged physical make-up, it does imply changes from time to time in the proportionate distribution of *outlay*, to the extent that those price-indexes diverged from one another.

But the components under each of those six heads change their own subweights not a little from time to time. Sometimes we made these changes deliberately, to take account of shifting habits of consumption, or the entry of new products; more often our hand was forced by lack of materials. In general, we arranged the sub-weighting of such series as we selected or were all we had from time to time, according to the detail in the budgets already cited, and failing that, in the half-light of general knowledge: such were our only grounds, for instance, for giving beef and mutton equal weights, and meat of all kinds about five times the weight of fish.[4]

The upshot is illustrated by Table 2, which takes as the unit of our composite commodity what a hundred pence would buy in 1451–75, and shows the articles that made up this unit about the beginning

[1] David Davies, Rector of Barkham, Berks., *The Case of Labourers in Husbandry* (1795). Sir Frederic Morton Eden, Bart., *The State of the Poor* (1797).
[2] *The Cost of Living Index Number: Method of Compilation.* Ministry of Labour (June 1934).
[3] Para. 12 of Supplement No. 2 (January 1948) to the *Industrial Relations Handbook* (Ministry of Labour, 1944).
[4] The detail of the subweighting is set out, with a table giving separate indexes for the six heads, in a duplicated paper of which a limited supply is available to applicants.

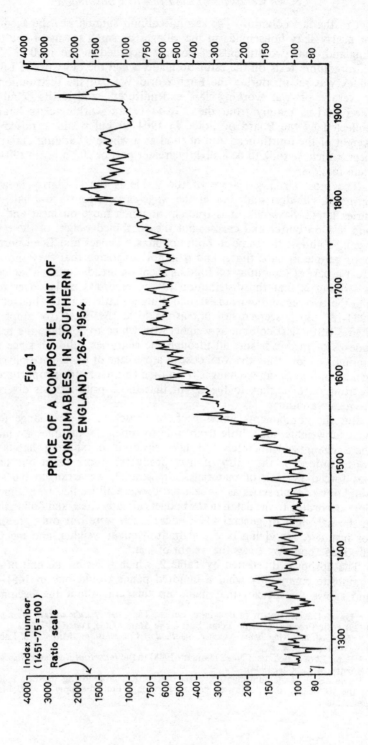

Fig. 1

PRICE OF A COMPOSITE UNIT OF
CONSUMABLES IN SOUTHERN
ENGLAND, 1264–1954

Index number
(1451–75=100)

Ratio scale

## FIG. 2

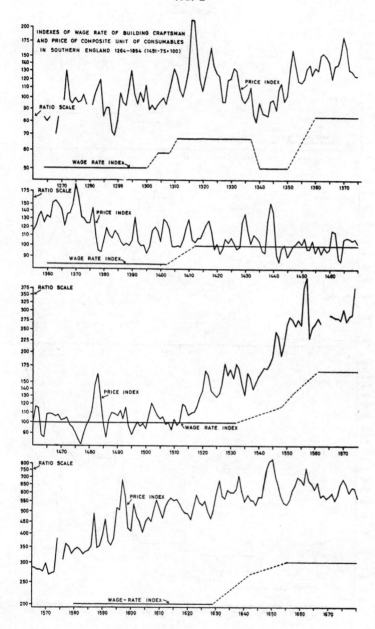

INDEXES OF WAGE RATE OF BUILDING CRAFTSMAN AND PRICE OF COMPOSITE UNIT OF CONSUMABLES IN SOUTHERN ENGLAND 1264–1954 (1451-75×100)

PRICE INDEX

RATIO SCALE

WAGE RATE INDEX

FIG. 2. CONTINUED

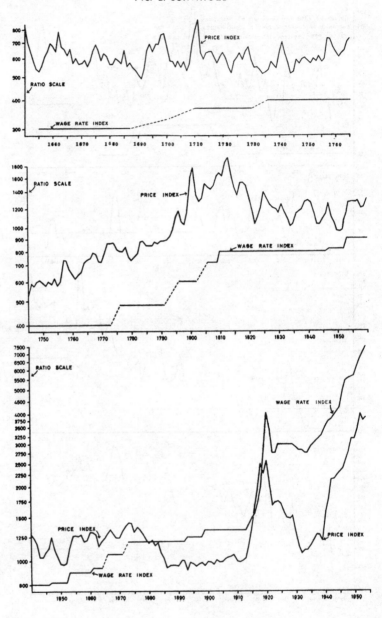

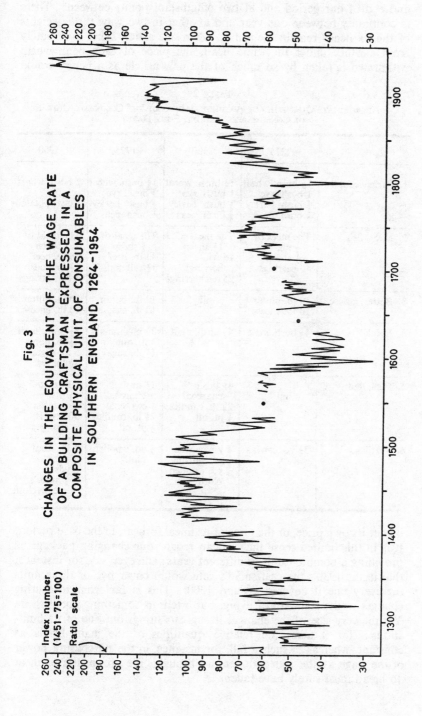

Fig. 3

CHANGES IN THE EQUIVALENT OF THE WAGE RATE
OF A BUILDING CRAFTSMAN EXPRESSED IN A
COMPOSITE PHYSICAL UNIT OF CONSUMABLES
IN SOUTHERN ENGLAND. 1264-1954

and end of our period and at two equidistant points between. There is continuity between one year and another in two ways: the weights of the six heads remain the same; when one article takes over outlay from another under the same head, the place of each pennyworth withdrawn is taken by so much of the new article as a penny would

TABLE 2

APPROXIMATE QUANTITIES OF ARTICLES MAKING UP THE COMPOSITE UNIT OF CONSUMABLES, AROUND FOUR DATES

| | 1275 | 1500 | 1725 | 1950 |
|---|---|---|---|---|
| 1. Farinaceous .. | 1¼ bush. wheat<br>1 bush. rye<br>½ bush. barley<br>⅜ bush. peas | 1¼ bush. wheat<br>1 bush. rye<br>½ bush. barley<br>⅜ bush. peas | 1½ bush. wheat<br>¾ bush. rye<br>⅓ bush. barley<br>½ bush. peas | 2 bush. wheat<br><br>1 cwt. potatoes |
| 2. Meat, fish .. | The meat of<br>½ pig<br>½ sheep<br>40 herrings | The meat of<br>1½ sheep<br>15 white herrings<br>25 red herrings | The meat of<br>½ sheep<br>33 lb. beef<br>1¼ salt cod | The meat of<br>⅜ sheep<br>28 lb. beef<br>1½ lb. cod<br>3 lb. herrings |
| 3. Butter, cheese | 10 lb. butter<br>10 lb. cheese | nil | 10 lb. butter<br>10 lb. cheese | 10 lb. butter<br>10 lb. cheese |
| 4. Drink .. | 4½ bush. malt | 4½ bush. malt | 3¼ bush. malt<br>3 lb. hops<br>1½ lb. sugar | 2⅓ bush. malt<br>2¼ lb. hops<br>5 lb. sugar<br>4⅛ lb. tea |
| 5. Fuel, light .. | nil | 4¼ bush. charcoal<br>2¾ lb. candles<br>½ pt. oil | 1½ bush. charcoal<br>1 cwt. coal<br>2⅛ lb. candles<br>½ pt. oil | 2 cwt. coal<br>5½ pts. paraffin<br>300 cu. ft. coal gas |
| 6. Textiles .. | 3¼ yd. canvas | ⅜ yd. canvas<br>½ yd. shirting<br>⅛ yd. woollen cloth | ⅛ yd. woollen cloth | ¾ lb. wool yarn<br>3 yds. printer's cotton cloth |

buy at its own price, or the price of its lineal forbear, in the base period. It is in this limited sense that we can regard our changing package as providing a common unit in different years: and even say, for instance, that in the 1930's the craftsman's rate would cover five of these units for every one it covered around 1300. This is far from measuring changes in the standard of living, but it tells us something about them. Yet the very size of the changes it suggests brings out one of its limitations: for it takes the relative quantities of the main heads as constant, whereas in such a fall, for instance, in the purchasing power of the wage as the sixteenth century brought, the proportion of meat to bread must surely have fallen.

## II

The sources we have drawn on for our prices are set out in Appendix A. Two of them are outstanding. We are reaping where other men have sown, and for any interest this study may afford, the credit belongs to Thorold Rogers and Beveridge.

Until early in the nineteenth century, most of our prices record what was paid by buyers in a local market or annual fair, or what a local purveyor charged for supplies delivered to the consumer's door. Rogers' prices come mostly from the accounts of the manors of Oxford colleges, and the provisioning of Oxford and Cambridge colleges themselves, with the similar household accounts of some great lay and monastic landlords. Most of the prices we have taken from Beveridge come from the accounts of colleges and hospitals, and from the Navy Victualling service. In sum, these prices give the terms on which raw or partially processed materials were available to consumers who bought locally in some bulk. But after Beveridge's records end, in the early nineteenth century, we have gone on with prices that are wholesale in the modern sense—quotations from the organised produce markets, and average values of imports or exports. We know how these show more and bigger movements than the prices paid for small quantities at retail. It is a further limitation that we have been able to include few fabricated articles. So our prices are not those at which the craftsman's wage was spent with the butcher, the baker, the candlestick maker; they do measure changes in the command of money over some of the main materials of consumption, at points where these are bought in some bulk, and when such changes were substantial and sustained they would come through to the craftsman; but even so, our index is still not responsive enough to changes in the costs of fabrication.

There are other respects in which these materials fall short. For one thing, they make no allowance for changes in quality: how like or unlike were the three quarters of wheat that were sold at Easington near Thame and helped make up our index for 1264, to the Manitoba No. 1 that is the subject of our last quotations? Changes in quantity as well as quality may have crept in, when provisioning went on, as it often did, for a long run of years at an unchanging price; or other adjustments, not recorded in the price, would have been made in the payment from time to time: our only remedy was to avoid all such constant series as far as possible, though sometimes they will have meant what they said. The worst shortcoming is the absence of some annual records altogether: especially for fuel and light in the earliest years, butter and cheese in the fifteenth and sixteenth centuries, and fish in the eighteenth. There are also many gaps, here and there, of a year or two at a time. It has been a matter of judgment, place by place, which of three possible courses to follow: simply accept the gap and carry the index on with the remaining series; transfer the weight of the missing series to some other that is close akin to it; fill the gap by interpolation,

To give our price-series their place in the index for the composite commodity, we had to express each as a relative to its own average in a common base-period. This is 1451–75, chosen because it lies within a long period of stability in the trend of prices—though it turns out to have been a time of exceptional prosperity. But of course many series do not run through it, and these we have had to set in their right relation to those that do. Often this raised no problem: if a new series differed from an old only by giving the price of another grade or region, and the two moved together through a number of years of overlap, then splicing was straightforward. But if either of these conditions was absent, we had to be wary of falsifying the whole later course of the new index by including some abnormality in the splice, or misplacing a turning-point by choosing the wrong place at which to join two series of divergent trends. Again, when the new series was not merely a variant of some old one, but brought a new commodity in—when hops appeared in the sixteenth century, for example, or potatoes in the eighteenth—we had to select the old series that seemed most akin to it, to join it to: so we joined hops to malt, and potatoes to peas. This involved the absurdity, if you will, of saying that potatoes cost four times as much in 1785 as in 1451–75, when there were none: but we can give an intelligible cast to this if we take potatoes and peas as two spokesmen, so to speak, for the one class of vegetables, and think of the one being brought in to supplement or take over from the other, just as when a series for beef becomes available we bring it in to supplement the price of mutton and fill out the index for meat.

### III

Our findings are summarised in Appendix B and displayed in the three figures. Many of them will be familiar to the economic historian. It is to his knowledge, and to the more detailed study of our present materials period by period, that we must look for answers to the questions they seem to raise.

The index of prices has two periods. each of about 130 years, 1380–1510, and 1630–1760, throughout which there is constancy in the general level, and this surprising stability, as it seems to us, was maintained through fluctuations of two or three years' span, due no doubt mostly to the harvest, whose violence seems no less extraordinary: what was the secret of this stability, and how was it held through such vibration ? There are also two periods, about 1270–1380, and 1815–1914, when a trend that is fairly level from end to end is modulated by " secondary secular movements ", as we call them now: what makes the difference between the two sorts of period ? The most marked feature of Fig. 1 is the extent, and persistence, of the Tudor inflation: what carried it on so far, and why did it end when it did ? For a century and more. it seems, prices will obey one all-powerful law; it changes, and a new law prevails; a war that would have cast the trend up to new heights in one dispensation is powerless to deflect it in another. Do we yet know what are the factors that set this stamp on an age; and why, after they have held on so long through such shakings, at last they give way, quickly and completely, to others ?

The simplest impression of the physical equivalent of the wage-rate, that Fig. 3 displays, is of a level much the same throughout, broken through only by a time of much greater prosperity from 1380 to 1510, and a rise that sets in at the last, from 1820 onwards, and carries us up to a new region altogether. We can go on to notice some differences in the level: the depths, for instance, to which it fell at the ends of the sixteenth century and the eighteenth, and the substantial rise from the Civil War to the 1740's. In considering all these things we want to know how far our building craftsman was representative of working men generally, whether wage-earners or not, and it is relevant here that the building labourer's rate did change in the same proportion as the craftsman's with great consistency from the Black Death to the First World War. If the movements of Fig. 3 were indeed not confined to certain crafts but were of some generality, then their size and shape mark deepgoing economic changes. Was it an advance in productivity, deserving the title of revolution, that about doubled the commodity equivalent between the Black Death and Agincourt, and held it at its new level for nearly a century ? A drastic fall set in about 1510: the level enjoyed at the accession of Henry VIII was not to be reached again until 1880; the lowest point we record in seven centuries was in 1597, the year of the *Midsummer Night's Dream*. Do we not see here a Malthusian crisis, the effect of a rapid growth of population impinging on an insufficiently expansive economy; such as perhaps we see also in the fall that set in again around 1750, until this time a commercial and industrial revolution came to save Britain from the fate of Ireland ?

## APPENDIX A

### LIST OF PRICE SERIES

ABBREVIATIONS

AS: Annual Statements of the Trade of the U.K.

B: Sir Wm. Beveridge and others: Prices and Wages in England from the Twelfth to the Nineteenth Century. Vol. I.

BPP: British Parliamentary Papers.

JRSS: Journal of the Royal Statistical Society, annual reports on wholesale prices by the Editor of *The Statist*.

PWH: Price and Wage History Research, manuscript materials, collected under the direction of Sir Wm. Beveridge, in the Institute of Historical Research, University of London.

R: J. E. Thorold Rogers: A History of Agriculture and Prices in England.

TN: Tooke and Newmarch: A History of Prices and of the State of the Circulation from 1792 to 1856.

WRP: Report on Wholesale and Retail Prices in the U.K., BPP 1903, LXVIII, 321.

DATES

Dates given for series record the length used here, either as a component of the final index or for splicing; the original is sometimes longer. We have entered the average price for a harvest year against the calendar year beginning during that harvest year, e.g. against Mich. 1400—Mich. 1401 we put the calendar year 1401.

SERIES

(01) *Wheat 1264–1703:* average of prices recorded, mostly in manorial and college accounts, in Southern England. R, I, 226–234; IV, 282–290; V, 268–274. (02) *Wheat 1583–1770:* mean of prices at Lady Day and Michaelmas, found in Oxford college accounts of payments of rent in kind. TN, VI, 427–436, from W. F. Lloyd, 1830. (03) *Wheat 1595–1826:* mean of prices at Lady Day and Michaelmas, taken by Eton College from the Windsor market, for the purpose of rent audit. 1595–1770, TN, VI, 352. 1646–1826, TN, II, 387–9. (04) *Wheat 1631–1818:* annual averages of prices paid by Winchester College. B, 18, 81–84. (05) *Wheat 1771–1954:* Gazette Average prices, England and Wales, weekly since 24 Nov. 1770 in the London Gazette, here from: 1771–1841, " Porter's Tables ", XI, 69 (BPP 1843, LVI); 1842–1902, WRP, 70–71; 1903–54, Statistical Abstract of the U.K. (06) *Wheat 1854–1907:* average value of wheat imported into the U.K.: 1854–70, " computed real values "; 1871+, " declared values ". WRP, 80; and AS. (07) *Wheat 1905–52:* market quotations for Northern Manitoba Wheat, No. 1 except 1924–38, when No. 2. Price at 1st Jan. 1906–12; thereafter at " end year "; price at 1st Jan., 1906 taken here as for end year 1905, and so on. *The Economist*, Annual Commercial History and Review, through 1953, then British Wholesale Prices. (08) *Barley 1264–1833:* average of prices recorded, mainly in manorial, college and church accounts, and in southern and eastern counties, but Durham included 1341–1541, and some northern counties 1771–1822. Entries sparse 1542–1728. PWH. (09) *Rye 1264–1540, 1688–1782:* same origins as 08; mainly Winchester manors and eastern counties down to 1454; 1455–1540 Dorset and Durham only; from 1688 Kent and Middlesex. PWH. (10) *Peas 1264–1685:* same origins as 01. R, I, 227–235; IV, 283–291; V, 269–275. (11) *Peas 1686–1790:* average price at which Navy Victualling bought peas under short-period contracts. B, 538–9, 567–9. (12) *Peas 1791–1809:* presumably for England and Wales; from " An Account of the Average Price of all sorts of Grain in each Year ", 1791–1821, BPP 1821, XVII, 11. (13) *Peas 1810–1833:* London Gazette Average prices, England and Wales, taken here from " Porter's Tables ", XI, 69 (BPP, 1843, LVI). (14) *Potatoes 1762–1830:* average price of old potatoes bought by the Lord Steward's department. B, 374–6, 427. (15) *Potatoes 1832–45:* 1832–36, middlings and middling whites from Borough and Spitalfields markets; 1837–45 Yorkshire reds, 1846–50 Yorkshire Regents, at Southwark Waterside. Averages of weekly quotations for October in each year, given in *The Christian Advocate* and *Mark Lane Express*. (16) *Potatoes 1846–84:* average of prices in Jan.-Apr. and Sept.-Dec. annually, of good English, mostly Kent Regents. A. Sauerbeck, " Prices of Commodities and the Precious Metals ", JRSS, XLIX (1886), 636. (17) *Potatoes 1885–1954:* London wholesale prices, grade A or good English. *The Economist*. (18) *Porci 1264–1460:* same origins as 01. 1264–1401, annual averages from R, I, 342–50. 1402–60, median or mean of entries from southern and eastern

counties, in R, III, 122–202. (19) *Muttons 1265–1582:* same origins as 01. 1265–1401, median of entries from southern and eastern counties, in R, II, 184–269. 1402–1582, 3-year moving average of highest price found in each year, reduced by a quarter throughout; a few exceptionally high entries omitted. R, IV, 346–54. (20) *Beef 1584–1659:* purchases by King's College, Cambridge; apparently annual averages. R, V, 347–51. (21) *Beef 1587–1767:* purchases by St. Bartholomew's Hospital, Sandwich, in August of each year. B, 219–21, 236–7. (22) *Beef 1602–21:* purchases by estate of Theydon Gernon, Essex; apparently annual average. R, V, 356. (23) *Mutton 1602–1700:* purchases of mutton by Eton College from the college butcher; annual averages. B, 112, 144–6. (24) *Mixed beef and mutton 1613–87:* purchases by Winchester College; weighted average of prices for the two kinds, including *ex gratia* payments to the butcher to compensate for losses. B, 33–5, 81–3. (25) *Beef 1683–1797:* Beef for salting bought by Navy Victualling, London. 1683–1747, from Arthur Young, Political Arithmetic, pp. 139–141, apparently annual averages; 1748–97, annual average of varying number of monthly entries in B, 548–53, 568–72. (26) *Beef 1688–1833:* purchases by St. Thomas's Hospital, Southwark; average of prices at Lady Day and Michaelmas. "Porter's Tables", BPP, 1835, XLIX, 390. (27) *Mutton 1701–1831:* market prices used to fix the money payments due from tenants of Eton College farms in lieu of rent sheep; average of prices at Lady Day and Michaelmas. B, 112, 146–7. (28) *Mutton 1725–1833:* as for 26. (29) *Beef 1789–1865:* annual average of monthly price (from 1792 mean of highest and lowest price on a day near end of month) at Smithfield market, London; extracted by Dr. A. H. John from contemporary sources (from 1796 onwards, the *Gentleman's Magazine*). (30) *Mutton 1796–1865:* as for 29 from 1796 onwards. (31) *Beef 1858–1954:* 1858–1914, mean of highest and lowest prices of inferior middling butcher's meat, Newgate or Smithfield, at beginning of each year; 1913–27, mean of prices of middling and prime at end of year; 1924–47, imported chilled hindquarters (Argentine 1924–38, New Zealand 1939–47); 1948 onwards, " beef imported ". *The Economist*, Annual Commercial History and Review through 1953, then British Wholesale Prices. (32) *Mutton 1858–1954:* 1858–90, mean of highest and lowest prices for middling butcher's meat, Newgate or Smithfield, and 1891–1914, price of middling, at beginning of year throughout; 1913–27, mean of middling and prime at end of year; 1924–54, imported (1924–38 New Zealand frozen wethers) at end of year. *The Economist,* Annual Commercial History and Review through 1953, then British Wholesale Prices. (33) *Herrings 1264–1400:* kind not specified; most of earlier entries from E. Anglia, and of later from monastic accounts esp. Wolrichston in Warwickshire. R, I, 635–640. (34) *White Herrings 1404–1590:* generally bought at Stourbridge fair. Through 1583, R, IV, 540–544; 1584–90, from entries in R, VI, 392–4. (35) *Red Herrings 1405–1561:* generally bought at Stourbridge fair. R, IV, 540–544. (36) *Haberden (salt cod) 1584–1703:* mostly from King's College, Cambridge, and probably mostly bought at Stourbridge fair. R, V, 427–8. (37) *Crimped (dried) cod 1783–1830:* Lord Steward's dept. B, 369–71, 370. (38) *Fresh cod 1783–1830:* Lord Steward's dept. B, 369–71, 420–1. (39) *Herrings 1827–1902:* average declared value per barrel exported, 1827–39, from " Porter's Tables " in various BPP, 1836–43; 1840–1902, WRP, 158. (40) *Herrings 1898–1938, 1945–54:* average value per cwt. of British takings landed. Annual Reports on Sea Fisheries, later Sea Fisheries Statistical Tables, of Board, later Ministry, of Agriculture. (41) *Cod 1898–1938, 1945–54:* as for 40. (42) *Cheese 1264–1429:* same origins as 01; numerous gaps in 14th century; 1401–1429, Hornchurch (Essex) only. R, I, 430–5; III, 209–212. (43) *Cheese 1573–1752:* Suffolk cheese bought by St. Bartholomew's Hospital, Sandwich. Numerous gaps. B, 223–5, 238–40. (44) *Cheese 1684–1758:* Suffolk cheese bought by Navy Victualling, London. B, 555–6, 576. (45) *Cheese 1703–96:* Gloucester cheese bought by Chelsea Hospital, London. B, 308, 313. (46) *Cheese 1713–1824:* Gloucester cheese bought by Greenwich Hospital. B, 261, 293, 295. (47) *Cheese 1756–1827:* Cheshire cheese bought by Navy Victualling, London. B, 555–6, 576. (48) *Cheese 1815–1902:* cheese (unspecified) bought by Bethlem Royal Hospital, London. Contract price 1815–71, thereafter open market. WRP, 150. (49) *Cheese 1854–1954:* average value per cwt. of cheese imported into U.K. AS. (50) *Butter 1264–1379:* same origins as 01. R, I, 430–434. (51) *Butter 1561–1702:* 1561–83, Oxford city accounts; 1584–1702, average of prices recorded mostly by New College Oxford, King's College, Cambridge, and Winchester. R, III, 217–8; V, 372–8. (52) *Butter 1659–1767:* fresh butter bought by St. Bartholomew's Hospital, Sandwich. B, 222–3, 236. (53) *Butter 1684–1827:* purchases by Navy Victualling, London. B, 555, 576. (54) *Butter 1805–1902:* contract prices paid by Royal Hospital, Greenwich. WRP, 139. (55) *Butter 1815–1902:* contract prices 1815–71, market prices 1872–1902, paid by Bethlem Royal Hospital, London. WRP, 140. (56) *Butter 1886–1954:* average value of butter imported into the U.K. AS. (57) *Malt 1266–1703:* specified as "first quality" through 1401, unspecified afterwards; same origins as 01. R, I, 227–235; IV, 283–291; V, 268–274. (58) *Malt 1596–1832:* Windsor market prices, average of Michaelmas and Lady Day, recorded by Eton College for assessing money due in lieu of malt rents. B, 111, 144–147. (59) *Malt 1684–1827:* price paid by Navy Victualling, London. B, 547–8, 574–5. (60) *Malt 1805–65:* contract price paid by Royal Hospital, Greenwich. J. R. McCulloch, Dictionary of Commerce (1882 edn.), 1138–40. (61) *Malt 1863–1954:* average declared value of exports. AS. (62) *Hops 1559–1594:* mainly Flemish; price paid by Eton College. B, 108, 143–4. (63) *Hops 1584–1703:* English; mainly Eton and King's College, Cambridge, with Winchester coming in from 1644. R, V, 289–301. (64) *Hops 1684–1827:* kind unspecified; bought by Navy Victualling, London. B, 539–40, 567–569. Some gaps filled according to movement of Greenwich Hospital price, B, 254–5, 292, 294. (65) *Hops 1805–64:* average contract price paid by Royal Hospital, Greenwich. WRP, 88. (66) *Hops 1854–1914:* average declared value of imports. AS. (67) *Hops 1906–54:* index no. of average price of home-grown hops. Ministry of Agriculture: Agricultural Statistics. (68) *Sugar 1689–1771:* brown, bought by Navy Victualling, London. Gaps after 1750 filled by reference to Navy Victualling, Plymouth. B, 557–8, 565. (69) *Sugar 1765–1831:* powder or Lisbon, bought by Lord Steward's dept. B, 383–5, 429–431. (70) *Sugar 1820–1954:* average declared export value. 1820–1902, WRP, 165; 1903–54, AS. (71) *Tea 1801–71:* average price in bond. WRP, 176–7. (72) *Tea 1854–1954:* average declared value of imports. 1854–1902, WRP, 173; 1903–54, AS. (73) *Charcoal 1441–1583:* mostly at Oxford and Cambridge. R, IV, 383–7. (74) *Charcoal 1442–1583:* as for 73. R, IV, 383–7. (75) *Charcoal 1551–1785:* price paid by Eton College. B, 119–22, 143–7. (76) *Charcoal 1584–1703:* at Oxford or Winchester. R, V, 398–405. (77) *Charcoal*

*1584–1703:* at Cambridge, mainly King's College. R, V, 398–405. (78) *Charcoal 1609–47:* at Oxford. R, V, 398–401. (79) *Charcoal 1576–1785:* price paid by Westminster (School and Abbey). B, 177–8, 193–5. (80) *Coal 1584–1703:* usually Newcastle coal, bought at Cambridge, mostly by King's College. R, V, 398–404. (81) *Coal 1586–1831:* bought for Westminster (School and Abbey) brewery 1586–1619, College 1620–1831. B, 173–7, 193–6. (82) *Coal 1654–1832:* bought for Eton College brewery. B, 116–9, 145–7. (83) *Coal 1717–1902:* Newcastle coal delivered Royal Naval Hospital, Greenwich. B, 264–7, 294–5. (84) *Coal 1846–1954:* price in London of Wallsend Hetton, 1846–1916, best Yorkshire house coal after 1916: JRSS. (85) *Candles 1321–1703:* same origins as 01. R, I, 439–44; IV, 376–80; V, 398–404. (86) *Candles 1645–1831:* price paid by Eton College, less tax. B, 128–9, 145–7. (87) *Candles 1703–1811:* price paid by Chelsea Hospital, less tax. B, 311–2, 313. (88) *Candles 1713–1868:* price paid by Greenwich Hospital, less tax. B, 271, 293–5. J. R. McCulloch, Dictionary of Commerce, 1138–40. (89) *Tallow 1846–1910:* town. JRSS. (90) *Oil 1402–1535:* olive and rape oil, mainly at Oxford and Cambridge. R, IV, 376–9. (91) *Oil 1567–1783:* train-oil bought for Naval Stores. B, 633–4, 670–4, 680. (92) *Oil 1783–1853:* Northern (1783–1839), Southern (1840–53), oil, without casks. TN, II, 394–5, 407; III, 297; IV, 430; VI, 504. (93) *Oil 1854–1880:* price exclusive of duty of train or blubber oil, from the Northern whale fishery and British North America: AS. (94) *Oil 1856–1912:* average import value of petroleum, illuminating and lubricating: AS. (95) *Oil 1903–54:* average import value of petroleum, lamp oil, later called Kerosene (burning oil): AS. (96) *Gas 1876–1954:* price paid by domestic consumers: 1876–1937, mean of prices of three London gas companies. Report from the Select Committee on Gas Undertakings, BPP, 1918, III, appx. 4. 1949–54, price of North Thames Gas Board, from Annual Reports; rise 1937–49 distributed by years according to rise in price of coal. (97) *Canvas 1265–1583:* same origins as 01. R, I, 587–92; IV, 583–88. (98) *Shirting 1402–1583, Sheeting or Shirting 1584–1701:* same origins as 01. R, IV, 583–88; V, 561–4. (99) *Linen and Canvas 1506–1673:* price paid by Eton College. B, 131–2, 143–5. (100) *Cloth 1394–1624:* bought by Winchester College for scholars and servants. B, 45–6, 85–89, 90. (101) *Cloth 1394–1554:* bought by Winchester College for fellows, stewards and others. B, 46–7, 85–7. (102) *Cloth 1402–1583:* average of three qualities of cloth, bought mainly by New College, Oxford and King's College, Cambridge. R, IV, 583–8. (103) *Cloth 1576–1757:* broad cloth bought for scholars of Westminster School. B, 182, 193–6. (104) *Cloth 1615–1757:* bought for scholars and choristers of Eton College. B, 130–1, 144–7. (105) *Cloth 1748–1829:* blue cloth bought by Greenwich Hospital. B, 273, 293, 295. (106) *Yarn, woollen and worsted, 1831–1954:* average declared value of exports. 1831–9, "Porter's Tables" in BPP; then AS. (107) *Cotton cloth 1812–60:* average price paid by printers per piece of 7/8–72 reed printing cloth. JRSS, 1861, 491–7. (108) *Cotton cloth 1858–1954:* 1858–1906, mean of 26 in. 66 reed printer's cloth and 40 in. 66 reed shirting; 1897–1950, 38 in. or 39 in. shirting; 1949–54, a printer's cloth. *The Economist*, Annual Commercial History and Review.

## APPENDIX B

### TABLE 3

INDEXES (1451–75 = 100) OF (1) PRICE OF COMPOSITE UNIT OF CONSUMABLES; (2) EQUIVALENT OF WAGE-RATE OF BUILDING CRAFTSMAN, EXPRESSED IN THE ABOVE COMPOSITE PHYSICAL UNIT; IN SOUTHERN ENGLAND, 1264–1954.

| | (1) | (2) | | (1) | (2) | | (1) | (2) | | (1) | (2) |
|---|---|---|---|---|---|---|---|---|---|---|---|
| 1260 | | | 1300 | 113 | 44 | 1340 | 96 | 52 | 1380 | 106 | 78 |
| 1261 | | | 1301 | 89 | — | 1341 | 86 | 58 | 1381 | 119 | 70 |
| 1262 | | | 1302 | 93 | — | 1342 | 85 | 59 | 1382 | 111 | 75 |
| 1263 | | | 1303 | 89 | — | 1343 | 84 | 60 | 1383 | 108 | 77 |
| 1264 | 83 | 60 | 1304 | 94 | 62 | 1344 | 97 | 52 | 1384 | 116 | 72 |
| 1265 | 80 | 63 | 1305 | 97 | 60 | 1345 | 98 | 51 | 1385 | 112 | 74 |
| 1266 | 83 | 60 | 1306 | 100 | 58 | 1346 | 88 | 57 | 1386 | 104 | 80 |
| 1267 | — | — | 1307 | 94 | 62 | 1347 | 109 | 46 | 1387 | 100 | 83 |
| 1268 | 70 | 71 | 1308 | 105 | 55 | 1348 | 116 | 43 | 1388 | 102 | 81 |
| 1269 | 83 | 60 | 1309 | 119 | — | 1349 | 97 | 52 | 1389 | 100 | 83 |
| | | | | | | | | | | | |
| 1270 | — | — | 1310 | 135 | — | 1350 | 102 | 49 | 1390 | 106 | 78 |
| 1271 | 98 | 51 | 1311 | 123 | 54 | 1351 | 134 | — | 1391 | 133 | 62 |
| 1272 | 130 | 38 | 1312 | 108 | 62 | 1352 | 160 | — | 1392 | 104 | 80 |
| 1273 | 98 | 51 | 1313 | 101 | 66 | 1353 | 138 | — | 1393 | 100 | 83 |
| 1274 | 95 | 53 | 1314 | 112 | 60 | 1354 | 117 | — | 1394 | 101 | 82 |
| 1275 | 100 | 50 | 1315 | 132 | 51 | 1355 | 115 | — | 1395 | 93 | 89 |
| 1276 | 96 | 52 | 1316 | 216 | 31 | 1356 | 121 | — | 1396 | 99 | 84 |
| 1277 | 97 | 52 | 1317 | 215 | 31 | 1357 | 133 | — | 1397 | 116 | 72 |
| 1278 | 103 | 49 | 1318 | 154 | 44 | 1358 | 139 | — | 1398 | 121 | 69 |
| 1279 | 94 | 53 | 1319 | 119 | 56 | 1359 | 126 | — | 1399 | 113 | 73 |
| | | | | | | | | | | | |
| 1280 | 94 | 53 | 1320 | 106 | 63 | 1360 | 135 | 61 | 1400 | 104 | 80 |
| 1281 | 93 | 54 | 1321 | 121 | 55 | 1361 | 131 | 63 | 1401 | 130 | 64 |
| 1282 | 104 | 48 | 1322 | 141 | 48 | 1362 | 153 | 54 | 1402 | 127 | 65 |
| 1283 | 111 | 45 | 1323 | 165 | 41 | 1363 | 155 | 54 | 1403 | 119 | — |
| 1284 | 120 | 42 | 1324 | 137 | 49 | 1364 | 151 | 55 | 1404 | 99 | — |
| 1285 | 83 | 60 | 1325 | 127 | 53 | 1365 | 143 | 58 | 1405 | 99 | — |
| 1286 | 91 | 55 | 1326 | 124 | 54 | 1366 | 121 | 69 | 1406 | 100 | — |
| 1287 | 91 | 55 | 1327 | 96 | 70 | 1367 | 137 | 61 | 1407 | 99 | — |
| 1288 | 72 | 69 | 1328 | 96 | 70 | 1368 | 139 | 60 | 1408 | 107 | — |
| 1289 | 69 | 72 | 1329 | 119 | 56 | 1369 | 150 | 55 | 1409 | 120 | — |
| | | | | | | | | | | | |
| 1290 | 80 | 63 | 1330 | 120 | 56 | 1370 | 184 | 45 | 1410 | 130 | — |
| 1291 | 106 | 47 | 1331 | 134 | 50 | 1371 | 164 | 51 | 1411 | 106 | — |
| 1292 | 96 | 52 | 1332 | 131 | 51 | 1372 | 132 | 63 | 1412 | 103 | 97 |
| 1293 | 93 | 54 | 1333 | 111 | 60 | 1373 | 131 | 63 | 1413 | 108 | 93 |
| 1294 | 110 | 45 | 1334 | 99 | 68 | 1374 | 125 | 66 | 1414 | 108 | 93 |
| 1295 | 131 | 38 | 1335 | 96 | 70 | 1375 | 125 | 66 | 1415 | 115 | 87 |
| 1296 | 104 | 48 | 1336 | 101 | 66 | 1376 | 146 | 57 | 1416 | 124 | 81 |
| 1297 | 93 | 54 | 1337 | 111 | 60 | 1377 | 112 | 74 | 1417 | 129 | 78 |
| 1298 | 106 | 47 | 1338 | 85 | — | 1378 | 95 | 87 | 1418 | 114 | 88 |
| 1299 | 96 | 52 | 1339 | 79 | — | 1379 | 94 | 88 | 1419 | 95 | 105 |

## APPENDIX B—*Continued*

| | (1) | (2) | | (1) | (2) | | (1) | (2) | | (1) | (2) |
|---|---|---|---|---|---|---|---|---|---|---|---|
| 1420 | 102 | 98 | 1470 | 102 | 98 | 1520 | 137 | 73 | 1570 | 300 | 56 |
| 1421 | 93 | 108 | 1471 | 103 | 97 | 1521 | 167 | 60 | 1571 | 265 | 63 |
| 1422 | 97 | 103 | 1472 | 104 | 96 | 1522 | 160 | 63 | 1572 | 270 | 62 |
| 1423 | 108 | 93 | 1473 | 97 | 103 | 1523 | 136 | 74 | 1573 | 274 | 61 |
| 1424 | 103 | 97 | 1474 | 95 | 105 | 1524 | 133 | 75 | 1574 | 374 | — |
| 1425 | 109 | 92 | 1475 | 90 | 111 | 1525 | 129 | 78 | 1575 | — | — |
| 1426 | 103 | 97 | 1476 | 85 | 118 | 1526 | 133 | 75 | 1576 | 309 | — |
| 1427 | 96 | 104 | 1477 | 81 | 123 | 1527 | 147 | 68 | 1577 | 363 | — |
| 1428 | 99 | 101 | 1478 | 89 | 112 | 1528 | 179 | 56 | 1578 | 351 | — |
| 1429 | 127 | 79 | 1479 | 97 | 103 | 1529 | 159 | 63 | 1579 | 326 | — |
| | | | | | | | | | | | |
| 1430 | 138 | 72 | 1480 | 103 | 97 | 1530 | 169 | 59 | 1580 | 342 | 58 |
| 1431 | 115 | 87 | 1481 | 115 | 87 | 1531 | 154 | 65 | 1581 | 347 | 58 |
| 1432 | 102 | 98 | 1482 | 145 | 69 | 1532 | 179 | 56 | 1582 | 343 | 58 |
| 1433 | 112 | 89 | 1483 | 162 | 62 | 1533 | 169 | — | 1583 | 324 | 62 |
| 1434 | 109 | 92 | 1484 | 128 | 78 | 1534 | 145 | — | 1584 | 333 | 60 |
| 1435 | 105 | 95 | 1485 | 99 | 101 | 1535 | 131 | — | 1585 | 338 | 59 |
| 1436 | 95 | 105 | 1486 | 86 | 116 | 1536 | 164 | — | 1586 | 352 | 57 |
| 1437 | 93 | 108 | 1487 | 103 | 97 | 1537 | 155 | — | 1587 | 491 | 41 |
| 1438 | 128 | 78 | 1488 | 110 | 90 | 1538 | 138 | — | 1588 | 346 | 58 |
| 1439 | 154 | 65 | 1489 | 109 | 92 | 1539 | 147 | — | 1589 | 354 | 56 |
| | | | | | | | | | | | |
| 1440 | 140 | 71 | 1490 | 106 | 94 | 1540 | 158 | — | 1590 | 396 | 51 |
| 1441 | 93 | 108 | 1491 | 112 | 89 | 1541 | 165 | — | 1591 | 459 | 44 |
| 1442 | 85 | 118 | 1492 | 103 | 97 | 1542 | 172 | — | 1592 | 370 | 54 |
| 1443 | 97 | 103 | 1493 | 117 | 85 | 1543 | 171 | — | 1593 | 356 | 56 |
| 1444 | 102 | 98 | 1494 | 96 | 104 | 1544 | 178 | — | 1594 | 381 | 52 |
| 1445 | 87 | 115 | 1495 | 89 | 112 | 1545 | 191 | — | 1595 | 515 | 39 |
| 1446 | 95 | 105 | 1496 | 94 | 106 | 1546 | 248 | — | 1596 | 505 | 40 |
| 1447 | 100 | 100 | 1497 | 101 | 99 | 1547 | 231 | — | 1597 | 685 | 29 |
| 1448 | 102 | 98 | 1498 | 96 | 104 | 1548 | 193 | 61 | 1598 | 579 | 35 |
| 1449 | 106 | 94 | 1499 | 99 | 101 | 1549 | 214 | — | 1599 | 474 | 42 |
| | | | | | | | | | | | |
| 1450 | 102 | 98 | 1500 | 94 | 106 | 1550 | 262 | — | 1600 | 459 | 44 |
| 1451 | 109 | 92 | 1501 | 107 | 93 | 1551 | 285 | — | 1601 | 536 | 37 |
| 1452 | 97 | 103 | 1502 | 122 | 82 | 1552 | 276 | 48 | 1602 | 471 | 42 |
| 1453 | 97 | 103 | 1503 | 114 | 88 | 1553 | 259 | — | 1603 | 448 | 45 |
| 1454 | 105 | 95 | 1504 | 107 | 93 | 1554 | 276 | — | 1604 | 404 | 50 |
| 1455 | 94 | 106 | 1505 | 103 | 97 | 1555 | 270 | — | 1605 | 448 | 45 |
| 1456 | 101 | 99 | 1506 | 106 | 94 | 1556 | 370 | — | 1606 | 468 | 43 |
| 1457 | 93 | 108 | 1507 | 98 | 102 | 1557 | 409 | — | 1607 | 449 | 45 |
| 1458 | 99 | 101 | 1508 | 100 | 100 | 1558 | 230 | — | 1608 | 507 | 39 |
| 1459 | 95 | 105 | 1509 | 92 | 109 | 1559 | 255 | — | 1609 | 559 | 36 |
| | | | | | | | | | | | |
| 1460 | 97 | 103 | 1510 | 103 | 97 | 1560 | 265 | — | 1610 | 503 | 40 |
| 1461 | 117 | 85 | 1511 | 97 | 103 | 1561 | 283 | 59 | 1611 | 463 | 43 |
| 1462 | 115 | 87 | 1512 | 101 | 99 | 1562 | 266 | 63 | 1612 | 524 | 38 |
| 1463 | 88 | 114 | 1513 | 120 | 83 | 1563 | — | — | 1613 | 549 | 36 |
| 1464 | 86 | 116 | 1514 | 118 | 85 | 1564 | — | — | 1614 | 567 | 35 |
| 1465 | 108 | 93 | 1515 | 107 | 93 | 1565 | 290 | 58 | 1615 | 561 | 36 |
| 1466 | 109 | 92 | 1516 | 110 | 90 | 1566 | 287 | 58 | 1616 | 562 | 36 |
| 1467 | 108 | 93 | 1517 | 111 | 90 | 1567 | 282 | 59 | 1617 | 537 | 37 |
| 1468 | 106 | 94 | 1518 | 116 | 86 | 1568 | 281 | 59 | 1618 | 524 | 38 |
| 1469 | 107 | 93 | 1519 | 129 | 78 | 1569 | 276 | 61 | 1619 | 494 | 40 |

## APPENDIX B—*Continued*

| | (1) | (2) | | (1) | (2) | | (1) | (2) | | (1) | (2) |
|---|---|---|---|---|---|---|---|---|---|---|---|
| 1620 | 485 | 41 | 1670 | 577 | 52 | 1720 | 635 | 58 | 1770 | 714 | 56 |
| 1621 | 461 | 43 | 1671 | 595 | 50 | 1721 | 604 | 61 | 1771 | 775 | 52 |
| 1622 | 523 | 38 | 1672 | 557 | 54 | 1722 | 554 | 66 | 1772 | 858 | 47 |
| 1623 | 588 | 34 | 1673 | 585 | 51 | 1723 | 525 | 70 | 1773 | 855 | 47 |
| 1624 | 543 | 37 | 1674 | 650 | 46 | 1724 | 589 | 62 | 1774 | 863 | — |
| 1625 | 534 | 37 | 1675 | 691 | 43 | 1725 | 610 | 60 | 1775 | 815 | — |
| 1626 | 552 | 36 | 1676 | 652 | 46 | 1726 | 637 | 58 | 1776 | 797 | 61 |
| 1627 | 496 | 40 | 1677 | 592 | 51 | 1727 | 596 | 62 | 1777 | 794 | 61 |
| 1628 | 466 | 43 | 1678 | 633 | 47 | 1728 | 649 | 57 | 1778 | 826 | 58 |
| 1629 | 510 | 39 | 1679 | 614 | 49 | 1729 | 681 | 54 | 1779 | 756 | 64 |
| 1630 | 595 | — | 1680 | 568 | 53 | 1730 | 599 | 61 | 1780 | 730 | 66 |
| 1631 | 682 | — | 1681 | 567 | 53 | 1731 | 553 | — | 1781 | 760 | 64 |
| 1632 | 580 | — | 1682 | 600 | 50 | 1732 | 557 | — | 1782 | 776 | 62 |
| 1633 | 565 | — | 1683 | 587 | 51 | 1733 | 544 | — | 1783 | 869 | 56 |
| 1634 | 611 | — | 1684 | 570 | 53 | 1734 | 518 | — | 1784 | 874 | 55 |
| 1635 | 597 | — | 1685 | 651 | 46 | 1735 | 529 | — | 1785 | 839 | 58 |
| 1636 | 593 | — | 1686 | 559 | 54 | 1736 | 539 | 74 | 1786 | 839 | 58 |
| 1637 | 621 | — | 1687 | 580 | 52 | 1737 | 581 | 69 | 1787 | 834 | 58 |
| 1638 | 707 | — | 1688 | 551 | — | 1738 | 563 | 71 | 1788 | 867 | 56 |
| 1639 | 607 | — | 1689 | 535 | — | 1739 | 547 | 73 | 1789 | 856 | 56 |
| 1640 | 546 | — | 1690 | 513 | — | 1740 | 644 | 62 | 1790 | 871 | 55 |
| 1641 | 586 | — | 1691 | 493 | — | 1741 | 712 | 56 | 1791 | 870 | 55 |
| 1642 | 557 | 48 | 1692 | 542 | — | 1742 | 631 | 63 | 1792 | 883 | — |
| 1643 | 553 | — | 1693 | 652 | — | 1743 | 579 | 69 | 1793 | 908 | — |
| 1644 | 531 | — | 1694 | 693 | — | 1744 | 518 | 77 | 1794 | 978 | — |
| 1645 | 574 | — | 1695 | 645 | — | 1745 | 528 | 76 | 1795 | 1091 | — |
| 1646 | 569 | — | 1696 | 697 | — | 1746 | 594 | 67 | 1796 | 1161 | 52 |
| 1647 | 667 | — | 1697 | 693 | — | 1747 | 574 | 70 | 1797 | 1045 | 57 |
| 1648 | 770 | — | 1698 | 767 | — | 1748 | 599 | 67 | 1798 | 1022 | 59 |
| 1649 | 821 | — | 1699 | 773 | — | 1749 | 609 | 66 | 1799 | 1148 | 52 |
| 1650 | 839 | — | 1700 | 671 | — | 1750 | 590 | 68 | 1800 | 1567 | 38 |
| 1651 | 704 | — | 1701 | 586 | 57 | 1751 | 574 | 70 | 1801 | 1751 | 34 |
| 1652 | 648 | — | 1702 | 582 | — | 1752 | 601 | 67 | 1802 | 1348 | 45 |
| 1653 | 579 | — | 1703 | 551 | — | 1753 | 585 | 68 | 1803 | 1268 | — |
| 1654 | 543 | — | 1704 | 587 | — | 1754 | 615 | 65 | 1804 | 1309 | — |
| 1655 | 531 | 56 | 1705 | 548 | — | 1755 | 578 | 69 | 1805 | 1521 | — |
| 1656 | 559 | 54 | 1706 | 583 | — | 1756 | 602 | 66 | 1806 | 1454 | 49 |
| 1657 | 612 | 49 | 1707 | 531 | — | 1757 | 733 | 55 | 1807 | 1427 | 50 |
| 1658 | 646 | 46 | 1708 | 571 | — | 1758 | 731 | 55 | 1808 | 1476 | 49 |
| 1659 | 700 | 43 | 1709 | 697 | — | 1759 | 673 | 59 | 1809 | 1619 | 44 |
| 1660 | 684 | 44 | 1710 | 798 | 46 | 1760 | 643 | 62 | 1810 | 1670 | 48 |
| 1661 | 648 | 46 | 1711 | 889 | 41 | 1761 | 614 | 65 | 1811 | 1622 | 49 |
| 1662 | 769 | 39 | 1712 | 638 | 58 | 1762 | 638 | 63 | 1812 | 1836 | 44 |
| 1663 | 675 | 44 | 1713 | 594 | 62 | 1763 | 655 | 61 | 1813 | 1881 | 43 |
| 1664 | 657 | 46 | 1714 | 635 | 58 | 1764 | 713 | 56 | 1814 | 1642 | 49 |
| 1665 | 616 | 49 | 1715 | 646 | 57 | 1765 | 738 | 54 | 1815 | 1467 | 55 |
| 1666 | 664 | 45 | 1716 | 645 | 57 | 1766 | 747 | 54 | 1816 | 1344 | 60 |
| 1667 | 577 | 52 | 1717 | 602 | 61 | 1767 | 790 | 51 | 1817 | 1526 | 52 |
| 1668 | 602 | 50 | 1718 | 575 | 64 | 1768 | 781 | 51 | 1818 | 1530 | 52 |
| 1669 | 572 | 52 | 1719 | 609 | 60 | 1769 | 717 | 56 | 1819 | 1492 | 54 |

## APPENDIX B—*Continued*

| | (1) | (2) | | (1) | (2) | | (1) | (2) | | (1) | (2) |
|---|---|---|---|---|---|---|---|---|---|---|---|
| 1820 | 1353 | 59 | 1860 | 1314 | 68 | 1900 | 994 | 134 | 1940 | 1574 | 222 |
| 1821 | 1190 | 67 | 1861 | 1302 | 72 | 1901 | 986 | 135 | 1941 | 1784 | 206 |
| 1822 | 1029 | 78 | 1862 | 1290 | 72 | 1902 | 963 | 138 | 1942 | 2130 | 176 |
| 1823 | 1099 | 73 | 1863 | 1144 | 82 | 1903 | 1004 | 133 | 1943 | 2145 | 183 |
| 1824 | 1193 | 67 | 1864 | 1200 | 78 | 1904 | 985 | 135 | 1944 | 2216 | 184 |
| 1825 | 1400 | 57 | 1865 | 1238 | — | 1905 | 989 | 135 | 1945 | 2282 | 186 |
| 1826 | 1323 | 60 | 1866 | 1296 | 82 | 1906 | 1016 | 131 | 1946 | 2364 | 208 |
| 1827 | 1237 | 65 | 1867 | 1346 | 79 | 1907 | 1031 | 129 | 1947 | 2580 | 210 |
| 1828 | 1201 | 67 | 1868 | 1291 | 82 | 1908 | 1043 | 128 | 1948 | 2781 | 198 |
| 1829 | 1189 | 67 | 1869 | 1244 | 86 | 1909 | 1058 | 126 | 1949 | 3145 | 178 |
| | | | | | | | | | | | |
| 1830 | 1146 | 70 | 1870 | 1241 | 86 | 1910 | 994 | 134 | 1950 | 3155 | 180 |
| 1831 | 1260 | 63 | 1871 | 1320 | 81 | 1911 | 984 | 135 | 1951 | 3656 | 170 |
| 1832 | 1167 | 69 | 1872 | 1378 | — | 1912 | 999 | 133 | 1952 | 3987 | 167 |
| 1833 | 1096 | 73 | 1873 | 1437 | 84 | 1913 | 1021 | 131 | 1953 | 3735 | 187 |
| 1834 | 1011 | 79 | 1874 | 1423 | 84 | 1914 | 1147 | 124 | 1954 | 3825 | 194 |
| 1835 | 1028 | 78 | 1875 | 1310 | 92 | 1915 | 1317 | 114 | | | |
| 1836 | 1141 | 70 | 1876 | 1370 | 88 | 1916 | 1652 | 94 | | | |
| 1837 | 1169 | 68 | 1877 | 1330 | 90 | 1917 | 1965 | 87 | | | |
| 1838 | 1177 | 68 | 1878 | 1281 | 94 | 1918 | 2497 | 80 | | | |
| 1839 | 1263 | 63 | 1879 | 1210 | 99 | 1919 | 2254 | 126 | | | |
| | | | | | | | | | | | |
| 1840 | 1286 | 62 | 1880 | 1174 | 102 | 1920 | 2591 | 154 | | | |
| 1841 | 1256 | 64 | 1881 | 1213 | 99 | 1921 | 2048 | 167 | | | |
| 1842 | 1161 | 69 | 1882 | 1140 | 105 | 1922 | 1672 | 164 | | | |
| 1843 | 1030 | 78 | 1883 | 1182 | 102 | 1923 | 1726 | 159 | | | |
| 1844 | 1029 | 78 | 1884 | 1071 | 112 | 1924 | 1740 | 172 | | | |
| 1845 | 1079 | 74 | 1885 | 1026 | 117 | 1925 | 1708 | 176 | | | |
| 1846 | 1122 | 71 | 1886 | 931 | 129 | 1926 | 1577 | 190 | | | |
| 1847 | 1257 | 65 | 1887 | 955 | 126 | 1927 | 1496 | 201 | | | |
| 1848 | 1105 | 74 | 1888 | 950 | 126 | 1928 | 1485 | 202 | | | |
| 1849 | 1035 | 79 | 1889 | 948 | 127 | 1929 | 1511 | 199 | | | |
| | | | | | | | | | | | |
| 1850 | 969 | 84 | 1890 | 947 | 127 | 1930 | 1275 | 229 | | | |
| 1851 | 961 | 85 | 1891 | 998 | 120 | 1931 | 1146 | 247 | | | |
| 1852 | 978 | 84 | 1892 | 996 | 120 | 1932 | 1065 | 266 | | | |
| 1853 | 1135 | 79 | 1893 | 914 | 137 | 1933 | 1107 | 248 | | | |
| 1854 | 1265 | 71 | 1894 | 982 | 127 | 1934 | 1097 | 251 | | | |
| 1855 | 1274 | 71 | 1895 | 968 | 129 | 1935 | 1149 | 254 | | | |
| 1856 | 1264 | 71 | 1896 | 947 | 132 | 1936 | 1211 | 248 | | | |
| 1857 | 1287 | 70 | 1897 | 963 | 130 | 1937 | 1275 | 242 | | | |
| 1858 | 1190 | 76 | 1898 | 982 | 127 | 1938 | 1274 | 249 | | | |
| 1859 | 1214 | 74 | 1899 | 950 | 140 | 1939 | 1209 | 269 | | | |

APPENDIX C

TABLES SHOWING SUB-WEIGHTING OF THE COMPONENT SERIES OF THE INDEX OF THE PRICE OF A COMPOSITE UNIT OF CONSUMABLES.

**I Farinaceous**

(i) *Wheat*

| | *Weighting of component series of the wheat index:* | | | | | | |
|---|---|---|---|---|---|---|---|
| | *01* | *02* | *03* | *04* | *05* | *06* | *07* |
| 1264–1582 | 1 | | | | | | |
| 1583–1594 | 5 | 1 | | | | | |
| 1595–1630 | 5 | 1 | 1 | | | | |
| 1631–1703 | 5 | 1 | 1 | 1 | | | |
| 1704–1770 | — | 1 | 1 | 1 | | | |
| 1771–1818 | — | — | 1 | 1 | 5 | | |
| 1819–1826 | — | — | 1 | — | 5 | | |
| 1827–1853 | — | — | — | — | 1 | | |
| 1854–1869 | — | — | — | — | 3 | 1 | |
| 1870–1884 | — | — | — | — | 2 | 1 | |
| 1885–1894 | — | — | — | — | 2 | 3 | |
| 1895–1907 | — | — | — | — | 1 | 3 | |
| 1908–1939 | — | — | — | — | 1 | — | 3 |
| 1940–1954 | — | — | — | — | 2 | — | 3 |

(ii) *Barley*

This was a single series.

(iii) *Rye*

This was a single series.

(iv) *Peas*

With certain adjustments these series were treated as continuous throughout.

(v) *Potatoes*

These series were treated as substantially continuous throughout.

*Combination of component series of the farinaceous index:*

This was made up of (a) wheat; (b) all other farinaceous;

(i) *Combination of all other farinaceous:*

|  | Barley | Rye | Peas | Potatoes |
|---|---|---|---|---|
| 1264–1540 | 25 | 50 | 25 | — |
| 1541–1687 | 75 | — | 25 | — |
| 1688–1734 | 25 | 50 | 25 | — |
| 1735–1784 | Barley and peas raised by one point each, and rye lowered by two points, every two years, e.g. | | | |
| 1735–1736 | 26 | 48 | 26 | |
| 1737–1738 | 27 | 46 | 27 | |
| ⋮ ⋮ | | | | |
| 1783–1784 | 50 | — | 50 | |
| 1785–1833 | Barley and peas each lose one point annually, and potatoes now coming in gain two points a year, e.g. | | | |
| 1785 | 49 | — | 49 | 2 |
| 1786 | 48 | — | 48 | 4 |
| ⋮ | | | | |
| 1833 | 1 | — | 1 | 98 |
| 1834–1954 | Potatoes are the sole component. | | | |

(ii) *Combination of wheat with "all other farinaceous" to form farinaceous index*

|  | (a) *wheat* | (b) *all other farinaceous* |
|---|---|---|
| 1264–1609 | 45 | 55 |
| 1610–1699 | (a) rises and (b) falls by one point in each decade, e.g. | |
| 1610–1619 | 46 | 54 |
| 1620–1629 | 47 | 53 |
| ⋮ ⋮ | | |
| 1690–1699 | 54 | 46 |
| 1700–1739 | 55 | 45 |
| 1740–1787 | (a) rises and (b) falls by one point each two years, e.g. | |
| 1740–1741 | 56 | 44 |
| 1742–1743 | 57 | 43 |
| ⋮ ⋮ | | |
| 1786–1787 | 79 | 21 |
| 1788–1954 | 80 | 20 |

APPENDIX C—*Continued*

## II Meat and Fish

(i) *Meat*

| | *Weighting of component series of the meat index:* | | | | | | | | | | |
|---|---|---|---|---|---|---|---|---|---|---|---|
| | *18* | *19* | *20* | *21* | *22* | *23* | *24* | *25* | *26* | *27* | *28* |
| 1264–1460 | 2 | 1 | | | | | | | | | |
| 1461–1582 | — | 1 | | | | | | | | | |
| 1584–1586 | — | — | 1 | | | | | | | | |
| 1587–1601 | — | — | 1 | 1 | | | | | | | |
| 1602–1612 | — | — | 1 | 1 | 1 | 3 | | | | | |
| 1613–1621 | — | — | 1 | 1 | 1 | 3 | 2 | | | | |
| 1622–1659 | — | — | 1 | 1 | — | 2 | 2 | | | | |
| 1660–1682 | — | — | — | 1 | — | 1 | 2 | | | | |
| 1683–1687 | — | — | — | ½ | — | 1 | 2 | ½ | | | |
| 1688–1700 | — | — | — | 1 | — | 3 | — | 1 | 1 | | |
| 1701–1724 | — | — | — | 1 | — | — | — | 1 | 1 | 3 | |
| 1725–1767 | — | — | — | 1 | — | — | — | 1 | 1 | 1½ | 1½ |

| | *25* | *26* | *27* | *28* | *29* | *30* | *31* | *32* |
|---|---|---|---|---|---|---|---|---|
| 1768–1788 | 1 | 1 | 1 | 1 | | | | |
| 1789–1795 | 1 | 1 | 1½ | 1½ | 1 | | | |
| 1796–1797 | 1 | 1 | 1 | 1 | 1 | 1 | | |
| 1798–1831 | — | 1½ | 1 | 1 | 1½ | 1 | | |
| 1832–1833 | — | 1 | — | 1 | 1 | 1 | | |
| 1834–1857 | — | — | — | — | 1 | 1 | | |
| 1858–1865 | — | — | — | — | 1 | 1 | 1 | 1 |
| 1866–1954 | — | — | — | — | — | — | 1 | 1 |

(ii) *Fish*

| | *Weighting of component series of the fish index:* | | | | | | | | |
|---|---|---|---|---|---|---|---|---|---|
| | *33* | *34* | *35* | *36* | *37* | *38* | *39* | *40* | *41* |
| 1264–1400 | 1 | | | | | | | | |
| 1404 | — | 1 | | | | | | | |
| 1405–1583 | — | 1 | 1 | | | | | | |
| 1584–1703 | — | — | — | 1 | | | | | |
| 1783–1826 | — | — | — | — | 1 | 1 | | | |
| 1827–1897 | — | — | — | — | — | — | 1 | | |
| 1898–1938 | — | — | — | — | — | — | — | 1 | 1 |
| 1945–1954 | — | — | — | — | — | — | — | 1 | 1 |

*Combination of the meat and fish indexes:*

These were combined throughout with the weights of 21 and 4 respectively.

APPENDIX C—*Continued*

### III Cheese and Butter

(i) *Cheese*

| | *Weighting of component series of the cheese index:* | | | | | | | |
|---|---|---|---|---|---|---|---|---|
| | 42 | 43 | 44 | 45 | 46 | 47 | 48 | 49 |
| 1264–1429 | 1 | | | | | | | |
| 1573–1683 | — | 1 | | | | | | |
| 1684–1702 | — | 1 | 1 | | | | | |
| 1703–1712 | — | 1 | 1 | 1 | | | | |
| 1713–1752 | — | 1 | 1 | 1 | 1 | | | |
| 1753–1755 | — | — | 1 | 1 | 1 | | | |
| 1756–1758 | — | — | 1 | 1 | 1 | 1 | | |
| 1759–1796 | — | — | — | 1 | 1 | 1 | | |
| 1797–1814 | — | — | — | — | 1 | 1 | | |
| 1815–1824 | — | — | — | — | 1 | 1 | 1 | |
| 1825–1827 | — | — | — | — | — | 1 | 1 | |
| 1828–1853 | — | — | — | — | — | — | 1 | |
| 1854–1902 | — | — | — | — | — | — | 1 | 4 |
| 1903–1954 | — | — | — | — | — | — | — | 1 |

(ii) *Butter*

| | *Weighting of component series of the butter index:* | | | | | | |
|---|---|---|---|---|---|---|---|
| | 50 | 51 | 52 | 53 | 54 | 55 | 56 |
| 1264–1379 | 1 | | | | | | |
| 1561–1658 | — | 1 | | | | | |
| 1659–1683 | — | 1 | 1 | | | | |
| 1684–1702 | — | 1 | 1 | 1 | | | |
| 1703–1767 | — | — | 1 | 1 | | | |
| 1768–1804 | — | — | — | 1 | | | |
| 1805–1814 | — | — | — | 1 | 1 | | |
| 1815–1827 | — | — | — | 1 | 1 | 1 | |
| 1828–1885 | — | — | — | — | 1 | 1 | |
| 1886–1902 | — | — | — | — | 1 | 1 | 2 |
| 1903–1954 | — | — | — | — | — | — | 1 |

*Combination of the cheese and butter index:*

These were combined throughout with the weights of 5 and $7\frac{1}{2}$ respectively.

APPENDIX C—*Continued*

## IV Drink

(i) *Malt*

| | *Weighting of component series of the malt index:* | | | | |
|---|---|---|---|---|---|
| | 57 | 58 | 59 | 60 | 61 |
| 1264–1595 | 1 | | | | |
| 1596–1683 | 1 | 1 | | | |
| 1684–1703 | 1 | 1 | 1 | | |
| 1704–1804 | — | 1 | 1 | | |
| 1805–1827 | — | 1 | 1 | 1 | |
| 1828–1832 | — | 1 | — | 1 | |
| 1833–1862 | — | — | — | 1 | |
| 1863–1865 | — | — | — | 1 | 1 |
| 1866–1954 | — | — | — | — | 1 |

(ii) *Hops*

| | *Weighting of component series of the hops index:* | | | | | |
|---|---|---|---|---|---|---|
| | 62 | 63 | 64 | 65 | 66 | 67 |
| 1559–1583 | 1 | | | | | |
| 1584–1594 | 1 | 1 | | | | |
| 1595–1683 | — | 1 | | | | |
| 1684–1703 | — | 1 | 1 | | | |
| 1704–1804 | — | — | 1 | | | |
| 1805–1827 | — | — | 1 | 1 | | |
| 1828–1853 | — | — | — | 1 | | |
| 1854–1864 | — | — | — | 1 | 1 | |
| 1865–1905 | — | — | — | — | 1 | |
| 1906–1914 | — | — | — | — | 1 | 1 |
| 1915–1954 | — | — | — | — | — | 1 |

(iii) *Sugar*

| | *Weighting of component series of the sugar index:* | | |
|---|---|---|---|
| | 68 | 69 | 70 |
| 1689–1764 | 1 | | |
| 1765–1771 | 1 | 1 | |
| 1772–1819 | — | 1 | |
| 1820–1831 | — | 1 | 1 |
| 1832–1954 | — | — | 1 |

APPENDIX C—*Continued*

(iv) *Tea*

<table>
<tr><td colspan="3">Weighting of component series of the tea index:</td></tr>
<tr><td></td><td>71</td><td>72</td></tr>
<tr><td>1801–1853</td><td>1</td><td></td></tr>
<tr><td>1854–1871</td><td>1</td><td>1</td></tr>
<tr><td>1872–1954</td><td>—</td><td>1</td></tr>
</table>

*Combination of component series of the "drink" index:*

| | Malt | Hops | Sugar | Tea |
|---|---|---|---|---|
| 1264–1558 | 22½ | | | |
| 1559–1608 | 20 | 2½ | | |
| 1609–1658 | 19½ | 3 | | |
| 1659–1688 | 19 | 3½ | | |
| 1689–1740 | 18 | 3½ | 1 | |
| 1741–1790 | 17 | 3½ | 2 | |
| 1791–1800 | 16 | 3½ | 3 | |
| 1801–1820 | 15½ | 3 | 3 | 1 |
| 1821–1830 | 14½ | 3 | 3 | 2 |
| 1831–1840 | 14 | 2½ | 3 | 3 |
| 1841–1954 | 12½ | 2½ | 3½ | 4 |

## V  Fuel and Light

(i) *Charcoal*

| | Weighting of component series of the charcoal index: | | | | | | |
|---|---|---|---|---|---|---|---|
| | *73* | *74* | *75* | *76* | *77* | *78* | *79* |
| 1441–1550 | 1 | 1 | | | | | |
| 1551–1575 | ½ | ½ | 1 | | | | |
| 1576–1583 | ½ | ½ | 1 | — | — | — | 1 |
| 1584–1608 | — | — | 1 | 1 | 1 | — | 1 |
| 1609–1647 | — | — | 1 | ½ | 1 | ½ | 1 |
| 1648–1703 | — | — | 1 | 1 | 1 | — | 1 |
| 1704–1785 | — | — | 1 | — | — | — | 1 |

(ii) *Coal*

| | Weighting of component series of the coal index: | | | | |
| | 80 | 81 | 82 | 83 | 84 |
| --- | --- | --- | --- | --- | --- |
| 1584–1653 | 1 | 1 | | | |
| 1654–1703 | 1 | 1 | 1 | | |
| 1704–1716 | — | 1 | 1 | | |
| 1717–1831 | — | 1 | 1 | 1 | |
| 1832–1845 | — | — | — | 1 | |
| 1846–1902 | — | — | — | 1 | 1 |
| 1903–1954 | — | — | — | — | 1 |

(iii) *Candles*

| | Weighting of component series of the candles index: | | | | |
| | 85 | 86 | 87 | 88 | 89 |
| --- | --- | --- | --- | --- | --- |
| 1321–1644 | 1 | | | | |
| 1645–1702 | 1 | 1 | | | |
| 1703 | 1 | 1 | 1 | | |
| 1704–1712 | — | 1 | 1 | | |
| 1713–1811 | — | 1 | 1 | 1 | |
| 1812–1831 | — | 1 | — | 1 | |
| 1832–1845 | — | — | — | 1 | |
| 1846–1868 | — | — | — | 1 | 1 |
| 1869–1910 | — | — | — | — | 1 |

(iv) *Oil, non-mineral*

Series 90 stands on its own base; series 91, 92 and 93 were treated as continuous.

(v) *Oil, mineral, and gas*

| | Weighting of component series of the index for oil, mineral, and gas: | | |
| | 94 | 95 | 96 |
| --- | --- | --- | --- |
| 1856–1875 | 1 | | |
| 1876–1895 | 3 | — | 1 |
| 1896–1902 | 2 | — | 2 |
| 1903–1912 | 1 | 1 | 2 |
| 1913–1925 | — | 2 | 2 |
| 1926–1954 | — | 1 | 3 |

*Combination of component series of the fuel and light index:*

|  | Charcoal | Coal | Candles | Oil, non-mineral | Oil, mineral, and gas |
|---|---|---|---|---|---|
| 1321–1401 | — | — | 1 | — | — |
| 1402–1440 | — | — | 4 | 1 | — |
| 1441–1535 | 5 | — | 4 | 1 | — |
| 1536–1566 | 5 | — | 4 | — | — |
| 1567–1583 | 5 | — | 4 | 1 | — |
| 1584–1635 | 4 | 1 | 4 | 1 | — |
| 1636–1685 | 3 | 2 | 4 | 1 | — |
| 1686–1735 | 2 | 3 | 4 | 1 | — |
| 1736–1785 | 1 | 4 | 4 | 1 | — |
| 1786–1855 | — | 5 | 4 | 1 | — |
| 1856–1880 | — | 7 | 3 | 1 | 1 |
| 1881–1890 | — | 7 | 3 | — | 2 |
| 1891–1900 | — | 7 | 2 | — | 3 |
| 1901–1910 | — | 7 | 1 | — | 4 |
| 1911–1954 | — | 7 | — | — | 5 |

## VI Textiles

*Weighting of component series of the textiles index:*

|  | 97 | 98 | 99 | 100 | 101 | 102 | 103 | 104 |
|---|---|---|---|---|---|---|---|---|
| 1264–1393 | 1 |  |  |  |  |  |  |  |
| 1394–1401 | 2 | — | — | 1½ | 1½ |  |  |  |
| 1402–1505 | 1 | 1 | — | 1 | 1 | 1 |  |  |
| 1506–1554 | 1 | 1 | 1 | 1½ | 1½ | 1½ |  |  |
| 1555–1575 | 1 | 1 | 1 | 2¼ | — | 2¼ |  |  |
| 1576–1583 | 1 | 1 | 1 | 1½ | — | 1½ | 1½ |  |
| 1584–1614 | — | 1 | 1 | 1½ | — | — | 1½ |  |
| 1615–1624 | — | 1 | 1 | 1 | — | — | 1 | 1 |
| 1625–1673 | — | 1 | 1 | — | — | — | 1½ | 1½ |
| 1674–1701 | — | 2 | — | — | — | — | 1½ | 1½ |

|  | 103 | 104 | 105 | 106 | 107 | 108 |
|---|---|---|---|---|---|---|
| 1702–1747 | 1 | 1 |  |  |  |  |
| 1748–1757 | 1 | 1 | 1 |  |  |  |
| 1758–1811 | — | — | 1 |  |  |  |
| 1812–1829 | — | — | 1 | — | 1 |  |
| 1830 | — | — | — | — | 1 |  |
| 1831–1857 | — | — | — | 1 | 1 |  |
| 1858–1860 | — | — | — | 1 | ½ | ½ |
| 1861–1954 | — | — | — | 1 | — | 1 |

APPENDIX C—*Continued*

TABLES SHOWING METHOD OF COMBINING COMPONENT SERIES
WITHIN EACH COMMODITY GROUP

*Note on splicing*

Not every series used in the construction of this index extends over the base period of 1451–75; when a new series becomes available it must be introduced into the calculation in index-number form. This means fixing an average level, in index number points, for some part at least of its course, which will fairly represent the relation which its price at that time bears to the prices of similar articles in the base period. The object of splicing is to fix this average level.

The general method of splicing consists of three steps:

(i) Choose a commodity whose price-series is already in continuous relation with the past and which is most similar in kind to the new commodity to be introduced;

(ii) Choose a run of years common to both the existing and the new series such as to avoid years of extreme or erratic movements and during which both series are fairly stable or follow similar trends;

(iii) Calculate a multiplier such that if it is applied to the prices in the new series throughout the chosen period, it will yield index numbers whose average value over the period will be the same as that of the old series in its existing index-number form. This multiplier is then applied to the whole run of the new series.

### I Farinaceous

(i) *Wheat*

01 expressed as an index with base 1451–75
02 spliced to 01 at 1600–07
03 spliced to 01 and 02 combined at 1600–07
04 spliced to 01, 02 and 03 combined at 1632–38
05 spliced to 03 and 04 combined at 1775–82
06 spliced to 05 at 1889–1902
07 spliced to 05 at 1908–54

(ii) *Barley*

08 expressed as an index with base 1451–75.

(iii) *Rye*

09, as 08 above, prices from 1688 onwards being treated as continuous with those before the gap beginning in 1541.

(iv) *Peas*

10 expressed as an index with base 1451–75.
11 lowered by 10% throughout and treated, so adjusted, as continuous with 10 at 1685–86 and with 12 at 1790–91.
13 spliced to 12 at 1810–19 (but 12 not used in index after 1809).

(v) *Potatoes*

Original prices of 15, 16 and 17 taken to be substantially continuous one with another.

15 and 16 spliced to index for peas at 1832–59, (for this purpose 13 continued after ceasing to be used as a component of the main index).

Last entry of 14 given, in 1830, the same *index* value as the first entry of 15, in 1832; the rest of 14 converted proportionally to index number values.

## II  Meat and Fish

(i) *Meat*

18 expressed as an index with base 1451–75.

19, as 18 above.

The average of 20 over 1584–85 given the same number of index points as 19 had over 1581–82; the rest of 20 converted proportionally.

21 and 22 adjusted to give price per 14lb; then each converted by the same factor as 20.

23 spliced to 20 at 1614–34.

24 spliced to 20 at 1616–34.

25 spliced to 21 at 1683–1767.

26 spliced to 21 at 1719–67.

27 spliced to 23 at 1701–1831.

28 spliced to 27 at 1725–1831.

29 spliced to 26 at 1789–1833.

30 spliced to 27 at 1796–1831.

31 spliced to 29 at 1858–65.

32 spliced to 30 at 1858–65.

(ii) *Fish*

34 expressed as an index with base 1451–75.

Prices of 33 halved to bring the unit of quotation in line with 34 and the resultant series expressed as relative to the base period.

35 spliced to 34 at 1451–75.

36 spliced to 34 at 1584–90, but used alone from 1584.

37 and 38 given the same index values over 1783–7 as 36 had over 1699–1703, it being assumed from the indications of the Lord Steward's accounts given by Beveridge that there was no considerable change in the price of fish over this period.

39 spliced to 37 and 38 combined at 1827–30 and used alone from 1827.

40 and 41 were combined and spliced to 39 at 1898–1902; they were used alone from 1898.

APPENDIX C—*Continued*

### III Cheese and Butter

(i) *Cheese*

In the absence of any entries over the usual base period, 42 was spliced to the index for meat at 1272–1305, after being expressed in terms of the wey.

43 taken as continuous with the adjusted series for 42.

44 spliced to 43 at 1687–1707.

45 spliced to 43 and 44 combined at 1703–52.

46 spliced to 43 and 44 combined at 1713–52.

47 spliced to 45 and 46 combined at 1756–1780.

48 spliced to 46 and 47 combined at 1815–24.

49 spliced to 48 at 1854–1902.

(ii) *Butter*

50 spliced to 42 (cheese) at 1278–1340, after being expressed in terms of pounds instead of gallons.

51 taken as continuous with 50 after adjustment.

52 spliced to 51 at 1672–1701.

53 spliced to 52 at 1719–67.

54 spliced to 53 at 1805–27.

55 spliced to 53 and 54 combined at 1815–1827.

56 spliced to 54 and 55 combined at 1886–1902.

### IV Drink

(i) *Malt*

57 expressed as an index with base 1451–75.

58 spliced to 57 at 1596–1625.

59 spliced to 57 at 1684–1703.

60 spliced to 58 and 59 combined at 1805–27.

61 spliced to 60 at 1863–65.

(ii) *Hops*

62 spliced to 57 (malt) at 1559–94.

63 spliced to 62 at 1584–91.

64 spliced to 63 at 1684–1703.

65 spliced to 64 at 1805–27.

66 spliced to 65 at 1854–64.

67 spliced to 66 at 1906–14.

(iii) *Sugar*

68 spliced to the combined index for malt over 1712–51.

69 spliced to 68 at 1765–71.

70 spliced to 69 at 1820–31.

(iv) *Tea*

    71 spliced to the combined index for malt and hops at 1845–69.
    72 spliced to 71 at 1854–71.

## V Fuel and Light

 (i) *Charcoal*

    73 expressed as an index with base 1451–75.
    74, as 73 above.
    75 spliced to 73 and 74 combined at 1551–83.
    76 spliced to 75 at 1586–1607.
    77 spliced to 75 at 1586–1607.
    78 spliced to 76 at 1609–15 with 1646–7.
    79 spliced to 73 and 74 combined at 1576–83.

 (ii) *Coal*

    80 spliced to combined index for charcoal at 1586–1635.
    81, as 80 above.
    82 spliced to 80 at 1654–1703.
    83 spliced to 81 at 1717–66.
    84 spliced to 83 at 1879–1902.

(iii) *Candles*

    85 expressed as an index with base 1451–75.
    86 spliced to 85 at 1645–1703.
    87 spliced to 86 at 1703–42.
    88 spliced to 86 at 1713–52.
    89 spliced to 88 at 1846–63.

(iv) *Oil, non-mineral*

    90 expressed as an index with base 1451–75.
    91 spliced to 85 (candles) at 1567–1637.
    92 and 93 taken as continuous with 91.

 (v) *Oil, mineral, and gas*

    94 spliced to the combined index for coal, candles and oil, non-mineral,
        at 1883–1912.
    95 spliced to 94 at 1903–1912.
    96, as 94 above.

APPENDIX C—*Continued*

## VI Textiles

97 expressed as an index with base 1451–75.

98, as 97 above.

99 spliced to 97 and 98 combined at 1506–45.

100, as 97 above.

101, as 97 above.

102, as 97 above.

103 spliced to 100 at 1576–1615.

104 spliced to 100 and 103 combined at 1615–24.

105 spliced to 103 and 104 combined at 1748–57.

First entry for 106, in 1831, given same index-number value as 105, in 1829.

107 spliced to 105 at 1812–29.

108 spliced to 107 at 1858–1860.

INDEXES OF PRICES OF COMPONENTS OF COMPOSITE UNIT OF

CONSUMABLES, MAINLY IN SOUTHERN ENGLAND, 1264–1954

(BASE 1451–75 = 100)

*Key to columns:*

col 1, Fa; Farinaceous.                 col 2, M; Meat, fish.

col 3, B; Butter, cheese.               col 4, D; Drink (malt, hops, sugar, tea).

col 5, Fu; Fuel and light.              col 6, T; Textiles.

col 7, W; Whole Composite Commodity.

| Year | 1.Fa | 2.M | 3.B | 4.D | 5.Fu | 6.T | 7.W |
|------|------|------|------|------|------|------|------|
| 1264 | 76 | 110 | 76 | — | — | — | 83 |
| 65 | 84 | 80 | 72 | — | — | 72 | 80 |
| 66 | 74 | — | 108 | 63 | — | 60 | 83 |
| 67 | 75 | — | — | 98 | — | 48 | — |
| 68 | 77 | 67 | 78 | — | — | 43 | 70 |
| 69 | 103 | 54 | 122 | — | — | 31 | 83 |
| 1270 | 91 | — | — | — | — | 60 | — |
| 71 | 129 | 51 | 92 | 144 | — | 63 | 98 |
| 72 | 142 | 170 | 107 | — | — | 31 | 130 |
| 73 | 118 | 104 | 81 | 122 | — | 28 | 98 |
| 74 | 120 | 78 | 99 | — | — | 36 | 95 |
| 75 | 136 | 82 | 100 | 130 | — | 24 | 100 |
| 76 | 98 | 108 | 94 | 120 | — | — | 96 |
| 77 | 126 | 79 | 103 | — | — | 30 | 97 |
| 78 | 104 | 103 | 108 | 126 | — | 52 | 103 |
| 79 | 84 | 110 | 101 | 111 | — | 39 | 94 |

APPENDIX C—*Continued*

| Year | 1.Fa | 2.M | 3.B | 4.D | 5.Fu | 6.T | 7.W |
|------|------|-----|-----|-----|------|-----|-----|
| 1280 | 99 | 99 | 108 | 111 | — | 33 | 94 |
| 81 | 93 | 83 | 96 | 126 | — | 49 | 93 |
| 82 | 117 | 96 | 104 | 133 | — | — | 104 |
| 83 | 115 | 82 | 89 | 187 | — | 52 | 111 |
| 84 | 133 | 119 | 91 | 180 | — | 24 | 120 |
| 85 | 96 | 84 | 90 | — | — | 29 | 83 |
| 86 | 102 | 94 | 91 | 111 | — | 31 | 91 |
| 87 | 91 | 74 | 99 | 132 | — | 43 | 91 |
| 88 | 56 | 78 | 92 | 93 | — | 30 | 72 |
| 89 | 59 | 72 | 108 | 73 | — | 30 | 69 |
| 1290 | 88 | 74 | 94 | 93 | — | 40 | 80 |
| 91 | 127 | 66 | 97 | 174 | — | 40 | 106 |
| 92 | 117 | 64 | 104 | 142 | — | 36 | 96 |
| 93 | 103 | 84 | 94 | 124 | — | 41 | 93 |
| 94 | 160 | 73 | 96 | 150 | — | 47 | 110 |
| 95 | 182 | 88 | 93 | 198 | — | 57 | 131 |
| 96 | 124 | 83 | 91 | 142 | — | 60 | 104 |
| 97 | 98 | 83 | 88 | 129 | — | 44 | 93 |
| 98 | 111 | 85 | 91 | 163 | — | 54 | 106 |
| 99 | 105 | 82 | 104 | 116 | — | 62 | 96 |
| 1300 | 101 | 116 | 102 | 144 | — | 81 | 113 |
| 01 | 84 | 72 | 104 | 126 | — | 47 | 89 |
| 02 | 89 | 90 | 98 | 115 | — | 59 | 93 |
| 03 | 92 | 85 | 100 | 102 | — | 57 | 89 |
| 04 | 82 | 108 | 85 | 120 | — | 50 | 94 |
| 05 | 111 | 86 | 81 | 132 | — | 50 | 97 |
| 06 | 105 | 92 | — | 135 | — | 50 | 100 |
| 07 | 92 | 99 | 94 | 111 | — | 55 | 94 |
| 08 | 105 | 139 | 92 | 93 | — | — | 105 |
| 09 | 135 | 81 | 92 | 165 | — | 91 | 119 |
| 1310 | 147 | 116 | 143 | 170 | — | 84 | 135 |
| 11 | 135 | 117 | 139 | — | — | 78 | 123 |
| 12 | 92 | 135 | 131 | 102 | — | 69 | 108 |
| 13 | 94 | 110 | 131 | 95 | — | 75 | 101 |
| 14 | 103 | 110 | 131 | 132 | — | 78 | 112 |
| 15 | 147 | 111 | 140 | 167 | — | 78 | 132 |
| 16 | 302 | 118 | 160 | 362 | — | 67 | 216 |
| 17 | 308 | 138 | 150 | 344 | — | 54 | 215 |
| 18 | 150 | 110 | 142 | 261 | — | 66 | 154 |
| 19 | 89 | 150 | 132 | 125 | — | 78 | 119 |
| 1320 | 100 | 119 | 126 | 102 | — | 78 | 106 |
| 21 | 117 | 112 | 136 | 131 | 179 | 78 | 121 |
| 22 | 226 | 98 | 174 | 139 | 119 | 71 | 141 |
| 23 | 183 | 105 | 166 | 269 | 159 | 70 | 165 |
| 24 | 130 | 124 | 154 | 181 | 179 | 53 | 137 |

APPENDIX C—*Continued*

| Year | 1.Fa | 2.M | 3.B | 4.D | 5.Fu | 6.T | 7.W |
|------|------|-----|-----|-----|------|-----|-----|
| 1325 | 144 | 93 | 137 | 154 | 185 | 70 | 127 |
| 26 | 105 | 106 | 139 | 158 | — | 89 | 124 |
| 27 | 76 | 94 | 106 | 106 | — | 69 | 96 |
| 28 | 78 | 115 | 120 | 97 | 129 | 45 | 96 |
| 29 | 131 | 104 | 124 | 128 | 159 | 84 | 119 |
| 1330 | 121 | 94 | 106 | 178 | 159 | 60 | 120 |
| 31 | 135 | 88 | 112 | 225 | 159 | 68 | 134 |
| 32 | 163 | 117 | 103 | 173 | — | 56 | 131 |
| 33 | 100 | 115 | 104 | 134 | 119 | 78 | 111 |
| 34 | 79 | 96 | 125 | 109 | 159 | 60 | 99 |
| 35 | 83 | 85 | 121 | 100 | — | 65 | 96 |
| 36 | 98 | 92 | 125 | 111 | 159 | 45 | 101 |
| 37 | 93 | 120 | 124 | 127 | 149 | 61 | 111 |
| 38 | 67 | 78 | 97 | 86 | 159 | 66 | 85 |
| 39 | 59 | 68 | 108 | 72 | 119 | 90 | 79 |
| 1340 | 109 | 83 | 108 | 89 | 159 | 65 | 96 |
| 41 | 74 | 79 | 104 | 96 | 129 | 55 | 86 |
| 42 | 71 | 82 | 92 | 101 | 144 | 43 | 85 |
| 43 | 83 | 84 | 86 | 100 | 119 | 36 | 84 |
| 44 | 105 | 86 | 108 | 102 | 144 | 58 | 97 |
| 45 | 72 | 94 | 162 | 94 | 159 | 56 | 98 |
| 46 | 75 | 78 | 112 | 94 | 139 | 62 | 88 |
| 47 | 127 | 88 | 123 | 124 | 159 | 54 | 109 |
| 48 | 125 | 103 | 124 | 152 | 119 | 55 | 116 |
| 49 | 80 | 90 | 119 | 113 | 159 | 55 | 97 |
| 1350 | 103 | 80 | 123 | 117 | 159 | 66 | 102 |
| 51 | 148 | 90 | 131 | 184 | 146 | 102 | 134 |
| 52 | 188 | 120 | 119 | 230 | 152 | — | 160 |
| 53 | 138 | 120 | 140 | 163 | 159 | — | 138 |
| 54 | 77 | 117 | 117 | 126 | 169 | 132 | 117 |
| 55 | 76 | 107 | 110 | 125 | 167 | — | 115 |
| 56 | 108 | 85 | 130 | 124 | 169 | 118 | 121 |
| 57 | 123 | 98 | 118 | 158 | — | 168 | 133 |
| 58 | 136 | 101 | 121 | 144 | — | 216 | 139 |
| 59 | 110 | 111 | 117 | 133 | 159 | 156 | 126 |
| 1360 | 105 | 115 | 168 | 149 | 172 | 144 | 135 |
| 61 | 119 | 104 | 123 | 186 | 159 | 96 | 131 |
| 62 | 130 | 104 | 118 | 270 | 179 | 100 | 153 |
| 63 | 143 | 123 | 142 | 213 | 159 | 144 | 155 |
| 64 | 141 | 149 | 139 | 167 | 166 | — | 151 |
| 65 | 130 | 134 | 107 | 167 | 179 | 150 | 143 |
| 66 | 111 | 137 | 124 | 109 | 159 | 102 | 121 |
| 67 | 120 | 130 | 123 | 149 | 199 | 132 | 137 |
| 68 | 157 | 114 | 116 | 167 | 199 | 96 | 139 |
| 69 | 156 | 122 | 123 | 167 | 189 | 168 | 150 |

APPENDIX C—*Continued*

| Year | 1.Fa | 2.M | 3.B | 4.D | 5.Fu | 6.T | 7.W |
|------|------|-----|-----|-----|------|-----|-----|
| 1370 | 231 | 137 | 156 | 244 | 166 | — | 184 |
| 71 | 161 | 188 | 146 | 186 | 172 | 96 | 164 |
| 72 | 120 | 140 | 154 | 116 | 159 | — | 132 |
| 73 | 132 | 129 | 111 | 118 | 159 | 156 | 131 |
| 74 | 109 | 122 | 110 | 118 | 169 | — | 125 |
| 75 | 144 | 103 | 127 | 102 | 159 | 156 | 125 |
| 76 | 143 | 116 | 154 | 159 | 166 | 168 | 146 |
| 77 | 92 | 109 | 117 | 115 | 159 | 108 | 112 |
| 78 | 70 | 110 | 99 | 93 | 159 | 66 | 95 |
| 79 | 73 | 96 | 117 | 84 | 169 | — | 94 |
| 1380 | 102 | 97 | 107 | 114 | 159 | 85 | 106 |
| 81 | 113 | 112 | — | 131 | — | — | 119 |
| 82 | 103 | 101 | 107 | 111 | 159 | 120 | 111 |
| 83 | 104 | 100 | 107 | 125 | 139 | 84 | 108 |
| 84 | 100 | 119 | 107 | 135 | 146 | 94 | 116 |
| 85 | 98 | 119 | — | 116 | 159 | — | 112 |
| 86 | 102 | 92 | 107 | 124 | 149 | 66 | 104 |
| 87 | 81 | 114 | 102 | 105 | 136 | 72 | 100 |
| 88 | 64 | 132 | 107 | 95 | 132 | 96 | 102 |
| 89 | 69 | 104 | 86 | 108 | 139 | 120 | 100 |
| 1390 | 100 | 100 | 107 | 110 | 139 | — | 106 |
| 91 | 168 | 102 | 86 | 198 | 126 | 72 | 133 |
| 92 | 93 | 107 | 107 | 115 | 139 | 75 | 104 |
| 93 | 69 | 107 | 107 | 103 | 132 | 108 | 100 |
| 94 | 74 | 101 | 118 | 103 | 149 | 92 | 101 |
| 95 | 79 | 97 | 96 | 99 | 119 | 80 | 93 |
| 96 | 95 | 84 | 107 | 115 | 119 | 88 | 99 |
| 97 | 110 | 118 | 132 | 125 | 119 | 89 | 116 |
| 98 | 124 | 119 | 112 | 147 | 119 | — | 121 |
| 99 | 96 | 109 | 118 | 134 | 146 | 85 | 113 |
| 1400 | 106 | 102 | 102 | 116 | 119 | 80 | 104 |
| 01 | 139 | 106 | 100 | 193 | 119 | 87 | 130 |
| 02 | 154 | — | 111 | 149 | 126 | 97 | 127 |
| 03 | 125 | 114 | 118 | 134 | 121 | 91 | 119 |
| 04 | 89 | 102 | 103 | 100 | 127 | 89 | 99 |
| 05 | 72 | 97 | 118 | 106 | 123 | — | 99 |
| 06 | 77 | 112 | 107 | 91 | 121 | 107 | 100 |
| 07 | 85 | 99 | 109 | 99 | 121 | 101 | 99 |
| 08 | 84 | 97 | 111 | 135 | 124 | 101 | 107 |
| 09 | 135 | 96 | 128 | 143 | 118 | 94 | 120 |
| 1410 | 165 | 124 | 116 | 131 | 117 | 107 | 130 |
| 11 | 104 | 98 | 107 | 113 | 118 | 104 | 106 |
| 12 | 89 | 101 | 103 | 110 | 117 | 107 | 103 |
| 13 | 94 | 97 | 128 | 120 | 117 | — | 108 |
| 14 | 86 | 109 | 128 | 111 | 121 | 109 | 108 |

APPENDIX C—*Continued*

| Year | 1.Fa | 2.M | 3.B | 4.D | 5.Fu | 6.T | 7.W |
|------|------|-----|-----|-----|------|-----|-----|
| 1415 | 92 | 108 | 121 | 140 | 122 | 113 | 115 |
| 16 | 125 | 115 | 120 | 143 | 117 | 112 | 124 |
| 17 | 138 | 118 | — | 157 | 116 | 102 | 129 |
| 18 | 116 | 107 | 118 | 125 | 110 | 100 | 114 |
| 19 | 109 | 86 | — | 91 | 108 | 103 | 95 |
| 1420 | 94 | 92 | 107 | 117 | 104 | 103 | 102 |
| 21 | 105 | 62 | 86 | 115 | 108 | 93 | 93 |
| 22 | 92 | 84 | 107 | 101 | 114 | 105 | 97 |
| 23 | 87 | 107 | — | 129 | 114 | — | 108 |
| 24 | 87 | 104 | 96 | 119 | 104 | 101 | 103 |
| 25 | 100 | 106 | — | 126 | 116 | 94 | 109 |
| 26 | 80 | 105 | — | 124 | 118 | 89 | 103 |
| 27 | 77 | 93 | 100 | 98 | 117 | 109 | 96 |
| 28 | 84 | 93 | 100 | 95 | 116 | 128 | 99 |
| 29 | 135 | 97 | 143 | 151 | 136 | 109 | 127 |
| 1430 | 147 | 106 | — | 200 | 136 | 107 | 138 |
| 31 | 109 | 98 | — | 153 | 116 | 103 | 115 |
| 32 | 88 | 102 | — | 110 | 116 | 98 | 102 |
| 33 | 130 | 100 | — | 120 | 124 | 95 | 112 |
| 34 | 117 | 96 | — | 127 | 122 | 99 | 109 |
| 35 | 104 | 111 | — | 94 | 122 | 99 | 105 |
| 36 | 96 | 101 | — | 74 | 118 | 99 | 95 |
| 37 | 95 | 88 | — | 97 | 112 | 90 | 93 |
| 38 | 161 | 103 | — | 152 | 112 | 112 | 128 |
| 39 | 261 | 105 | — | 186 | 118 | 96 | 154 |
| 1440 | 118 | 137 | — | 200 | 111 | 93 | 140 |
| 41 | 73 | 100 | — | 83 | 131 | 99 | 93 |
| 42 | 74 | 88 | — | 70 | 119 | 97 | 85 |
| 43 | 74 | 100 | — | 101 | 124 | 99 | 97 |
| 44 | 90 | 113 | — | 91 | 115 | 97 | 102 |
| 45 | 73 | 93 | — | 73 | 103 | 105 | 87 |
| 46 | 92 | 97 | — | 81 | 132 | 97 | 95 |
| 47 | 105 | 100 | — | 97 | 96 | 97 | 100 |
| 48 | 96 | 106 | — | 100 | 108 | 102 | 102 |
| 49 | 96 | 114 | — | 106 | 104 | 95 | 106 |
| 1450 | 91 | 114 | — | 98 | 94 | 96 | 102 |
| 51 | 127 | 98 | — | 118 | 99 | 99 | 109 |
| 52 | 107 | 94 | — | 96 | 90 | 96 | 97 |
| 53 | 106 | 96 | — | 88 | 107 | 93 | 97 |
| 54 | 96 | 105 | — | 123 | 105 | 90 | 105 |
| 55 | 79 | 94 | — | 95 | 104 | 108 | 94 |
| 56 | 95 | 97 | — | 113 | 91 | 106 | 101 |
| 57 | 81 | 101 | — | 86 | 96 | 99 | 93 |
| 58 | 100 | 101 | — | 92 | 105 | 100 | 99 |
| 59 | 100 | 101 | — | 76 | 108 | 100 | 95 |

APPENDIX C—*Continued*

| Year | 1.Fa | 2.M | 3.B | 4.D | 5.Fu | 6.T | 7.W |
|------|------|-----|-----|-----|------|-----|-----|
| 1460 | 91 | 104 | — | 87 | 103 | 99 | 97 |
| 61 | 150 | 102 | — | 121 | 104 | — | 117 |
| 62 | 141 | 98 | — | 124 | 106 | 112 | 115 |
| 63 | 86 | 101 | — | 65 | 78 | — | 88 |
| 64 | 71 | 92 | — | 84 | 91 | 92 | 86 |
| 65 | 93 | 107 | — | 136 | 93 | 95 | 108 |
| 66 | 103 | 103 | — | 121 | 123 | 107 | 109 |
| 67 | 97 | 119 | — | 102 | 100 | 109 | 108 |
| 68 | 104 | 114 | — | 106 | 99 | 94 | 106 |
| 69 | 102 | 122 | — | 84 | 98 | 120 | 107 |
| 1470 | 113 | 101 | — | 84 | 123 | 112 | 102 |
| 71 | 117 | 97 | — | 103 | 102 | 96 | 103 |
| 72 | 115 | 89 | — | 133 | 93 | 86 | 104 |
| 73 | 87 | 104 | — | 91 | 90 | 108 | 97 |
| 74 | 84 | 103 | — | 86 | 83 | 115 | 95 |
| 75 | 88 | 87 | — | 85 | 99 | 103 | 90 |
| 76 | 95 | 78 | — | 65 | 95 | 119 | 85 |
| 77 | 98 | 70 | — | 66 | 93 | 105 | 81 |
| 78 | 114 | 81 | — | 70 | 93 | 107 | 89 |
| 79 | 113 | 75 | — | 120 | 92 | 100 | 97 |
| 1480 | 110 | — | — | 98 | 87 | 105 | 103 |
| 81 | 118 | — | — | 120 | 107 | 103 | 115 |
| 82 | 161 | — | — | 163 | 102 | 99 | 145 |
| 83 | 215 | 143 | — | 195 | 97 | 112 | 162 |
| 84 | 144 | 127 | — | 132 | 106 | 110 | 128 |
| 85 | 101 | 95 | — | 107 | 80 | 103 | 99 |
| 86 | 90 | 82 | — | 65 | 91 | 130 | 86 |
| 87 | 130 | 93 | — | 93 | 90 | 114 | 103 |
| 88 | 108 | 117 | — | 107 | 97 | 108 | 110 |
| 89 | 109 | 120 | — | 81 | 86 | 136 | 109 |
| 1490 | 103 | 117 | — | 98 | 87 | 102 | 106 |
| 91 | 120 | 111 | — | 111 | 93 | 114 | 112 |
| 92 | 112 | — | — | 91 | 77 | 121 | 103 |
| 93 | 143 | — | — | 109 | 81 | 113 | 117 |
| 94 | 93 | — | — | 93 | 81 | 118 | 96 |
| 95 | 84 | — | — | 91 | 79 | 108 | 89 |
| 96 | 80 | 113 | — | 66 | 89 | 110 | 94 |
| 97 | 114 | 102 | — | 84 | 87 | 119 | 101 |
| 98 | 110 | 95 | — | 78 | 91 | 108 | 96 |
| 99 | 107 | 81 | — | 127 | 73 | 105 | 99 |
| 1500 | 93 | 88 | — | 100 | 76 | 114 | 94 |
| 01 | 127 | — | — | 99 | 91 | 107 | 107 |
| 02 | 139 | — | — | 125 | 82 | 111 | 122 |
| 03 | 130 | — | — | 102 | 98 | 126 | 114 |
| 04 | 129 | 103 | — | 95 | 96 | 116 | 107 |

APPENDIX C—*Continued*

| Year | 1.Fa | 2.M | 3.B | 4.D | 5.Fu | 6.T | 7.W |
|------|------|-----|-----|-----|------|-----|-----|
| 1505 | 111 | 99 | — | 107 | 90 | 104 | 103 |
| 06 | 123 | 101 | — | 108 | 84 | 105 | 106 |
| 07 | 107 | — | — | 91 | 85 | 105 | 98 |
| 08 | 120 | — | — | 79 | 85 | 117 | 100 |
| 09 | 85 | — | — | 89 | 92 | 114 | 92 |
| 1510 | 74 | 126 | — | 86 | 85 | 119 | 103 |
| 11 | 85 | 115 | — | 68 | 88 | 119 | 97 |
| 12 | 112 | — | — | 92 | 90 | 109 | 101 |
| 13 | 136 | — | — | 120 | 89 | 109 | 120 |
| 14 | 123 | — | — | — | 91 | 132 | 118 |
| 15 | 128 | — | — | 82 | 112 | 122 | 107 |
| 16 | 126 | — | — | 100 | 97 | 109 | 110 |
| 17 | 109 | 110 | — | 107 | 107 | 124 | 111 |
| 18 | 114 | 119 | — | 110 | 100 | 128 | 116 |
| 19 | 112 | 133 | — | 155 | 95 | 115 | 129 |
| 1520 | 140 | 158 | — | 130 | 89 | 111 | 137 |
| 21 | 201 | 167 | — | 180 | 95 | 134 | 167 |
| 22 | 172 | 187 | — | 156 | 92 | 108 | 160 |
| 23 | 110 | 170 | — | 120 | 94 | 126 | 136 |
| 24 | 98 | 184 | — | 93 | 92 | 131 | 133 |
| 25 | 98 | 165 | — | 131 | 106 | 126 | 129 |
| 26 | 100 | 160 | — | 131 | 101 | 124 | 133 |
| 27 | 193 | 156 | — | 110 | 97 | 142 | 147 |
| 28 | 218 | 149 | — | 257 | 97 | 117 | 179 |
| 29 | 193 | 154 | — | 158 | 94 | 159 | 159 |
| 1530 | 208 | 171 | — | 164 | 102 | 152 | 169 |
| 31 | 151 | 177 | — | 151 | 100 | 129 | 154 |
| 32 | 193 | 175 | — | 225 | 109 | 126 | 179 |
| 33 | 214 | 156 | — | 191 | 93 | 138 | 169 |
| 34 | 138 | 155 | — | 151 | 98 | 146 | 145 |
| 35 | 112 | 158 | — | 104 | 92 | 156 | 131 |
| 36 | 214 | 158 | — | 167 | 100 | 137 | 164 |
| 37 | 173 | 162 | — | 151 | 100 | 144 | 155 |
| 38 | 135 | 163 | — | 104 | 100 | 147 | 138 |
| 39 | 132 | 168 | — | 139 | 103 | 148 | 147 |
| 1540 | 144 | 190 | — | 144 | 96 | 149 | 158 |
| 41 | 148 | 203 | — | — | 88 | 155 | 165 |
| 42 | 160 | 220 | — | 135 | 102 | 154 | 172 |
| 43 | 162 | 225 | — | 122 | 98 | 157 | 171 |
| 44 | 174 | 232 | — | 130 | 98 | 155 | 178 |
| 45 | 170 | 245 | — | — | 105 | 153 | 191 |
| 46 | 293 | 263 | — | 279 | 125 | 147 | 248 |
| 47 | 156 | 273 | — | 297 | 132 | 169 | 231 |
| 48 | 135 | 274 | — | 149 | 138 | 153 | 193 |
| 49 | 152 | 296 | — | 190 | 140 | 154 | 214 |

APPENDIX C—*Continued*

| Year | 1.Fa | 2.M | 3.B | 4.D | 5.Fu | 6.T | 7.W |
|------|------|-----|-----|-----|------|-----|-----|
| 1550 | 307 | 283 | — | 260 | 153 | 199 | 262 |
| 51 | 339 | 316 | — | 297 | 155 | 159 | 285 |
| 52 | 383 | 329 | — | 149 | 178 | 232 | 276 |
| 53 | 209 | 346 | — | 223 | 186 | 184 | 259 |
| 54 | 235 | 346 | — | 260 | 180 | 218 | 276 |
| 55 | 283 | 308 | — | — | 174 | 165 | 270 |
| 56 | 504 | 322 | — | — | 177 | 174 | 370 |
| 57 | 558 | 303 | — | 669 | 188 | 157 | 409 |
| 58 | 178 | 302 | — | — | 195 | 208 | 230 |
| 59 | 175 | 297 | — | 298 | 215 | 201 | 255 |
| 1560 | 208 | 321 | — | 279 | 230 | 183 | 265 |
| 61 | 253 | 330 | 370 | 262 | 229 | 221 | 283 |
| 62 | 236 | — | 370 | 227 | 216 | 199 | 266 |
| 63 | 225 | — | — | 348 | 217 | 232 | — |
| 64 | 337 | — | — | 321 | 213 | 229 | — |
| 65 | 214 | 326 | 339 | 356 | 207 | 225 | 290 |
| 66 | 222 | 315 | 370 | 327 | 219 | 219 | 287 |
| 67 | 257 | 302 | — | 325 | 211 | 225 | 282 |
| 68 | 271 | 310 | — | 291 | 215 | 234 | 281 |
| 69 | 265 | 304 | — | 284 | 220 | 231 | 276 |
| 1570 | 260 | 320 | 431 | 293 | 217 | 253 | 300 |
| 71 | 246 | 326 | — | 215 | 220 | 232 | 265 |
| 72 | 215 | 332 | 370 | 241 | 227 | 215 | 270 |
| 73 | 276 | — | 246 | 243 | 214 | 274 | 274 |
| 74 | 424 | — | 381 | 484 | 225 | 216 | 374 |
| 75 | 273 | — | — | 279 | 237 | 202 | — |
| 76 | 316 | — | 362 | 303 | 229 | 223 | 309 |
| 77 | 436 | — | 370 | 399 | 245 | 254 | 363 |
| 78 | 425 | — | 341 | 398 | 237 | 232 | 351 |
| 79 | 367 | — | 339 | 347 | 229 | 218 | 326 |
| 1580 | 388 | — | 349 | 371 | 247 | 236 | 342 |
| 81 | 381 | 353 | 370 | 395 | 235 | 241 | 347 |
| 82 | 422 | 347 | — | 362 | 231 | 242 | 343 |
| 83 | 337 | — | 342 | 334 | 233 | 255 | 324 |
| 84 | 352 | 370 | 373 | 331 | 236 | 255 | 333 |
| 85 | 344 | 345 | 436 | 320 | 254 | 297 | 338 |
| 86 | 565 | 352 | 426 | 218 | 260 | 234 | 352 |
| 87 | 731 | 430 | 446 | 522 | 272 | 326 | 491 |
| 88 | 346 | 407 | 430 | 317 | 267 | 236 | 346 |
| 89 | 392 | 403 | 408 | 317 | 286 | 248 | 354 |
| 1590 | 471 | 382 | 498 | 407 | 285 | 251 | 396 |
| 91 | 554 | 416 | 513 | 565 | 270 | 259 | 459 |
| 92 | 350 | 432 | 452 | 365 | 268 | 265 | 370 |
| 93 | 336 | 414 | 462 | 347 | 263 | 236 | 356 |
| 94 | 419 | 405 | 500 | 350 | 270 | 278 | 381 |

APPENDIX C—Continued

| Year | 1.Fa | 2.M | 3.B | 4.D | 5.Fu | 6.T | 7.W |
|---|---|---|---|---|---|---|---|
| 1595 | 724 | 416 | 588 | 615 | 254 | 278 | 515 |
| 96 | 680 | 441 | 567 | 587 | 278 | 280 | 505 |
| 97 | 1138 | 447 | 484 | 1025 | 278 | 270 | 685 |
| 98 | 818 | 464 | 528 | 784 | 294 | 279 | 579 |
| 99 | 526 | 474 | 513 | 568 | 301 | 289 | 474 |
| 1600 | 532 | 485 | 547 | 482 | 293 | 263 | 459 |
| 01 | 708 | 497 | 580 | 629 | 314 | 263 | 536 |
| 02 | 494 | 468 | 597 | 550 | 305 | 267 | 471 |
| 03 | 548 | 470 | 404 | 503 | 279 | 290 | 448 |
| 04 | 411 | 449 | 495 | 407 | 268 | 286 | 404 |
| 05 | 513 | 481 | 454 | 481 | 306 | 297 | 448 |
| 06 | 524 | 482 | 508 | 542 | 293 | 278 | 468 |
| 07 | 516 | 465 | 511 | 486 | 292 | 271 | 449 |
| 08 | 658 | 481 | 557 | 570 | 304 | 276 | 507 |
| 09 | 704 | 506 | 582 | 713 | 325 | 273 | 559 |
| 1610 | 541 | 500 | 578 | 619 | 326 | 271 | 503 |
| 11 | 544 | 517 | 499 | 456 | 339 | 277 | 463 |
| 12 | 661 | 495 | 608 | 591 | 320 | 277 | 524 |
| 13 | 733 | 513 | 586 | 630 | 323 | 275 | 549 |
| 14 | 760 | 520 | 670 | 637 | 326 | 272 | 567 |
| 15 | 671 | 542 | 665 | 659 | 355 | 271 | 561 |
| 16 | 679 | 550 | 621 | 667 | 360 | 274 | 562 |
| 17 | 750 | 532 | 549 | 562 | 339 | 271 | 537 |
| 18 | 658 | 532 | 637 | 535 | 336 | 270 | 524 |
| 19 | 518 | 533 | 600 | 549 | 328 | 270 | 494 |
| 1620 | 469 | 541 | 625 | 505 | 335 | 313 | 485 |
| 21 | 418 | 534 | 586 | 498 | 330 | 272 | 461 |
| 22 | 686 | 521 | 554 | 563 | 343 | 268 | 523 |
| 23 | 808 | 527 | 452 | 798 | 331 | 270 | 588 |
| 24 | 637 | 535 | 595 | 664 | 327 | 268 | 543 |
| 25 | 683 | 546 | 647 | 537 | 345 | 266 | 534 |
| 26 | 760 | 548 | 499 | 637 | 320 | 260 | 552 |
| 27 | 519 | 555 | 547 | 566 | 330 | 268 | 496 |
| 28 | 428 | 544 | 520 | 531 | 340 | 278 | 466 |
| 29 | 547 | 553 | 499 | 608 | 342 | 294 | 510 |
| 1630 | 759 | 542 | 711 | 711 | 430 | 269 | 595 |
| 31 | 1055 | 537 | 499 | 956 | 335 | 266 | 682 |
| 32 | 688 | 539 | 616 | 761 | 327 | 275 | 580 |
| 33 | 728 | 541 | — | 697 | 331 | 275 | 565 |
| 34 | 754 | 548 | 609 | 829 | 343 | 277 | 611 |
| 35 | 699 | 575 | 684 | 740 | 359 | 277 | 597 |
| 36 | 745 | 569 | 629 | 714 | 370 | 282 | 593 |
| 37 | 785 | 576 | 685 | 771 | 356 | 278 | 621 |
| 38 | 923 | 596 | 557 | 1076 | 358 | 280 | 707 |
| 39 | 698 | 586 | 616 | 803 | 370 | 282 | 607 |

APPENDIX C—*Continued*

| Year | 1.Fa | 2.M | 3.B | 4.D | 5.Fu | 6.T | 7.W |
|------|------|-----|-----|-----|------|-----|-----|
| 1640 | 561 | 582 | 701 | 616 | 364 | 283 | 546 |
| 41 | 669 | 588 | 680 | 687 | 411 | 279 | 586 |
| 42 | 587 | 574 | 603 | 684 | 426 | 279 | 557 |
| 43 | 614 | 577 | 610 | 632 | 440 | 279 | 553 |
| 44 | 522 | 564 | 698 | 566 | 491 | 279 | 531 |
| 45 | 627 | 579 | 595 | 723 | 425 | 282 | 574 |
| 46 | 660 | 602 | 582 | 656 | 407 | 288 | 569 |
| 47 | 899 | 625 | 796 | 728 | 424 | 294 | 667 |
| 48 | 1089 | 656 | 847 | 956 | 427 | 293 | 770 |
| 49 | 1267 | 685 | 916 | 949 | 443 | 295 | 821 |
| 1650 | 1145 | 770 | 885 | 1060 | 443 | 293 | 839 |
| 51 | 831 | 770 | 791 | 784 | 448 | 297 | 704 |
| 52 | 742 | 725 | 749 | 678 | 442 | 318 | 648 |
| 53 | 595 | 684 | 425 | 712 | 472 | 318 | 579 |
| 54 | 466 | 653 | 633 | 602 | 471 | 297 | 543 |
| 55 | 409 | 623 | 739 | 578 | 449 | 301 | 531 |
| 56 | 585 | 603 | 670 | 623 | 426 | 285 | 559 |
| 57 | 679 | 622 | 642 | 772 | 432 | 273 | 612 |
| 58 | 766 | 676 | 739 | 701 | 450 | 320 | 646 |
| 59 | 902 | 680 | 790 | 803 | 463 | 289 | 700 |
| 1660 | 863 | 660 | 709 | 833 | 460 | 283 | 684 |
| 61 | 797 | 654 | 708 | 740 | 460 | 282 | 648 |
| 62 | 1181 | 660 | 668 | 925 | 461 | 331 | 769 |
| 63 | 822 | 666 | 668 | 853 | 460 | 275 | 675 |
| 64 | 843 | 676 | 660 | 739 | 463 | 286 | 657 |
| 65 | 704 | 689 | 662 | 649 | 494 | 300 | 616 |
| 66 | 721 | 715 | 688 | 789 | 510 | 317 | 664 |
| 67 | 620 | 681 | — | 553 | 531 | 317 | 577 |
| 68 | 754 | 638 | 661 | 592 | 483 | 322 | 602 |
| 69 | 647 | 607 | 607 | 620 | 442 | 338 | 572 |
| 1670 | 675 | 591 | — | 645 | 438 | 338 | 577 |
| 71 | 757 | 593 | 648 | 636 | 434 | 307 | 595 |
| 72 | 678 | 594 | 632 | 543 | 447 | 304 | 557 |
| 73 | 735 | 575 | 637 | 612 | 508 | 310 | 585 |
| 74 | 856 | 607 | 726 | 733 | 458 | 300 | 650 |
| 75 | 832 | 645 | 642 | 890 | 478 | 379 | 691 |
| 76 | 649 | 624 | 1027 | 740 | 460 | 295 | 652 |
| 77 | 712 | 634 | 611 | 628 | 489 | 289 | 592 |
| 78 | 806 | 624 | 683 | 699 | 466 | 306 | 633 |
| 79 | 768 | 645 | 648 | 647 | 456 | 306 | 614 |
| 1680 | 731 | 612 | 587 | 553 | 450 | 296 | 568 |
| 81 | 750 | 628 | 580 | 547 | 427 | 261 | 567 |
| 82 | 699 | 617 | 703 | 691 | 415 | 256 | 600 |
| 83 | 673 | 612 | 576 | 731 | 403 | 256 | 587 |
| 84 | 709 | 634 | 481 | 644 | 427 | 263 | 570 |

APPENDIX C—*Continued*

| Year | 1.Fa | 2.M | 3.B | 4.D | 5.Fu | 6.T | 7.W |
|------|------|------|------|------|------|------|------|
| 1685 | 869 | 654 | 674 | 730 | 437 | 263 | 651 |
| 86 | 575 | 618 | 573 | 670 | 404 | 293 | 559 |
| 87 | 614 | 623 | 586 | 719 | 400 | 293 | 580 |
| 88 | 465 | 654 | 573 | 700 | 391 | 290 | 551 |
| 89 | 517 | 655 | 596 | 522 | 441 | 339 | 535 |
| 1690 | 507 | 645 | 583 | 468 | 466 | 299 | 513 |
| 91 | 474 | 616 | 613 | 435 | 453 | 283 | 493 |
| 92 | 658 | 607 | 603 | 497 | 465 | 290 | 542 |
| 93 | 881 | 693 | 654 | 664 | 470 | 290 | 652 |
| 94 | 951 | 693 | 705 | 745 | 495 | 290 | 693 |
| 95 | 752 | 726 | 684 | 675 | 529 | 290 | 645 |
| 96 | 810 | 742 | 687 | 829 | 538 | 290 | 697 |
| 97 | 820 | 718 | 649 | 848 | 506 | 318 | 693 |
| 98 | 990 | 723 | 702 | 1001 | 471 | 318 | 767 |
| 99 | 929 | 704 | 703 | 1125 | 461 | 281 | 773 |
| 1700 | 775 | 651 | 648 | 910 | 432 | 281 | 671 |
| 01 | 608 | 660 | 600 | 664 | 455 | 321 | 586 |
| 02 | 548 | 668 | 681 | 636 | 495 | 321 | 582 |
| 03 | 487 | 627 | 632 | 625 | 513 | 311 | 551 |
| 04 | 724 | 607 | 518 | 661 | 510 | 311 | 587 |
| 05 | 521 | 618 | 494 | 667 | 510 | 311 | 548 |
| 06 | 478 | 586 | 675 | 806 | 480 | 311 | 583 |
| 07 | 448 | 572 | 562 | 679 | 485 | 311 | 531 |
| 08 | 601 | 590 | 479 | 750 | 484 | 311 | 571 |
| 09 | 1007 | 629 | 570 | 843 | 516 | 311 | 697 |
| 1710 | 1219 | 716 | 647 | 966 | 512 | 311 | 798 |
| 11 | 994 | 764 | 1242 | 1180 | 527 | 311 | 889 |
| 12 | 716 | 641 | 638 | 790 | 513 | 311 | 638 |
| 13 | 689 | 642 | 508 | 686 | 512 | 311 | 594 |
| 14 | 832 | 647 | 459 | 771 | 502 | 311 | 635 |
| 15 | 713 | 645 | 489 | 910 | 503 | 311 | 646 |
| 16 | 758 | 693 | 553 | 776 | 499 | 311 | 645 |
| 17 | 622 | 652 | 466 | 796 | 512 | 311 | 602 |
| 18 | 589 | 659 | 483 | 692 | 507 | 311 | 575 |
| 19 | 552 | 665 | 514 | 849 | 515 | 311 | 609 |
| 1720 | 663 | 679 | 521 | 846 | 506 | 311 | 635 |
| 21 | 596 | 617 | 566 | 821 | 488 | 311 | 604 |
| 22 | 503 | 631 | 554 | 674 | 482 | 311 | 554 |
| 23 | 505 | 582 | 518 | 621 | 467 | 311 | 525 |
| 24 | 624 | 631 | 548 | 733 | 459 | 311 | 589 |
| 25 | 724 | 622 | 540 | 747 | 465 | 311 | 610 |
| 26 | 709 | 649 | 558 | 840 | 480 | 311 | 637 |
| 27 | 659 | 636 | 583 | 704 | 472 | 311 | 596 |
| 28 | 837 | 658 | 568 | 759 | 484 | 311 | 649 |
| 29 | 777 | 721 | 632 | 842 | 508 | 311 | 681 |

APPENDIX C—*Continued*

| Year | 1.Fa | 2.M | 3.B | 4.D | 5.Fu | 6.T | 7.W |
|------|------|-----|-----|-----|------|-----|-----|
| 1730 | 576 | 674 | 652 | 695 | 513 | 311 | 599 |
| 31 | 515 | 635 | 611 | 609 | 521 | 311 | 553 |
| 32 | 448 | 612 | 566 | 747 | 494 | 311 | 557 |
| 33 | 446 | 576 | 505 | 764 | 484 | 311 | 544 |
| 34 | 520 | 540 | 507 | 625 | 475 | 311 | 518 |
| 35 | 605 | 520 | 514 | 627 | 445 | 311 | 529 |
| 36 | 610 | 564 | 515 | 630 | 413 | 311 | 539 |
| 37 | 598 | 558 | 571 | 799 | 421 | 311 | 581 |
| 38 | 571 | 588 | 572 | 713 | 430 | 311 | 563 |
| 39 | 550 | 599 | 545 | 652 | 453 | 311 | 547 |
| 1740 | 755 | 684 | 594 | 760 | 507 | 311 | 644 |
| 41 | 843 | 744 | 741 | 829 | 529 | 311 | 712 |
| 42 | 555 | 720 | 720 | 755 | 554 | 311 | 631 |
| 43 | 479 | 631 | 603 | 765 | 523 | 311 | 579 |
| 44 | 415 | 577 | 542 | 638 | 537 | 311 | 518 |
| 45 | 435 | 585 | 494 | 693 | 512 | 311 | 528 |
| 46 | 545 | 613 | 619 | 786 | 509 | 311 | 594 |
| 47 | 541 | 630 | 675 | 658 | 500 | 311 | 574 |
| 48 | 544 | 679 | 626 | 741 | 483 | 311 | 599 |
| 49 | 575 | 623 | 649 | 800 | 510 | 311 | 609 |
| 1750 | 540 | 586 | 692 | 770 | 499 | 311 | 590 |
| 51 | 581 | 607 | 610 | 691 | 478 | 311 | 574 |
| 52 | 666 | 607 | 606 | 743 | 459 | 311 | 601 |
| 53 | 656 | 609 | 614 | 677 | 464 | 302 | 585 |
| 54 | 619 | 676 | 688 | 715 | 495 | 302 | 615 |
| 55 | 535 | 660 | 704 | 630 | 534 | 300 | 578 |
| 56 | 640 | 677 | 688 | 616 | 572 | 300 | 602 |
| 57 | 1000 | 716 | 734 | 812 | 559 | 300 | 733 |
| 58 | 864 | 744 | 731 | 893 | 572 | 300 | 731 |
| 59 | 672 | 718 | 734 | 831 | 567 | 300 | 673 |
| 1760 | 581 | 661 | 673 | 880 | 555 | 300 | 643 |
| 61 | 551 | 680 | 706 | 733 | 573 | 300 | 614 |
| 62 | 605 | 686 | 746 | 760 | 581 | 300 | 638 |
| 63 | 638 | 646 | 716 | 880 | 543 | 300 | 655 |
| 64 | 745 | 696 | 733 | 970 | 555 | 308 | 713 |
| 65 | 810 | 707 | 774 | 987 | 552 | 314 | 738 |
| 66 | 803 | 786 | 717 | 980 | 542 | 315 | 747 |
| 67 | 1036 | 829 | 730 | 911 | 546 | 306 | 790 |
| 68 | 995 | 807 | 751 | 926 | 551 | 296 | 781 |
| 69 | 775 | 791 | 762 | 849 | 547 | 296 | 717 |
| 1770 | 803 | 757 | 806 | 831 | 548 | 284 | 714 |
| 71 | 943 | 806 | 854 | 890 | 566 | 284 | 775 |
| 72 | 1032 | 847 | 888 | 1104 | 586 | 296 | 858 |
| 73 | 1076 | 828 | 932 | 1059 | 574 | 284 | 855 |
| 74 | 1057 | 850 | 881 | 1114 | 564 | 284 | 863 |

*A Perspective of Wages and Prices*

APPENDIX C—*Continued*

| Year | 1.Fa | 2.M | 3.B | 4.D | 5.Fu | 6.T | 7.W |
|------|------|------|------|------|------|-----|------|
| 1775 | 1011 | 847 | 756 | 1014 | 567 | 284 | 815 |
| 76 | 849 | 839 | 841 | 1037 | 601 | 273 | 797 |
| 77 | 926 | 837 | 971 | 886 | 601 | 273 | 794 |
| 78 | 903 | 849 | 1066 | 981 | 605 | 273 | 826 |
| 79 | 739 | 836 | 1002 | 864 | 601 | 273 | 756 |
| 1780 | 756 | 786 | 908 | 835 | 615 | 273 | 730 |
| 81 | 938 | 768 | 757 | 906 | 634 | 273 | 760 |
| 82 | 951 | 786 | 774 | 927 | 655 | 282 | 776 |
| 83 | 1074 | 824 | 814 | 1188 | 589 | 284 | 869 |
| 84 | 1027 | 864 | 845 | 1193 | 574 | 287 | 874 |
| 85 | 902 | 888 | 809 | 1140 | 580 | 288 | 839 |
| 86 | 866 | 894 | 856 | 1140 | 564 | 293 | 839 |
| 87 | 880 | 912 | 843 | 1086 | 576 | 296 | 834 |
| 88 | 957 | 926 | 819 | 1164 | 574 | 296 | 867 |
| 89 | 1023 | 928 | 734 | 1099 | 578 | 296 | 856 |
| 1790 | 1090 | 899 | 804 | 1094 | 591 | 296 | 871 |
| 91 | 988 | 958 | 866 | 1076 | 594 | 303 | 870 |
| 92 | 888 | 960 | 902 | 1217 | 606 | 271 | 883 |
| 93 | 1018 | 944 | 905 | 1215 | 640 | 268 | 908 |
| 94 | 1089 | 974 | 941 | 1395 | 666 | 284 | 978 |
| 95 | 1490 | 1079 | 1072 | 1329 | 738 | 284 | 1091 |
| 96 | 1582 | 1237 | 1090 | 1364 | 742 | 288 | 1161 |
| 97 | 1092 | 1248 | 1066 | 1290 | 736 | 288 | 1045 |
| 98 | 1069 | 1160 | 1081 | 1298 | 730 | 288 | 1022 |
| 99 | 1332 | 1277 | 1062 | 1477 | 819 | 288 | 1148 |
| 1800 | 2229 | 1523 | 1204 | 2180 | 848 | 288 | 1567 |
| 01 | 2428 | 1750 | 1284 | 2536 | 805 | 288 | 1751 |
| 02 | 1389 | 1636 | 1287 | 1801 | 788 | 288 | 1348 |
| 03 | 1161 | 1583 | 1226 | 1713 | 874 | 288 | 1268 |
| 04 | 1213 | 1563 | 1247 | 1852 | 910 | 288 | 1309 |
| 05 | 1725 | 1495 | 1400 | 2316 | 895 | 309 | 1521 |
| 06 | 1520 | 1548 | 1352 | 2172 | 876 | 315 | 1454 |
| 07 | 1496 | 1516 | 1416 | 2083 | 846 | 315 | 1427 |
| 08 | 1594 | 1550 | 1556 | 2083 | 908 | 303 | 1476 |
| 09 | 1871 | 1691 | 1585 | 2238 | 1099 | 303 | 1619 |
| 1810 | 2039 | 1757 | 1605 | 2262 | 1020 | 299 | 1670 |
| 11 | 1845 | 1772 | 1787 | 2126 | 946 | 299 | 1622 |
| 12 | 2390 | 1860 | 1828 | 2444 | 991 | 322 | 1836 |
| 13 | 2211 | 2012 | 1712 | 2679 | 1057 | 322 | 1881 |
| 14 | 1513 | 1916 | 1726 | 2313 | 1091 | 339 | 1642 |
| 15 | 1339 | 1596 | 1722 | 2073 | 986 | 358 | 1467 |
| 16 | 1471 | 1398 | 1244 | 1945 | 829 | 364 | 1344 |
| 17 | 1940 | 1344 | 1163 | 2438 | 835 | 364 | 1526 |
| 18 | 1706 | 1566 | 1508 | 2204 | 937 | 341 | 1530 |
| 19 | 1458 | 1657 | 1482 | 2220 | 833 | 310 | 1492 |

APPENDIX C—*Continued*

| Year | 1.Fa | 2.M | 3.B | 4.D | 5.Fu | 6.T | 7.W |
|------|------|------|------|------|------|------|------|
| 1820 | 1314 | 1582 | 1236 | 1985 | 778 | 280 | 1353 |
| 21 | 1124 | 1278 | 1174 | 1832 | 730 | 256 | 1190 |
| 22 | 930 | 1002 | 1029 | 1686 | 688 | 264 | 1029 |
| 23 | 1062 | 1156 | 1014 | 1721 | 684 | 260 | 1099 |
| 24 | 1229 | 1255 | 1111 | 1807 | 637 | 267 | 1193 |
| 25 | 1336 | 1495 | 1349 | 2265 | 660 | 254 | 1400 |
| 26 | 1178 | 1447 | 1320 | 2137 | 657 | 241 | 1323 |
| 27 | 1155 | 1417 | 1254 | 1852 | 647 | 237 | 1237 |
| 28 | 1167 | 1335 | 1165 | 1834 | 643 | 224 | 1201 |
| 29 | 1263 | 1266 | 1094 | 1818 | 623 | 216 | 1189 |
| 1830 | 1228 | 1185 | 1007 | 1802 | 615 | 215 | 1146 |
| 31 | 1396 | 1260 | 1178 | 1982 | 608 | 218 | 1260 |
| 32 | 1131 | 1202 | 1143 | 1909 | 525 | 226 | 1167 |
| 33 | 1090 | 1212 | 1100 | 1670 | 418 | 243 | 1096 |
| 34 | 881 | 1073 | 1031 | 1663 | 412 | 263 | 1011 |
| 35 | 828 | 1076 | 1031 | 1768 | 433 | 274 | 1028 |
| 36 | 975 | 1288 | 1161 | 1816 | 457 | 287 | 1141 |
| 37 | 1103 | 1312 | 1276 | 1739 | 506 | 256 | 1169 |
| 38 | 1309 | 1286 | 1228 | 1654 | 494 | 250 | 1177 |
| 39 | 1399 | 1365 | 1271 | 1831 | 524 | 256 | 1263 |
| 1840 | 1369 | 1369 | 1281 | 1980 | 471 | 233 | 1286 |
| 41 | 1285 | 1365 | 1340 | 1887 | 482 | 223 | 1254 |
| 42 | 1150 | 1253 | 1303 | 1745 | 484 | 205 | 1161 |
| 43 | 1027 | 1119 | 1176 | 1501 | 475 | 197 | 1030 |
| 44 | 1054 | 1050 | 1090 | 1597 | 443 | 220 | 1029 |
| 45 | 1159 | 1174 | 1194 | 1535 | 433 | 214 | 1079 |
| 46 | 1281 | 1218 | 1233 | 1561 | 421 | 192 | 1122 |
| 47 | 1636 | 1337 | 1288 | 1667 | 472 | 191 | 1257 |
| 48 | 1197 | 1268 | 1281 | 1484 | 444 | 173 | 1105 |
| 49 | 1019 | 1101 | 1215 | 1557 | 419 | 179 | 1035 |
| 1850 | 923 | 1058 | 1075 | 1458 | 425 | 203 | 969 |
| 51 | 851 | 1047 | 1062 | 1521 | 407 | 192 | 961 |
| 52 | 946 | 1170 | 1024 | 1388 | 417 | 193 | 978 |
| 53 | 1286 | 1151 | 1097 | 1731 | 511 | 200 | 1135 |
| 54 | 1530 | 1346 | 1270 | 1758 | 600 | 188 | 1265 |
| 55 | 1504 | 1354 | 1243 | 1839 | 567 | 182 | 1274 |
| 56 | 1366 | 1398 | 1321 | 1813 | 581 | 195 | 1264 |
| 57 | 1263 | 1475 | 1322 | 1873 | 687 | 218 | 1287 |
| 58 | 1016 | 1453 | 1259 | 1744 | 621 | 220 | 1190 |
| 59 | 985 | 1493 | 1283 | 1805 | 623 | 242 | 1214 |
| 1860 | 1213 | 1491 | 1344 | 2001 | 648 | 254 | 1314 |
| 61 | 1249 | 1586 | 1297 | 1872 | 569 | 241 | 1302 |
| 62 | 1240 | 1578 | 1225 | 1875 | 536 | 256 | 1290 |
| 63 | 994 | 1246 | 1308 | 1723 | 557 | 328 | 1144 |
| 64 | 881 | 1580 | 1287 | 1680 | 577 | 373 | 1200 |

APPENDIX C—*Continued*

| Year | 1.Fa | 2.M | 3.B | 4.D | 5.Fu | 6.T | 7.W |
|------|------|------|------|------|------|------|------|
| 1865 | 934  | 1666 | 1350 | 1654 | 644 | 363 | 1238 |
| 66   | 1068 | 1654 | 1412 | 1770 | 660 | 353 | 1296 |
| 67   | 1436 | 1626 | 1313 | 1800 | 593 | 309 | 1346 |
| 68   | 1398 | 1500 | 1265 | 1789 | 575 | 264 | 1291 |
| 69   | 1031 | 1549 | 1339 | 1802 | 572 | 278 | 1244 |
| 1870 | 1027 | 1601 | 1311 | 1759 | 562 | 268 | 1241 |
| 71   | 1138 | 1801 | 1332 | 1789 | 547 | 258 | 1320 |
| 72   | 1328 | 1820 | 1287 | 1843 | 622 | 282 | 1378 |
| 73   | 1418 | 1928 | 1347 | 1869 | 629 | 285 | 1437 |
| 74   | 1207 | 1947 | 1427 | 1951 | 562 | 285 | 1423 |
| 75   | 1053 | 1785 | 1399 | 1784 | 550 | 288 | 1310 |
| 76   | 1147 | 2030 | 1424 | 1702 | 523 | 260 | 1370 |
| 77   | 1298 | 1732 | 1487 | 1704 | 496 | 248 | 1330 |
| 78   | 1220 | 1693 | 1436 | 1657 | 440 | 229 | 1281 |
| 79   | 1109 | 1650 | 1217 | 1634 | 411 | 200 | 1210 |
| 1880 | 1126 | 1507 | 1230 | 1596 | 409 | 228 | 1174 |
| 81   | 1007 | 1991 | 1318 | 1294 | 426 | 205 | 1213 |
| 82   | 1024 | 1546 | 1480 | 1358 | 438 | 202 | 1140 |
| 83   | 994  | 1830 | 1414 | 1303 | 441 | 185 | 1182 |
| 84   | 809  | 1613 | 1395 | 1231 | 422 | 185 | 1071 |
| 85   | 745  | 1599 | 1315 | 1157 | 395 | 184 | 1026 |
| 86   | 779  | 1282 | 1269 | 1091 | 376 | 180 | 931  |
| 87   | 794  | 1360 | 1323 | 1068 | 386 | 183 | 955  |
| 88   | 790  | 1316 | 1321 | 1100 | 378 | 179 | 950  |
| 89   | 777  | 1260 | 1299 | 1116 | 387 | 180 | 948  |
| 1890 | 709  | 1356 | 1253 | 1135 | 408 | 187 | 947  |
| 91   | 840  | 1433 | 1289 | 1143 | 411 | 179 | 998  |
| 92   | 715  | 1524 | 1300 | 1146 | 407 | 171 | 996  |
| 93   | 630  | 1337 | 1247 | 1095 | 401 | 171 | 914  |
| 94   | 547  | 1755 | 1187 | 1053 | 372 | 167 | 982  |
| 95   | 597  | 1743 | 1126 | 999  | 368 | 159 | 968  |
| 96   | 573  | 1696 | 1125 | 973  | 352 | 178 | 947  |
| 97   | 698  | 1651 | 1122 | 998  | 353 | 155 | 963  |
| 98   | 801  | 1630 | 1110 | 1025 | 359 | 146 | 982  |
| 99   | 638  | 1605 | 1159 | 1024 | 372 | 143 | 950  |
| 1900 | 694  | 1700 | 1202 | 991  | 497 | 154 | 994  |
| 01   | 706  | 1691 | 1189 | 988  | 427 | 153 | 986  |
| 02   | 621  | 1668 | 1204 | 992  | 409 | 141 | 963  |
| 03   | 694  | 1751 | 1231 | 1011 | 372 | 146 | 1004 |
| 04   | 797  | 1607 | 1172 | 1018 | 368 | 167 | 985  |
| 05   | 684  | 1677 | 1245 | 1018 | 350 | 174 | 989  |
| 06   | 668  | 1764 | 1312 | 1000 | 372 | 198 | 1016 |
| 07   | 733  | 1752 | 1299 | 1008 | 421 | 205 | 1031 |
| 08   | 883  | 1639 | 1372 | 1032 | 394 | 187 | 1043 |
| 09   | 855  | 1716 | 1331 | 1074 | 381 | 176 | 1058 |

APPENDIX C—*Continued*

| Year | 1.Fa | 2.M | 3.B | 4.D | 5.Fu | 6.T | 7.W |
|------|------|------|------|------|------|------|------|
| 1910 | 777 | 1519 | 1349 | 1055 | 372 | 202 | 994 |
| 11 | 858 | 1334 | 1386 | 1115 | 371 | 214 | 984 |
| 12 | 868 | 1319 | 1443 | 1134 | 433 | 196 | 999 |
| 13 | 829 | 1408 | 1407 | 1195 | 439 | 208 | 1021 |
| 14 | 1016 | 1796 | 1468 | 1120 | 436 | 212 | 1147 |
| 15 | 1319 | 1819 | 1732 | 1354 | 577 | 277 | 1317 |
| 16 | 2049 | 2028 | 2146 | 1742 | 566 | 359 | 1664 |
| 17 | 1675 | 2753 | 2636 | 2260 | 641 | 448 | 1965 |
| 18 | 1837 | 4082 | 3042 | 2544 | 822 | 760 | 2497 |
| 19 | 1631 | 2945 | 3123 | 2778 | 925 | 849 | 2254 |
| 1920 | 2104 | 2979 | 3475 | 3573 | 902 | 960 | 2591 |
| 21 | 1383 | 2924 | 2892 | 2458 | 823 | 514 | 2048 |
| 22 | 1064 | 2508 | 2121 | 2055 | 713 | 409 | 1672 |
| 23 | 1112 | 2815 | 2178 | 1907 | 649 | 400 | 1726 |
| 24 | 1641 | 2536 | 2246 | 1761 | 589 | 455 | 1740 |
| 25 | 1398 | 2430 | 2226 | 1966 | 614 | 436 | 1708 |
| 26 | 1320 | 2249 | 2033 | 1779 | 670 | 368 | 1577 |
| 27 | 1268 | 2059 | 2024 | 1738 | 549 | 336 | 1496 |
| 28 | 1128 | 2033 | 2108 | 1795 | 510 | 367 | 1485 |
| 29 | 1071 | 2443 | 2082 | 1514 | 540 | 358 | 1511 |
| 1930 | 790 | 2097 | 1703 | 1326 | 557 | 315 | 1275 |
| 31 | 1071 | 1599 | 1400 | 1270 | 541 | 250 | 1146 |
| 32 | 747 | 1627 | 1230 | 1266 | 526 | 248 | 1065 |
| 33 | 708 | 1844 | 985 | 1393 | 513 | 238 | 1107 |
| 34 | 788 | 1834 | 882 | 1340 | 478 | 262 | 1097 |
| 35 | 989 | 1811 | 1018 | 1344 | 480 | 259 | 1149 |
| 36 | 1298 | 1798 | 1152 | 1265 | 519 | 273 | 1211 |
| 37 | 1239 | 1862 | 1265 | 1442 | 548 | 308 | 1275 |
| 38 | 790 | 1949 | 1339 | 1698 | 569 | 295 | 1274 |
| 39 | 832 | 1982 | 1359 | 1332 | 568 | 282 | 1209 |
| 1940 | 1027 | 2377 | 1559 | 2131 | 631 | 419 | 1574 |
| 41 | 1217 | 2401 | 1602 | 2775 | 689 | 513 | 1784 |
| 42 | 1132 | 2784 | 1686 | 3890 | 728 | 537 | 2130 |
| 43 | 1255 | 2808 | 1772 | 3697 | 775 | 645 | 2145 |
| 44 | 1215 | 2832 | 1772 | 3992 | 836 | 658 | 2216 |
| 45 | 1433 | 2856 | 2084 | 3846 | 895 | 706 | 2282 |
| 46 | 1422 | 2895 | 2310 | 4043 | 931 | 701 | 2364 |
| 47 | 1727 | 2799 | 2689 | 4498 | 991 | 822 | 2580 |
| 48 | 2086 | 2959 | 3188 | 4543 | 1125 | 955 | 2781 |
| 49 | 2390 | 4223 | 3483 | 4309 | 1125 | 980 | 3145 |
| 1950 | 2446 | 4218 | 3473 | 4203 | 1118 | 1178 | 3155 |
| 51 | 2744 | 4893 | 3797 | 4901 | 1229 | 1715 | 3656 |
| 52 | 2815 | 5893 | 4035 | 5299 | 1366 | 1208 | 3987 |
| 53 | 2679 | 5387 | 4222 | 4699 | 1419 | 1290 | 3735 |
| 54 | 2608 | 5900 | 4319 | 4516 | 1448 | 1311 | 3825 |

# 3

## Wage-rates and Prices: Evidence for Population Pressure in the Sixteenth Century[1]

In an earlier paper[2] we gave estimates showing that the basketful of consumables which the English building craftsman could buy with a day's pay began about 1510 to contract progressively, and by 1630 had shrunk to perhaps as little as two-fifths of what it had been through much of the fifteenth century. Since the builder's labourer suffered equally, and he may be regarded as representative of unskilled wage-earners at large, there is reason to believe that the decline was not peculiar to building but afflicted other wage-earners too. It was catastrophic. So far as we know, there is nothing like it anywhere else in wage history. Yet one can read a great deal about the sixteenth century without finding any mention of it, and with some reason, for there was no great outburst to set historians looking for a great social constriction as its origin. Did it really happen in anything like the severity that the figures suggest? If it did, what caused it?

### I

Certainly those who have worked before us on similar materials have found it in them, and in much the same degree. Malthus, for example—though he was using only the prices of grain—said in his *Principles*,[3] " From the end of the reign of Henry VII to the end of the reign of Elizabeth . . . it is an unquestionable fact that the corn wages of labour fell in an extraordinary degree, and towards the latter end of the century they would not command much above one-third of the quantity of wheat which they did at the beginning of it. " Thorold Rogers was emphatic. " I have shown, " he said,[4] " that from the earliest recorded annals, through nearly three centuries, the condition of the English labourer was that of plenty and hope, that from perfectly intelligible causes it sunk within a century to so low a level as to make

[1] We are under a special obligation to Dr. D. C. Coleman and Professor F. J. Fisher of the London School of Economics, to the former for making available to us his knowledge of the European price history of the time, and to both for taking much pains to help us with criticism and suggestion in this field of theirs into which our own pursuit of wage movements has led us. They have brought many improvements to our paper, but are in no wise implicated in its treatment or conclusions.

[2] " Seven Centuries of the Prices of Consumables, compared with Builders' Wage-rates ", *Economica*, Nov. 1956. This used wage series from our " Seven Centuries of Building Wages ", *Economica*, August 1955.

[3] T. R. Malthus, *Principles of Political Economy*, 2nd edn. (1826), c. IV, sec. IV, p. 240.

[4] J. E. Thorold Rogers, *Six Centuries of Work and Wages* (1884), c. XIX.

the workman practically helpless, and that the lowest point was reached just about the outbreak of the great war between King and Parliament. " Knoop and Jones, in their study of the mason,[1] formed their own index of his daily money wage on the average of Oxford, Cambridge and London Bridge, and compared it with an index of the price of food that they formed from Thorold Rogers by combining series for twelve articles, from wheat to pigeons, at equal weights. They found that through 1593–1632 the amount of food the mason's daily wage would buy was from 38 to 40 per cent. of what it had been in 1451–75: our own estimate for a more inclusive basketful is just 40 per cent. Clapham, making his own reconnaissance, found that over the sixteenth century day-wages on the land about doubled while food prices rose nearly sixfold: " this sounds desperate and it was certainly very bad ".[2]

We can add evidence that the purchasing power of builders' wage-rates fell at much the same time, and to much the same extent, in France and Alsace. This evidence is displayed in Figure 1. The materials and methods we describe in our Appendix, but we may mention the main points here.

The French wages and prices are from the Vicomte d'Avenel. It is not hard to call his tables in question[3]—he averaged quotations drawn now here now there from all over France, he lumped what must have been very various articles together under such broad ingenuous heads as " fish ", " clothing " or " wine ". None the less, from nearly six centuries he did collect some 56,000 quotations, and when he gives us the average of those falling within each period of as much as twenty-five years at a time, we can look for some consistency in the results. More compact and continuous series each drawn from one district only—Poitou, Rouen, the Ile de France—are reported[4] as showing some variations in the timing and extent of movements but agreeing in finding a great fall in the purchasing power of the wage-rate during the sixteenth century. In our Appendix we give particulars of the materials from Poitou, and the indexes appear in Table 3. The index of food prices does not differ widely from that from d'Avenel; the wages do not rise so much before 1600; over the whole span an implied fall in the amount of food the wage-rate would buy to 35 per cent. of what it had been compares with our estimate of 37 per cent. from d'Avenel. The closeness is fortuitous, because the wage series in Poitou is fragmentary, and unlike that from d'Avenel contains wages with board, which would have risen less than those without, but at

---

[1] D. Knoop & G. P. Jones, *The Mediaeval Mason* (1933), pp. 204–15 & Appendix I.

[2] Sir John Clapham: *A Concise Economic History of Britain* (1949), pp. 186–7, 211.

[3] Cf. F. Simiand: *Recherches Anciennes et Nouvelles sur le Mouvement Général des Prix du 16e au 19e Siècle* (1932), pp. 122–5.

[4] J. U. Nef, " Prices and Industrial Capitalism in France and England, 1540–1640 ", *Economic History Review*, VII (1937), 2, reprinted in *Essays in Economic History*, ed. E. M. Carus-Wilson (1954).

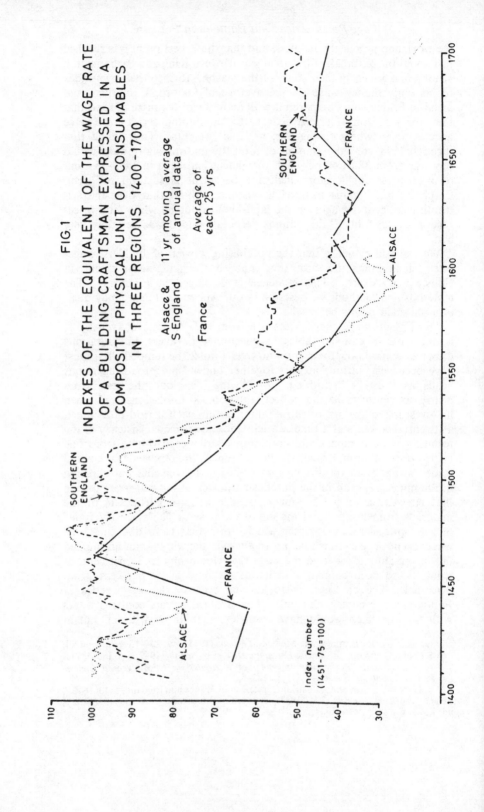

FIG.1

INDEXES OF THE EQUIVALENT OF THE WAGE RATE
OF A BUILDING CRAFTSMAN EXPRESSED IN A
COMPOSITE PHYSICAL UNIT OF CONSUMABLES
IN THREE REGIONS 1400-1700

Alsace &      11 yr moving average
S England     of annual data

France        Average of
              each 25 yrs

Index number
(1451-75=100)

SOUTHERN
ENGLAND

SOUTHERN
ENGLAND

FRANCE

FRANCE

ALSACE

ALSACE

least there is agreement in the finding of a great fall. But most of all, when we find that the changes indicated by d'Avenel's tables, though extraordinary in themselves, are closely similar to those we find in England and Alsace, we can call in a rule of evidence to justify a kind of circular reasoning: it is improbable that erroneous materials would have led to outcomes so strikingly similar; but if the materials are authenticated they substantiate the outcome. We may add that our French series also yield an outcome similar to that of our English for some time before the comparison displayed here opens in 1401.[1]

Wages and prices in Alsace come from the two volumes published by the Abbé Hanauer in 1876–8. He did for Alsace essentially what Thorold Rogers did for southern England. In the archives mainly of Colmar, Strasbourg and Basle he extracted quotations from the accounts of the time, especially those of monasteries and hospitals, and from municipal records and market reports. He printed them in some fulness of original detail, with careful commentary. But his entries for prices are scanty in the fifteenth century, save for grain, and those for wages do not carry us beyond 1610.

The wage-rates we have used are those of three types of craftsman in France—masons; carpenters; painters, tilers, and plasterers— and those of the first two only in Alsace. In both regions they are wages for the day, without board.

To trace the movement of the prices of consumables we copied as closely as we could the make-up of the composite unit we used for England, except that since Drink which mostly meant malt in England was represented only by wine in France and Alsace, we transferred 10 out of the $22\frac{1}{2}$ points of its weight to Farinaceous. In Alsace, moreover, we had no adequate series for fish, cheese, or textiles. The number of components is generally smaller than in England. The upshot is a composite commodity made up as in Table 1, but not all the components were available throughout the three centuries.

Fig. 1 suggests that in all three countries the day's wage of the building craftsman at the end of the sixteenth century would buy less than half of what it had commanded in the second half of the fifteenth; in France and Alsace the fall appears as rather greater than in England. The English and Alsatian series agree in showing the downturn as setting in sharply between 1509 and 1513. The English and French series, which alone are available after 1605, agree in showing a check to the rate of fall about 1600, and some recovery after the 1630's.

Here are strong grounds for believing that the lot of the building craftsman in all three regions was sadly worsened. But was it really worsened as much as our estimates by themselves suggest? Earlier

[1] The purchasing power of the builders' wage-rate in composite units of con-sumables comes out as follows·

(1451–75 = 100).

| 25 yrs. beginning: | 1276 | 1301 | 1326 | 1351 | 1376 |
|---|---|---|---|---|---|
| France | 57 | 49 | 58 | 58 | 63 |
| S. England | 52 | 53 | 57 | 59 | 77 |

discussion[1] has given reasons to believe they overstate it. Processed products like bread and beer will not have risen in price so much as grain and malt: the price of the loaf, for example, will have had to cover not the cost of grain only but wages for milling, transporting, and baking, and as these did not go up as much as grain, the loaf will have gone up rather less too. This consideration is important. If the prices wage-earners paid at retail were made up, say, as to two-thirds of such wholesale costs of foods and materials as we have used, and as to the

TABLE 1

CONSTITUTION AND COMPONENT SERIES OF COMPOSITE UNIT OF CONSUMABLES, FRANCE AND ALSACE, 1401–1700.

| Constitution of composite commodity | | Component series | |
|---|---|---|---|
| | Weight | France | Alsace |
| 1. Farinaceous .. | 30 | Wheat, rye | Wheat, rye, barley |
| 2. Meat, fish .. | 25 | Beef, pork, " fish " | Central tendency of beef, veal, mutton, and pork. No fish |
| 3. Butter, cheese .. | 12½ | Butter, cheese | Butter, no cheese |
| 4. Drink .. .. | 12½ | " Wine " | Châtenois ordinaire |
| Subtotal, Food .. | 80 | | |
| 5. Fuel and light .. | 7½ | Oil, candles, fire-wood | Central tendencies of hardwood, softwood and faggots. Oil, candles, tapers |
| 6. Textiles .. .. | 12½ | " Clothing ", linen | Nil |
| TOTAL .. | 100 | | |

other third of wages, an English index of retail prices starting at the base of 100 in 1451–75 would have gone up to only 380 by the end of the sixteenth century, against the 475 of our index, and the basketful would be well over 50 per cent. of its initial size instead of around 40. The sixteenth century also saw significant improvements in methods of manufacture. These things help to explain why the money equivalent of a mason's daily board, where it was entered in the English accounts, rose from 2d. in 1495 to no more than 5d. in 1591–1610, whereas to keep pace with our index of prices it would have had to be 9½d. It is also possible that annual money earnings in England rose more than the daily rate we have followed, because workers combined to keep down the normal day and the stint they would do in it, and so got more overtime; and because the Reformation reduced the number of holidays—Knoop and Jones reckon this will have raised by a fifth the number of days available for work in the year.

[1] Knoop and Jones, *op. cit.*; J. U. Nef, *loc. cit.*

So the equivalent in commodities at retail of the annual money receipts of a wage-earner will have fallen less than our index of the equivalent in foodstuffs and materials at wholesale of his pay for a day. Even so, the fall remains very great, and it still poses the problem why it did not cause an upheaval. Part of the answer may be that it was a fall from a high level, so that great though it was it still left the wage-earner with a subsistence: " the wages the most difficult to be accounted for, " Malthus[1] remarked, " are the high corn wages of the fifteenth, rather than the low corn wages of the sixteenth century ". But the most important consideration remains: many wage-earners occupied land, raised much of their own food, and save for rising rents were insulated from its increasing scarcity. There was a spectrum, from the largely self-subsistent smallholder who occasionally did jobs to get some income in cash, through the workman mainly dependent on his wages but also cultivating a plot, to the landless labourer. It was only the last who felt the full force of the blast.

None the less, a blast it was. There seems no doubt that we are confronted with a great impoverishment. From the Rhine to the Thames, the standard of living of one section of the working population was brought down progressively for more than a century. There can be few parallels to this at other times. Why did it happen now ?

## II

Thorold Rogers found his " perfectly intelligible causes " in a deliberate course of oppression and exploitation of the labourer by the ruling class. Can we think there was such a policy, adopted at the same time and pursued to the same outcome over the same period, in all three of our regions ?

But Malthus found the cause in a factor that might well have come into play in several regions at the same time. The last half of the fifteenth century, he wrote,[2] saw wages which, in terms of corn, " were evidently peculiar, and could not therefore be permanent. This indeed is evident, not only by comparing them with previous and subsequent periods, but by considering their positive amount. Earnings of the value of nearly two pecks or half a bushel of wheat a day would allow of the earliest marriages, and the maintenance of the largest families. They are nearly the same as the earnings of the labourer in the United States. . . . . Considering the extraordinary high corn wages at this period, and that they could only fall very gradually, the stimulus must have continued to operate with considerable force during the greatest part of the century. In fact, depopulation was loudly complained of at the end of the 15th and beginning of the 16th centuries, and a redundancy of population was acknowledged at the end of the 16th. And it was this

---

[1] *Principles*, 2nd edn., p. 242
[2] *Principles*, 2nd edn., pp. 252, 256.

change in the state of population, and not the discovery of the American mines, which occasioned so marked a fall in the corn wages of labour. "

We do at least know it was possible that an increase of population occurred at this time. It is generally reckoned, with much reserve, that the population of England and Wales was from $2\frac{1}{2}$ to 3 millions about 1500, and, with more confidence, that it was about 5.8 millions in 1700.[1] Within two centuries there was something like a doubling. It might have taken place by steady accretion throughout, yet borne with different pressure on the labour market at different times, according to different rates of industrial development; or it may have impinged rather suddenly about 1510, and run for some time then at a higher pace than it maintained later. We do not know. But the great course of growth that began in the eighteenth century does seem to have set in rather suddenly, in the 1750's. This movement too was common to a number of countries. K. F. Helleiner, in a recent survey[2] of the evidence, has concluded: " At least two periods of secular increase can be tolerably well identified in the demographic history of medieval and modern Europe, the first extending from about the middle of the eleventh to the end of the thirteenth, the second from the middle of the fifteenth to the end of the sixteenth century. What the exact rates of growth during these earlier phases of expansion were it is impossible to ascertain, but their order of magnitude can be estimated with some confidence, and there can be no doubt that it was comparable to that observed in the early phases of the Vital Revolution " of the eighteenth century.

This comparison reminds us that we do not have to accept Malthus' account of the immediate cause of population growth in the sixteenth century. The fact that in the eighteenth century the available records for Norway and Sweden agree with those for England and Wales in indicating that " while the birth-rate fluctuated round a high level, the death-rate fell "[3] strengthens the finding for each country and suggests a common cause. A lowered virulence of bacteria or virus seems a possible explanation of a fall in mortality occurring at much the same time in several countries with different economic and social structures. This provides a suggestion for the sixteenth century. If indeed it was high real earnings that through earlier marriages caused a rise in population then, we have to explain why those earnings seem to have been sustained for some ninety years, from about 1420 to 1510[4], before their effect on population reacted in turn on them. The alternative possibility is open that the modus was a fall in the death-rate, and the cause some factor other than earnings.

[1] e.g. Clapham, *op. cit.*, pp. 78, 186.
[2] K. F. Helleiner, " The Vital Revolution Reconsidered ", *Canadian Journal of Economics and Political Science*, 23, 1, Feb. 1957.
[3] A. M. Carr-Saunders: *World Population*, p. 62.
[4] Appx. B to Phelps Brown and Hopkins, " Seven Centuries of the Prices of Consumables, compared with Builders' Wage-rates ", *Economica*, Nov. 1956.

If a big increase in population did impinge on the England of the early sixteenth century, we can see how it would have tended to bring about the effects we actually find. In some districts and by various methods the outputs of food and wool were increased, but we should not expect agriculture to have the capacity for expansion, extensively or intensively, that could raise either its labour force or its product proportionately to the rise in population. The overspill of labour would have had to go into what industrial employments it could find: the output of industrial products would be raised, and the extra labour would have its share in that output to offer in exchange for the available supplies of food. But those supplies would not have risen so much: there would have to be a squeeze, and it would be the occupations in which the job-hungry overspill was competing that would have to bear most of it. That was Clapham's view. " The main trouble, " he wrote,[1] " came from a growing population in a rural society in which the number of separate agricultural holdings was certainly not growing. Many of the new mouths went to Town or the towns or picked up some trade in the country. Some took to the roads or to crime. All who could added to the family earnings by any available sort of by-employment for some member of the family—spinning, nailmaking, or whatever it might be. The rest worked for what wages they could get . . . "

If it was population pressure that lay behind the fall in the purchasing power of the wage-rate, then the check to the fall after the turn of the century might mark a reduction of the pressure. There are indications that this could have come about. " The seventeenth century, " D. C. Coleman has noted,[2] " ushered in by the famine of 1596–7, brought renewed and severe outbreaks of plague, more harvest failures, wars, worsening climatic conditions and various other pointers towards higher mortality and a markedly reduced rate of population growth ". But the other side of the balance may have been changing too, and the expansion of agriculture—growth in the number it could employ, or in the output per man, or both—would have worked to the same effect.

Our explanation both of fall and check implies changes in the terms of trade between agriculture and industry: as population pressure mounted, we should expect these terms to move against industry, and when the pressure was checked we should expect their movement to be checked too. We can now add evidence that this did in fact happen very markedly in all three of our regions within just the same period as the fall in the purchasing power of the wage-rate. Fig. 2 illustrates this. It confronts us with a movement of prices quite distinct from the general raising that came about at this time through increased supplies of silver and a smaller silver content in the coinage. We have traced it by taking the price index of the food component of our composite commodity in each region, and dividing it into an index of the prices

[1] *Op. cit.*, p. 211.
[2] D. C. Coleman, " Labour in the English Economy of the Seventeenth Century ", *Economic History Review* (2), 8, 3, April 1956.

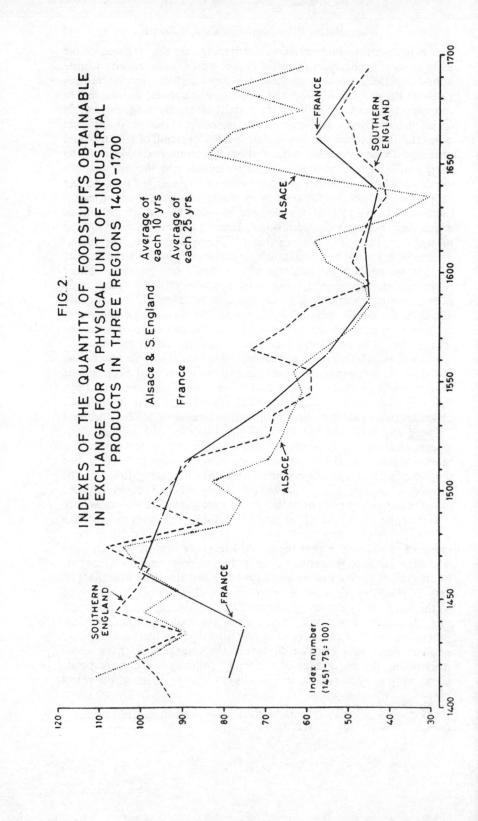

FIG. 2.

INDEXES OF THE QUANTITY OF FOODSTUFFS OBTAINABLE
IN EXCHANGE FOR A PHYSICAL UNIT OF INDUSTRIAL
PRODUCTS IN THREE REGIONS 1400-1700

Alsace & S. England    Average of
                       each 10 yrs

France                 Average of
                       each 25 yrs.

Index number
(1451-75 = 100)

of the fuel and light, and textiles (except in Alsace) which we had in the composite commodity, together with some building materials and metals—bricks and lime, iron and lead in Alsace; laths, plain tiles, and bricks, with lead and solder, in southern England; no building materials, but iron, copper and lead in France. The fall of the quotient in all three countries marks the extent to which the prices of foodstuffs rose more than those of our sample of industrial products. It sets in at the same time as the purchasing power of the builder's wage-rate begins to fall. It goes on until in all three regions the quantity of foodstuffs that a unit of industrial products will command in exchange is less than half what it was in 1510. Then at the turn of the century the rate of fall is checked, about the same time as that of the purchasing power of the wage-rate. In England and France both kinds of index first show a clear rise again after 1640. Evidently the shrinking of the wage-earner's basketful was due at least in part to a change in the terms of trade between workshop and farm.

We can go farther than that. The similarity of Figs. 1 and 2 shows that the change in the terms of trade resembled that in the basketful not in direction and timing only but in magnitude. We can draw an inference: the similarity of the sets of curves in the two Figures implies that our prices of industrial products behaved not unlike the wage-rate.[1] This in fact they did, in each country, at least in this sense, that though they rose more than the wage-rate, they did not rise anything like so much more as the price of food did. This is the position in 1601–20, the base being 1451–75 = 100 :—

| Index of | Alsace | Southern England | France |
|---|---|---|---|
| Prices of foodstuffs          ..     .. | 517 | 555 | 729 |
| Prices of some industrial products | 294 | 265 | 335 |
| Builders' wage-rates          ..     .. | 150 | 200 | 268 |

In considering the relation between the last two rows here, moreover, we have to make some allowance for the extent to which the cost of farm products, as raw materials, entered into the prices of fuel and light, and textiles. We conclude that the contraction of the wage-earner's basketful was mostly due to the changed terms of trade between workshop and farm. Probably he did come to get a smaller share of his own industrial product, but what he lost in that way was small compared with what he lost when he came to exchange his product for foodstuffs.

[1] In Fig. 1 we have the quotients of (*a*) wage-rates, divided by (*b*) the price of a composite unit of consumables. In Fig. 2 we have the quotients of (*c*) prices of some industrial products, divided by (*d*) prices of foodstuffs. Since (*d*) is the main component of (*b*) and highly correlated with it, the similarity of the quotients implies some similarity between (*a*) and (*c*).

It follows that Keynes was misled when he argued in the *Treatise*[1] that the general rise in prices had stimulated industrial growth by widening profit margins. As Nef[2] indicated in 1937, the figures Keynes relied on marked a shrinkage of the foodstuffs in the industrial wage-earner's basketful much more than any widening of the margin between his wage and the price of his product.

So the theory that population pressure was at the root of the fall in the purchasing power of the wage-rate receives support from the observed movement of the terms of trade between farm and workshop in all three of our present regions. We must remind ourselves that farm and workshop were not so distinct then as now; but what we see is the growth of population making them more so. If by a wage-earner we mean one whose income in kind from any land he occupies is sub-sidiary, so that his material wellbeing depends mainly on his wages, then we believe it is generally reckoned that in the first half of the six-teenth century about a third of the occupied population in England were wage-earners: they were, Clapham[3] says, " becoming a more im-portant social group, destined to be a majority well before the next century was over ". The existence of a majority of mainly landless wage-earners—nearly four of every five in the occupied population of Victorian Britain—is a product of population pressure. Wage-earning is not a career that men seek for its own sake; and when there were only three million people in all England and Wales we should not expect many of them to be wage-earners, any more than in a young colony or frontier community of more recent years. But when numbers mounted there were more and more who could not succeed to a holding of land or a niche already fixed in the economic establishment, and had to " look out for a place ".[4] As industry grew it found here the materials of that broad, numerically preponderant class of wage-earners that characterises industrialism. But industrialism did not create that class, it found jobs for it.

We have been concerned with the impoverishment of the wage-earner: the other side of the medal is the enrichment of those who sold farm produce or leased farms at rents they could raise. The cost of labour (if the builder's labourer is representative) and the costs of some leading industrial products were halved in terms of foodstuffs. This pervasive and deepgoing change must have trans-formed the real incomes of those who were able to share in the higher real earnings of farming as a business.

---

[1] J. M. Keynes, *A Treatise on Money* (1930), Vol. II, c. 30, (i).
[2] *Op. cit.*
[3] *Op. cit.* pp. 212–13.
[4] Various facets of the relation between the supply of labour and the economy of the times are illuminated by D. C. Coleman, *loc. cit.*

## APPENDIX ON SOURCES AND METHODS

ALSACE

*Source*: L'Abbé A. Hanauer, *Études Économiques sur l'Alsace Ancienne et Moderne*, 2 vols. (Paris, 1876–8.) Unless otherwise stated all page references are to Vol. II.

*Unit of money*: The wage-rates we have used are all given in one unit of account, the denier. Prices originally quoted in various units were reduced by Hanauer to common terms of the 19th century franc of 4.50 grams silver. We used these terms for all components of our price index and then converted this to an index of prices expressed in the denier as the unit of account by use of Table III, Monnaies Strasbourgeoises, at pp. 496–7 of Vol. I.

*Wage-rates*: We entered in one graph the rates per day in summer given at pp. 417–20 for master carpenters, masons, and gâcheurs (building labourers). These show much stability. By inspection we took out a single rate as representative of the craftsmen.

*Prices*: (1) *Composite unit of consumables*. We followed the make-up of the English unit (*Economica*, Nov. 1956, p. 297, Table 1) as far as possible, but here we had no adequate series for fish, cheese, or textiles; and drink was represented by wine alone, whereas in England at this time it was mostly malt, so we transferred 10 points of the English weight for drink to farinaceous. We estimated the components as follows: 1. *Farinaceous*. Pp. 92–97, wheat, rye and barley, in Strasbourg; combined at equal weights. Gaps in rye filled graphically in accordance with the movements of rye at Basle, pp. 82–4. 2. *Meat*. We graphed prices of beef, veal, mutton and pork at Strasbourg, pp. 187–190, and traced a central tendency by freehand; entries for earlier years are few, and we took the price as constant until after 1536. 3. *Butter*. We graphed prices from pp. 286–7, and traced the central tendency by freehand; we took the price as constant until after 1540. 4. *Drink*. No entry before 1478. From pp. 331–4 we took Châtenois ordinaire, and filled gaps, 1478–1610 according to the movement of some associated series in the same table, 1611–1700 by graphical comparison with all the other series except Châtenois edel. 5. *Fuel and Light*. (*a*) We took prices of hardwood, softwood and faggots from pp. 394–7; 1401–1610, we traced a central tendency by freehand, neglecting faggots before 1535; 1611–1700, we took the mean of the central tendencies of softwood and faggots. (*b*) We took prices of candles, oil, and tapers from pp. 374–9; 1401–1610, we combined indexes of the three at equal weights; 1611–1700, we traced a single central tendency by freehand. We combined (*a*) and (*b*) at equal weights. *Weights of components*: 1, 30; 2, 25; 3, 12$\frac{1}{2}$; 4, 12$\frac{1}{2}$; 5, 7$\frac{1}{2}$; total, 87$\frac{1}{2}$.

(2) *Indexes of prices of foodstuffs and of industrial products*. The index for foodstuffs is provided by components 1—4 of the composite unit above, combined as there weighted. We made that for industrial products by combining at equal weights component 5, Fuel and Light, with the two following series: (*a*) Metals. Average of entries in each decade, iron pp. 581–2, lead p. 583. 1401–90, lead only; 1491–1580, iron and lead at equal weights; 1581–1670, the previous combined index carried on in proportion to the movement of iron only; no index after 1670. We spliced the index for iron to that for lead at 1491–1580. (*b*) Building materials. We combined " grosses briques " and lime, pp. 432–5, at equal weights, 1411–1700.

SOUTHERN ENGLAND

*Sources*: J. E. Thorold Rogers, *History of Agriculture and Prices in England*, Vols. IV and V; Sir William Beveridge, *Prices and Wages in England*, Vol. I; present authors in *Economica*, Nov. 1956.

*Unit of money*: The unit of account, throughout.

*Index of purchasing power of wage-rate over composite unit of consumables*; in Fig. 1, 11 yr. moving average of col. 2, Appx. B of article in *Economica*, Nov. 1956.

*Indexes of prices of foodstuffs and of industrial products*. The index for foodstuffs is provided by components 1—4 of the composite unit in *Economica*, Nov. 1956, as there weighted. We made that for industrial products by combining at equal weights components 5 and 6 of that composite unit and indexes for (*a*) building materials and (*b*) metals which we made as follows: (*a*) Thorold Rogers, Vol. IV, p. 473, and Vol. V, pp. 544–5, decennial averages, prices of laths, plain tiles, and bricks; we combined the indexes at equal weights. (*b*) From Thorold Rogers, Vol. IV, p. 488, we made an index for lead by meaning indexes for lead in pigs and lead rolled, and an index for solder, all 1401–1582. We continued the two series by splicing to them at 1571–80 indexes for sheet lead and solder respectively from prices of Naval Stores in Beveridge, pp. 652–3, 658, 677–8 (lead series A). We combined the indexes for lead and solder at equal weights throughout.

FRANCE

*Source*: *Séances et Travaux de l'Académie des Sciences Morales et Politiques. Compte Rendu*. 1892, 2me semestre. (Paris, 1892.) Pp. 349– 419, Rapport sur deux Concours pour le Prix Rossi, by E. Levasseur. ·

*Unit of money*: all wages and prices expressed by d'Avenel in the 19th century franc of 4.50 grams silver; final indexes converted by us to indexes of prices in the livre tournois as unit of account, by using Table I at p. 399— see note at pp. 357–8.

*Wage-rates*: pp. 410–11, Table IX. We combined at equal weights indexes for wages for the day, without board, of (i) masons, (ii) carpenters, (iii) painters, tilers, and plasterers.

*Prices*. (1) *Composite unit of consumables*. We followed the make-up of the English unit (*Economica*, Nov. 1956, p. 297, Table 1) but as for Alsace gave farinaceous a weight of 30 and drink one of 12½. We estimated the components as follows: 1. *Farinaceous*. At p. 414 Table XII expresses the day's wage of a labourer without board in units of wheat and rye; by applying the annual (250 days') wage of the labourer given in col. 13 of Table IX at pp. 410–11 we obtained the implied price-indexes of wheat and rye, which we combined with weights of 1, 2 respectively. 2. *Meat and fish*. From Table XII we got price-indexes for beef and pork in the same way as for wheat and rye, and we combined them at equal weights. We took an index of the price of fish (unspecified) from the reciprocal of col. 8 of Table XVI at p. 418, from 1301, but omitting 1351–75. Weights: Meat 21, Fish 4. 3. *Butter and cheese*. We obtained indexes for butter and cheese from cols. 10, 9 of Table XVI, and combined them at equal weights. 4. *Drink*. We derived an index for wine (unspecified) in the same way as those of grain and meat from Table XII, accepting the entries only from 1276. 5. *Fuel and Light*. We took indexes of prices of oil, candles and fire wood from 1301 onwards from reciprocals of cols. 21, 22, 23 of Table XVI, and combined them with weights

1, 4, 5 respectively.  6. *Textiles*.  We took indexes of prices of clothing (unspecified) and linen from reciprocals of cols. 17, 19 of Table XVI, and combined them with equal weights.  *Weights of components*: 1, 30; 2, 25; 3, 12½;  4, 12½;  5, 7½;  6, 12½;  total, 100.

(2) *Indexes of prices of foodstuffs and of industrial products*.  The index for foodstuffs is provided by components 1—4 of the composite unit above, combined as there weighted.  That for industrial products we made by combining at equal weights components 5, 6 above and an index of prices of metals which we made by combining at equal weights indexes for iron, copper and lead from Table XIV at p. 416.

MATERIALS FOR HAUT POITOU ALONE

*Source*:  Paul Raveau, *L'Agriculture et les Classes Paysannes*: *la transformation de la propriété dans le Haut Poitou au 16ᵉ· siècle* (Paris, 1926), preliminary study on " Pouvoir d'Achat de la Livre ".

*Unit of money*:  the unit of account.  We got our indexes by dividing later entries into that for 1461–72 in each column of Table 1, p. xxxii.

*Wage rates*:  Apparently all available entries have been taken together; mention is made of joiners, carpenters, and masons, but also of mowers, and household staff; wages with board as well as without.

*Prices*:  a composite unit of foodstuffs made up of four series only with weights as follows—wheat 30, cattle 25, " various foodstuffs " 12½, " wine " 12½.  All four are available only for five periods; we extended the index they yield there over other periods in proportion to the combined movement of series continuously available.

TABLE 2

ALSACE: INDEXES OF (1) MONEY WAGE-RATES OF BUILDERS, (2) THE PRICE OF A COMPOSITE UNIT OF CONSUMABLES, AND (3) THE POWER OF THE WAGE-RATE TO COMMAND SUCH UNITS, IN THE 15TH, 16TH AND 17TH CENTURIES. 1451–75 = 100.

(1) 1401–1555 : 100                 1586–95 : 133
    1556–85 : 117                  1596–1610 : 150

| Year | (2) index of composite unit | (3) (1) ÷ col. (2) | Year | (2) index of composite unit | (3) (1) ÷ col. (2) | Year | (2) index of composite unit | (3) (1) ÷ col. (2) |
|---|---|---|---|---|---|---|---|---|
| 1401 | 104 | 96 | 1450 | 102 | 98 | 1499 | 107 | 93 |
| 1402 | 93 | 108 | 1451 | 104 | 96 | 1500 | 123 | 81 |
| 1403 | — | — | 1452 | 103 | 97 | 1501 | 127 | 79 |
| 1404 | 107 | 93 | 1453 | 103 | 97 | 1502 | 121 | 83 |
| 1405 | 98 | 102 | 1454 | 116 | 86 | 1503 | 114 | 88 |
| 1406 | 104 | 96 | 1455 | 116 | 86 | 1504 | 112 | 89 |
| 1407 | — | — | 1456 | 117 | 85 | 1505 | 101 | 99 |
| 1408 | 102 | 98 | 1457 | — | — | 1506 | 101 | 99 |
| 1409 | 93 | 108 | 1458 | — | — | 1507 | 99 | 101 |
| 1410 | 96 | 104 | 1459 | 130 | 77 | 1508 | 106 | 94 |
| 1411 | 100 | 100 | 1460 | 111 | 90 | 1509 | 92 | 109 |
| 1412 | 111 | 90 | 1461 | 104 | 96 | 1510 | 90 | 111 |
| 1413 | 100 | 100 | 1462 | 101 | 99 | 1511 | 122 | 82 |
| 1414 | 98 | 102 | 1463 | 98 | 102 | 1512 | 125 | 80 |
| 1415 | 102 | 98 | 1464 | 86 | 116 | 1513 | 124 | 81 |
| 1416 | 117 | 85 | 1465 | 97 | 103 | 1514 | 112 | 89 |
| 1417 | 100 | 100 | 1466 | 97 | 103 | 1515 | 130 | 77 |
| 1418 | 96 | 104 | 1467 | 100 | 100 | 1516 | 161 | 62 |
| 1419 | 97 | 103 | 1468 | 98 | 102 | 1517 | 175 | 57 |
| 1420 | 90 | 111 | 1469 | 96 | 104 | 1518 | 134 | 75 |
| 1421 | 108 | 93 | 1470 | 93 | 108 | 1519 | 107 | 93 |
| 1422 | 104 | 96 | 1471 | 93 | 108 | 1520 | 127 | 79 |
| 1423 | 98 | 102 | 1472 | 92 | 109 | 1521 | 128 | 78 |
| 1424 | 104 | 96 | 1473 | 97 | 103 | 1522 | 128 | 78 |
| 1425 | 107 | 93 | 1474 | — | — | 1523 | 118 | 85 |
| 1426 | 111 | 90 | 1475 | 89 | 112 | 1524 | 129 | 78 |
| 1427 | 104 | 96 | 1476 | 91 | 110 | 1525 | 123 | 81 |
| 1428 | 114 | 88 | 1477 | 99 | 101 | 1526 | 115 | 87 |
| 1429 | 133 | 75 | 1478 | 96 | 104 | 1527 | 125 | 80 |
| 1430 | 133 | 75 | 1479 | — | — | 1528 | 158 | 63 |
| 1431 | 129 | 78 | 1480 | 96 | 104 | 1529 | 165 | 61 |
| 1432 | 118 | 85 | 1481 | 150 | 67 | 1530 | 192 | 52 |
| 1433 | 109 | 92 | 1482 | 150 | 67 | 1531 | 174 | 57 |
| 1434 | 115 | 87 | 1483 | 120 | 83 | 1532 | 160 | 63 |
| 1435 | 108 | 93 | 1484 | 94 | 106 | 1533 | 157 | 64 |
| 1436 | 116 | 86 | 1485 | 104 | 96 | 1534 | 152 | 66 |
| 1437 | 117 | 85 | 1486 | 123 | 81 | 1535 | 143 | 70 |
| 1438 | 149 | 67 | 1487 | 118 | 85 | 1536 | 138 | 72 |
| 1439 | 147 | 68 | 1488 | 119 | 84 | 1537 | 148 | 68 |
| 1440 | 157 | 64 | 1489 | 131 | 76 | 1538 | 186 | 54 |
| 1441 | 152 | 66 | 1490 | 139 | 72 | 1539 | 135 | 74 |
| 1442 | 125 | 80 | 1491 | 153 | 65 | 1540 | 143 | 70 |
| 1443 | 116 | 86 | 1492 | 139 | 72 | 1541 | 130 | 77 |
| 1444 | 128 | 78 | 1493 | 123 | 81 | 1542 | 141 | 71 |
| 1445 | 119 | 84 | 1494 | 109 | 92 | 1543 | 194 | 52 |
| 1446 | 122 | 82 | 1495 | 96 | 104 | 1544 | 232 | 43 |
| 1447 | 113 | 88 | 1496 | 99 | 101 | 1545 | 218 | 46 |
| 1448 | 109 | 92 | 1497 | — | — | 1546 | 191 | 52 |
| 1449 | 100 | 100 | 1498 | 106 | 94 | 1547 | 161 | 62 |

TABLE 2 (*continued*)

| Year | (2) index of composite unit | (3) (1) ÷ col. (2) | Year | (2) index of composite unit | (3) (1) ÷ col. (2) | Year | (2) index of composite unit | (3) (1) ÷ col. (2) |
|------|-----|----|------|------|----|------|------|----|
| 1548 .. | 178 | 56 | 1599 .. | 384 | 39 | 1650 .. | 611 | |
| 1549 .. | 189 | 53 | 1600 .. | 438 | 34 | 1651 .. | 625 | |
| 1550 .. | 209 | 48 | 1601 .. | 503 | 30 | 1652 .. | 520 | |
| 1551 .. | 232 | 43 | 1602 .. | 520 | 29 | 1653 .. | 379 | |
| 1552 .. | 239 | 42 | 1603 .. | 501 | 30 | 1654 .. | 381 | |
| 1553 .. | 186 | 54 | 1604 .. | 430 | 35 | 1655 .. | 352 | |
| 1554 .. | 191 | 52 | 1605 .. | 385 | 39 | 1656 .. | 344 | |
| 1555 .. | 210 | 48 | 1606 .. | 410 | 37 | 1657 .. | 348 | |
| 1556 .. | 243 | 48 | 1607 .. | 465 | 32 | 1658 .. | 431 | |
| 1557 .. | 217 | 54 | 1608 .. | 462 | 32 | 1659 .. | 407 | |
| 1558 .. | 196 | 60 | 1609 .. | 550 | 27 | 1660 .. | 394 | |
| 1559 .. | 226 | 52 | 1610 .. | 591 | 25 | 1661 .. | 492 | |
| 1560 .. | 232 | 50 | 1611 .. | 568 | | 1662 .. | 609 | |
| 1561 .. | 276 | 42 | 1612 .. | 575 | | 1663 .. | 472 | |
| 1562 .. | 331 | 35 | 1613 .. | 494 | | 1664 .. | 387 | |
| 1563 .. | 225 | 52 | 1614 .. | 533 | | 1665 .. | 401 | |
| 1564 .. | 225 | 52 | 1615 .. | 549 | | 1666 .. | 392 | |
| 1565 .. | 293 | 40 | 1616 .. | 488 | | 1667 .. | 390 | |
| 1566 .. | 327 | 36 | 1617 .. | 420 | | 1668 .. | 361 | |
| 1567 .. | 275 | 43 | 1618 .. | 435 | | 1669 .. | 353 | |
| 1568 .. | 236 | 50 | 1619 .. | 392 | | 1670 .. | 376 | |
| 1569 .. | 250 | 47 | 1620 .. | 483 | | 1671 .. | 355 | |
| 1570 .. | 305 | 38 | 1621 .. | 549 | | 1672 .. | 340 | |
| 1571 .. | 400 | 29 | 1622 .. | 1684 | | 1673 .. | 376 | |
| 1572 .. | 353 | 33 | 1623 .. | 2428 | | 1674 .. | 512 | |
| 1573 .. | 508 | 23 | 1624 .. | 672 | | 1675 .. | 722 | |
| 1574 .. | 468 | 25 | 1625 .. | 623 | | 1676 .. | 829 | |
| 1575 .. | 308 | 38 | 1626 .. | 742 | | 1677 .. | 651 | |
| 1576 .. | 295 | 40 | 1627 .. | 660 | | 1678 .. | 666 | |
| 1577 .. | 278 | 42 | 1628 .. | 757 | | 1679 .. | 642 | |
| 1578 .. | 258 | 45 | 1629 .. | 720 | | 1680 .. | 640 | |
| 1579 .. | 385 | 30 | 1630 .. | 707 | | 1681 .. | 636 | |
| 1580 .. | 366 | 32 | 1631 .. | 596 | | 1682 .. | 534 | |
| 1581 .. | 437 | 27 | 1632 .. | 559 | | 1683 .. | 471 | |
| 1582 .. | 360 | 33 | 1633 .. | 631 | | 1684 .. | 473 | |
| 1583 .. | 332 | 35 | 1634 .. | 863 | | 1685 .. | 509 | |
| 1584 .. | 306 | 38 | 1635 .. | 1150 | | 1686 .. | 468 | |
| 1585 .. | 388 | 30 | 1636 .. | 1599 | | 1687 .. | 473 | |
| 1586 .. | 534 | 25 | 1637 .. | 1541 | | 1688 .. | 479 | |
| 1587 .. | 468 | 28 | 1638 .. | 1625 | | 1689 .. | 631 | |
| 1588 .. | 541 | 25 | 1639 .. | 1460 | | 1690 .. | 821 | |
| 1589 .. | 554 | 24 | 1640 .. | 899 | | 1691 .. | 928 | |
| 1590 .. | 464 | 29 | 1641 .. | 868 | | 1692 .. | 837 | |
| 1591 .. | 454 | 29 | 1642 .. | 855 | | 1693 .. | 960 | |
| 1592 .. | 496 | 27 | 1643 .. | 722 | | 1694 .. | 1107 | |
| 1593 .. | 544 | 24 | 1644 .. | 779 | | 1695 .. | 699 | |
| 1594 .. | 513 | 26 | 1645 .. | 594 | | 1696 .. | 613 | |
| 1595 .. | 572 | 23 | 1646 .. | 451 | | 1697 .. | 580 | |
| 1596 .. | 549 | 27 | 1647 .. | 374 | | 1698 .. | 808 | |
| 1597 .. | 514 | 29 | 1648 .. | 433 | | 1699 .. | 1005 | |
| 1598 .. | 450 | 33 | 1649 .. | 531 | | 1700 .. | 709 | |

TABLE 3

FRANCE: INDEXES OF (1) MONEY WAGE-RATES OF BUILDERS, (2) THE PRICE OF A COMPOSITE UNIT OF CONSUMABLES, (3) THE POWER OF THE WAGE-RATE TO COMMAND SUCH UNITS, 1276–1700, (4) THE PRICE OF THE FOODSTUFFS COMPRISED IN THE COMPOSITE UNIT, 1451–1625.

HAUT POITOU : INDEXES OF (5) MONEY WAGE-RATES, (6) THE PRICE OF A COMPOSITE UNIT OF FOODSTUFFS, 1461–1640.

1451–75 = 100.

|  | | | France | | | | Haut Poitou | |
|---|---|---|---|---|---|---|---|---|
|  | | | (1) | (2) | (3) | (4) | (5) | (6) |
| 1276–1300 | .. | .. | 31 | 54 | 57 | | | |
| 1301–1325 | .. | .. | 41 | 83 | 49 | | | |
| 1326–1350 | .. | .. | 50 | 86 | 58 | | | |
| 1351–1375 | .. | .. | 81 | 139 | 58 | | | |
| 1376–1400 | .. | .. | 71 | 112 | 63 | | | |
| 1401–1425 | .. | .. | 89 | 134 | 66 | | | |
| 1426–1450 | .. | .. | 92 | 149 | 62 | | | |
| 1451–1475 | .. | .. | 100 | 100 | 100 | 100 | 100[1] | 100[1] |
| 1476–1500 | .. | .. | 109 | 128 | 85 | 132 | 92 | 144 |
| 1501–1525 | .. | .. | 112 | 161 | 70 | 168 | 101 | 188 |
| 1526–1550 | .. | .. | 156 | 265 | 59 | 276 | 117 | 240 |
| 1551–1575 | .. | .. | 179 | 411 | 44 | 449 | | 497 |
| 1576–1600 | .. | .. | 258 | 759 | 34 | 853 | 215[2] | 779 |
| 1601–1625 | .. | .. | 268 | 638 | 42 | 729 | 281 | 775 |
| 1626–1650 | .. | .. | 326 | 949 | 34 | | 284[3] | |
| 1651–1675 | .. | .. | 405 | 888 | 46 | | | |
| 1676–1700 | .. | .. | 428 | 951 | 45 | | | |

[1] 1461–1472 only
[2] 1576–1589 only
[3] 1630–1640 only

## TABLE 4

ALSACE, SOUTHERN ENGLAND, FRANCE. INDEXES OF (1) PRICE OF A COMPOSITE UNIT OF FOODSTUFFS, (2) PRICE OF A SAMPLE OF INDUSTRIAL PRODUCTS, (3) QUANTITY OF FOODSTUFFS COMMANDED IN EXCHANGE BY A UNIT OF INDUSTRIAL PRODUCTS IN OUR SAMPLE, I.E. (2)÷(1), IN THE 15TH, 16TH AND 17TH CENTURIES.
1451–75=100

| | *Alsace* | | | *England* | | | *France* | | | |
|---|---|---|---|---|---|---|---|---|---|---|
| | (1) | (2) | (3) | (1) | (2) | (3) | (1) | (2) | (3) | |
| 1401–1410 .. | — | — | — | 115 | 107 | 93 | | | | |
| 1411–1420 .. | 99 | 110 | 111 | 111 | 107 | 96 | 140 | 110 | 79 .. | 1401–1425 |
| 1421–1430 .. | 110 | 107 | 97 | 107 | 108 | 101 | | | | |
| 1431–1440 .. | 127 | 113 | 89 | 118 | 106 | 90 | 156 | 117 | 75 .. | 1426–1450 |
| 1441–1450 .. | 118 | 117 | 99 | 95 | 101 | 106 | | | | |
| 1451–1460 .. | 113 | 103 | 91 | 98 | 99 | 101 | | | | |
| 1461–1470 .. | 98 | 98 | 100 | 105 | 103 | 98 | 100 | 100 | 100 .. | 1451–1475 |
| 1471–1480 .. | 95 | 99 | 104 | 93 | 100 | 108 | | | | |
| 1481–1490 .. | 127 | 100 | 79 | 121 | 103 | 85 | 132 | 125 | 95 .. | 1476–1500 |
| 1491–1500 .. | 120 | 92 | 77 | 100 | 97 | 97 | | | | |
| 1501–1510 .. | 108 | 89 | 82 | 106 | 98 | 92 | | | | |
| 1511–1520 .. | 134 | 92 | 69 | 116 | 102 | 88 | 168 | 151 | 90 .. | 1501–1525 |
| 1521–1530 .. | 141 | 94 | 67 | 159 | 110 | 69 | | | | |
| 1531–1540 .. | 157 | 101 | 64 | 161 | 110 | 68 | 276 | 194 | 70 .. | 1526–1550 |
| 1541–1550 .. | 188 | 115 | 61 | 217 | 127 | 59 | | | | |
| 1551–1560 .. | 221 | 140 | 63 | 315 | 186 | 59 | | | | |
| 1561–1570 .. | 280 | 156 | 56 | 298 | 218 | 73 | 449 | 245 | 55 .. | 1551–1575 |
| 1571–1580 .. | 376 | 183 | 49 | 341 | 223 | 65 | | | | |
| 1581–1590 .. | 453 | 204 | 45 | 389 | 230 | 59 | 853 | 385 | 45 .. | 1576–1600 |
| 1591–1600 .. | 507 | 231 | 46 | 530 | 238 | 45 | | | | |
| 1601–1610 .. | 494 | 271 | 55 | 527 | 256 | 49 | | | | |
| 1611–1620 .. | 540 | 316 | 59 | 583 | 274 | 47 | 729 | 335 | 46 .. | 1601–1625 |
| 1621–1630 .. | 1057 | 425 | 40 | 585 | 264 | 45 | | | | |
| 1631–1640 .. | 1169 | 348 | 30 | 687 | 281 | 41 | 1091 | 466 | 43 .. | 1626–1650 |
| 1641–1650 .. | 668 | 411 | 62 | 723 | 306 | 42 | | | | |
| 1651–1660 .. | 448 | 376 | 84 | 687 | 327 | 48 | | | | |
| 1661–1670 .. | 453 | 353 | 78 | 702 | 343 | 49 | 980 | 569 | 58 .. | 1651–1675 |
| 1671–1680 .. | 616 | 376 | 61 | 675 | 351 | 52 | | | | |
| 1681–1690 .. | 588 | 456 | 78 | 631 | 310 | 49 | 1067 | 519 | 49 .. | 1676–1700 |
| 1691–1700 .. | 889 | 542 | 61 | 737 | 331 | 45 | | | | |

# 4

## Builders' Wage-rates, Prices and Population: Some Further Evidence[1]

### I

In two previous papers[2] we gave estimates indicating that the basketful of consumables which the building craftsman could buy with his day's pay contracted greatly in the course of the sixteenth century in Southern England, France and Alsace, until in all three it was less than half as big as it had been. Our estimates also indicated that this had come about despite the builders' money wage-rate having risen in much the same proportion as the prices of industrial products: the prices of foodstuffs had risen very much more, so that the quantity of foodstuffs which the industrial worker could obtain in exchange for a unit of his own produce was greatly reduced. We suggested that this wide movement of the terms of trade between workshop and farm, itself also common to all three regions, might have a common cause in the increase of population: if the agriculture of the time could not absorb many of the extra hands, most of them must work in industry if they were to work at all, and so the output of industry would be increased relatively to that of agriculture, and industrial products and the labour that made them would alike be cheapened in terms of food. We can now add estimates which will show whether anything of the same kind seems to have happened in Münster, Augsburg, Vienna and Valencia.

In all four, the wages and prices alike come from the books kept mainly by religious foundations and hospitals. Münster provides some accounts from the municipality, but more from the cathedral, five monasteries, and ten local offices of the bishop's administration; there are many more quotations from the country than the city, but all are from within forty square miles. All the figures for Augsburg come from its hospital. It is the city hospital too, that yields a large part of our figures for Vienna, but many come also from the Klosterneuburg monastery seven miles or so away—from the accounts kept in its

[1] It was only through the generous guidance to the sources given us by Dr. D. C. Coleman that this study was made possible; and we are indebted to him too for reading and discussing this paper in draft. We also thank Mrs. Meyrick Browne, who carried through the whole study of Augsburg, and made the index of French land prices; Dr. Dipak Mazumdar, who made the first survey of the Spanish materials; Mrs. Faye Bayley, who took part in the work on Vienna, and carried through the computations for Valencia; and Miss Sheila Chantler, who drew the Figures. We are grateful to Professors E. M. Carus-Wilson and F. J. Fisher for their kindness in reading our paper in draft.

[2] " Seven Centuries of the Prices of Consumables, compared with Builders' Wage-rates ", *Economica*, November, 1956; " Wage-rates and Prices: Evidence for Population Pressure in the Sixteenth Century ", *Economica*, November, 1957.

own offices and by the priests of its parishes. In Valencia, the accounts of the cathedral provide the costs of builders' work, those of the Hospital dels Inocents the prices of consumables; from 1501 onwards the municipal accounts yield wages. Many of the various foundations owned their own land, and recorded not only the prices at which they bought supplies for their residents, but those at which they sold farm produce, or accepted it in payment of rent or tithe.

We have set out in the Appendix the details of our own secondary sources, and of our methods, but would record here how much we owe to the immense labours of the original searchers and gatherers—Georg Wiebe, Moritz Elsas, Karl Pribram, and Earl Hamilton.

The pattern of the building craftsman's wage-rates is much the same in most of these records as in those we have drawn on before, and again we have struck no averages (save that these were all we had for Münster) but tried instead to pick out a continuous line of rates which were representative in so far as they were recurrent. But some features of the present records are unusual. Generally, a graph of wages can be immediately distinguished from one of prices by its lack of sustained falls and falling trends, but here there are two clear cases of a cut. In Valencia rates generally were reduced substantially in the 1460's: the master carpenter came down from 60 diners a day to 51, the labourer —though this rather later—from 33 to 24. There they stayed till about 1488, when they went back to what they had been. There was little change in prices before or during the cut. In Vienna in 1667 the wage-rates stood where they had been, the one for the past 26 and the other for the past 40 years, the journeyman at 22 kroner a day and the labourer at 15; but by 1670, the one was down to 19½ kroner, the other to 12, and there they stayed through 1682. It turned out that at the new level the journeyman was soon to be as well off as before, for prices went down too; but not the labourer, who had been cut deeper; and in any case the cuts were made just when six successive years of higher prices had reduced the purchasing power of the going rate. Valencian wages also compose one unusual pattern. Most of the rates recorded there fall into the familiar pattern of tramlines, the same two rates cropping up for years together; but the master carpenter's rate, though on tramlines from 1465 onwards, in 1419–64 looks much more like a price series, with quotations at fine intervals, and short-period fluctuations about the majestic arc of a long-period rise and fall. It does seem that there was something unusual in the terms of engagement of the master carpenters by the municipality and cathedral of Valencia at this time; but on further scrutiny we thought the unusual element lay in the variety and fineness of the variations, rather than in any gradual rise and fall of a central value, which itself could quite possibly have remained unchanged, as the rates of the other craftsmen evidently did then.

The commodities whose prices we combined appear in Table I. The list is very like that for the three regions we studied before. The table notices some of the biggest gaps, but there were many others, and we had to use our judgment as before how best to bridge each gap where it occurred.

TABLE I

COMMODITIES ENTERING INTO COMPOSITE UNIT OF CONSUMABLES; WITH OTHER PRODUCTS USED IN INDEX OF PRICES OF INDUSTRIAL PRODUCTS

|  | MÜNSTER | AUGSBURG | VIENNA | VALENCIA |
|---|---|---|---|---|
| 1. FARINACEOUS | Barley, rye, wheat, oats, peas | Barley, rye, oats, peas, spelt; from 1674 only, wheat | (Not before 1486) barley, " Korn ", wheat | Wheat; from 1504 and 1512 only, rice, carob beans |
| Weight | 20 | 20 | 20 | 30 |
| 2. MEAT AND FISH | Fat oxen, calves, pigs, fat sheep; herrings, stockfish | Beef, veal, suet, dripping; carp | Hungarian oxen; calves, whole sheep, half or quarter sheep; herrings, sturgeon | Beef (not after 1446); mutton, hens (except 1449 – 1502); lard (from 1502); sardines, hake (not after 1495); tuna (except 1451 – 1503); dried cod (from 1555) |
| Weight | 25 | 25 | 37½ | 25 |
| 3. BUTTER & CHEESE | Butter, cheese | Milk; from 1580 only, Dutch cheese | None | Cheese (except 1551–1600) |
| Weight | 12½ | 12½ | — | 12½ |
| 4. DRINK | Wine, malt, five sorts of beer | From 1641, brown beer | Five sorts of beer; heuriger wine | Wine |
| Weight | 22½ | 22½ | 22½ | 12½ |
| 5. FUEL AND LIGHT | Charcoal; tallow, tallow candles, wax | Tallow, linseed oil | Soft firewood, charcoal; tallow candles, raw tallow, olive oil | Firewood; olive oil (not after 1500); charcoal (from 1512) |
| Weight | 7½ | 7½ | 7½ | 7½ |
| 6. TEXTILES | Four sorts of linen, five sorts of cloth | Several qualities of twill | Hemp, thread, coarse woollen cloth | Flax; linen, bedticks (from 1552) |
| Weight | 12½ | 12½ | 12½ | 12½ |
| Total | 100 | 100 | 100 | 100 |
| ADDITIONAL INDUSTRIAL PRODUCTS | Salt, bricks, tiles, nails, paper, men's shoes | Bavarian salt; lime, bricks; writing paper | Bricks, tiles, shingles, lime, pitch, three sorts of planks, laths; three sorts of nails | Plaster of Paris, lime, bricks; nails, large (not after 1500) |

So with some piecing and patching we arrived at an index of the price of a composite unit of consumables in each city. When we confront these indexes with those of the craftsman's wage-rate, what do we find ?

The outstanding finding is that in all four places the basketful a day's pay would buy shrank drastically during the 16th century, just as it did in the three regions we studied before. Indexes of the size of the basketful are displayed in Fig. 1. In Fig. 2 they may be compared with those for the other three regions: the base of those three has been changed here to 1521–30, which we chose for the present four because it is the earliest decade that brings Vienna in; also we have smoothed the outlines by taking decennial averages, save for France, which runs in quarter-centuries. The extent of agreement springs to the eye. It is instanced numerically in Table II.

TABLE II

INDEXES OF THE EQUIVALENT OF THE WAGE-RATE OF A BUILDING CRAFTSMAN
EXPRESSED IN A COMPOSITE PHYSICAL UNIT OF CONSUMABLES
Base 1521–30=100

|  | 1476–1500 | 1521–30 | 1551–60 | 1591–1600 |
|---|---|---|---|---|
| S. England .. | 146 | 100 | (72)* | 65 |
| France .. .. | 131 | 100 | — | 52† |
| Alsace .. .. | 118 | 100 | 68 | 39 |
| Münster .. | 143 | 100 | 70 | — |
| Augsburg .. | — | 100 | 78 | 60 |
| Vienna .. | — | 100 | 69 | 48 |
| Valencia .. | 119 | 100 | 67 | 59 |

\* 1552 only. † 1576–1600.

That Valencia should show so great a fall—a halving of the basketful the craftsman had been buying at the end of the fifteenth century—was unexpected, when Earl Hamilton had found[1] that real wages in Spain in the last decade of the sixteenth century were only about 10 per cent. lower than they had been in the first, and that they then rose again " by leaps and bounds " until in 1611–20 they were higher than ever before since 1500. Hamilton's price index, though unweighted, differs little from ours, but his money wage index[2] differs greatly—in the course of the sixteenth century ours rises by a half, his threefold. This extraordinary disparity may arise from our following only carpenters, stonecutters and masons in Valencia, whereas he combines " wages covering from about 50 to almost 100 grades of labour ",[3] not necessarily the same in each of the three half-centuries from 1501 to 1650, and not in Valencia only but in Andalusia, New Castile and Old Castile as well. " The greatest defect . . . consists of the abnormally high

[1] Earl J. Hamilton, *American Treasure and the Price Revolution in Spain, 1501–1650* (Harvard, 1934), pp. 277–282.
[2] *Op. cit.*, p. 271, Table 27.
[3] *Op. cit.*, p. 270.

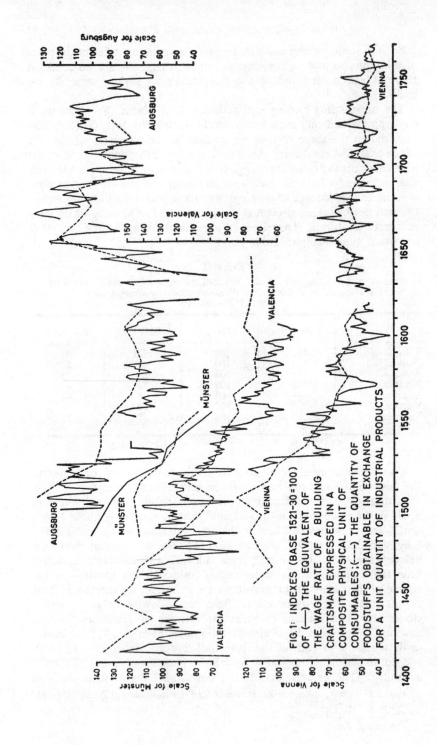

FIG.1: INDEXES (BASE 1521-30=100) OF (——) THE EQUIVALENT OF THE WAGE RATE OF A BUILDING CRAFTSMAN EXPRESSED IN A COMPOSITE PHYSICAL UNIT OF CONSUMABLES;(---) THE QUANTITY OF FOODSTUFFS OBTAINABLE IN EXCHANGE FOR A UNIT QUANTITY OF INDUSTRIAL PRODUCTS

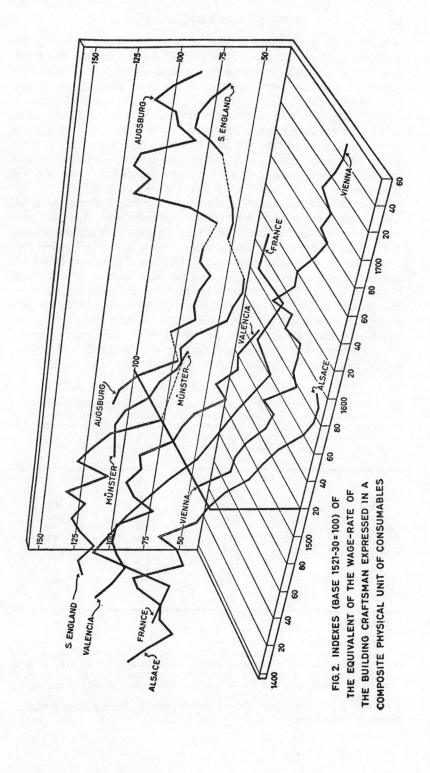

FIG. 2. INDEXES (BASE 1521-30=100) OF
THE EQUIVALENT OF THE WAGE-RATE OF
THE BUILDING CRAFTSMAN EXPRESSED IN A
COMPOSITE PHYSICAL UNIT OF CONSUMABLES

percentage of professional labour included."[1]  Some points in his statistical methods are not clear to us.[2]  From his estimate of a three-fold rise we can only come back to the Valencian builders' rates in his Appendix VII—the journeyman carpenter and journeyman mason, both 48 diners a day in 1502–05, 72 in 1599–1600; the master mason rising by absolutely as much but proportionately less, from 60 diners to 84; the mason's helper rising more, from 30 diners to 60, but still only doubling.  The rise of a half which we take as representative is borne out by the agreement which appears here as elsewhere between the implied fall in the commodity equivalent of the wage, and the movement of the terms of trade between workshop and farm.

This movement of the terms of trade, which Fig. 1 illustrates for all four places, is the second salient feature of our findings.  Again it agrees with what we found before in Southern England, France and Alsace. We can add now that it seems to have taken place in Sweden too. From the price indexes compiled by Dr. Ingrid Hammarström[3] for Stockholm and district we have made combined indexes of barley and butter on the one hand, and iron, bricks, lime, and cloth on the other. The price of barley, Dr. Hammarström says, was representative of that of rye, the most important bread grain, and we have given it twice the weight of butter; but our index for foodstuffs rests on rye and butter alone.  When we compare it with that for the industrial products, we get the index of the terms of trade in the third column of Table III.

TABLE III

STOCKHOLM AND DISTRICT, 1460–1559: INDEXES OF (1) PRICES OF BARLEY (WEIGHT 2) AND BUTTER (WEIGHT 1); (2) PRICES OF OSMUND IRON, BRICKS, LIME AND NAARDEN CLOTH (AT EQUAL WEIGHTS); (3) QUANTITY OF BARLEY AND BUTTER OBTAINABLE IN EXCHANGE FOR A UNIT OF INDUSTRIAL PRODUCT, VIZ. (2) ÷ (1) FROM DR. INGRID HAMMARSTRÖM'S MATERIALS Base 1460–69 = 100

|         | | | | (1) | (2) | (3) |
|---------|---|---|---|-----|-----|-----|
| 1460–69 | .. | .. | .. | 100 | 100 | 100 |
| 1470–79 | .. | .. | .. | 99 | 107 | 108 |
| 1480–89 | .. | .. | .. | 106 | 113 | 107 |
| 1490–99 | .. | .. | .. | 128 | 98 | 77 |
| 1500–09 | .. | .. | .. | 118 | 100 | 85 |
| 1510–19 | .. | .. | .. | 164 | 112 | 68 |
| 1520–29 | .. | .. | .. | *372 | *176 | *47 |
| 1530–39 | .. | .. | .. | 308 | 195 | 63 |
| 1540–49 | .. | .. | .. | 500 | 231 | 46 |
| 1550–59 | .. | .. | .. | 781 | 306 | 39 |

* 1525–29 only.

[1] *Op. cit.*, p. 270.

[2] Viz. the adjustment, if any, for divergences between the purchasing powers of the units of account in different provinces; how changes in the array of series available from year to year were dealt with; the extrapolation for Andalusia in 1501–50, described in *op. cit.*, p. 272, n. 1; how indexes computed for periods without overlap were subsequently spliced.

[3] " The ' Price Revolution ' of the Sixteenth Century: Some Swedish Evidence." *Scandinavian Economic History Review*, V. 2, 1957.

Evidently we are confronted with a movement of wide extent, and we have to look for an equally general cause. Our own suggestion has been that this lay in a growth of population. We can now add two pieces of evidence which tend to bear this out.

The first is the relationship between the population of certain German cities and food prices there, to which Elsas has drawn attention.[1] Admittedly the cities could have waxed and waned independently of population in the aggregate, and in the Thirty Years' War no doubt some did; but we know that the sixteenth century saw the growth of European cities generally,[2] and this may well have been the outlet that the growth of population found—when the death rate was so high in the cities, they could grow only through migration from the countryside. Elsas may therefore have been putting his finger on a factor of some generality when in his commentary on Frankfurt he said: " The lag of wages behind the rise of prices in the sixteenth century may be occasioned by the great accession to the labour force which the cities drew in from the countryside ".[3]

The second piece of evidence comes from France. Among the innumerable prices d'Avenel collected[4]—the last of all his tables contains six quotations for wooden legs—are the prices of land.[5] Much more goes to settling the price per hectare that any one parcel of land will fetch than the scarcity of land as a whole at the time relative to other factors of production; but when we aggregate many prices, as d'Avenel did, we can expect particularities to cancel one another out and let the prevailing influence of scarcity appear. This expectation gains support by the agreement between the movements of the averages d'Avenel presents separately for arable, pasture, vineyards and woodland: the price of woodland does not show so great a fall as the other prices between 1200 and 1475, and rises less afterwards; in both fall and rise pasture moves less than vineyards and arable; but with those exceptions the trends and the movements from one quarter-century to the next mostly agree. We have therefore made bold to form a combined index, with weights arable 6, pasture 2, vineyards 1, woodland 1; and compare it with our existing index for the building craftsman's wage-rate,[6] so as to see how the relative scarcities of land and at least one kind of industrial labour may have changed from time to time. The results are set out in Table IV and illustrated in Fig. 3, where the contemporary changes in the equivalent of the wage-rate

[1] M. J. Elsas, *Umriss einer Geschichte der Preise und Löhne in Deutschland*, vol. I (1936), pp. 77–82.

[2] Roger Mols, S. J., *Introduction à la démographie historique des villes de l'Europe du XIVᵉ au XVIIIᵉ siècle* (Louvain, 3 vols. 1954–6), vol. II, Aperçu d'Ensemble; review by K. F. Helleiner, *Journal of Economic History*, March, 1958.

[3] *Op. cit.*, vol. II.B, p. 68.

[4] Vicomte G. d'Avenel: *Histoire économique de la propriété, des salaires, des denrées, et de tous les prix en général, depuis l'an 1200 jusqu'en 1800.* Vols. I, II, 1894; III, IV, 1898; V, 1909; VI, 1912; VI(b), ?; VII, 1926.

[5] *Op. cit.*, vol. II, p. 884.

[6] *Economica*, November, 1957, p. 305, Table 3.

in units of basic consumables[1] are also shown. It will be seen that from 1276 to 1700 the craftsman's wage generally rose relatively to the price of land when the basketful of consumables it would buy was also rising, and conversely; the most marked exception is in the quarter-century

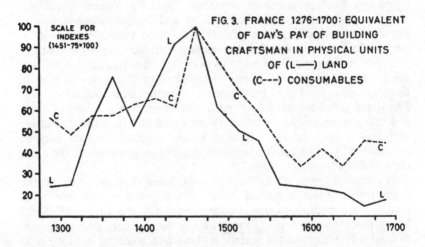

FIG. 3. FRANCE 1276-1700: EQUIVALENT OF DAY'S PAY OF BUILDING CRAFTSMAN IN PHYSICAL UNITS OF (L——) LAND (C---) CONSUMABLES

after the Black Death, and arises from a fall in the price of land then. The outcome is not unexpected, for in effect all we find now is that the price of land moved in sympathy with that of its produce; but it is something to have this direct indication of the changing scarcity of land writ large. It is generally consistent with the assumption that the growth of population in France was slower (it may even have been negative at times) between 1300 and 1475, more rapid thereafter until 1600, and then checked again.

TABLE IV

FRANCE, 1276–1700: INDEXES OF (1) PRICES PER HECTARE (IN LIVRES TOURNOIS) OF FOUR KINDS OF LAND; (2) WAGE-RATE (IN LIVRES TOURNOIS) OF BUILDING CRAFTS-MAN; (3) QUANTITY OF LAND OBTAINABLE IN EXCHANGE FOR A UNIT OF THE BUILDING CRAFTSMAN'S WORK, VIZ. (2) ÷ (1)
Base 1451–75 = 100

|  | (1) | (2) | (3) |  | (1) | (2) | (3) |
|---|---|---|---|---|---|---|---|
| 1276–1300 | 131 | 31 | 24 | 1501–25 .. | 218 | 112 | 51 |
| 1301–25 .. | 166 | 41 | 25 | 1526–50 .. | 338 | 156 | 46 |
| 1326–50 .. | 90 | 50 | 55 | 1551–75 .. | 728 | 179 | 25 |
| 1351–75 .. | 106 | 81 | 76 | 1576–1600 | 1062 | 258 | 24 |
| 1376–1400 | 134 | 71 | 53 | 1601–25 .. | 1188 | 268 | 23 |
| 1401–25 .. | 124 | 89 | 72 | 1626–50 .. | 1537 | 326 | 21 |
| 1426–50 .. | 100 | 92 | 92 | 1651–75 .. | 2635 | 405 | 15 |
| 1451–75 .. | 100 | 100 | 100 | 1676–1700 | 2418 | 428 | 18 |
| 1476–1500 | 175 | 109 | 62 | | | | |

[1] Also from Table 3, *loc. cit.*

One other feature of the comparisons in Fig. 2 remains for notice: the three places for which we have estimates through the seventeenth and eighteenth centuries behave very differently then. In Vienna the craftsman's basketful increases at first after 1600, from less than half its bulk of the 1520's to nearly two-thirds about 1650, but then it slips back, and from the 1690's to 1760 it lies around the size it had been brought down to at its most meagre around 1610. In Southern England it not only recovers much as in Vienna down to 1650, but goes on increasing gently until the 1740's, when it is getting on for double what it had been at its worst, and is not much smaller than in the 1520's; but from 1750 it begins to shrink again. In Augsburg it behaves quite otherwise: with the end of the Thirty Years' War it doubles in a matter of only twenty years, and though it fluctuates in size thereafter, and its tendency is to shrink, it remains for most of a hundred years not far from its bulk of the 1520's. The contrast between Vienna and Augsburg seems the more striking at first because Augsburg had been stricken in the war as Vienna had not: but what mattered afterwards was not the rubble in the city itself but the terms on which it could now draw in supplies from the countryside around. In all three places the terms of this trade moved in close agreement with the changes in the size of the basketful, for which they provide a first explanation. They would themselves be consistent with our main conjecture, if in fact the population of southern Germany had been reduced through the Thirty Years War to little more than its figure of a hundred years before; whereas that of Lower Austria had kept up, and grew again somewhat after 1650, and that of Southern England grew more slowly if at all after 1600, until in the 1750's it began to rise rapidly again. According to Roger Mols,[1] the population of Augsburg doubled in a hundred years to reach 40–50,000 about 1600, but in 1645 it was only 21,000, and as late as 1790 it still did not exceed 50,000; whereas Vienna, in 1600 about the same size as Augsburg, had more than 100,000 inhabitants by 1700.

## II

In Southern England we were also able to trace the labourer's rate over much of five centuries, and found that in settled periods from first to last down to 1914 it was commonly two-thirds of the craftsman's. This persistence of a rule of thumb, as we must think it, was remarkable. Does it appear elsewhere? In Vienna, yes: in the 1520's the tiler's and mason's labourers got six kronen a day against the nine kronen of the journeyman carpenter and mason; after 1750 the tiler's labourer got 18 to the journeyman's 27; and the ratio of two to three held pretty well throughout except that from 1670 onwards the mason's labourer lay somewhat below it. But in two other of our cities it seems to have been mostly otherwise: the differential was wider to start with, but then when rates generally rose it narrowed. In Valencia the prevailing

[1] *Op. cit.*, vol. II, pp. 510–12.

rates down to 1550 seem to have been 48 for the journeyman against not 32 but 30 for the labourer; but then the labourer rose more, not relatively only but absolutely, to attain first three-quarters, and then by 1589 five-sixths, of the journeyman's rate. In Augsburg it is the mortar-mixer who is best recorded. His rate seems to have been higher by as much as a quarter than the mere labourer's, but even so was only four-sevenths of the journeyman mason's early in the sixteenth century; then his more rapid rise lifted the ratio by the 1570's to three-quarters or over. There it seems to have stayed until 1713, when it was shifted back to the two-thirds so familiar elsewhere. So in the eighteenth century the differential between the skilled and the unskilled was the same (at least for the mortar-mixer) in Augsburg as it was generally in Vienna and Southern England.

## III

Our present sources provide household budgets in Germany and Spain for comparison with the weights of the composite commodity that we adopted in the light of English evidence alone, but later used elsewhere with little change. The comparison is shown in Table V.

TABLE V

DIVISION OF OUTLAY DERIVED FROM GERMAN,
SPANISH AND ENGLISH HOUSEHOLD BUDGETS

|  | Original | | Common items only | | | |
|---|---|---|---|---|---|---|
|  | Germany, (Palatinate) 1500–1700 | Spain, 16th century | Germany, (Palatinate) 1500–1700 | Spain, 16th century | S. England Davies & Eden, 1790's | Adopted by present authors |
|  | (1) % | (2) % | (3) % | (4) % | (5) % | (6) % |
| 1. Farinaceous | 36 | 25 | 46 | 36 | 53 | 20 |
| 2. Meat, fish .. | 11 | 23½ | 14 | 33½ | 12 | 25 |
| 3. Butter, cheese | 9 | 2 | 12 | 3 | 7 | 12½ |
| 4. Drink .. | 6 | 10 | 8 | 14 | 9 | 22½ |
| Subtotal, Food.. | 62 | 60½ | 80 | 86½ | 81 | 80 |
| 5. Fuel and light | 8 | 5 | 10 | 7 | 7½ | 7½ |
| 6. Textiles .. | 8 | 4½ | 10 | 6½ | 11½ | 12½ |
| TOTAL, (1)–(6) .. | 78 | 70 | 100 | 100 | 100 | 100 |
| 7. Other .. | 22* | 30† | | | | |
| TOTAL, (1)–(7) .. | 100 | 100 | | | | |

* Other foodstuffs 6, shoes 4, rent 8, various 4.
† Miscellaneous, but not including rent.
*Sources :* Col. (1), G. Wiebe, *Zur Geschichte der Preisrevolution des XVI. und XVII. Jahrhunderts* (Leipzig, 1895), pp. 176–7. Col. (2), Earl J. Hamilton, *American Treasure and the Price Revolution in Spain, 1501–1650* (Harvard, 1934), pp. 275–6. Cols. (3) and (4): calculated by raising rows (1)–(6) in cols. (1) and (2) in equal proportions so as to make their totals 100. Cols. (5) and (6): *Economica,* November, 1956, p. 297.

It lends support to the view that we gave too little weight to breadstuffs. Our chosen proportions, it is true, are closely akin to those (not shown in the Table) of the British urban wage-earners' budgets of 1904, and (taking the two kinds of animal produce together) William Savernak's household in Dorset in the 1450's, but in the setting of seven centuries these were both times of exceptional prosperity. So we have recalculated our index of prices for Southern England with new weights for food more like cols. (3)–(5) of Table V:

|  | Original index % | Present re-calculation % |
|---|---|---|
| 1. Farinaceous | 20 | 50 |
| 2. Meat, fish .. | 25 | 12½ |
| 3. Butter, cheese | 12½ | 7½ |
| 4. Drink | 22½ | 10 |
| Subtotal, Food | 80 | 80 |

But until 1855 the outcome proves to be so little changed that there is no need to set the new series out. It usually rises higher in a year of dearth, and drops lower in one of plenty, because grain fluctuated more widely than meat; but there is no divergence of trend, nor sustained difference of level, except that through most of 1659–85 the new index runs four or five per cent. above the old, and through 1818–46 often as much as ten per cent. below it. In 1855, however, a very different story begins, for the relative price of grain now falls steeply, and by 1895 the new index lies for the moment below 750 while the old is over 950. But this is a period in which the weights of the budgets of 1904 become increasingly appropriate.

There is a noteworthy implication of this fact that in the last hundred years meat has been so much dearer relatively to grain than in the six hundred years before: we must beware of supposing that wage-earners in those earlier years would have bought as little meat as the poor have in more recent times. "That island of England breeds very valiant creatures . . . give them great meals of beef, and iron and steel, they will eat like wolves, and fight like devils." It was possible to write that when the Tudor decline in the purchasing power of wages had already run most of its course.

## APPENDIX ON SOURCES AND METHODS

MÜNSTER

*Source:* G. Wiebe, *Zur Geschichte der Preisrevolution des XVI. und XVII. Jahrhunderts* (Leipzig, 1895).

*Unit of Money:* Some of the original quotations were in the golden gulden, some in silver marks, shillings, pence, and (later) thalers. Wiebe reduced them all to their contemporary equivalents in grams of gold, and our indexes follow his tables. Until 1539 Münster was effectively on a bimetallic standard, but as the weight of silver exchangeable for a unit weight of gold changed little, our indexes effectively show the movements of quotations in the unit of account. From 1539 onwards the silver thaler became the unit of account, and we are told that in 1545–60 silver depreciated relatively to gold by 2·7 to 6·7 per cent., so quotations in the unit of account would have risen to that extent more than our indexes.

*Wage-rates:* pp. 335–7, quotations mostly for wages when the employer provided food. After comparison mainly of series for carpenters, masons and tilers, the helpers of each, also sawyers and day labourers, we took out a representative series, whose movements differed little from those of the carpenter's wage, when food was provided, for the summer day.

*Prices:* (1) *Composite unit of consumables :* pp. 325–334. We followed the make-up of the English unit (*Economica*, November, 1956, p. 297, Table I). 1. *Farinaceous.* Rye, wheat and barley at equal weights, oats and peas at half weights. 2. *Meat and fish.* Fat oxen, calves, pigs, and fat sheep at equal weights, total subweight 21; herrings and stock-fish at equal weights, total subweight 4. 3. *Butter and Cheese* at equal weights. 4. *Drink.* Wine, malt and beer (average of five sorts) at equal weights. 5. *Fuel and light.* Tallow, tallow candles, and wax, sub-weights 1 each; charcoal, subweight $4\frac{1}{2}$. 6. *Textiles.* Linen (average of four sorts) and cloth (average of five sorts) at equal weights.

(2) *Indexes of prices of foodstuffs and of industrial products.* The index for foodstuffs is provided by components 1–4 of the composite unit above, combined as there weighted. We made that for industrial products by combining at equal weights the series for linen and cloth in (6) above with others for salt, bricks, tiles, nails, paper, and men's shoes, pp. 330–4.

AUGSBURG

*Source:* M. J. Elsas, *Umriss einer Geschichte der Preise und Löhne in Deutschland*, vol. I (Leiden, 1936). All the extracts we used are from the accounts of the Augsburg hospital.

*Unit of money :* the Augsburg pfennig as unit of account throughout.

*Wage-rates:* We graphed the rates given at pp. 726–36 for mortar-mixers, unskilled building labourers, journeyman masons, and journeyman carpenters, and then took out by inspection a series representative of the craftsmen's rate.

*Prices:* (1) *Composite unit of consumables.* We followed the make-up of the English unit (*Economica*, November, 1956, p. 297, Table I) as far as possible, but until 1641 we had no entries for Drink, and transferred its weight to Farinaceous. We estimated the components as follows; the brackets after each commodity contain the weight we gave it in calculating the index for the whole component : 1. *Farinaceous.* Pp. 360–72, 383–5, 593–8, rye (8), barley (3), oats (3), peas (2), spelt (4 through 1673, 2 from 1674), and, from

1674 only, wheat (2). We spliced wheat to the mean of the others over 1674–85.
2. *Meat and fish.* Pp. 386–8, 392–6, 601–5, 607–14, beef (10), veal (5, transferred to beef in absence of veal 1499–1511, 1542–89), suet (3), dripping (3),
carp (4, transferred *pro rata* to the other four in absence of carp before 1551).
The entries for veal and suet were mostly of sales, those for the other three
mostly of purchases. We spliced carp to the mean of the other four over
1551–64. 3. *Butter and cheese.* Pp. 390–1, 600–4, milk (5, transferred to
cheese 1647–56, 1670–1711), and, from 1580 only, Dutch cheese (7½, transferred to milk until 1580). We spliced cheese to milk over 1580–95. 4. *Drink.*
Pp. 405–6, 616, 618–20, brown beer. There are early entries ending with
1536, but we used the series only from its resumption in 1641, and until then
transferred the weight of Drink to Farinaceous. We spliced brown beer
to the mean of the series in Farinaceous over 1652–89. 5. *Fuel and light.*
Pp. 408–10, 615–21, tallow (5), linseed oil (2½). 6. *Textiles.* Pp. 413–4,
615–20, twill: the quotations comprise different qualities.

(2) *Indexes of prices of foodstuffs and of industrial products.* The index for
foodstuffs is given by components 1–4 of the composite unit of consumables,
combined as weighted there. That for industrial products we made by
combining at equal weights the series for textiles in component 6 above and
the following: pp. 401–3, 418–25, 607–13, 615–20, 622–4, salt, Bavarian,
in blocks; lime, by the barrel through 1573, by the peck from 1574—we
spliced the second series to the first over 1557–74; bricks; writing paper.

VIENNA
  *Source:* A. F. Pribram, *Materialien zur Geschichte der Preise und Löhne in
Österreich*, vol. I (Vienna, 1938). Data here all from Vienna city hospital
and the Klosterneuburg monastery, referred to here as WB and SK respectively.
  *Unit of money:* the kreuzer as unit of account throughout.
  *Wage-rates:* pp. 177–83, 344–50, 235–7, 515–20. Journeymen carpenters,
masons and tilers in WB and SK; labourers of the last two in WB, and we
are told that the SK rates for the mason's labourer were the same as the
WB; tiler's labourer from 1636 at SK (p. 236, note H). Wage without
board, for the summer day throughout, except that for the tilers there was no
seasonal difference. By graphical inspection we took out a single rate as
representative of the journeymen, mainly the carpenters and masons.
  *Prices:* (1) *Composite unit of consumables.* We followed the make-up of
the English unit (*Economica*, November, 1956, p. 297, Table 1), except that
here we had no series for butter and cheese, whose weight we transferred to
meat, and that we have had to compute the index before 1486 without any
farinaceous component. There is no fish through 1607–91. We estimated
the components as follows: 1. *Farinaceous.* SK 1486–1528, pp. 204–5,
447–9; WB 1527–1779, pp. 133–4, 269–74. Barley, " corn " (specified for
SK as ' Traid, Korn, selten Roggen '), and wheat at equal weights throughout.
We adjusted the quotations from harvest to calendar years by taking the price
for the calendar year 1486 to be made up of half the prices for the harvest
years 1485, 1486, and so on. We reduced the SK series of 1485–1528 by
one-sixteenth to offset the larger SK bushel (p. 104), and took the adjusted
series as continuous with the WB series which were all we used after 1528.
Through 1690–1751 and again from 1752 onwards we adjusted prices to
offset changes in the size of the bushel (pp. 101–2). 2. *Meat and fish.* Meat:
pp. 215–6 and 465–72, 1445–1535, SK oxen (Hungarian), calves, whole sheep.

half or quarter sheep; pp. 151–4 and 287–92, 1533–1735, WB oxen (Hungarian), sheep, with calves beginning only in 1565 and spliced to oxen over 1565–78. We joined the SK to the WB series as follows: we spliced SK oxen to WB at 1533–35, SK calves to SK oxen over 1516–33, and SK whole sheep to WB sheep at 1533–35, and we applied the factor calculated for this last splice to SK half or quarter sheep. We gave equal weights to the unweighted means of the series for cattle and sheep. Fish: pp. 220–1 and 471–6, SK herrings 1445–1533 and 1735–65, sturgeon 1445–1583 and 1694–1769; pp. 158 and 290–2, WB herrings 1528–1606 and 1692–1734. We spliced SK to WB herrings over 1528, 1531, 1533, and again over 1692–1729. We gave herrings and sturgeon equal weights throughout. We combined meat and fish with weights $33\frac{1}{2}$ (including the $12\frac{1}{2}$ transferred from butter and cheese) and 4. 4. *Drink*. Beer all WB, pp. 146–9 and 300–02, 307–8: 1527–1653 Iglauer, 1528–78 Freistädter, 1535–1616 Schweinitzer, 1583–1616 Regensberger, all prices of purchases; 1565–1653, Spital, ordinary, price of sales. We spliced the Regensberger to the Iglauer over 1595–1603. The Spital stands on its own base in 1535–44, though we have not included its entries at that time in the index. Wine, SK, pp. 213–4 and 462–4, 1450–1750 sales, 1483–1748 retail; WB, pp. 143–5 and 308–11, 1526–1756 sales, 1526–1770 retail, 1592–1770 purchases. The WB wines are all heuriger (first-year) and the prices are for the harvest year: we entered the price for harvest year 1525 against calendar year 1526, and so on. We spliced SK to WB, retail over 1526–33, sales over 1553–87; and WB purchases to retail over 1630–62. We combined the unweighted means of beer, wine with weights 3 and 1. 5. *Fuel and light*. Fuel: pp. 163–4, 295–7, 321–6, WB, 1527–1603 and 1634–1779, soft firewood, with fir (p. 332) used for interpolation 1746–62; 1551–1665, charcoal. We spliced charcoal to firewood over 1582–97. We combined the two series with equal weights to give an index for fuel. Light: pp. 171–3, 311–4, 316, 327, 335–8, WB, tallow candles, (i) with black wick, 1439–1512, 1553–84, 1630–1781, (ii) with cotton wick 1630–1781, raw tallow 1527–58; pp. 233, 508–11, SK tallow candles, 1448–1582. We spliced candles (i) to raw tallow over 1555–8, and (ii) to (i) over 1680–1702. We combined these series at equal weights to get an index for candles. Pp. 232, 508–14, SK olive oil, 1442–1532, 1646–1771; pp. 170–1, 316, WB olive (lighting) oil, 1722–79. We spliced SK oil to SK candles over 1520–9, and where there were two series for oil combined them at equal weights so as to have a single index for oil throughout. We combined the three indexes with weights fuel 5, candles 4, oil 1. 6. *Textiles*. Pp. 222–3, 499–501, SK hemp, 1443–1532, adjusted from harvest to calendar years; pp. 168–9, 321–30, WB thread (cheap sort) 1527–1703, coarse woollen cloth 1527–1778. We spliced hemp to thread at 1527, 1531, and formed an index with weights hemp and thread combined 1, cloth 3.

(2) *Indexes of prices of foodstuffs and of industrial products.* The index for foodstuffs is provided by components 1–4 of the composite unit above, combined as there weighted. That for industrial products we made by combining with equal weights the indexes for components 5 and 6 above with indexes for building materials and ironwork which we formed as follows. *Building materials :* the following six indexes combined at equal weights— *bricks*, mean of WB (without delivery charge) pp. 162, 586, and SK pp. 224, 630; *tiles* (without delivery charge), WB, pp. 162, 586; *shingles*, mean of WB, pp. 165, 586, 8, and SK, small, pp. 225, 630; *lime*, WB, pp. 161, 586, combined at equal weights with mean of SK series 1, 2, 4, pp. 223–4, 628;

*pitch*, WB, pp. 174, 592, 4; *timber*, unweighted mean of WB ordinary planks, carpenter's planks, bench planks, and laths, pp. 165, 586, 588. *Ironwork:* unweighted mean of three SK series for *nails*—large shingle, partition, large lath, pp. 228–9, 634.

## Valencia

*Sources:* Earl J. Hamilton, (M) *Money, Prices and Wages in Valencia, Aragon, and Navarre, 1351–1500* (Harvard, 1936); (A) *American Treasure and the Price Revolution in Spain, 1501–1650* (Harvard, 1934).

*Unit of money:* the diner as unit of account throughout.

*Wage-rates:* We graphed the quotations for the following: 1392–1500, carpenters, masons and stonecutters, masters and helpers, with journeyman masons, and unskilled labourers; 1501–1600, carpenters, masons and stonecutters, masters and journeymen, with mason's helper to 1650. By inspection we took out a rate representative of the movements of the craftsmen's rates generally, and at the level of the master carpenter's rate down to 1500, the journeyman carpenter's thereafter; we joined the two by assigning to the first entry of the second the same index-number value as appeared for the last entries of the first. We also took out a series representative of the carpenters' and masons' helpers with the unskilled labourers in 1392–1500, and continued this without any change of rate at 1500, but now on the showing of the mason's helper alone, down to 1638.

*Prices:* (1) *Composite unit of consumables.* We followed the make-up of the English unit (*Economica*, November, 1956, p. 297, Table 1) but because Drink meant wine not beer gave it a weight of only $12\frac{1}{2}$ and transferred the rest of its English weight to Farinaceous, whose weight becomes 30. We estimated the components as follows. Prices are from M, Appendix III, and A, Appendix III.D, IV.D, V.D. 1. *Farinaceous*. We spliced carob beans and rice to wheat over 1520–60. 2. *Meat and fish*. We took the predominant values of beef, mutton and hens in the 1440's as an approximation to the required base in 1451–75, when wheat prices lay about the same level as in the 1440's. We spliced lard to mutton over 1505–30, and cod to tuna over 1558–68. Sub-weights: before 1451, beef 8, mutton 8, hens 5; before 1501, sardines 1, tuna $1\frac{1}{2}$, hake $1\frac{1}{2}$; from 1501, mutton 13, hens 4, lard 4, tuna 2, dried cod 2. 3. *Butter and cheese*. Cheese only. In the absence of any series even for cheese through 1551–1601, we extrapolated the index for all foodstuffs in 1550 in proportion to the combined movement of the remaining foodstuffs. 4. *Drink*. Wine only. 5. *Fuel and light*. We spliced charcoal to firewood over 1520–40. Sub-weights, before 1501, firewood 5, olive oil $2\frac{1}{2}$; from 1501, firewood 4, charcoal $3\frac{1}{2}$. 6. *Textiles*. We spliced linen and bedticks to flax over 1552–66. Sub-weights from 1552, flax 3, linen 3, bedticks $6\frac{1}{2}$.

(2) *Indexes of prices of foodstuffs and of industrial products.* The index for foodstuffs is provided by components 1–4 of the composite unit above, combined as there weighted. We made that for industrial products by combining at equal weights firewood, plaster of Paris, lime, bricks, and (not after 1500) nails, large.

TABLE VI

BUILDERS' WAGE-RATES IN MÜNSTER, AUGSBURG,
VIENNA AND VALENCIA, FOR VARIOUS PERIODS
WITHIN 1413–1796

1. MÜNSTER. Index of craftsman's rate for summer day, in units of gold; base 1467–1500, when the rate for the carpenter, summer day, employer providing food, was about 0·192 grams gold, that is, about 0·072 gulden, or 1·4 schilling.

| 1467–1500 | .. 100 | 1531–40 .. | .. 84 |
|---|---|---|---|
| 1501–10 .. | .. 80 | 1541–50 .. | .. 79 |
| 1511–20 .. | .. 83 | 1551–60 .. | .. 74 |
| 1521–30 .. | .. 77 | | |

2. AUGSBURG. (1) Craftsman's rate as represented mainly by the mason, in pfennig for summer day. (2) Unskilled rate as represented mainly by the mortar-mixer, in pfennig per day, summer and winter not distinguished. Both apparently without board.

| (1) | | (2) | | (1) | | (2) | |
|---|---|---|---|---|---|---|---|
| | d. | | d. | | d. | | d. |
| 1499–1538 | 28 | 1502–19 .. | 16 | 1604–21 .. | 63 | 1606–24 .. | n.a. |
| 1539–52 .. | n.a. | 1520–37 .. | n.a. | 1622–29 .. | n.a. | 1625–30 .. | 52·5 |
| 1553–68 .. | 35 | 1538 | 19 | 1630–44 .. | 77 | 1631–52 .. | n.a. |
| 1569–1603 | 45·5 | 1539–52 .. | n.a. | 1645–65 .. | 84 | 1653–66 .. | 63 |
| | | 1553–65 .. | 24·5 | 1666–67 .. | n.a. | 1667–74 .. | n.a. |
| | | 1566–7 .. | n.a. | 1668–1712 | 91 | 1675–1763 .. | 70 |
| | | 1568 .. | 30·5 | 1713–96 .. | 105 | | |
| | | 1569–72 .. | 31·5 | | | | |
| | | 1573 .. | 34·5 | | | | |
| | | 1574–1605 | 35 | | | | |

3. VIENNA. Craftsman's rate, represented mainly by masons and carpenters, in kronen for a summer day, without board.

| | | Kr. | | | Kr. |
|---|---|---|---|---|---|
| 1520–43 .. | .. | 9 | 1641–69 .. | .. | 22 |
| 1544–74 .. | .. | 10 | 1670–82 .. | .. | 19·5 |
| 1574–79 | Rising to 12 | | 1682–90 | Rising to 24 | |
| 1579–1600 .. | .. | 12 | 1690–1711 .. | .. | 24 |
| 1600–02 | Rising to 15 | | 1712–20 .. | .. | 24·5 |
| 1602–18 .. | .. | 15 | 1721–79 .. | .. | 25·5 |
| 1618–41 | Rising to 22 | | | | |

4. VALENCIA. Index of craftsman's rate, represented mainly by the master and journeyman carpenters, in diners per day (the rate was the same throughout the year) without board for the most part. Base 1451–75=100, when the master carpenter's rate was 57d.

| 1392–1463 .. | .. 105 | 1561–78 .. | .. 132 |
|---|---|---|---|
| 1463–73 | Falling to 89 | 1579–85 .. | .. 145 |
| 1473–87 .. | .. 89 | 1586–1607 .. | .. 158 |
| 1488–1560 .. | .. 105 | | |

TABLE VII

INDEXES (1521–30=100) OF (1) PRICE OF COMPOSITE UNIT OF CONSUMABLES, (2) EQUIVALENT OF WAGE-RATE OF BUILDING CRAFTSMAN, EXPRESSED IN THE ABOVE PHYSICAL UNIT, IN MÜNSTER (M), AUGSBURG (A), VIENNA (W) AND VALENCIA (V), FOR PERIODS WITHIN 1413–1770

(a) MÜNSTER 1467–1560

|  | M.1 | M.2 |  | M.1 | M.2 |  | M.1 | M.2 |  | M.1 | M.2 |
|---|---|---|---|---|---|---|---|---|---|---|---|
| 1467–1500 | 90 | 143 | 1511–20 | 90 | 121 | 1531–40 | 113 | 97 | 1551–60 | 137 | 70 |
| 1501–10 | 81 | 130 | 1521–30 | 100 | 100 | 1541–50 | 123 | 84 |  |  |  |

(b) VALENCIA 1413–98 (*contd. in* (c))

|  | V.1 | V.2 |  | V.1 | V.2 |  | V.1 | V.2 |  | V.1 | V.2 |
|---|---|---|---|---|---|---|---|---|---|---|---|
| 1413 | 111 | 90 | 1435 | 91 | 110 | 1457 | 81 | 122 | 1479 | 87 | 97 |
| 1414 | 78 | 128 | 1436 | 88 | 113 | 1458 | 71 | 141 | 1480 | 84 | 101 |
| 1415 | 77 | 130 | 1437 | 90 | 111 | 1459 | 76 | 131 | 1481 | 67 | 126 |
| 1416 | 64 | 156 | 1438 | 91 | 109 | 1460 | 75 | 132 | 1482 | 74 | 114 |
| 1417 | 67 | 149 | 1439 | 87 | 115 | 1461 | 69 | 144 | 1483 | 69 | 122 |
| 1418 | 69 | 144 | 1440 | 85 | 117 | 1462 | 77 | 130 | 1484 | 76 | 111 |
| 1419 | 71 | 141 | 1441 | 76 | 131 | 1463 | 76 | 131 | 1485 | 100 | 85 |
| 1420 | 72 | 138 | 1442 | 84 | 118 | 1464 | 77 | 128 | 1486 | 77 | 110 |
| 1421 | 80 | 125 | 1443 | 81 | 123 | 1465 | 70 | 138 | 1487 | 76 | 111 |
| 1422 | 78 | 127 | 1444 | 81 | 123 | 1466 | 68 | 139 | 1488 | 74 | 134 |
| 1423 | 74 | 134 | 1445 | 81 | 122 | 1467 | 73 | 129 | 1489 | 76 | 131 |
| 1424 | 75 | 132 | 1446 | 82 | 121 | 1468 | 73 | 127 | 1490 | 75 | 132 |
| 1425 | 79 | 126 | 1447 | 83 | 120 | 1469 | 75 | 121 | 1491 | 86 | 116 |
| 1426 | 84 | 119 | 1448 | 71 | 141 | 1470 | 83 | 108 | 1492 | 78 | 128 |
| 1427 | 93 | 107 | 1449 | 79 | 126 | 1471 | 79 | 111 | 1493 | 81 | 122 |
| 1428 | 82 | 121 | 1450 | 77 | 130 | 1472 | 74 | 116 | 1494 | 84 | 118 |
| 1429 | 71 | 139 | 1451 | 79 | 126 | 1473 | 83 | 102 | 1495 | 79 | 126 |
| 1430 | 83 | 120 | 1452 | 81 | 123 | 1474 | 101 | 84 | 1496 | 82 | 121 |
| 1431 | 78 | 128 | 1453 | 74 | 134 | 1475 | 84 | 101 | 1497 | 80 | 125 |
| 1432 | 81 | 122 | 1454 | 70 | 142 | 1476 | 68 | 123 | 1498 | 82 | 121 |
| 1433 | 79 | 126 | 1455 | 73 | 136 | 1477 | 69 | 122 |  |  |  |
| 1434 | 75 | 132 | 1456 | 81 | 123 | 1478 | 82 | 103 |  |  |  |

(c) AUGSBURG 1499–1753, VIENNA 1520–1770,

VALENCIA (*contd.*) 1499–1607

|  | A.1 | A.2 | W.1 | W.2 | V.1 | V.2 |  | A.1 | A.2 | W.1 | W.2 | V.1 | V.2 |
|---|---|---|---|---|---|---|---|---|---|---|---|---|---|
| 1499 | 77 | 122 | 91 |  | 76 | 131 | 1514 | 77 | 124 | 91 |  | 79 | 126 |
| 1500 | 97 | 97 | 79 |  | 71 | 141 | 1515 | 88 | 108 | 92 |  | 81 | 123 |
| 1501 | 100 | 95 | 79 |  | 70 | 142 | 1516 | 102 | 93 | 86 |  | 91 | 109 |
| 1502 | 89 | 107 | 80 |  | 96 | 104 | 1517 | 100 | 95 | 86 |  | 87 | 114 |
| 1503 | 96 | 99 | 86 |  | 114 | 87 | 1518 | 81 | 117 | 86 |  | 84 | 119 |
| 1504 | 93 | 102 | 91 |  | 84 | 119 | 1519 | 89 | 107 | 89 |  | 85 | 117 |
| 1505 | 74 | 129 | 87 |  | 87 | 114 | 1520 | 85 | 111 | 87 | 112 | 79 | 126 |
| 1506 | 73 | 130 | 86 |  | 84 | 118 | 1521 | 80 | 119 | 86 | 114 | 111 | 89 |
| 1507 | 77 | 124 | 81 |  | 84 | 119 | 1522 | 83 | 115 | 84 | 118 | 115 | 86 |
| 1508 | 80 | 119 | 75 |  | 82 | 121 | 1523 | 81 | 117 | 86 | 114 | 91 | 110 |
| 1509 | 92 | 103 | 86 |  | 82 | 121 | 1524 | 86 | 110 | 91 | 108 | 92 | 108 |
| 1510 | 92 | 103 | 87 |  | 85 | 117 | 1525 | 77 | 124 | 104 | 95 | 98 | 101 |
| 1511 | 96 | 99 | 86 |  | 85 | 117 | 1526 | 104 | 91 | 109 | 90 | 94 | 105 |
| 1512 | 80 | 119 | 80 |  | 81 | 122 | 1527 | 98 | 96 | 99 | 99 | 101 | 99 |
| 1513 | 79 | 120 | 90 |  | 82 | 121 | 1528 | 94 | 100 | 100 | 98 | 99 | 100 |

| | A.1 | A.2 | W.1 | W.2 | V.1 | V.2 | | A.1 | A.2 | W.1 | W.2 | V.1 | V.2 |
|---|---|---|---|---|---|---|---|---|---|---|---|---|---|
| 1529 | 150 | 63 | 102 | 95 | 97 | 102 | 1590 | 292 | 52 | 241 | 55 | 226 | 66 |
| 1530 | 147 | 64 | 141 | 69 | 101 | 98 | 1591 | 253 | 61 | 247 | 53 | 239 | 62 |
| 1531 | 144 | 66 | 124 | 79 | 104 | 95 | 1592 | 235 | 66 | 213 | 61 | 264 | 57 |
| 1532 | 140 | 68 | 130 | 75 | 106 | 94 | 1593 | 255 | 60 | 232 | 56 | 263 | 57 |
| 1533 | 160 | 59 | 141 | 69 | 101 | 99 | 1594 | 265 | 58 | 258 | 51 | 242 | 62 |
| 1534 | 155 | 61 | 127 | 77 | 107 | 93 | 1595 | 238 | 64 | 286 | 46 | 236 | 63 |
| 1535 | 120 | 79 | 127 | 77 | 103 | 97 | 1596 | 224 | 69 | 257 | 51 | 222 | 68 |
| 1536 | 100 | 95 | 125 | 79 | 104 | 96 | 1597 | 258 | 59 | 266 | 49 | 241 | 62 |
| 1537 | 121 | 79 | 125 | 79 | 98 | 101 | 1598 | 288 | 53 | 295 | 44 | 272 | 55 |
| 1538 | 121 | 79 | 124 | 79 | 104 | 95 | 1599 | 262 | 59 | 336 | 39 | 295 | 51 |
| 1539 | 121 | | 115 | 85 | 108 | 92 | 1600 | 305 | 50 | 389 | 33 | 276 | 54 |
| 1540 | 154 | | 115 | 85 | 109 | 91 | 1601 | 295 | 52 | 354 | 41 | 285 | 52 |
| 1541 | 124 | | 127 | 77 | 107 | 93 | 1602 | 292 | 52 | 332 | 49 | 287 | 52 |
| 1542 | 136 | | 130 | 75 | 111 | 89 | 1603 | 272 | 57 | 347 | 47 | 315 | 48 |
| 1543 | 151 | | 122 | 80 | 102 | 97 | 1604 | 261 | 82 | 333 | 49 | 290 | 52 |
| 1544 | 146 | | 135 | 80 | 98 | 101 | 1605 | 272 | 79 | 290 | 56 | 277 | 54 |
| 1545 | 138 | | 156 | 70 | 111 | 89 | 1606 | 284 | 75 | 321 | 51 | 262 | 57 |
| 1546 | 133 | | 166 | 66 | 126 | 79 | 1607 | 288 | 74 | 356 | 46 | 249 | 60 |
| 1547 | 131 | | 147 | 75 | 106 | 94 | 1608 | 286 | 74 | 322 | 49 | 245 | |
| 1548 | 126 | | 130 | 83 | 115 | 86 | 1609 | 305 | 70 | 324 | 50 | 246 | |
| 1549 | 149 | | 122 | 89 | 126 | 79 | 1610 | 320 | 67 | 308 | 53 | 262 | |
| 1550 | 170 | | 149 | 73 | 130 | 77 | 1611 | 330 | 64 | 305 | 53 | 256 | |
| 1551 | 185 | | 156 | 70 | 130 | 76 | 1612 | 326 | 66 | 298 | 55 | 268 | |
| 1552 | 163 | | 157 | 69 | 145 | 69 | 1613 | 318 | 68 | 314 | 52 | 269 | |
| 1553 | 156 | 76 | 155 | 71 | 157 | 63 | 1614 | 369 | 58 | 383 | 43 | 285 | |
| 1554 | 144 | 82 | 130 | 83 | 148 | 67 | 1615 | 332 | 64 | 348 | 47 | 250 | |
| 1555 | 143 | 83 | 151 | 72 | 146 | 68 | 1616 | 322 | 67 | 347 | 47 | 259 | |
| 1556 | 136 | 87 | 156 | 65 | 146 | 68 | 1617 | 285 | 75 | 337 | 48 | 285 | |
| 1557 | 144 | 83 | 158 | 69 | 175 | 57 | 1618 | 268 | 80 | 361 | 45 | 285 | |
| 1558 | 155 | 76 | 152 | 71 | 153 | 65 | 1619 | 299 | 72 | 366 | 45 | 265 | |
| 1559 | 185 | 64 | 165 | 67 | 151 | 66 | 1620 | 323 | 67 | 494 | | 263 | |
| 1560 | 173 | 69 | 217 | 50 | 150 | 66 | 1621 | 567 | 37 | 523 | | 265 | |
| 1561 | 168 | 71 | 185 | 59 | 150 | 84 | 1622 | 1364 | | 955 | | 264 | |
| 1562 | 180 | 66 | 166 | 65 | 156 | 80 | 1623 | 574 | | 1901 | | 288 | |
| 1563 | 171 | 70 | 172 | 64 | 163 | 77 | 1624 | 467 | | 830 | | 269 | |
| 1564 | 165 | 72 | 170 | 64 | 153 | 82 | 1625 | 539 | | 597 | | 265 | |
| 1565 | 176 | 68 | 172 | 64 | 170 | 73 | 1626 | 502 | | 409 | 47 | 293 | |
| 1566 | 206 | 58 | 176 | 62 | 176 | 71 | 1627 | 472 | | 438 | 44 | 294 | |
| 1567 | 209 | 57 | 183 | 60 | 169 | 74 | 1628 | 468 | | 406 | 48 | 302 | |
| 1568 | 173 | 69 | 191 | 57 | 182 | 69 | 1629 | 387 | | 378 | 53 | 296 | |
| 1569 | 232 | 67 | 222 | 49 | 180 | 70 | 1630 | 339 | 76 | 429 | 48 | 320 | |
| 1570 | 351 | 44 | 268 | 41 | 187 | 67 | 1631 | 312 | 84 | 353 | 59 | 327 | |
| 1571 | 303 | 51 | 277 | 40 | 196 | 64 | 1632 | 474 | 55 | 329 | 64 | 315 | |
| 1572 | 255 | 60 | 260 | 42 | 177 | 70 | 1633 | 788 | | 334 | 64 | 304 | |
| 1573 | 272 | 57 | 220 | 50 | 203 | 62 | 1634 | 1072 | | 343 | 64 | 309 | |
| 1574 | 290 | 53 | 216 | 51 | 212 | 59 | 1635 | 830 | 32 | 368 | 60 | 306 | |
| 1575 | 197 | 79 | 221 | 52 | 210 | 60 | 1636 | 583 | 45 | 429 | 52 | 289 | |
| 1576 | 191 | 81 | 203 | 58 | 208 | 60 | 1637 | 483 | 55 | 429 | 53 | 356 | |
| 1577 | 192 | 80 | 177 | 69 | 190 | 66 | 1638 | 399 | 66 | 482 | 48 | 328 | |
| 1578 | 210 | 73 | 187 | 68 | 216 | 58 | 1639 | 354 | 74 | 441 | 53 | 286 | |
| 1579 | 235 | 66 | 182 | 71 | 211 | 65 | 1640 | 376 | 70 | 387 | 62 | 278 | |
| 1580 | 225 | 69 | 210 | 63 | 205 | 67 | 1641 | 398 | 66 | 388 | 62 | 288 | |
| 1581 | 202 | 76 | 203 | 64 | 210 | 65 | 1642 | 356 | 73 | 411 | 59 | 292 | |
| 1582 | 205 | 76 | 185 | 71 | 223 | 62 | 1643 | 327 | 80 | 424 | 56 | 308 | |
| 1583 | 187 | 82 | 200 | 65 | 240 | 57 | 1644 | 301 | 86 | 448 | 53 | 385 | |
| 1584 | 223 | 69 | 201 | 65 | 233 | 59 | 1645 | 296 | 96 | 492 | 48 | 318 | |
| 1585 | 245 | 62 | 208 | 63 | 219 | 63 | 1646 | 352 | 81 | 438 | 55 | 313 | |
| 1586 | 286 | 53 | 210 | 63 | 199 | 75 | 1647 | 355 | 80 | 454 | 53 | 351 | |
| 1587 | 265 | 58 | 207 | 64 | 217 | 69 | 1648 | 425 | 67 | 427 | 56 | 297 | |
| 1588 | 257 | 60 | 201 | 65 | 229 | 65 | 1649 | 484 | 59 | 416 | 58 | 342 | |
| 1589 | 310 | 49 | 208 | 63 | 244 | 61 | 1650 | 337 | 84 | 414 | 58 | 328 | |

| | A.1 | A.2 | W.1 | W.2 | | A.1 | A.2 | W.1 | W.2 | | A.1 | A.2 | W.1 | W.2 |
|---|---|---|---|---|---|---|---|---|---|---|---|---|---|---|
| 1651 | 285 | 100 | 392 | 61 | 1691 | 370 | 83 | 507 | 52 | 1731 | 355 | 100 | 498 | 56 |
| 1652 | 291 | 98 | 372 | 64 | 1692 | 413 | 75 | 497 | 52 | 1732 | 323 | 110 | 507 | 55 |
| 1653 | 278 | 103 | 389 | 62 | 1693 | 481 | 64 | 515 | 51 | 1733 | 314 | 114 | 490 | 56 |
| 1654 | 226 | 126 | 378 | 64 | 1694 | 397 | 78 | 574 | 45 | 1734 | 317 | 112 | 487 | 57 |
| 1655 | 225 | 127 | 382 | 63 | 1695 | 332 | 93 | 616 | 42 | 1735 | 345 | 104 | 513 | 54 |
| 1656 | 238 | 119 | 312 | 77 | 1696 | 302 | 103 | 603 | 44 | 1736 | 362 | 98 | 483 | 57 |
| 1657 | 324 | 121 | 364 | 66 | 1697 | 307 | 100 | 665 | 39 | 1737 | 375 | 95 | 544 | 51 |
| 1658 | 242 | 118 | 317 | 75 | 1698 | 372 | 83 | 656 | 40 | 1738 | 393 | 91 | 553 | 50 |
| 1659 | 248 | 115 | 292 | 82 | 1699 | 444 | 70 | 638 | 41 | 1739 | 409 | 87 | 583 | 48 |
| 1660 | 275 | 104 | 333 | 72 | 1700 | 379 | 81 | 755 | 35 | 1740 | 495 | 72 | 633 | 44 |
| 1661 | 332 | 85 | 372 | 64 | 1701 | 377 | 82 | 706 | 37 | 1741 | 473 | 75 | 624 | 44 |
| 1662 | 317 | 90 | 396 | 60 | 1702 | 346 | 90 | 636 | 41 | 1742 | 469 | 76 | 593 | 47 |
| 1663 | 315 | 91 | 468 | 52 | 1703 | 381 | 81 | 540 | 48 | 1743 | 440 | 81 | 644 | 43 |
| 1664 | 312 | 92 | 515 | 47 | 1704 | 386 | 80 | 469 | 56 | 1744 | 393 | 91 | 582 | 48 |
| 1665 | 278 | 103 | 570 | 42 | 1705 | 332 | 93 | 492 | 53 | 1745 | 422 | 84 | 593 | 47 |
| 1666 | 267 | | 432 | 56 | 1706 | 300 | 103 | 497 | 52 | 1746 | 436 | 82 | 633 | 44 |
| 1667 | 260 | | 432 | 56 | 1707 | 296 | 105 | 472 | 56 | 1747 | 393 | 91 | 582 | 48 |
| 1668 | 255 | 121 | 367 | 65 | 1708 | 321 | 96 | 493 | 53 | 1748 | 383 | 93 | 553 | 50 |
| 1669 | 249 | 124 | 316 | 76 | 1709 | 349 | 88 | 542 | 48 | 1749 | 405 | 88 | 519 | 53 |
| 1670 | 233 | 132 | 349 | 61 | 1710 | 339 | 91 | 567 | 46 | 1750 | 552 | 64 | 470 | 59 |
| 1671 | 226 | 136 | 337 | 63 | 1711 | 377 | 82 | 487 | 54 | 1751 | 552 | 64 | 456 | 61 |
| 1672 | 227 | 135 | 327 | 65 | 1712 | 433 | 71 | 560 | 48 | 1752 | 525 | 68 | 562 | 49 |
| 1673 | 237 | 130 | 328 | 65 | 1713 | 366 | 97 | 579 | 46 | 1753 | 526 | 68 | 572 | 48 |
| 1674 | 266 | 116 | 331 | 64 | 1714 | 362 | 98 | 615 | 44 | 1754 | | | 592 | 47 |
| 1675 | 285 | 108 | 352 | 60 | 1715 | 362 | 98 | 612 | 44 | 1755 | | | 567 | 49 |
| 1676 | 282 | 109 | 341 | 63 | 1716 | 387 | 92 | 603 | 44 | 1756 | | | 621 | 44 |
| 1677 | 269 | 115 | 394 | 54 | 1717 | 352 | 100 | 599 | 44 | 1757 | | | 739 | 37 |
| 1678 | 285 | 108 | 368 | 58 | 1718 | 339 | 105 | 668 | 40 | 1758 | | | 847 | 33 |
| 1679 | 302 | 103 | 428 | 50 | 1719 | 353 | 100 | 689 | 39 | 1759 | | | 787 | 35 |
| 1680 | 314 | 98 | 353 | 60 | 1720 | 354 | 100 | 621 | 43 | 1760 | | | 615 | 45 |
| 1681 | 279 | 110 | 311 | 68 | 1721 | 339 | 105 | 592 | 47 | 1761 | | | 594 | 47 |
| 1682 | 260 | 119 | 329 | 64 | 1722 | 326 | 109 | 509 | 55 | 1762 | | | 614 | 45 |
| 1683 | 266 | 116 | 369 | 60 | 1723 | 325 | 109 | 462 | 60 | 1763 | | | 597 | 47 |
| 1684 | 283 | 109 | 533 | 42 | 1724 | 344 | 104 | 437 | 64 | 1764 | | | 609 | 46 |
| 1685 | 245 | 126 | 613 | 37 | 1725 | 333 | 107 | 500 | 56 | 1765 | | | 603 | 46 |
| 1686 | 247 | 124 | 572 | 41 | 1726 | 352 | 102 | 532 | 52 | 1766 | | | 656 | 42 |
| 1687 | 255 | 121 | 587 | 41 | 1727 | 324 | 110 | 578 | 48 | 1767 | | | 673 | 41 |
| 1688 | 291 | 106 | 499 | 50 | 1728 | 335 | 106 | 534 | 52 | 1768 | | | 680 | 41 |
| 1689 | 312 | 98 | 569 | 45 | 1729 | 335 | 106 | 507 | 55 | 1769 | | | 630 | 44 |
| 1690 | 306 | 100 | 515 | 51 | 1730 | 324 | 110 | 480 | 58 | 1770 | | | 670 | 41 |

## TABLE VIII

INDEXES OF (1) PRICE OF A COMPOSITE UNIT OF FOODSTUFFS, (2) PRICE OF A SAMPLE OF INDUSTRIAL PRODUCTS, (3) QUANTITY OF FOODSTUFFS COMMANDED IN EXCHANGE BY A UNIT OF INDUSTRIAL PRODUCTS IN OUR SAMPLE, I.E. (2)÷(1), DECENNIAL AVERAGES

1521–30=100

| | MÜNSTER | | | AUGSBURG | | | VIENNA | | | VALENCIA | | |
|---|---|---|---|---|---|---|---|---|---|---|---|---|
| | (1) | (2) | (3) | (1) | (2) | (3) | (1) | (2) | (3) | (1) | (2) | (3) |
| 1411–20 .. | | | | | | | | | | 76 | 126 | 166 |
| 1421–30 .. | | | | | | | | | | 80 | 122 | 153 |
| 1431–40 .. | | | | | | | | | | 86 | 118 | 136 |
| 1441–50 .. | | | | | | | | | | 80 | 127 | 159 |
| 1451–60 .. | | | | | | | 69 | 79 | 115 | 77 | 114 | 148 |
| 1461–70 .. | | | | | | | 81 | 84 | 104 | 74 | 107 | 144 |
| 1471–80 .. | | | | | | | 79 | 88 | 111 | 83 | 108 | 130 |
| 1481–90 .. | *87 | *99 | *114 | | | | 86 | 101 | 117 | 78 | 93 | 119 |
| 1491–1500 .. | | | | | | | 89 | 98 | 110 | 83 | 89 | 108 |
| 1501–10 .. | 78 | 91 | 117 | 83 | 115 | 138 | 79 | 99 | 125 | 89 | 88 | 99 |
| 1511–20 .. | 89 | 101 | 113 | 84 | 101 | 121 | 86 | 91 | 106 | 82 | 95 | 116 |
| 1521–30 .. | 100 | 100 | 100 | 100 | 100 | 100 | 100 | 100 | 100 | 100 | 100 | 100 |
| 1531–40 .. | 114 | 106 | 93 | 134 | 130 | 97 | 128 | 108 | 84 | 107 | 102 | 96 |
| 1541–50 .. | 126 | 113 | 90 | 140 | 136 | 97 | 142 | 110 | 77 | 116 | 107 | 92 |
| 1551–60 .. | 148 | 115 | 78 | 157 | 140 | 89 | 168 | 114 | 68 | 158 | 134 | 84 |
| 1561–70 .. | | | | 208 | 165 | 79 | 202 | 131 | 65 | 177 | 154 | 87 |
| 1571–80 .. | | | | 243 | 180 | 74 | 232 | 134 | 58 | 218 | 159 | 73 |
| 1581–90 .. | * average of | | | 258 | 185 | 72 | 219 | 140 | 64 | 239 | 178 | 74 |
| 1591–1600 .. | 1467–1500 | | | 274 | 208 | 76 | 296 | 166 | 56 | 279 | 202 | 72 |
| 1601–10 .. | | | | 292 | 240 | 82 | 349 | 205 | 59 | 296 | 236 | 80 |
| 1611–20 .. | | | | 330 | 233 | 71 | 387 | 201 | 52 | 293 | 226 | 77 |
| 1621–30 .. | | | | — | — | — | — | — | — | 311 | 234 | 75 |
| 1631–40 .. | | | | 625 | 303 | 48 | 427 | 248 | 58 | 337 | 254 | 75 |
| 1641–50 .. | | | | 380 | 317 | 83 | 477 | 253 | 53 | 355 | 270 | 76 |
| 1651–60 .. | | | | 260 | 318 | 122 | 382 | 248 | 65 | | | |
| 1661–70 .. | | | | 289 | 317 | 110 | 466 | 244 | 52 | | | |
| 1671–80 .. | | | | 287 | 290 | 101 | 392 | 221 | 56 | | | |
| 1681–90 .. | | | | 289 | 311 | 108 | 549 | 294 | 54 | | | |
| 1691–1700 .. | | | | 400 | 295 | 74 | 684 | 306 | 45 | | | |
| 1701–10 .. | | | | 359 | 344 | 96 | 598 | 304 | 51 | | | |
| 1711–20 .. | | | | 394 | 305 | 77 | 675 | 309 | 46 | | | |
| 1721–30 .. | | | | 361 | 320 | 89 | 569 | 274 | 48 | | | |
| 1731–40 .. | | | | 398 | — | — | 613 | 270 | 44 | | | |
| 1741–50 .. | | | | 464 | 392 | 84 | 674 | 310 | 46 | | | |
| 1751–60 .. | | | | 587 | — | — | 753 | 300 | 40 | | | |
| 1761–70 .. | | | | | | | 755 | 329 | 44 | | | |
| 1771–80 .. | | | | | | | 730 | 342 | 47 | | | |

# 5

## Seven Centuries of Wages and Prices: Some Earlier Estimates[1]

In two earlier papers[2] we sketched an outline of the movements of builders' wage-rates, and the prices of some of the materials of consumption, in southern England since 1264. In this paper we compare our findings with those of some earlier investigators. It will be found that the most striking features of the record have long been known : what is surprising is that they have been so little discussed and assimilated.

Our own mainstay, Thorold Rogers, does not seem to have compiled any index-numbers, but in his *Six Centuries of Work and Wages* (1884) he threw into his argument an occasional reckoning of the change in the general level of prices between one era and another. Thus in Chapter XIX, after citing wages in 1449–50 and 1877, he said ," now a multiple of twelve will fairly represent, except in house-rent, the general difference in the cost of living " then and now ; our own index stands at 104 for 1449–50, and 1228 for 1875–84. In another place (Chapter XVII) he said that to meet its needs in 1770 as fully as in 1495, a family would need to spend $7\frac{1}{2}$ times as much : our index gives 101 for 1490–9, 784 for 1765–74. But when he compared that change in prices with the change in the aggregate pay of seven kinds of agricultural labour over the same span, his figures imply that the commodity equivalent of the pay had fallen to between a third and a quarter of what it had been, and here our own estimates for builders' wage-rates show a much smaller fall, to just over a half. A third incidental reckoning of the change in prices differs from ours greatly : in Chapter VI he gave another multiple of twelve, this time for the span from 1260 to 1760, but our corresponding multiple is $8 \cdot 2$ ; and as against this inference that " the labourer in the time of Henry III was paid better than he was in the first year of George III ", we should say that for the building craftsman there seems to have been little or no difference.

[1] We gratefully acknowledge the interest and help of Professors E. F. Jacob, M. G. Kendall and B. S. Yamey, and the collaboration of Mrs. Meyrick Browne in the study of Playfair.

[2] " Seven Centuries of Building Wages ", *Economica*, August 1955 ; " Seven Centuries of the Prices of Consumables, compared with Builders' Wage-rates ", *Economica*, November 1956. Supplementary materials appeared in our " Wage-rates and Prices : Evidence for Population Pressure in the Sixteenth Century ", *Economica*, November 1957, and " Builders' Wage-rates, Prices and Population : some further Evidence ", *Economica*, February 1959.

But his main findings about the course of change in the purchasing power of wages agree closely enough with ours. He said (Chapter XIX) :

> I have shown that from the earliest recorded annals, through nearly three centuries, the condition of the English labourer was that of plenty and hope, that from perfectly intelligible causes it sunk within a century to so low a level as to make the workmen practically helpless, and that the lowest point was reached just about the outbreak of the great war between King and Parliament. From this time it gradually improved, till in the first half of the eighteenth century, though still far below the level of the fifteenth, it achieved comparative plenty. Then it began to sink again, and the workmen experienced the direst misery during the great continental war. Latterly, almost within our own memory and knowledge, it has experienced a slow and partial improvement.

He went on to say that at the time of writing, say 1883, the more advanced wage-earners " have at last regained the relative rate of wages which they earned in the fifteenth century, though, perhaps, in some particulars, the recovery is not complete " ; we might compare the finding, in our own paper of November 1956, that " the level enjoyed at the accession of Henry VIII was not to be reached again until 1880 ".

In Palgrave's *Dictionary of Political Economy*, A. W. Flux used Thorold Rogers' materials to arrive at " a summary view of the results". He took from Rogers two statements of the amount of food needed to support a family of four for a year : one, the " grain diet ", contained 3 qrs. of wheat, 3 qrs. of malt, and 2 qrs. of oatmeal (*Six Centuries of Work and Wages*, Chapter XIV) ; the other, the " meat diet ", contained 4 qrs. of wheat, 2 qrs. of malt, and 800 lbs. of meat (*History of Agriculture and Prices*, Vol. I, Chapter XXIX). Reckoning the cost of these diets year by year, and comparing it with the current annual earnings (in 47 weeks) of the carpenter and the labourer, Flux obtained the number of weeks that each had to work in order to provision his household for the whole year. Table 1 compares his results for the carpenter and the two diets with ours for the building craftsman and the composite unit of consumables.

It will be seen that in our reckoning the craftsman appears to have gained more than in Flux's between the 13th and 15th centuries, and to have been set back less when things were at their worst for him, in 1583–1642. These differences do not arise from the wage-rates that Flux took out, which agree closely with ours : they must be due to differences in the contents of the basket and/or the prices taken for them. But the differences concern only the exact measure, not the direction and magnitude of the movements.

Some seventy years before Thorold Rogers, in 1811, Arthur Young entered on a study of price history, when his sight was all but gone. This study, he tells us, " occupied myself, an amanuensis, and an accountant, with other occasional assistance, much the greater part

TABLE 1

COMPARISON OF A. W. FLUX'S SUMMARY OF THOROLD ROGERS' MATERIALS WITH
FINDINGS OF PRESENT AUTHORS

|  | | (1) | (2) | (3) | (4) | (5) |
|---|---|---|---|---|---|---|
| 1261–1350 | .. | 28 | 31 | 156 | 141 | 171 |
| 1351–1400 | .. | 20 | 23 | 111 | 105 | 132 |
| 1401–1540 | .. | 18 | 22 | 100 | 100 | 100 |
| 1541–1582 | .. | 27 | 33 | 150 | 150 | 157 |
| 1583–1642 | .. | 46 | 53 | 256 | 241 | 214 |
| 1643–1702 | .. | 34 | 40 | 189 | 182 | 188 |

Col. (1) : A. W. Flux : Number of weeks a carpenter had to
work to obtain grain diet for a year.
Col. (2) : Ditto, to obtain meat diet.
Col. (3) : Col. (1) as index, 1401–1540=100.
Col. (4) : Col. (2) as index, 1401–1540=100.
Col. (5) : Present authors : Index of number of days a building
craftsman had to work to obtain composite unit of
consumables, 1401–1540=100.

of ten months ". " At my advanced age, " he added—he was seventy
—" and labouring under a great personal calamity, (I hope and trust
from the mercy of God), my voluntary pursuits should be directed to
higher purposes than worldly objects . . . But in truth, when I began
the work, I had not the least conception how far it would carry me ;
and I was gradually immersed in a great range of enquiry before I
perceived the extent of it "—how well we understand that ! He published the results in 1812 as *An Enquiry into the Progressive Value of
Money in England.* Before it appeared, he had been couched for
cataract. " A week after the operation Wilberforce came to his
darkened bedside, told him of the death of the Duke of Gratton,
and painted so vivid a picture of the loss sustained by agriculture that
Young burst into tears and destroyed the last hope of recovering
the use of his eyes."[1]

We cannot compare our prices directly with his, because he had
been at pains to reduce his " to the standard of our present money ",
that is, he expressed them in units of silver. But since his prices and
wages were both adjusted in this way, we can divide the one into the
other so as to get a commodity equivalent of the wage in a form
comparable with ours. In Table 2 we follow him in giving our findings
as index numbers based on 1804–10, or, for his building wages, 1801–11
—evidently he thought the difference inconsiderable.

The figure given for a time of extensive change like the sixteenth
century will depend much on whether the quotations used cover the
whole hundred years or give more weight to some part of them :
if our own figure were based on the second half alone it would agree
well enough with Young's. No such problem arises in so level a tract

[1] *Dictionary of National Biography*, Vol. 63, p. 361 b.

TABLE 2

INDEXES OF COMMODITY EQUIVALENT OF WAGE-RATES OF ENGLISH CARPENTERS AND MASONS : 1804–10=100.

|  | 14th century | 15th century | 16th century | 17th century | 18th century |
|---|---|---|---|---|---|
| 1. In terms of corn* .. <br> (a) Young .. .. | 80 | 190 | 90 | 80 | 110 |
| (b) Present authors .. | 139 | 211 | 122 | 85 | 124 |
| 2. In terms of foodstuffs generally† .. .. <br> (a) Young .. .. |  |  | 85 | 85–90 | 125 |
| (b) Present authors .. |  |  | 131 | 97 | 130 |

* *Young*: wheat, barley, oats; *present authors*: wheat, barley, rye through 1782, peas, some potatoes from 1785.
† *Young*: wheat with beef, mutton, pork, bacon, butter, cheese ; *present authors*: above farinaceous with pork, mutton, beef from 1584, fish, cheese except 1430–1572, butter except 1380–1560, malt, hops from 1559, sugar from 1689, tea from 1801.

as the fifteenth century, and Young agreed with us in finding this to be a plateau of exceptional elevation. But we differ widely on the extent to which the previous century lay below it.

William Playfair was a contemporary of Young's. Son of the manse, and brother of a mathematician and geologist who became a professor at Edinburgh, he began his own chequered career as a draughtsman with Boulton and Watt. He went to Paris, and is thought to have taken part in the storming of the Bastille. Returning to London, he published many pamphlets on current affairs, and applied himself especially to the display of statistics. His training as a draughtsman was allied with great natural ingenuity, and the " stained copper-plate charts " that he provided liberally are works of high technical proficiency and so of beauty. He has been called the father of the chart. In his *Lineal Arithmetic* (1798) he states the case for the graphical mode of presentation with all the force of conciseness : " In a numerical table there are as many distinct ideas given, and to be remembered, as there are sums, the order and progression, therefore, of those sums are also to be recollected by *another* effort of memory, while this mode unites *proportion, progression,* and *quantity* all under one simple impression of vision, and consequently one act of memory. " The simple impression led him to arresting insights. Looking upon the charts displaying " the physical powers of each distinct nation " in his *Statistical Breviary* (1801), he exclaimed (pp. 7–8):

> What thinking man who considers the important part that the small republic of Holland has acted, while Russia lay as if congealed in an eternal winter, but will conclude, that if ever the people in those different countries come to be in any degree similar in civilization and intelligence,

the importance of the smaller must sink into great inferiority, and in general, that if ever the different countries in the world should come to be nearly upon a par in respect of arts, civilization and knowledge, the scale of their importance must be strangely altered, and accordingly it is daily altering.

And again, in the *Lineal Arithmetic* (p. 27) :

> We may consider what *all the Russias united* would be, were they as well cultivated and civilized as England, and if Manufactures flourished there under a free government. The immense empire would in that event be able to swallow up all the other powers of Europe, in case of war ; and, in times of peace, might have every necessary of life, and almost every article of luxury, without importing a single cask of goods from any European nation.

But our concern is with wages and prices. The history of these he displayed in his *Letter on our Agricultural Distresses* (3rd edn., 1822), where he compared " the wages of good mechanics, such as smiths masons, and carpenters " with the price of wheat. He found (p. 31)

> that never at any former period was wheat so cheap, in proportion to the price of mechanical labour, as it is at this time, when a good workman may, with ten or eleven days' wages, purchase a quarter of wheat. This never was the case in England before, except perhaps at the time of the civil wars between the houses of York and Lancaster ; but between that and the present time there can be no comparison, as it is evident that, both before and after, wheat was not the material from which bread was made that was used even by the middling classes.

He noticed the great fall in the purchasing power of wages in the 16th century (p. 55):

> How then did the working man do in Queen Elizabeth's time ? That is a question not very easy to answer, but certainly he and his family could not eat wheaten bread, yet those are still termed " the happy days of good Queen Bess ! " . . . There were no potatoes in those days, and other sorts of grain probably bore nearly the same proportion to the price of wheat that they do now : so that the only answer that can be given is, that the condition of the working classes must now be far better than it was then, so far as being better consists in eating farinaceous food.

Yet though Playfair discerned the high plateau of the 15th century and the sharpness of the declivity that followed, his materials were poor. His prices for wheat he says he took from the *Wealth of Nations*, but actually they run constantly lower than the Windsor prices that Adam Smith reproduced, and coincide rather with those that Playfair himself included in his edition of the *Wealth of Nations* and ascribed to " Mr. Oddy, a gentleman who has been very largely concerned in the corn trade."[1]  Their movement agrees fairly well from 1610 onwards

---

[1] The eleventh edition of the *Wealth of Nations*, " with notes, supplementary chapters, and a life of Dr. Smith, by William Playfair ", 1805, Vol. II, pp. 356–7. J. Jepson Oddy was the author of *European Commerce : Showing New and Secure Channels of Trade with the Continent of Europe*, 1805.

with our index of grain prices, but in 1565–99 they run much higher—they lie 30 per cent. then above their level in 1610–29, whereas our index, far from dropping, more than doubles meanwhile. As for his wages, he gives no source at all : his graph simply shows a smoothly rising trend starting at 5s. a week in 1565, with phases of steeper rise in 1700–20 and since 1770 ; but from a table he gives (*Letter . . . ,* App. D, p. 53) of the number of days the mechanic had to work to obtain a quarter of wheat, we can calculate the implied daily wage. Table 3 compares his findings with ours.

TABLE 3

COMPARISON OF FINDINGS BY WILLIAM PLAYFAIR WITH THOSE OF PRESENT AUTHORS.

| | (1) d. | (2) d. | (3) | (4) | (5) |
|---|---|---|---|---|---|
| 1565–99 .. .. | 7·7 | 11·3 | 73 | 430 | 125 |
| 1600–24 .. .. | 10·3 | 12·0 | 37½ | 220 | 165 |
| 1625–49 .. .. | 11·6 | 14·3 | 43 | 253 | 165 |
| 1650–74 .. .. | 12·5 | 17·9 | 38 | 224 | 137 |
| 1675–99 .. .. | 13·2 | 18·5 | 35 | 206 | 132 |
| 1700–24 .. .. | 17·1 | 21·6 | 23½ | 138 | 112 |
| 1725–49 .. .. | 20·8 | 23·3 | 17 | 100 | 100 |
| 1750–74 .. .. | 32·3 | 24·0 | 14 | 82 | 112 |
| 1775–99 .. .. | 41·3 | 30·5 | 14½ | 85 | 114 |
| 1800–19 .. .. | 72·6 | 43·75 | 14 | 82 | 137 |

Col. (1) : Playfair's daily wage of " good mechanics ".
Col. (2) : Present authors' daily wage of building craftsman.
Col. (3) : Playfair's estimate of number of days a mechanic had to work to obtain a quarter of wheat.
Col. (4) : (3) as index number, 1725–49=100.
Col. (5) : Present authors' index of number of days a building craftsman had to work to obtain a composite unit of consumables, 1725–49=100.

If William Playfair was father of the chart, William Fleetwood was father of the index number. A Fellow of King's College in Cambridge, he had gained much acceptance as a preacher at the court of Queen Anne, then retired to a country living in Buckinghamshire in order to devote himself to study. There he was approached with a question of conscience concerning the limitation on the income of those admitted to Fellowships at All Souls College, Oxford.[1] By the founder's statute no one could be admitted who had an estate of more than five pounds a year : the question was " whether he who is actually possessed of an estate of six pounds per annum, as money and things

---

[1] Fleetwood did not name the college, but his answer takes the form of " a letter to a student in the university of Oxford ", the statutes " were made betwixt the years 1440 and 1460 " (pp. 8–9), the founder was male (p. 11), and 1439 was " very near to the time of foundation " (p. 138) : All Souls was founded in 1438 by Archbishop Chichele, and its statutes, issued in 1443, provided that an estate worth a hundred shillings a year disqualified for Fellowship. (*Statutes of the Colleges of Oxford.* All Souls, 67.)

go now, may safely take that oath, upon presumption that six pounds now is not worth what five pounds was when that statute was made ? " Fleetwood published his answer in 1707 in his *Chronicon Preciosum ; Or, an Account of English Money, the Price of Corn, and Other Commodities, for the Last Six Hundred Years.* Having decided that it was the real and not the monetary income that mattered, he had to find how the purchasing power of money had changed. He wrote (pp. 166–7) :

> To know somewhat more distinctly whereabouts an equivalent to your ancient five pounds will come, you are . . . to observe how much corn, meat, drink, or cloth, might have been purchased 250 years ago with five pounds, and to see how much of the modern money will be requisite to purchase the same quantity of corn, meat, drink, or cloth, nowadays. To this end, you must neither take a very dear year, to your prejudice, nor a very cheap one, in your own favour, nor indeed any single year, to be your rule ; but you must take the price of every particular commodity, for as many years as you can (20, if you have them) and put them all together ; and then find out the common price ; and afterwards take the same course with the price of things, for these last 20 years ; and see what proportion they will bear to one another.

So comparing the prices of 1440–60 with those of 1686–1706, Fleetwood found that wheat, oats, beans, and meat and dairy produce had all come to cost about six times what they had done, ale about five and a third times, and " good cloth, such as was to serve the best Doctor in your university for his gown ", five times. (Our own corresponding multiples are, for grain 7·2, meat and fish 6·4, drink 7·2, textiles 3·1.) Putting these things together, and evidently giving bread and meat a greater weight than ale and cloth, Fleetwood concluded (p. 169) : " I can see no causes why £28 or £30 per annum should now be accounted a greater estate than £5 was heretofore, betwixt 1440 and 1460. " That is a ratio of 5·6 or 6 to one : our own estimate, for our whole composite commodity, comes out at 6·1.— The next year, Fleetwood was made Bishop of St. Asaph's.

# 6

# The Share of Wages in National Income[1]

1. KEYNES wrote in 1939 [1] that " the stability of the proportion of the national dividend accruing to labour " was " one of the most surprising, yet best-established, facts in the whole range of economic statistics, both for Great Britain and for the United States "; he thought it " a bit of a miracle." The records which are now available for a number of countries qualify the impression of stability suggested to Keynes by such estimates as he had before him,[2] for they show the share of wages in national income as following trends of change for many years together, undergoing sharp alterations in the short run, and varying often, though not regularly, with the trade cycle. These movements call for explanation, and the short-period shifts in particular may bring to light some causes of changes in the distribution of national income. Yet it still remains true that the changes in the share of wages in national incomes are not so great as we should expect when we look at the often wide swings of the corresponding shares within particular industries, and this relative stability also calls for explanation. It is also true that when big changes occur in money wage-rates, the accompanying changes in the share of wages are relatively small, and this has evident implications for the connection between the levels of wages and other incomes, and the possibility of changing the distribution of national income by changing money wage-rates.

2. Applying economic analysis to the share of wages would be easier, if this share was the remuneration of a constant proportion of the whole working population; but in fact a main cause of the long-period changes in the share of wages has been simply the change in the relative number of wage-earners. Such changes have sometimes been considerable, and Table I gives some indications of their extent.

Two processes have been at work. As countries become

---

[1] J. M. Keynes, "Relative Movements of Real Wages and Output," in ECONOMIC JOURNAL, Vol. XLIX, 1939, pp. 48–9.

[2] These were Kalecki's figures for Great Britain in 1880, 1911 and 1924–35, and the U.S.A. in 1919–34. (M. Kalecki, " The Determinants of Distribution of the National Income," in *Econometrica*, Vol. 6, No. 2, April 1938; reprinted with revision of the statistics in *Readings in the Theory of Income Distribution*.) The estimates for the United Kingdom in the present paper agree with Kalecki's in putting 1880 very close to 1924, but make 1911 different from these, and show wide movements in the years between. Kalecki's figures are shares of gross, ours of net, home-produced income.

industrialised the number of wage-earners rises relatively to the self-employed, the family workers and the small employers, who are numerous in agriculture. But the proportion of wage-earners is lowered by the growth in the relative numbers of technicians and administrators, both within manufacturing itself

TABLE I

*The Number of Wage-earners (within given Definitions) as a Percentage of all Occupied Persons, or of all Persons of Working Age*

| Germany. | | Great Britain. | | U.S.A. | |
|---|---|---|---|---|---|
| Year. | %. | Year. | %. | Year. | %. |
| 1907 | 54 | 1881 | 81 | 1900 | 50½ |
| 1925 | 50 | 1911 | 74 | 1910 | 54 |
| 1939 | 51 | 1931 | 72 | 1930 | 47 |

*Sources :* Germany : *Statistisches Handbuch von Deutschland 1928–44 (Landerrat des Amerikanischen Besatzungsgebiets,* 1949), Table 12, p. 31. Great Britain : see Appendix to present article. U.S.A. : T. M. Sogge, " Industrial Classes in the U.S. in 1930," in *Journal of the American Statistical Association,* 1933, p. 199.

and in the whole economy, which raises the relative number of salaried posts, while the increase of educational opportunities raises the relative number of people qualified to fill them.

3. This second process has brought about so great a social change, that the old division between wage-earners and other people means much less than it used to. Perhaps there was a time when the line could be drawn with confidence, because it coincided with a social distinction marked by men's dress and speech and their esteem for one another. In some Western countries that is no longer so, but wage-earners and salary-earners are mixed together in family and district, and are not divided by social distinction. Nor are they demarcated by income : more than a quarter of the British salary-earners in 1938 are estimated to have been earning no more than £125 a year, which was about the average earning of the wage-earners then, and nearly three-fifths of them no more than £250.[1] The distinction by the term of engagement—weekly or by the month or longer period—is not of much significance. What remains is the line firms usually draw between " operatives " and " staff," and this is the line that the British White Papers on National Income

[1] Table II at p. 88 of J. G. Marley and H. Campion, *Changes in Salaries in Great Britain, 1924 to 1939*, at pp. 84–94 of A. L. Bowley, *Studies in the National Income 1924–1938*.

have been trying to follow.[1]  This grouping, though often without
a clear counterpart outside manufacturing, does mark off as wages
a block of incomes distinguished, like profits, by its comparative
variability through the trade cycle.  This block, moreover, is
constituted mainly of the incomes which, with raw material
charges, make up most of direct costs, so that changes in them are
more closely connected than changes in other incomes with the
movements of product prices.

4. The shift of the occupied population from wage-earning
jobs, so defined, to others, in itself tends to reduce the share of
wages in national income, and is connected with another process
which likewise has its distributive effects.  This is the internal
shift, within each of our two groups, " wage-earners " and " other
occupied people," between jobs at different levels of pay.  Bowley
has shown[2] that about half the rise in the earnings of the average
wage-earner in Great Britain between 1880 and 1910 was due to
people moving into the better-paid jobs.  Such shifts can come
about by changes in the relative numbers in different industries,
or in different grades within any one industry; and each of these
changes can be made both by those who move from one job to
another, and by those entering employment for the first time.
It is reasonable to expect that there is tendency for the relative
numbers of wage-earners in the higher-paid grades to rise, but we
do not know much about this distribution and its changes.[3]  We
know even less about the relative numbers in different grades of
salary.  It would be natural to expect to find here some attrac-

---

[1] " For manufacturing industries, mining and quarrying and gas, water and
electricity, the definition of wage-earners corresponds to that used for " operatives " in the Census of Production; and for other industries the division of total
numbers employed between wage-earners and salary-earners has been made, as
far as is possible with limited data, consistent with this.  The term wage-earner
thus covers factory workers, operative workers in transport such as drivers and
conductors, storemen, warehousemen, porters, messengers, postmen, waiters,
cooks and domestic servants.  Conversely, the term salary-earner covers all
those engaged in a clerical, technical, professional or managerial capacity, or
who are attached to an office, such as commercial travellers and canvassers.  All
shop-assistants are treated as salary-earners.  All policemen and all firemen are
also included among salary-earners.  Members of the Armed Forces are treated
as an entirely separate category.  It is emphasised that the distinction between
wage-earners and salary-earners is not based on the distinction between employees
paid weekly or monthly or on the amount of money earned, but upon occupation."
Note to Table 7 at pp. 59–60 of *National Income and Expenditure of the United
Kingdom, 1946 to 1950* (Cmd. 8203 of 1951).

[2] A. L. Bowley, *Wages and Income in the United Kingdom since 1860*, Appendix
C.

[3] The evidence for the United Kingdom is summarised by A. L. Bowley in
the first part of Ch. III of his *Wages and Income in the United Kingdom since
1860*.

tion of the higher rates, and an increase in the number qualified to fill the posts that carry them. But if we had the figures we still could not trace this influence, because they would also show the effect of " the shift to salaries," the " immigration " of many who, had the distribution of the occupied population remained constant, must have been wage-earners; and probably most of these have gone into the lower-paid ranks of the salaried.[1]

5. These shifts account for some otherwise perplexing changes in the relations between wages and other incomes. If, for example, we ask whether the average wage-earner in the United Kingdom has fared better or worse than the community as a whole, we find that on the eve of the Second World War the average wage-rate bore very much the same ratio to national income per head of the whole occupied population, as it had done in the 1880s; but at the same time the average income of occupied people other than wage-earners, reckoned on certain assumptions,[2] had fallen from about $7\frac{1}{2}$ times to no more than $4\frac{1}{2}$ times the wage-earner's income.[3] At first sight it looks as though this were

[1] A rough check may be made as follows. From the *Occupation Tables of the Census of England and Wales, 1931*, we take out the numbers in 1921 and 1931 in all those employing, salaried and professional occupations, which can be regarded with confidence as predominantly (a) relatively high-paid and (b) relatively low-paid. We omit doubtful classes, so our enumeration is not exhaustive. The higher paid are chiefly employers, managers, professional and those above the clerical grades in public administration. The lower paid are mainly subordinate staff in mining, shop assistants, insurance agents, draughtsmen, typists and clerks. We find :

|  | 1921. | 1931. | Increase, |
|---|---|---|---|
|  | (in thousands) |  | %. |
| Higher paid . . . . | 532 | 608 | 14 |
| Lower paid . . . | 1,717 | 2,129 | 24 |

We can follow smaller selections in a consistent form through earlier years (*Census 1911, England and Wales*, Vol. X, p. 540, Table 26). Here the higher paid are : merchants; brokers, agents and factors; accountants; auctioneers; barristers and solicitors; physicians and surgeons; vets. The lower paid are : commercial clerks; insurance officials, clerks and agents; railway officials and clerks. Such small selections are liable to be affected by changes in the size of particular industries and callings, but the outcome is at least not in conflict with our presumption :

|  | 1891. | 1901. | 1911. |
|---|---|---|---|
| Higher paid (000s) . . . | 107 | 117 | 124 |
| *Increase on 1891* (%) . . | | *8* | *16* |
| Lower paid (000s) . . . | 322 | 489 | 663 |
| *Increase on 1891* (%) . . | | *52* | *106* |

[2] It is assumed that all national income other than wages accrues to " other occupied people." In fact, some of this income accrues to wage-earners, and some to institutions, foreigners and unoccupied persons, not included in " other occupied people."

[3] Phelps Brown and Hopkins, "The Course of Wage-Rates in Five Countries, 1860–1939 " (*Oxford Economic Papers*, II, 2, June 1950).

arithmetically impossible, as though the relation between wages and other income could not change while that between wages and the sum of the two remained the same; but an example will show how this can come about.  Suppose that, while other things remain the same, the number of wage-earners is reduced and that of salary-earners is raised by the same amount, through an addition to the number of clerks; and suppose, as is quite possible, that this occurs in such a way as to leave the average earnings of wage-earners unchanged, while the new clerks receive salaries equal to these average wage-earnings.  Then national income per head of the whole occupied population will be the same, and the average wage, being itself unchanged, will bear the same relation to it as before.  But among occupied people other than wage-earners, there has been an increase in numbers, and it has gone into the bottom of the salary scale, so the average income of these other people will be reduced, and it will bear a lower ratio than before to the average wage.

The apparent paradoxes which arise when we compare the incomes of groups of changing composition also appear when the average incomes of wage-earners and of other people *both* fall relatively to that of the whole occupied population.  A shift of population from wage-earning to other occupations will generally (apart from the case last supposed) tend to raise the average income of the whole occupied population, by shifting its centre of gravity higher up the scale of pay, and so it will tend to lower the ratio of the average wage-earner's income to this average of the whole.  But at the same time, within the ranks of the other people themselves, the centre of gravity will very probably shift downwards, because the new-comers mostly go into the lower-paid posts; and profits and income from property will be spread, arithmetically, over more heads.  So the average income of other people will tend to fall, and like that of the wage-earners it will bear a lower ratio to the average income of the whole occupied population.

6. The ideas just introduced can be given more precision by a numerical illustration.  The proportions (not the absolute figures) are those of the United Kingdom in the 1880s.  Suppose that a country has an occupied population of 20 millions, of whom 16 millions are wage-earners; and let the national income be £10,000 millions, of which £4,000 millions goes to wages.  Then the average earnings of a wage-earner are $\dfrac{£4,000 \text{ million}}{16 \text{ millions}}$, or £250 a year.  Let us assume that the whole national income accrues to occupied persons (whereas in the actual world some part accrues

to unoccupied persons, corporations and foreigners); then national income per head of the occupied population is $\dfrac{\text{£10,000 million}}{\text{20 millions}}$, or £500 a year. The average earnings of a wage-earner, at £250 a year, are one-half this average income per head of the whole occupied population. Let us now further assume that the whole return to property accrues to occupied persons other than wage-earners (whereas actually some does accrue to wage-earners); then the average income of the occupied person who is not a wage-earner is $\dfrac{\text{£6,000 million}}{\text{4 millions}}$, or £1,500 a year. This is six times the £250 of the average wage-earner.

It is convenient to have symbols for the expressions here. Let us call $r$ the ratio of the average earnings of wage-earners to national income per head of the whole occupied population;[1] and $s$ the ratio of the average income of occupied people other than wage-earners (on the above assumptions) to the average earnings of the wage-earners. In the present example we have $r = \dfrac{\text{£250}}{\text{£500}} = 0.5$, and $s = \dfrac{\text{£1,500}}{\text{£250}} = 6.0$. There is also the share of wages as a whole in the national income; let this be $p$: here $p = \dfrac{\text{£4,000 million}}{\text{£10,000 million}} = 0.4$. Let the proportion of wage-earners in the whole occupied population be $t$: here $t = \dfrac{\text{16 millions}}{\text{20 millions}} = 0.8$.

We can use our example to show how $s$ can fall without necessarily raising $r$.[2] Suppose that the number of wage-earners falls by a million, from 16 millions to 15 millions, and that this is accompanied by an equal proportionate fall in total wages, so that the average income of the wage-earners remains unchanged. Suppose also that these million are transferred to clerical jobs which yield them the same average income as that of the wage-earners; then one-sixteenth of the former total of wages, or £250

---

[1] This is akin to the wage-income ratio calculated in Phelps Brown and Hopkins, " The Course of Wage-Rates in Five Countries, 1860–1939 " (*Oxford Economic Papers*, II, 2, June 1950); but not the same, because the wage-income ratio used indexes of wage-*rates*, and $r$ uses wage-*earnings*.

[2] Formally, the relations are these. Let there be $N$ occupied people, of whom a proportion $t$ are wage-earners. Let the average income of wage-earners be $w$, and of others $v$. Then: $s = \dfrac{v}{w}$. National income per head of the occupied population is:

$$\frac{1}{N}(Ntw + N(1 - t)v) = tw + (1 - t)v$$

and

$$r = \frac{w}{tw + (1 - t)v} = \frac{1}{t + s(1 - t)}$$

A fall in $s$ can be offset by a fall in $t$ so as to prevent a rise in $r$.

million, will have been shifted to other incomes, which become £6,250 million, while the number of " other people " rises from 4 millions to 5 millions. National income remains the same, and so does *r*, but the average income of " other people " falls from £1,500 to £1,250, and *s* falls from 6·0 to 5·0.

It will be seen that *r* and *s* can be reckoned directly from the internal proportions of the economy, without using absolute figures.[1] Thus, if, as in our first example, the wage-earners being 0·8 of all occupied people receive 0·4 of all income, we can see that *r*, the ratio of the average earnings of wage-earners to national

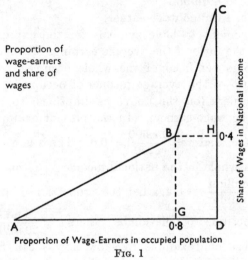

Proportion of wage-earners and share of wages

Share of Wages in National Income

Proportion of Wage-Earners in occupied population

Fɪɢ. 1

income a head of the whole occupied population, will be $\dfrac{0\cdot4}{0\cdot8} = 0\cdot5$.

Similarly, the ratio of the average income of " other people " to national income a head of the whole occupied population will be $\dfrac{(1-0\cdot4)}{(1-0\cdot8)}$, or $\dfrac{0\cdot6}{0\cdot2}$. If we divide this by *r*, the common denominators (national income a head) will cancel out, and we are left with the ratio of the average income of " other people " to the average earnings of wage-earners, that is, with *s* : $\dfrac{0\cdot6}{0\cdot2} \div \dfrac{0\cdot4}{0\cdot8} = 6\cdot0$.

7. This can be used to show the course of change in a diagram. In Fig. 1 the proportion of all occupied people who are wage-earners is measured along *AD*, and the share *p* of wages in national

[1] If the national income is *Y*,

$$r = \frac{pY}{tN} \div \frac{Y}{N} = \frac{p}{t}$$

$$s = \frac{(1-p)Y}{(1-t)N} \div \frac{pY}{tN} = \frac{(1-p)t}{(1-t)p}$$

income is measured up $DC$. In our example, the wage-earners made up 0·8 of all occupied people, and received 0·4 of the national income. These figures are represented by the point $B$ (0·8, 0·4). We join $AB$, $BC$, and drop perpendiculars from $B$ to $AD$ at $G$ and to $DC$ at H. We now have a representation of each of $p$, $t$, $r$, and $s$.

$p$ is represented by the vertical distance $BG$.

$t$ is represented by the horizontal distance $AG$.

$r$ is represented by the slope of the radian $AB$, here $\dfrac{0·4}{0·8} = 0·5$.

$s$ is represented by the ratio of the slope of $BC$ to that of $AB$,

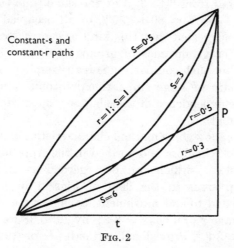

Constant-$s$ and constant-$r$ paths

Fig. 2

here $\dfrac{0·6}{0·2} \div \dfrac{0·4}{0·8} = 6·0$. This is not directly presented to the eye, but through any position of $B$ we can draw a curve [1] showing how $B$ will move if $s$ is to remain constant while other proportions change. A number of such constant-$s$ curves are shown with some constant-$r$ lines in Fig. 2.

If in the course of time $B$ moves, its path shows the changes in $p$, $t$, $r$ and $s$, and this brings to the eye the necessity of some at first sight unexpected changes in the pattern of distribution when $t$, the proportion of wage-earners in the whole occupied population, is changing. If the share of wages in national income remains constant, the $B$-path will be a horizontal straight line, and evidently this will mean changes in both $r$ and $s$ : constancy in

[1] If $s = \dfrac{(1 - p)t}{(1 - t)p} = $ a constant, say $k$, we have

$$p = \frac{t}{t + k(1 - t)}$$

the share of wages, that is, is generally possible only if average wage-earnings are rising or falling relatively to other incomes. If, on the other hand, the share of wages changes, there are two criteria of an unchanged relation between wages and other incomes. If average wage-earnings bear a steady ratio to the average income of the whole occupied population, the $B$-path moves along a constant-$r$ line, that is, along a radian through $A$ to the momentary position of $B$. If they bear a steady ratio to the incomes of " other people," the $B$-path moves along a constant-$s$ curve. In some parts of the field constancy in one respect implies big changes in others : while $r$ remains unchanged, for instance, at 0·5, $s$ will fall from 6 to 3, if at the same time the number of wage-earners falls from 80 to 50% of all occupied people. We have already suggested that this kind of contrast comes of comparing the average incomes of groups of diverse and changing composition, but such comparison is really implicit in any reckoning of the share of wages in national income, and the $B$-path brings out the dependence of this share on the composition of the occupied population.

8. $B$-paths show some marked characteristics in practice. One for the United Kingdom is described in the Appendix and shown in Figs. 3 and 4, which can be regarded as enlargements of postage-stamp areas in the field of Figs. 1 or 2. A striking feature is the end-to-end movement, to higher $r$ and lower $s$ : in 1870–71 we have $r = 0·46$, $s = 8·2$; by 1937–38 we have reached $r = 0·55$, $s = 3·8$. Provisional estimates [1] for 1948–50 suggest a further transit, to around $r = 0·63$, $s = 2·7$. This remarkable change is not the outcome of a year-by-year progression, but is the net result of certain sharp shifts; these we must try to explain. Yet such shifts are exceptional : for the most part there is relatively little to-and-fro movement, and for a number of years together the path follows a linear trend which lies not far from a constant-$r$ line. Other paths estimated for Germany, Sweden and the United States are similar in this respect. There are some substantial exceptions, and we can trace some cyclical movement, especially in 1929–38, yet it remains remarkable that the $B$-paths should contain so many linear stretches, and that these should often approximate to a constant-$r$ line.

Is this what we should expect ? The $B$-path shows the joint effect of " inter-grade migration," *i.e.*, changes in the distribution

---

[1] We must emphasise their provisional nature. They are believed to be internally consistent, but the absolute figures are probably not continuous with those of 1938.

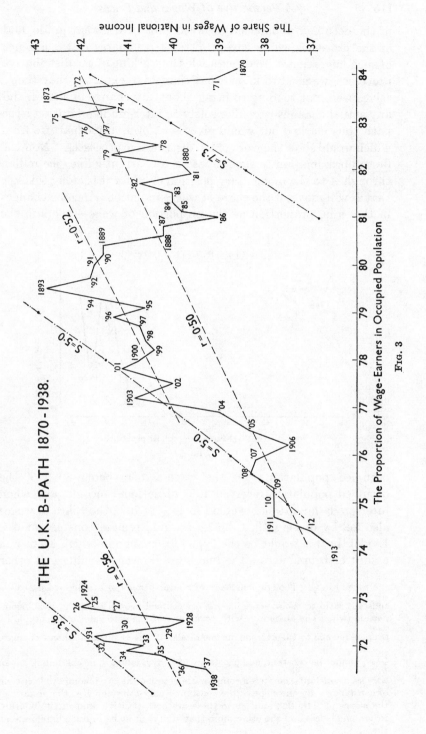

THE U.K. B-PATH 1870-1938.

FIG. 3

of the occupied population between jobs of different grade, and of the processes which govern distributive shares in the absence of such migration. To disentangle the working of the distributive processes, we need to know what changes to expect if they themselves were not tending to bring about any change of shares, and any actual changes were due solely to inter-grade migration : the path thus marked out would give us a norm, any departure from which would show the work of the distributive processes. Now the first approximation to such a path is a constant-$r$ line, the radian through $A$ to the momentary position of $B$, for it is along this line that $B$ will move, if the share of wages in national income changes in the same proportion as the proportion of wage-earners in the

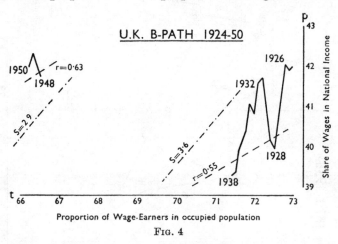

Proportion of Wage-Earners in occupied population

Fig. 4

occupied population : [1] if the wage-earners being 80% of the occupied population received 40% of national income, and when inter-grade migration lowered the 80% to 70% the share of wages also fell by one-eighth, to 35%, $r$ would remain constant at 0·5. Evidently this would be the type of a change in which there was a shift of people across the line between wage-earning and other

---

[1] Since $r = \dfrac{p}{t}$. Though constancy of $r$ means that the average wage bears a constant ratio to the average income of occupied people generally, it is incompatible (when $t$ is changing) with constancy of the ratio of " other people's " average income to the average income of all; if $\dfrac{p}{t}$ is a constant when $t$ changes, $\dfrac{1-p}{1-t}$ cannot be constant, and constancy of $r$, with falling $t$, means falling $s$. In a sense, a constant-$s$ curve is a compromise between the two incompatible criteria of constancy : for the slope of the constant-$s$ curve through $B$ is the product of the slopes of $AB$, $BC$, and (since these are both positive, and in the relevant region one is less and the other more than unity) must be intermediate between them.

jobs, but no one's personal income was altered, and the change in the share of wages was only the arithmetic counterpart of the change in the relative number of wage-earners. This can be only a first approximation : our initial distinction between migration and distributive processes is not absolute, and in practice the migration will affect relative rates of pay. Yet these attendant changes are likely to offset one another. Let us take, as the most likely case, a fall in the relative number of wage-earners through a growth of " white-collar " jobs. The migration will tend to raise the relative pay of wage-earners and lower that of the salaried. The additional salary-earners will mostly receive somewhat more than the wage-earners whom statistically they replace. The first of these changes tends to raise $r$, the second to lower it. Perhaps in the short run the second will be the stronger, and then our $B$-path will fall rather more steeply than a constant-$r$ line. But it will hardly fall so steeply as to cross a constant-$s$ curve, for the migration will tend to lower the average income of other people, probably by increasing the relative numbers in the lower-salary grades, and certainly by raising the number of heads over which property income and profits are (arithmetically) spread. We may conclude that our hypothetical $B$-path, to show the consequences of inter-grade migration in the absence of changes in distributive processes, is likely to follow a constant-$r$ line, or a course intermediate between that and a constant-$s$ curve.

This is a fair account of what the linear segments of the $B$-path in the United Kingdom and the United States actually do. We can therefore treat these segments as periods in which, save for migration effects, the share of wages was fairly steady. How can we account for this ? Does it arise out of the working of the distributive processes, or does it only show the inertia of statistical aggregates ?

9. We shall try to throw some light on this by a study of changes in the internal structure of British national income since 1870. Sources, methods and tables are set out in the Appendix. We have estimated wages, profits, salaries and rents annually as making up the home-produced national income between them. Wages and profits both vary considerably with the trade cycle, and together make up what we may call the fluctuating sector of national income. Salaries and rents are relatively unaffected by the cycle, and make up what we may call the stable sector of national income. In Fig. 5 we show the course of wages as a share of the fluctuating sector, and the fluctuating sector itself as a share of the whole national income. We see here how the comparative steadiness

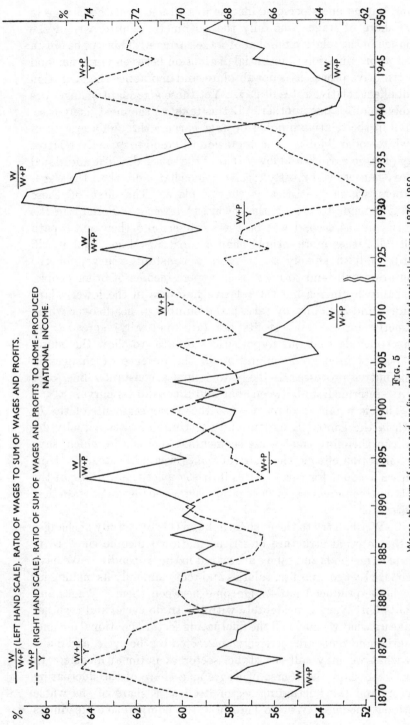

Fig. 5

Wages, the sum of wages and profits, and home-produced national income, 1870-1950.

of the share of wages arises out of a compensation between shares which themselves are not at all steady. The share of wages in the fluctuating sector itself varies; but at the same time the share of this sector in the whole national income varies in the opposite direction, so as to compensate roughly the changes in the relations between wages and profits and leave wages a fairly steady share of the whole. Generally, in a recession wages fell less than profits, but wages and profits together fell more than the stable sector; in a recovery the opposite usually happened; and in each case the effect was to leave wages much the same share of the whole.

10. But this compensation was in a sense accidental, depending as it did upon a particular combination of relative sizes of different components in national income with the extent of cyclical fluctuation in two of them. We do not expect to find it everywhere. In the United States, for example, the share of wages in national income usually declined in the recession, and rose in the recovery : a rise of 5 points in the unemployment index [1] usually went with a fall of about 1 point in the percentage share of wages, and vice versa.

Nor was the compensation complete in the United Kingdom, where there was a residual cyclical motion. It is interesting that this was different in different periods. From 1870 to the mid-1890s the share of wages usually went down in a recession and rose in a recovery, but from the mid-1890s to 1914 it did the opposite. In both periods the ratio of (home-produced) profits to wages went down in a recession and rose in recovery, but in the later period its movement per unit change in the unemployment rate was much bigger than before. Other evidence suggests that we have come on a difference here between two types of market environment. From 1873–1894 the trends of prices, the long-term rate of interest and the ratio of profits to wages were all downwards; from 1894 to 1914 they all rose. In para. 15 we we shall return to the distributive consequences of these differences between types of market environment.

11. The compensation we have traced has been between aggregates, and Dunlop [2] has shown how within these there may be further compensations between the various fluctuations of different industries and the attendant changes in their relative

---

[1] P. H. Douglas's " Combined Index," *Real Wages in the United States, 1890–1926*, Table 172, p. 460.

[2] J. T. Dunlop, *Wage Determination under Trade Unions* (British edition, Blackwell, 1950), Ch. VIII.

contributions to national income. So we have no reason to infer from such stability as we find in the aggregate share of wages any similar stability within the industry, and still less within the firm.

12. The division of British national income illustrated by Fig. 5 brings to light not only the compensation between cyclical movements, but also a main source of redistribution in the longer run. In the 1880s rent was over 14% of national income; to-day it is less than 5%. Down to 1913, the fall in its share was presumably due to the agricultural depression after 1873 and then to the effects of rising prices and money incomes on the share of contractual payments; since then this last effect has been enhanced by greater rises in prices and incomes and by rent control. As a matter of arithmetic, the withdrawal from landlords of over 9% of national income would make possible a rise of nearly a quarter in the income of the wage-earners, without reducing any other incomes. Similar influences will have affected the share of profits, so far as these contain fixed-interest payments, and of salaries, so far as these are slow to be adjusted, though here the predominant influence in depressing relative incomes has been the great increase in the supply of educated people. All these influences have borne upon the years since the Second World War, when the share of wages in national income has been higher than before, not because wages have borne a higher ratio to profits, but because the shares of rent and salaries have contracted. These considerations prevent us from treating the difference between wages and total national income as determined simply by the gross margins realised by firms between direct costs and selling prices.

13. Yet it does seem that we must invoke some stability of policy in the firm to explain the facts. When we abstract from the factors just dealt with, we are left with the relation of wages to profits, and though this is far from constant, it does show a fairly stable pattern of cyclical variation. We have also to explain why short-run changes in distributive shares are usually quite small, even when wage-rates and prices have changed sharply.[1] We can account for these things by assuming that

---

[1] Evidence for several countries in the recent years of big changes in the price and cost structure is cited at pp. 63–7 of *Wages* (a) *General Report* (I.L.O., 1948). New Zealand after the return of a Labour government in 1936, and France in and after " l'expérience Blum," are instructive cases, because here the nitiative clearly came on the side of wages. See A. E. C. Hare, *Report on Industrial Relations in New Zealand;* M. Kalecki, " The Lesson of the Blum Experiment," ECONOMIC JOURNAL, March 1938 and R. Marjolin, " Reflections on the Blum Experiment," *Economica,* May 1938.

firms—using that term to cover income-producing units of many kinds—make or accept adjustments between costs, output and selling price, and that the pattern on which these adjustments are made does not change rapidly, so that at any time we can expect a given stage of the trade cycle to be associated with a determinate margin of profit or loss, and a change made sharply on the side either of costs or of price to be followed by adjustments which prevent it from taking a marked and sustained effect on that margin. The pattern of adjustment cannot be reduced to any simple form, such as that $MR = MC$, or that price is set at a certain gross margin over direct cost, for actual situations and policy are too various for this : we have to cover all sorts of firm, from the strong monopolist to the seller who has to take whatever price the market gives him, and all sorts of phase, from the peak of the cycle to the trough. Generally, a firm's pattern of adjustment will depend on its internal cost structure, the extent of competition or monopoly power in the markets for its factors and products, and the temperament and strategy of its management. The practical outcome will vary with cyclical changes in orders and prospects. But we may reasonably suppose that the pattern itself does not change rapidly, and if that is so, then we can account for the stability in the course of distribution by stability in the propensities of management.

14. But we also have evidence that the pattern of adjustment does undergo changes : in particular, we noticed that the linear segments of the $B$-path were sometimes ended by sharp shifts—in the United Kingdom there were such shifts in 1870–72, 1888–89, 1903–5, 1926–28, and bigger ones within the gaps 1913–24, and (probably) 1938–48. These shifts move the $B$-path to a new value of $r$ or $s$, and differ from cyclical changes through having no rebound : once displaced, the $B$-path accepts the new situation, so to speak, and generally proceeds on something like a constant-$r$ course with the new value of $r$. It is probable that these shifts mark a change in the economy, and not merely a jump in the estimates of wages and national income, for their size, though it may lie within the margin of error of these estimates in any one year, seems greater than could arise from discontinuities in them between one year and another.

We shall try first to explain the four shifts in years of peace. The first two, those of 1870–72 and 1888–89, were both towards a higher value of $r$ and a higher share of wages in national income; the later two, 1903–5 and 1926–28, were the other way. Then is not trade-union activity the explanation ? Both the first two shifts occurred in periods of exceptional trade-union growth and initiative.[1]  The shift of 1903–5, on the other hand, falls in the shadow of the Taff Vale decision, when the unions were virtually unable to strike; and that of 1926–28 falls after the collapse of the General Strike.  It is tempting to conclude that the causes of these shifts lie in the strength of trade-union pressure.  But if this is so, we should expect to find shifts at other times of special trade-union activity or weakness, notably the collapse of 1879 and the belligerence of 1909–13 [2]; yet through 1879 the $B$-path followed the same linear trend as from 1872 to 1888; and though from 1910 there came a sharp rise in money wage-rates after a decade of little change, the $B$-path follows very nearly a constant-$r$ line throughout 1905–13.  We may add that in 1946–50, in which trade-union bargaining power has generally been reckoned exceptionally high, though exercised with restraint, and in which the money earnings of industrial workers have risen by about a third,[3] the ratio of wages to profits has not been higher than in the inter-war years.  So if trade-union strength does have something to do with the shifts, it cannot be the whole story.  If union strength tends to raise the share of wages in national income, we have to explain why it did this in 1870–72 and 1888–89, but not in 1909–13 and 1946–50.  If union weakness tends to lower the share, we have to explain why it did so in 1903–5 and 1926–28, but not in 1879–81.

15.  We could do this if we supposed that at different times the generality of firms have a different ability to maintain or raise profit margins.  When trade-union strength raises wages, at one

---

[1] " There were, during the nineteenth century, three high tides in the Trade Union history of our country, 1833–34, 1872–74, and 1889–90 " (S. and B. Webb, *The History of Trade Unionism*, 1920 edn., p. 328).  Of twenty-eight unions listed by the Webbs, the membership nearly doubled between 1870 and 1875 (*ibid.*, Appendix VI).  Of 1889 they write, " already in 1888 the revival of trade had led to a marked increase in Trade Union membership.  This normal growth now received a great impulse from the sensational events of the Dock strike.  Even the oldest and most aristocratic unions were affected by the revivalistic fervour of the new leaders " (*ibid.*, p. 406).

[2] " The year 1879 was as distinctly a low-water mark of the Trade Union Movement as 1873–74 registered a full tide of prosperity. . . . In some districts, such as South Wales, Trade Unionism practically ceased to exist.  The total membership of the Trade Union Movement returned, it is probable, to the level of 1871 " (S. and B. Webb, *op. cit.*, pp. 349–50).  In 1909 began the period of direct action, syndicalism and rank-and-file movements.  Between 1909 and 1913 the total membership of British trade unions rose from under 2½ millions to nearly 4 millions (*ibid.*, Appendix VI).  " The number of disputes reported to the Labour Dept., which had sunk in 1908 to only 399, rose in 1911 to 903, and culminated in the latter half of 1913 and the first half of 1914 in the outbreak of something like a hundred and fifty strikes per month " (*ibid.*, p. 690).

[3] *Ministry of Labour Gazette*, September 1951, p. 345.

time firms may be unable to raise prices proportionally; but at another they can ride the punch, and raise their prices so as to maintain their profit margins.   Similarly, when unions are weak, at one time firms may have to accept prices so low as to give no wider margin than before, but at another they may be able to raise prices without wages following after, or lower prices less than in proportion to costs.   In the first kind of period union strength will raise the share of wages, and union weakness will not lower it; in the second, the opposite holds.[1]   Outcomes of the first kind appear in 1870–72, 1879–80, 1888–89; of the second, in 1903–05, 1909–13, 1926–28, 1946–50.

Now there is a marked contrast between the conditions of the market prevailing in these two groups of cases.   In the first the market environment was that of " the Great Depression."   The shift of 1870–72, it is true, seems to be an exception, for " the Great Depression " is usually dated only from 1873.   It may be that this apparent shift lies within the margin of error of estimates which we are warned are none too firm at that time.[2]   Yet there is no reason why the onset of the non-cyclical conditions of twenty years should have coincided with a particular turning point of the cycle : [3]   The *Economist*, in its review of 1872,[4] remarked that " the increased cost of production has been so great that profits have been materially diminished," and this in the midst of the boom—evidently there was some resistance to the raising of prices.   If this is so, we can put all three cases of our first group in a setting of rapidly rising productivity, improved communications, improving terms of trade, falling prices and a falling long-term rate of interest.   Those of the second group come from more varied settings, but 1903–5 and 1909–13 are from the period whose contrast with " the Great Depression " was marked by the

---

[1] If we apply this distinction to movements of the wages/profit ratio we must formulate it as a tendency to modulate the cyclical movement of that ratio, noticed in para. 10, and say, for instance, that in the first kind of period union strength will cause the wages/profit ratio to rise more than it usually does in a recession, and fall less than it usually does in a recovery; and so on.

[2] P. 52 of A. R. Prest, " National Income of the United Kingdom, 1870–1946," in ECONOMIC JOURNAL, March 1948.

[3] " It is our main impression that as early as in the 'sixties there is a beginning tendency to a fall in prices. . . . Reviewing the individual commodity prices, we find, it is true, in most cases rising prices prior to 1870. . . . Nevertheless, we venture to think that these underlying forces during these years have been preparing the way for a fall, and that the apparent rise is an optical illusion, due to the extraordinary cyclical rise in 1872–73." J. Pedersen and O. S. Petersen, *An Analysis of Price Behaviour during the Period 1855–1913*, pp. 135–6.

[4] *Economist*, March 15, 1873, " Commercial History and Review of 1872," p. 114.

changed trend of productivity, prices and the rate of interest. This was a period in which firms found it much easier to obtain advances in product prices : " in general, the severity of competition probably increased between 1873 and 1900, and probably decreased between 1900 and 1914." [1] The " cost plus world " of inflationary pressure since 1945 is evidently a much stronger case of the same sort of thing. The years 1926–28 are very different, for prices if anything were falling then, but the post-mortem on the depression of 1929 has made us aware how misleading that course of prices was. A rapid rise in productivity, especially through the realisation of the economies of scale in new industries, reduced unit costs, and so raised profits despite constant or falling prices.[2] So though 1926–28 were not years of rising prices as were the other years of their group, they were years of a widening profit margin : the conditions of the market allowed firms, in effect, to raise prices relatively to costs.

The contrast between the two groups, then, is that between a market environment which resists firms' maintaining or raising prices so as to widen or maintain profit margins, and one which allows this. In the first sort of environment, if the unions are strong they can squeeze profits between rising wages and market-controlled prices; if they are weak, the market will keep prices down to the resultant level of costs so that profits do not rise. In the second sort, if the trade unions are strong they can only push the whole cost and price structure up with them, and profits keep pace with wages; if they are weak, profits may draw ahead of wages.

16. This hypothesis agrees with the difference we noted in para. 10 between the variation of the share of wages during the trade cycle, in the years 1870–93, and 1929–38 on the one hand, and 1894–1914 on the other. We should now say that one and the same phase of the trade cycle will have a different influence on the distribution of income according as it falls in one or another sort of market environment. The rising phase of the cycle will usually bring a tendency towards higher money wage-rates, and strengthen the unions; but whether or not this raises wages relatively to profits, depends on whether the market environment is " hard " or " soft." But we should note that no such difference

---

[1] W. W. Rostow, *British Economy of the Nineteenth Century*, Appendix, p. 235.

[2] For the sources of the rise in productivity, see R. S. Sayers, " The Springs of Technical Progress in Britain, 1919–39," in Economic Journal, June 1950. For the rise in profits 1925–28, see Table I of R. S. Hope, " Profits in British Industry from 1924 to 1935," in *Oxford Economic Papers*, June 1949.

in the cyclical behaviour of the share of wages appears in the United States : perhaps because it was a protected market.

17. We have spoken of " the market environment " [1] to indicate that in different periods firms have been under different degrees of constraint by their markets, without suggesting that these conditions could be characterised by the movements of one variable, such as a price index, or necessarily showed the regularity of long waves. The determinants of the market environment are complex, and revealed only to a study of each period, but they are likely to comprise such factors as : the rate of massive application of new techniques; alternations between development of sources and " reaping the harvest " of primary products; the supply of money; the extent of combination; and " the policy of Europe." [2] It lies beyond our scope to pursue these things here. But the reality of a market environment persisting through several cycles in succession is supported by the associated movements of the price-level and the rate of interest in Great Britain since the end of the eighteenth century.[3]

18. We may now apply these ideas to the explanation of the shifts in the British *B*-path through the periods of the two World Wars. From Fig. 5 we see that shifts in the same direction have come about in different ways. In 1924 the combined share of wages and profits in national income was a little lower than in 1913; what had shifted the *B*-path was the big rise in the ratio of wages to profits. In 1948, on the contrary, the ratio of wages to profits was about the same as before the war, and what had shifted the *B*-path was the rise in the combined share of wages and profits, relatively to salaries and rent. The contrast is what we might expect on our present hypotheses. We do not know at what point between 1913 and 1924 the effective change was made, but it seems probable that profits rose relatively to wages during

---

[1] " I believe that changes in the methods of business and the amounts of the commodities, or, as we may say, changes in the commercial environment, have much greater effects in disturbing prices than changes in these supplies of the precious metals "; Marshall, Q. 9696 of evidence before the Gold and Silver Commission, 1887.

[2] Cf., for example, Marshall's application to the 1880s of Tooke's reasons for the fall in prices 1814–37, in his answers to questions put by the Royal Commission on the Depression of Trade, 1886 (*Official Papers*, by Alfred Marshall, pp. 4–5); the study of " the Great Depression " in Chs. III, IV, VII and IX of W. W. Rostow, *British Economy in the Nineteenth Century*; G. C. Allen, " Economic Progress, Retrospect and Prospect," in ECONOMIC JOURNAL, September 1950; J. Pedersen and O. S. Petersen, *An Analysis of Price Behaviour during the Period 1855–1913*, pp. 131, 135–46.

[3] See J. M. Keynes, *A Treatise on Money*, Vol. II, Ch. 30, (viii), " The ' Gibson Paradox '."

the First World War, as we know they did during the Second, and that in the inflation the combined share of profits and wages rose relatively to the fixed or more slowly adjusted rents and salaries. But the First World War was followed by a sharp deflation, and it seems probable that this both restored the share of rents and salaries, and squeezed profit margins so as to bring about the big rise we find in the ratio of wages to profits—the effect we expect from the conjunction of a "hard" market environment with trade-union strength, albeit this was shown only in defence. The Second World War, however, was not soon followed by a deflation : so the squeezing of the shares of rents and salaries was not reversed, but, on the other hand, in the "soft" market environment, the rises in money wages did not raise the ratio of wages to profits.

19. We have seen how particular conjunctions of the trade cycle, union activity and the market environment brought about short-period changes in the relation between profits and wages, marked by shifts in the $B$-path. But these shifts were not soon reversed like cyclical changes, and we have also to consider the implications of that. For some time after the shift, firms generally must have gone on working with the range of margins which the shift had left them, and which changed only through such gradual processes as had been operative before the shift. The implication must be that firms' "patterns of adjustment" generally were malleable, in the sense that a level of margins once imposed by force of circumstances came to be accepted as normal. But this malleability, within the range of our observations, does not imply that changes in the return to risk-capital and enterprise set up no reactions on the side of supply. Such reactions must take time to make themselves felt, and so cannot be traced by the methods of this study, which itself gives no reason to affirm or doubt their importance to the course of distribution and economic progress.

20. The present evidence has led us towards hypotheses containing some elements of a theory of distribution applicable to the United Kingdom within the period studied, which we may summarise as follows :

(a) When we allow for the effects of the changing proportion of wage-earners in the occupied population we find more steadiness than at first appears in the share of wages in national income.

(b) But this steadiness of lengths of the $B$-path was due in the first place to internal compensation between distributive shares, which themselves were far from steady through the trade cycle.

(*c*) Over the longer period there has been a reduction in the shares of rent and (latterly) of salaries.

(*d*) When we take away this "stable sector" of rent and salaries, we are left with wages and profits, which carried most of the fluctuation of national income between them, and showed a cyclical variation relatively to one another. The comparative regularity of this variation, and also the narrowness of its movements in comparison with those in prices and money incomes, we attribute to the stability of *the pattern of adjustment* by which firms regulate the relations between costs, output and prices. This pattern depends on such factors as the internal cost structure of the firm, the extent of competition or monopoly power in its markets, and the temperament of its management.

(*e*) In a given firm or industry the prevailing pattern of adjustment yielded certain profit margins through the course of a cycle. But the extent of such margins depended on *the market environment* in which the cycle was set : that is, on whether the combined effect of such non-cyclical conditions as productivity, monetary supply and public policy was repressive or conducive to the maintenance or raising of prices.

(*f*) The course of the trade cycle brought changes in the demand for labour, and corresponding changes in the effective strength of trade unions. From time to time there were some greater and in part exogenous changes in union strength. Whether these changes affected the relative size of wages and profits depended on the market environment. When that was repressive to price rises, union strength raised the share of wages and union weakness did not lower it; but when the market environment was conducive to price rises, wage rises did not increase the share of wages, and with union weakness the share of profit rose.

(*g*) At certain times the conjunctions described in (*f*) brought shifts in the share of wages, whose persistence implied a change imposed on the patterns of adjustment generally, so that larger or smaller profit margins came to be accepted as normal.

APPENDIX : STATISTICAL SOURCES AND METHODS

A. NET HOME-PRODUCED NATIONAL INCOME. *1870–1913* : Estimates of the net national income are given by A. R. Prest, " National Income of the U.K. 1870–1946," ECONOMIC JOURNAL, March 1948. We deducted the estimates of gross income from overseas investments given in C. K. Hobson, *Export of Capital*, p. 204; and those for 1912 and 1913 given in J. H. Lenfant, *British Capital Export 1900–1914* (Table III, p. 521), a London Ph.D. thesis. We have made no attempt to add back any income generated at home but excluded in these years because paid out to persons abroad; this amount was put by Stamp at £6·5 million in 1913 (*British Incomes and Property*, p. 424). *1924–38* : J. R. N. Stone gives an index of national income in *Analysis of Market Demand*, J.R.S.S., 1945 p. 335, item V. We used this to carry back the estimate of net national income for 1938 given in the White Paper on National Income of 1951, Cmd. 8203, p. 17, items 14 − (3 + 4). A series of net income from overseas investment is given by the *Board of Trade Journal*. A summary of these figures 1929–38 is given in the League of Nations *Balance of Payments*, 1938, p. 125. We took estimates for earlier years from earlier issues of the same report. We lowered this series by the ratio 163 : 200, the ratio of the Cmd. 8203 (p. 17, item 13) 1938 figure to the B.O.T. 1938 figure, and subtracted the resulting series from our estimates of net national income, to get net home-produced national income 1924–38. *1939–45* : We made estimates by adding the series in B, C, D, E below. *1946–50* : Cmd. 8203, p. 17, items 12 − (3 + 4).

B. WAGES. *1870–1913* : Estimates of the annual wages bill 1880–1914, excluding shop assistants, are given in A. L. Bowley, *Wages and Income in the U.K. since 1860*, Table XII, p. 76. We assumed that the earnings of shop assistants 1870–80 varied in proportion to estimates of the total wages bill (including shop assistants) given by Bowley in ECONOMIC JOURNAL, 1904, p. 459, col. 4, and we subtracted them from these estimates to get annual wage earnings, excluding shop assistants, 1870–80. *1924–38* : We raised the estimates of annual wage earnings given in A. L. Bowley, *Studies in the National Income*, Table III, p. 58, by the ratio of the Cmd. 8203 figure for 1938 (p. 17, item 1) to Bowley's 1938 figure. *1939–45* : The National Income White Paper of 1947, Cmd. 7099, gives estimates of wages for the war years. We raised the first differences of this series by the ratio of the difference between the 1938 and 1946 figures of Cmd. 8203 to the corresponding difference in Cmd. 7099, and used these raised first differences to interpolate between the 1938 and 1946 figures in Cmd. 8203. *1946–50* : Cmd. 8203, p. 17, item 1.

C. SALARIES. *1870–1913* : Figures of intermediate incomes 1870–1914 are given in Prest (*op. cit.*, p. 57). We added the earnings of shop assistants to these to get estimates of salaries 1870–1913. We obtained estimates of the earnings of shop assistants, for 1870–79 as in para. B above, and for 1880–1913 from the difference between the two wages-bill series in Bowley's *Wages and Income in U.K.*, Table XII, p. 76. *1924–38* : (i) Estimates of the earnings of shop assistants and of non-wage-earners below the taxation limit are given in Bowley's *Studies in the National Income*, Table IX, p. 81, rows 4 and 6. (ii) The annual Reports of the Commissioners of His Majesty's Inland Revenue give values of the actual income assessed under Schedule E for each financial year, and distinguish " manual wage earners " from " others." We took the assessments of " others " in each financial year to state salaries earned in the preceding calendar year, as during this period Schedule E assessments were made one year in arrears. (iii) We added the series in (i) to that in (ii) to get a series of salaries 1924–38. Our resultant total for 1938 was £1,130 million, which compared with the estimate of salaries for 1938 in Cmd. 8203 (p. 17, item 2) of £1,110 million. We reduced our series throughout in the proportion of 111 to 113. *1939–45* : We made estimates by the same method as in B. *1946–50* : Cmd. 8203, p. 17, item 2.

D. RENT. *1870–1913* : Gross income assessed under Schedule A for Houses, Land and Other Property is given by Stamp, *British Incomes and Property*,

Table A.4, pp. 49–51. We corrected the three series for re-assessment by averaging the incomes over each period between re-assessments, and we took these averages to refer to the middle year in each period. We converted each series into net income by subtracting $\frac{1}{8}$ from "lands," $\frac{1}{6}$ from "houses" and $\frac{1}{7}$ from "other property." These fractions represent estimates for repairs allowances (Stamp, *op. cit.*, p. 61), the major difference between gross and net rent. Thus we got a series of net rent for the mid-re-assessment years. The values for other years we obtained by freehand interpolation. *1924–38*: The Annual

TABLE 2

*Factor Distribution of the Home Produced National Income in the United Kingdom,*
1870–1950. £ million.

|  | 1 | 2 | 3 | 4 | 5 | 6 | 7 |
|---|---|---|---|---|---|---|---|
|  | Rent. | Salaries. | Wages. | Home profits. | Home national income. | Wage-earners as % occupied population. | Wages as % national income. |
| 1870 | 126 | 143 | 342 | 274 | 885 | 84·1 | 38·6 |
| 1871 | 128 | 142 | 368 | 303 | 941 | 83·9 | 39·1 |
| 1872 | 130 | 143 | 417 | 303 | 993 | 83·7 | 42·0 |
| 1873 | 133 | 144 | 461 | 345 | 1,083 | 83·5 | 42·6 |
| 1874 | 136 | 145 | 445 | 355 | 1,081 | 83·3 | 41·2 |
| 1875 | 139 | 146 | 439 | 311 | 1,035 | 83·1 | 42·4 |
| 1876 | 142 | 145 | 435 | 319 | 1,041 | 82·9 | 41·8 |
| 1877 | 146 | 146 | 434 | 319 | 1,045 | 82·7 | 41·5 |
| 1878 | 150 | 147 | 413 | 314 | 1,024 | 82·5 | 40·3 |
| 1879 | 154 | 148 | 402 | 269 | 973 | 82·3 | 41·3 |
| 1880 | 157 | 152 | 407 | 307 | 1,023 | 82·1 | 39·8 |
| 1881 | 159 | 158 | 421 | 324 | 1,062 | 81·9 | 39·6 |
| 1882 | 162 | 168 | 449 | 324 | 1,103 | 81·7 | 40·7 |
| 1883 | 163 | 174 | 451 | 340 | 1,128 | 81·5 | 40·0 |
| 1884 | 164 | 179 | 432 | 304 | 1,079 | 81·3 | 40·0 |
| 1885 | 165 | 184 | 419 | 286 | 1,054 | 81·1 | 39·8 |
| 1886 | 165 | 190 | 414 | 293 | 1,062 | 81·0 | 39·0 |
| 1887 | 166 | 198 | 437 | 285 | 1,086 | 80·8 | 40·2 |
| 1888 | 166 | 207 | 467 | 323 | 1,163 | 80·6 | 40·2 |
| 1889 | 167 | 216 | 518 | 346 | 1,247 | 80·4 | 41·5 |
| 1890 | 168 | 226 | 543 | 370 | 1,307 | 80·2 | 41·5 |
| 1891 | 169 | 231 | 541 | 355 | 1,296 | 80·0 | 41·7 |
| 1892 | 170 | 237 | 531 | 332 | 1,270 | 79·7 | 41·8 |
| 1893 | 172 | 243 | 529 | 295 | 1,239 | 79·5 | 42·7 |
| 1894 | 174 | 250 | 537 | 328 | 1,289 | 79·3 | 41·7 |
| 1895 | 176 | 257 | 549 | 369 | 1,351 | 79·1 | 40·6 |
| 1896 | 179 | 265 | 569 | 364 | 1,377 | 78·9 | 41·3 |
| 1897 | 181 | 271 | 581 | 393 | 1,426 | 78·7 | 40·7 |
| 1898 | 185 | 281 | 610 | 426 | 1,502 | 78·4 | 40·6 |
| 1899 | 188 | 289 | 635 | 461 | 1,573 | 78·2 | 40·4 |
| 1900 | 192 | 297 | 674 | 494 | 1,657 | 78·0 | 40·7 |
| 1901 | 196 | 303 | 667 | 455 | 1,621 | 77·8 | 41·1 |
| 1902 | 201 | 309 | 654 | 469 | 1,633 | 77·5 | 40·0 |
| 1903 | 206 | 315 | 655 | 430 | 1,606 | 77·2 | 40·8 |
| 1904 | 209 | 319 | 637 | 468 | 1,633 | 76·9 | 39·0 |
| 1905 | 213 | 327 | 649 | 507 | 1,696 | 76·5 | 38·3 |
| 1906 | 217 | 336 | 679 | 577 | 1,809 | 76·2 | 37·5 |
| 1907 | 220 | 345 | 723 | 607 | 1,895 | 75·9 | 38·2 |
| 1908 | 224 | 349 | 682 | 525 | 1,780 | 75·6 | 38·3 |
| 1909 | 226 | 355 | 688 | 550 | 1,819 | 75·3 | 37·8 |
| 1910 | 228 | 365 | 717 | 587 | 1,897 | 75·0 | 37·8 |
| 1911 | 231 | 372 | 744 | 622 | 1,969 | 74·7 | 37·8 |
| 1912 | 233 | 390 | 772 | 692 | 2,087 | 74·4 | 37·0 |
| 1913 | 235 | 402 | 795 | 742 | 2,174 | 74·1 | 36·6 |

| | 1 | 2 | 3 | 4 | 5 | 6 | 7 |
|---|---|---|---|---|---|---|---|
| | Rent. | Salaries. | Wages. | Home profits. | Home national income. | Wage-earners as % occupied population. | Wages as % national income. |
| 1924 | 274 | 905 | 1,535 | 948 | 3,662 | 73·0 | 41·9 |
| 1925 | 281 | 907 | 1,560 | 983 | 3,731 | 72·9 | 41·8 |
| 1926 | 297 | 933 | 1,525 | 876 | 3,631 | 72·8 | 42·0 |
| 1927 | 311 | 944 | 1,596 | 1,016 | 3,867 | 72·7 | 41·3 |
| 1928 | 321 | 957 | 1,560 | 1,078 | 3,916 | 72·5 | 39·8 |
| 1929 | 331 | 979 | 1,566 | 1,028 | 3,904 | 72·4 | 40·1 |
| 1930 | 337 | 931 | 1,489 | 876 | 3,633 | 72·3 | 41·0 |
| 1931 | 342 | 902 | 1,376 | 679 | 3,299 | 72·2 | 41·7 |
| 1932 | 347 | 885 | 1,350 | 672 | 3,254 | 72·1 | 41·5 |
| 1933 | 349 | 906 | 1,376 | 747 | 3,378 | 72·0 | 40·7 |
| 1934 | 355 | 942 | 1,458 | 799 | 3,554 | 71·9 | 41·0 |
| 1935 | 365 | 995 | 1,535 | 910 | 3,805 | 71·8 | 40·3 |
| 1936 | 375 | 1,046 | 1,627 | 1,044 | 4,092 | 71·6 | 39·8 |
| 1937 | 407 | 1,087 | 1,720 | 1,166 | 4,380 | 71·5 | 39·3 |
| 1938 | 416 | 1,110 | 1,735 | 1,160 | 4,421 | 71·4 | 39·2 |
| 1939 | 445 | 1,158 | 1,844 | 1,369 | 4,816 | — | 38·3 |
| 1940 | 438 | 1,236 | 2,142 | 1,788 | 5,604 | — | 38·2 |
| 1941 | 434 | 1,386 | 2,466 | 2,159 | 6,445 | — | 38·3 |
| 1942 | 430 | 1,422 | 2,746 | 2,426 | 7,024 | — | 39·1 |
| 1943 | 430 | 1,482 | 2,905 | 2,566 | 7,383 | — | 39·3 |
| 1944 | 430 | 1,536 | 2,943 | 2,499 | 7,408 | — | 39·7 |
| 1945 | 434 | 1,614 | 2,877 | 2,402 | 7,327 | — | 39·3 |
| 1946 | 438 | 1,790 | 3,140 | 2,378 | 7,746 | — | 40·5 |
| 1947 | 456 | 1,960 | 3,580 | 2,772 | 8,768 | — | 40·8 |
| 1948 | 470 | 2,200 | 4,025 | 2,960 | 9,655 | 66·5 * | 41·7 |
| 1949 | 483 | 2,350 | 4,230 | 2,935 | 9,998 | 66·3 * | 42·3 |
| 1950 | 496 | 2,500 | 4,470 | 3,208 | 10,674 | 66·2 * | 41·9 |

* Provisional.

Reports of the Commissioners of Inland Revenue give figures of gross income assessed under Schedule A. From these we subtracted all items under the heading of " reductions." We took fiscal years to represent the calendar years in which the fiscal years began, *e.g.*, 1938–39 = 1938. Rent calculated in this way for 1938 (83rd Report, for the year ended March 31, 1940, Cmd. 6769, Table 14, p. 24) came to £382 million. We compared this with the estimate of rent for 1938 given in Cmd. 8203 (p. 17, item 11) of £416 million, and raised our series throughout in the ratio of 416 to 382. *1939–45* : We made estimates by the same method as in B. *1946–50* : Cmd. 8203, p. 17, item 11.

E. HOME PROFITS. *1870–1913* : Prest (*op. cit.*, p. 57) gives estimates of profits, to which we added his estimates of income evading taxation. From this series we subtracted estimates of income from abroad (as in A) and of rent (as in D). *1924–38* : Profits are a residual, the result of substracting the sum of the series in B, C, D, from A. For 1938 this is equal to the sum of items 5, 6, 7, 8, 9 and 10 of Table 6 in Cmd. 8203, p. 17. *1939–45* : We made estimates by the same method as in B. *1946–50* : Cmd. 8203, Table 6, p. 17, items 5–10.

F. NUMBERS OF WAGE-EARNERS AND OCCUPIED POPULATION. *1881–1911* : Bowley, *Wages and Income in the U.K.*, p. 91, gives estimates for the census years; we made estimates for intercensal years by linear interpolation. We made estimates of the percentage of wage-earners in occupied population 1870–88 by linear extrapolation of the movement of this percentage 1881–91. *1924–38* : Bowley, *Studies in National Income*, Table II, p. 56. *1948–51* : Provisional estimates, which are believed to be consistent with the figures for national income and wages used for the same years, but the coverage of which may not be continuous with that of 1938.

# 7

# The Climacteric of the 1890's: A Study in the Expanding Economy[1]

## I

**1.** It has been known for some time that a check to the rise of real wages, or of productivity, occurred in a number of countries about the end of the nineteenth century.

In his *Wealth and Income of the People of the United States*, in 1915, Dr. Willford I. King found that the real earnings of the American wage-earner, though not real income per head of the whole population, failed to rise between 1900 and 1912, and he attributed this to the closing of the internal frontier while the immigration of unskilled labour continued.

In 1920 A. L. Bowley, in his lecture on *The Change in the Distribution of the National Income 1880–1913*, stated that 'average real wages were very nearly stationary from the late '90's to 1913. . . . It was not uncommonly alleged immediately before the war that real wages had fallen. Though I do not accept the truth of this statement as being demonstrable on the evidence if the average of all wages is in question, yet it is undoubtedly true if we ignore the part of the progress due to the numerical increase of the better-paid occupations' (p. 19). For the population as a whole, 'average incomes were quite one-third greater in 1913 than in 1880' (since it happened that prices were much the same in those two years, Bowley could speak indifferently of money and real income here); 'but the increase was gained principally before 1900, since when it [*sc.* money income] barely kept pace with the diminishing value of money' (p. 26). 'I think . . . that the increase of luxury and the abundance of wealth which many people believe they observed before the war were illusions, fostered by the newspapers. I can find no statistical evidence that the rich as a class were getting rapidly richer in real income. . . . A considerable part of the impression of wealth was, I think, caused by the diversion of expenditure from other objects to motor-cars' (p. 20).

In 1933 G. T. Jones's *Increasing Return* found[2] that 'the 19th century was characterised by a progressive diminution in the quantity of resources consumed per unit of product in British manufacturing industries. By the close of the century, however, this movement had spent its force, so that real costs remained almost constant during the first decade

---

[1] The statistical studies, of which the ground was largely covered by S. J. Handfield-Jones before he went abroad, were completed by Bernard Weber, who in particular revised and extended the calculations of national capital reported in Appendix C. Sheila V. Hopkins carried out the work reported in Appendix A.       [2] pp. 247–8.

of the 20th century in at least three of the basic industries of Great Britain'—namely building, cotton, and pig-iron.[1] Jones attributed this partly to the balance of diseconomies consequent upon a growth of scale,[2] but more especially to easier working conditions for labour.[3] He further found that the efficiency of the Massachusetts cotton industry resembled that of Lancashire in reaching a maximum in 1900 and falling slightly in the next decade;[4] but real costs in the American pig-iron industry fell throughout 1900–12.[5]

In his *National Income and Outlay*, in 1937, Colin Clark noted a fall in the rate of growth of British real income a head in 1900–13: 'the curve was approaching a very definite ceiling.'[6]

In his *Conditions of Economic Progress*, in 1940, Colin Clark gave estimates of real income per head of the working population (after correction for changes in the length of the working week) which showed a check to the rate of rise appearing about 1900 or later in U.S.A., Canada, Great Britain, Australia, and France, but an unchecked rise in Germany, Switzerland, Sweden, Norway, Russia, and Italy.[7] Of Great Britain he said, 'productivity per worker-hour only increased slowly during the first fourteen years of this century';[8] of the U.S.A., 'productivity per worker per hour, which was rising sharply up to 1900, showed very little increase between 1900 and 1914';[9] of Australia, 'we have the remarkable feature of a very rapid growth of real income between 1886 and 1898 followed by a definite recession. Not until 1920 was the 1898 level of real income per head recovered.'[10]

In 1950 Phelps Brown and Hopkins[11] published estimates of real income per head of the occupied population in five countries. These showed that in Germany and the United Kingdom a rapid rise in real income per head was broken off between 1895 and 1900, after which there was little advance in the United Kingdom, and in Germany even some decline; but no such check was evident in the U.S.A. or in the fragmentary observations for France, and in Sweden a rapid rise was sustained. The same authors gave estimates of product wage-rates (i.e. money wage-rates divided by product prices), which are reproduced in Fig. 1, together with a similar series calculated subsequently for Belgium.[12] This figure gives a stronger impression of a check than do the income series, for in France, the United Kingdom, and the United States the ratio of wage-rates to the average income of the whole occupied population was probably lower in 1913 than in the

[1] pp. 93, 118, 143.    [2] pp. 255–6.
[3] See p. 248 for a general statement. There are particular observations at pp. 94, 96, 97, 118–19, 144.    [4] pp. 212, 214.
[5] pp. 238, 240.    [6] p. 271.    [7] Graph opposite p. 147, table opposite p. 148.
[8] p. 147.    [9] p. 158.    [10] p. 162.
[11] 'The Course of Wage Rates in Five Countries, 1860–1939', *Oxford Economic Papers*, June 1950.    [12] See Appendix A of the present article.

1890's. But such distributive shifts were of minor effect: even had product wage-rates fared no worse than other incomes, they would still have been checked.

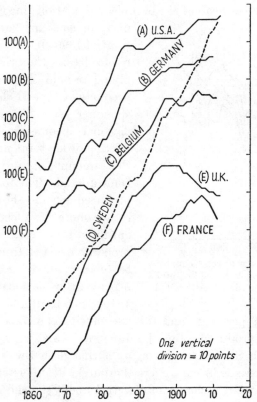

Fig. 1. Product Wage-rates. 5-yr. moving averages (1890–9=100).

## II

**2.** The object of the present paper is to examine the climacteric in the United Kingdom more closely. From the evidence so far cited it appears that the check to the rise in British real wage-rates was due in part to a distributive change,[1] but that even had wage-rates kept pace with average income they would have made little if any net gain between the late 1890's and 1913. This is in marked contrast with the sustained advance of earlier years. Does it arise only from some bias, perhaps, in the index numbers, or does it mark a real check to the economic progress of the country?

**3.** There are three factors on which the real income of the people of the United Kingdom depends: their efficiency in production; their net receipts of property income from overseas; and the terms on which they exchange

[1] The reasons for this are discussed in Phelps Brown and Hart, 'The Share of Wages in National Income', *Economic Journal*, June 1952.

their produce for that of the outside world. We have taken out estimates of the contributions of the last two factors, to see whether they played any part in the climacteric. The results are shown in Fig. 2.[1] Curve *A* shows total national income per head of the occupied population; income is expressed

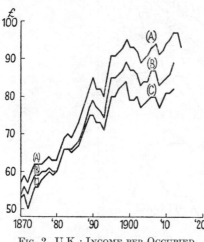

FIG. 2. U.K.: INCOME PER OCCUPIED PERSON, IN 1890–9 £s. (A) Total. (B) Home-produced. (C) (B) at 1881 terms of trade throughout.

in £s of constant purchasing power (that of 1890–9), to which it has been reduced from the original £s by applying an index of the prices of final products. Curve *B* shows the corresponding series for home-produced national income, reckoned by deducting from total national income the amount of property incomes from abroad. This curve of home-produced income shows if anything rather more of a check from 1899 onwards than total income does: property incomes from abroad seem to have made up rather less than 5 per cent. of national income in the 1870's, but from 1908 onwards they made up over 8 per cent., and this rise gave total income a better showing than home-produced. But the difference is not very great.

Then was the check brought on by a change in the terms of trade? Statistically, these lie in controversial ground,[2] but there can be no doubt that they underwent a change of direction about the end of the century. We have used Schlote's[3] indexes of the prices of imports and exports, and the result is shown in Fig. 3. From 1882 to 1900 there was a big fall of import prices relatively to export prices; after 1900 the movement though smaller was on balance the other way. So from 1882 to 1900 the rise in real income was being boosted by a change in the terms of trade, but after 1900 this factor operated in the opposite direction. How much did this contribute to the difference between the earlier rise and the later stagnation of real income a head? We can make a rough estimate by reckoning the value of the goods which would have had to be withdrawn from use at home in order to complete payment for the actual imports of each year, had these been bought at the terms of trade of 1882. The estimate is only rough, because if the terms of trade had been different, no doubt many

[1] Data, sources, and methods in Appendix B.

[2] The controversy is surveyed in W. W. Rostow, 'The Terms of Trade in Theory and Practice', *Economic History Review*, iii. 1, 1950. See also his 'The Historical Analysis of the Terms of Trade', ibid. iv. 1, 1951.

[3] *Entwicklung des Englischen Außenhandels*, Table 26.

other things would have been different too; but it gives us at least the
order of magnitude of the effects on real income which changes in the terms
of trade had from time to time. Deducting this from the figures of home-
produced national income gives us the series which, after reduction to £s of
constant purchasing power, appears as curve *C* of Fig. 2. This shows, as
we might expect, that the changes in the terms of trade made the rise of
real income more rapid than it would probably have been otherwise from

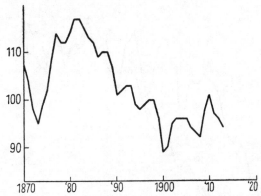

FIG. 3. U.K.: TERMS OF TRADE. Exports per unit of imports (Index, 1890–9=100).

1882 to 1900, whereas from 1900 to 1912 their effect was small: so the part
of the rise in real income which depended solely on the efficiency of British
production at home shows less check than real income as a whole, which
felt the impact of things beyond our control in the world market. Yet
when we have allowed for this, by far the greater part of the check remains.
Its causes must still be sought in productivity within the United Kingdom
itself.

4. Here our widest measure of output, short of the whole national
income, is Hoffmann's index,[1] which brings together many records of
physical output, some of them running back into the eighteenth century.
In 1861–1913 it has forty-three or more series, from a wide range of
industries.[2] The weights are proportional to the estimated total 'value
added' of each industry,[3] and if on the whole, at constant factor prices,
this varies from year to year in rough proportion to the physical output
of the industry, the index traces the growth in real terms of aggregate

---

[1] Walther Hoffmann, *Wachstum und Wachstumformen der englischen Industriewirtschaft
von 1700 bis zur Gegenwart* (Fischer, Jena, 1940). The index is also given in W. Hoffmann,
'Ein Index der industriellen Produktion für Großbritannien seit dem 18. Jahrhundert',
*Weltwirtschaftliches Archiv*, xl, 1934.

[2] The groups, with the number of series comprised in each in 1861–90, are: mining (7);
iron, steel, and machines (2); metal (non-ferrous) and metal wares (5); ships and vehicles (3);
wood (2); textiles (8); food, alcohol, and tobacco (9); paper (1); leather (2); rubber products
(1); chemicals (3). Three more series are used in 1891–1913.

[3] For 1861–90, estimated as at 1881; for 1891–1913, according to the Census of 1907.

'value added'. Hoffmann reckons that his series during these years represent around 70 per cent. of the value added by all industry, and according
to our estimate they cover more than 20 per cent. of the contemporary
occupied population of Great Britain.

To arrive at the changes in productivity in this field we took the number
of operatives within it from the occupational tables of the Census, and
divided the index of this number into Hoffmann's index of output.[1] The

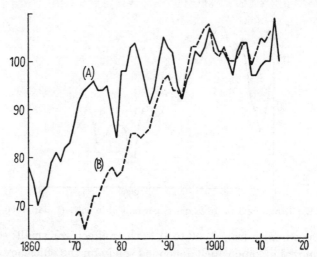

Fig. 4. (A) Output per Operative in Mining and Manufacturing
         (B) Home-produced Real Income per Occupied Person, at 1881 Terms of
             Trade
                    (A) G.B. (B) U.K. (1890–9=100).

upshot is shown in curve *A* of Fig. 4. The *fluctuations* here are those of the
trade cycle, for our numbers occupied year by year are obtained simply by
linear interpolation between one census and the next, and are not adjusted
for unemployment. But what concerns us here is the *trend*, and this shows
a marked slowing down after 1880 in the rate of rise, and an asymptotic
approach to a level no more than 5 per cent. above the average of the
nineties. So marked is the change, indeed, that the trend can be closely
approximated by a linear rise from 1860 to 1885, in which output a head
rose by nearly a third, and after that a barely rising course down to
1914.

Can this be due solely to bias in our materials? Our numbers are of
operatives only, not of all occupied: but the ratio of staff to operatives
will have risen rather than fallen in this period. In working on the censuses
we have encountered the difficulties of uncertain and changing classifica-

[1] Hoffmann's index, and the corresponding index of output a head, are at Table II, and
the estimated numbers occupied at Table III, in Appendix B.

tion with which all who use these tables are familiar: the treatment of dealers, and of labourers, is specially liable to mislead, and there are many other points at which a hazardous decision had to be made on what to take in and leave out. But our guiding principle was to take only those series which were continuously comparable, rather than to achieve the fullest count possible at any one time; so though our coverage is sometimes incomplete, the movements of our total between one census year and another should be reasonably representative, save for one source of error. This lies in the attribution to particular industries in later censuses of many who had appeared before only as general labourers. In 1891 there were some 879,000 general labourers recorded in Great Britain, but in 1911, despite the growth of population meanwhile, only 481,000. Let us suppose that the whole of the difference of almost 400,000 was due to labourers getting classified by industry, and that all those so classified appeared as additions to the labour force of Hoffmann's industries: if we corrected for this, we should raise output a head in 1911 from 100 to nearly 110 per cent. of the average of the 1890's. Even on this extreme assumption, the contrast between the earlier and later rates of growth would remain: in the 20 years from 1861 to 1881, a rise of about a third; in the 30 years from 1881 to 1911, a rise of about a tenth.

Alternatively, does the behaviour of our index of productivity arise out of changes in the distribution of the working population between industries, rather than from changes in the productivities of those industries themselves? Since 'value added' per operative differs in different industries, a redistribution of the working force towards industries in which 'value added' per operative was low could lower productivity in the aggregate, even though in each separate industry it had been rising. We have checked this possibility by estimating the effect of the actual redistribution of the working force on average 'value added' per operative, on the assumption that in each industry 'value added' was at its 1907 level throughout, and we find a sustained rise, amounting to about 8 per cent. in all between 1861 and 1911. The check, then, cannot be ascribed to the redistribution of the working force, which worked rather the other way.

There may, however, be a downward bias in our index, because Hoffmann's series make no allowance for the product becoming more highly fabricated as time goes on. Some allowance is due for this; we cannot tell how much.

With some reservations, then, we can accept our index as a check on the evidence of national income; indeed, in one respect it may be more reliable, for it does not depend, as the series for national income must do, upon appropriate representation of the general level of prices. Fig. 4

enables us to compare the movements of our two indexes, that is, real income per occupied person (at constant terms of trade), and output a head in the Hoffmann industries. There is one divergence—between 1885 and 1900 real income a head rose by more than a fifth, whereas in 1885 the rapid rise of productivity in the Hoffmann industries had already come to an end. After 1900, the two series follow remarkably similar courses;

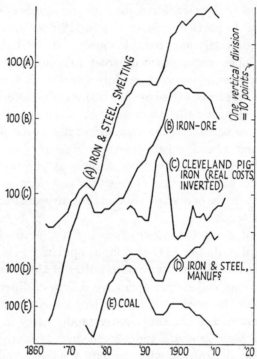

FIG. 5. U.K.: INDEXES OF OUTPUT PER OPERATIVE OR PER UNIT REAL COST.
5- or 7-yr. moving averages (1890–9 = 100).

and if we represented them with 1870 as base, we should see that the same holds for the years on the other side of the divergence, those, namely, from 1870 to 1885. For the most part, then, the two series bear each other out. What of the divergence? In part it was due to the influence on the Hoffmann index of coal-mining, in which output a head began to fall off before 1890; but even when allowance is made for this,[1] much of the divergence remains. It may well be due partly to a fall in our price index which, at a time of sharp movement in commodity prices, was excessive relatively to the less flexible money flows. The main impression remains one of agreement. There is no doubt about the check.

[1] The index of productivity in the Hoffmann coverage less coal is at col. 8 of Table II in Appendix B.

**5.** This change in general productivity can be explored by calculating indexes of output a head in those industries where we have records of output, and also can trace the number of operatives in a sufficiently comparable and consistent form. The results[1] appear in smoothed form in Figs. 5 and 6, together with two of G. T. Jones's estimates[2] of real cost per

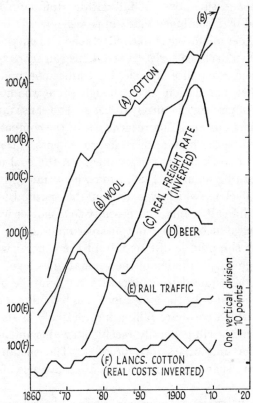

FIG. 6. U.K.: INDEXES OF OUTPUT PER OPERATIVE OR PER UNIT REAL COST.
5-, 7-, or 10-yr. moving averages (1890–9 = 100).

unit of output, which are inverted here so as to appear as indexes of output per unit of real cost. The estimates of the numbers occupied in particular industries are more liable to error than those for industry as a whole, and

---

[1] Data, sources, and methods are in Appendix B. These include estimates for shipbuilding, which are not illustrated in the Figures, because of the unsatisfactory nature of the only unit of output available—the unit of tonnage. Taking these estimates for what they are worth, we find a declining trend of tonnage per man between the 1880's and 1914.

[2] G. T. Jones, *Increasing Return* (1933). Jones's estimates of real cost were made by deflating the product price by an index of factor prices. When inverted, as here, they provide indexes of output per composite unit input of resources of all kinds, whereas our indexes are of output per operative only. Thus where equipment per head is increasing our index will rise more than the inverted G. T. Jones index, and this may account for some of the difference between the two types of index for cotton down to 1899 (Fig. 6). The G. T. Jones type is disturbed when the product price departs from the normal supply price, and this accounts for the peak in the 1890's in the Cleveland pig-iron series in Fig. 5.

the allocation of more labourers to particular industries in 1911 may distort the results for one industry. But the possibilities of error are not so great as to bring marked movements under suspicion.

Two industries stand out as reaching their highest output per operative early on, and considerably declining thereafter. The first of these is transport by rail, though this does not fall within Hoffmann's coverage. The traffic, measured by a combined index of passengers and freight, which the railways carried per operative employed, reached its maximum in the early seventies and then declined for 20 years. This can scarcely have been due to any lack of the economies of scale, for traffics continued to rise faster than the occupied population, even though there was an abrupt stop in 1901 to the rise of passenger journeys a head. The cause must be sought on the opposite side, in diminishing returns; or in the competitive increase of amenities offered to the public; or in improvements in the working hours and conditions of work of the railwaymen. In the coal-mines also there was an early turning-point, in 1886, from which time till 1914 there was a fairly steady decline, which was attributable certainly to the resort to deeper or more difficult seams, and possibly to a shorter working week per man not compensated by higher outputs per man-hour.

The index for shipping is different from the others: we have deflated an index of freights by an index of the general price level, so as to get the quantity of goods required to compensate the ton-mile of sea transport, and then inverted this. In the long run, though by no means in the short, an industry in which costs are falling more rapidly than they are in the aggregate elsewhere, will generally receive a smaller quantity of goods in exchange for the unit of its own product. The sustained fall of 'real freights' therefore suggests a sustained *relative* advance of productivity in sea transport.

Two other industries show no check—iron and steel manufactures, and wool.

This leaves four industries in which output per operative seems to have been checked about the turn of the century: cotton, in both its otherwise very different indexes; beer, in which economies of scale may have been cut back, for consumption a head began to fall from 1900; the mining of iron ore; and iron and steel smelting, in which output per operative continued to rise, but more slowly, though G. T. Jones's real costs of Cleveland pig-iron conflict with this.

In sum, the evidence needs cautious handling, and is by no means unanimous; so far as it goes, it shows a check or reversal of the rise of output per operative in six particular industries, at various dates from the seventies to the turn of the century; and no check in three others. The field surveyed is not wide, but so far as any generalization is warranted, it is that no concentration of effects or causes has been revealed: the rise of productivity was checked in some industries, and not in others; those in which the check appeared were of various kinds.

6. An index of output cannot usually include new industries until they have grown to some size and come of statistical age, and so it gives us no view of technical progress in its early stages. We must take care, therefore, not to read into the later course of productivity within Hoffmann's coverage a general verdict of stagnation. On the contrary, there was much technical development in the United Kingdom in the 20 years before the First World War, and a rapid expansion of still small industries which were to attain a massive development through and after the war.[1]

We may cite three here. The output of motor vehicles trebled between 1907 and 1913, when it was about 34,000—in 1934 it was over ten times as great.[2] The number of operatives whom the Census classified as manufacturing chemists, or as engaged in the manufacture of alkali, in Great Britain, rose by a half between 1901 and 1911.[3] In electricity, the expansion of a still small industry became very rapid at the turn of the century. The output sold by supply undertakings increased fifteenfold between 1899 and 1914.[4] Between 1901 and 1911 the number of operatives recorded by the Census as electricians or as manufacturing electrical equipment in Great Britain nearly doubled.[5]

Yet the rise of these industries, and of others such as rayon, aluminium, and aircraft, was big with promise rather than achievement. In the three we first cited, all the operatives together were less than a quarter of a million in 1911, when there were about $13\frac{1}{2}$ million wage-earners in Great Britain. Hoffmann's index in this period actually includes motor-cars, alkalis, and aluminium. Its omission of the others cannot give it any significant downward bias as a measure of current output: what it leaves out was significant for the future, but too small to make much difference for the time being.

7. We can supplement our study of industrial productivity with the estimates of output a head in agriculture shown in Fig. 7.[6] The more

---

[1] See R. S. Sayers, 'The Springs of Technical Progress in Britain, 1919–39', *E.J.*, June 1950; A. Plummer, *New British Industries in the Twentieth Century* (Pitman, 1937). In 1907 electrical engineering and contracting accounted for 4·5 per cent., and commercial vehicles and aircraft for 1·2 per cent., of the aggregate value of gross investment in fixed capital; in 1930 the corresponding percentages were 8·5 and 3·4 (Colin Clark, *Investment in Fixed Capital in Great Britain*, London and Cambridge Economic Service, Special Memo. No. 38, Sept. 1934).

[2] *The Motor Industry of Great Britain*, issued by the Statistical Dept. of the Society of Motor Manufacturers and Traders, 1936.

[3] *Census of England and Wales, 1911*, x, Table 26; *Census of Scotland, 1911*, ii, Table D.1.

[4] Garcke, *Manual of Electrical Undertakings*, vol. xvii, 1913–14, p. 6.

[5] *Census of England and Wales, 1911*, x, Table 26; *Census of Scotland, 1911*, ii, Table D.1.

[6] We are indebted for commentary and guidance here to Dr. J. R. Raeburn of the London School of Economics.

steeply rising curve shows the result of dividing Drescher's index[1] of the gross output of agriculture in Great Britain by our own figures for the numbers occupied there.[2] The other curve is E. M. Ojala's estimate[3] of value added (at 1911–13 prices) per person occupied in agriculture in the whole United Kingdom. The difference between the two curves can be accounted for by the first using the gross output of Great Britain alone and

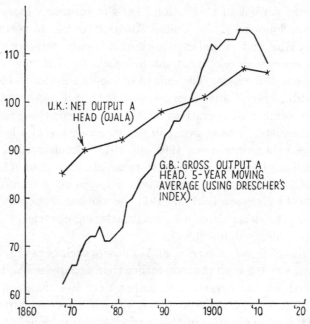

Fig. 7. Output per Person Occupied in Agriculture
(1890–9 = 100).

the second the net output of the whole United Kingdom, and subject to this they confirm each other closely.[4] The second is the more closely connected with our estimates of national income a head, and it is also based on

[1] Leo Drescher, 'Die Entwicklung der Agrarproduktion Großbritanniens und Irlands seit Beginn des 19. Jahrhunderts', *Weltwirtschaftliches Archiv*, xli, 1935, p. 270. We use the 'economic index of volume' in his Table 10; it is cited, on a different base, in col. 23 of Table II, Appendix B, of this article.

[2] Series 2, Table III, Appendix B.

[3] E. M. Ojala, *Agriculture and Economic Progress* (Oxford University Press, 1952), Table LV, p. 153, col. 4:

1867–9 = 100. *Output per worker in agriculture in the United Kingdom, averages of groups of years*

| 1867–9 | . | . | 100 | 1886–93. | . | 115 | 1911–13. | . | 124 | 1930–4. | . | 140 |
| 1870–6 | . | . | 106 | 1894–1903 | . | 119 | 1920–2 | . | . | 116 | 1935–9. | . | 127 |
| 1877–85 | . | . | 108 | 1904–10. | . | 126 | 1924–9 | . | . | 125 | | | |

In Fig. 7 these are shown as relatives to the average of 1890–9 (taken as 117·3) as base.

[4] (a) In Ojala's estimates the ratio of net to gross output falls from 77 per cent. in 1867–9 to about 67 per cent. through 1894–1913 (op. cit., Table XX, p. 215), so if a corresponding

more extensive materials; it suggests that the agriculture of the United Kingdom as a whole did not contribute much to the check to the rise of real income. The first serves to separate gross output a head in British agriculture from that of the very different rural economy of Ireland. Irish gross output a head seems to have been lower at all times than British, and to have risen less rapidly down to 1901, but much more rapidly thereafter.[1] When this element is removed, we are left with a course of change in Great Britain alone which in its set-back after 1900 resembles industrial productivity. Proximately, at least, this resemblance was a mere co-incidence, for the check in agriculture seems to have sprung from the changed course of agricultural prices. The near doubling of gross output a head between 1860 and 1900 came about through a moderate but fairly persistent increase in output being achieved by a rapidly falling labour force. This may have been made possible by continued technical improve-ment, the contraction of tillage to the best soils, and a general pressure on farmers to save labour, as product prices fell relatively to money wage-rates. In 1896 the price trend was reversed, and soon afterwards the rise in gross output a head came nearly to a stop. But though agriculture seems

correction were applied to the curve from Drescher in Fig. 7 it would be raised by about one-sixth at its start relatively to its end, and rise rather more slowly down to 1900.

(*b*) Drescher also gives a combined index for the whole United Kingdom and this shows close agreement with an index of gross output which Ojala also gives, except in the first 20 years, when it rises rather more rapidly. Irish output carried about a quarter of the weight of Drescher's combined index. Thus it is probable that Drescher's estimate for Great Britain alone would be borne out by the wider materials used by Ojala. The figures are:

*U.K.: gross output of agriculture, at constant prices*

1911–13 = 100. Col. (1): Drescher, op. cit., Table 10. Col. (2): Ojala, op. cit., Table XVIII, p. 210

|  | (1) | (2) |  | (1) | (2) |
|---|---|---|---|---|---|
| 1867–9 | 83 | 89 | 1894–1903 | 95 | 95 |
| 1870–6 | 87 | 93 | 1904–10 | 102 | 99 |
| 1877–85 | 85 | 90 | 1911–13 | 100 | 100 |
| 1886–93 | 93 | 94 |  |  |  |

[1] The numbers occupied in agriculture in Ireland may be obtained by subtracting our estimates of the number occupied in Great Britain (Appendix B, Table III, Series 2) from the numbers occupied in the United Kingdom given by Ojala, op. cit., Table XXXIII, p. 85, the earlier entries here being scaled down to give continuity through 1881. The results can be divided into Drescher's index of physical output in Ireland (average of 5 years centred on census year) to yield an index of productivity:

Col. (1): Numbers occupied in G.B., '000s. Col. (2): Numbers occupied in Ireland, '000s. Col. (3): Index of gross output a head in Ireland, 1871 = 100.

|  | (1) | (2) | (3) |  | (1) | (2) | (3) |
|---|---|---|---|---|---|---|---|
| 1871 | 1,477 | 1,242 | 100 | 1901 | 979 | 1,202 | 118 |
| 1881 | 1,327 | 1,152 | 104 | 1911 | 1,081 | 1,102 | 140 |
| 1891 | 1,205 | 1,200 | 110 |  |  |  |  |

Drescher (op. cit.) gives the aggregate value of British and Irish gross outputs (items within his index only) as £m.202 and £m.63 respectively in 1909–13. At this time the numbers occupied in the two areas were about equal, so Irish gross output a head seems to have been much lower than British, even when allowance is made for any relative under-representation of Ireland in the index (e.g. omission of horsebreeding). This seems to have been the position after 40 years of continuous and, latterly, rapid advance in Irish productivity.

in this way to have been governed mostly by the change in its own prices, this in turn was bound up with the changed relation between industry and agriculture, to which we return in paras. 12 and 13 below. If we have interpreted the records of British agriculture rightly, they suggest that the increased scarcity of farm products may have reinforced itself somewhat: there may be a general tendency for productivity to be checked where the product becomes scarcer, because higher prices make life easier for the producer.

### III

**8.** Our estimates are subject to a wide margin of error at some points, but contain enough agreement of independent evidence to make it clear that some checks to the rise of productivity in industry and agriculture underlay the set-backs to real income a head and real wages in the United Kingdom about the turn of the century. Why did these things come about ? We can narrow our search for causes, because we have good reason to believe that the check was not peculiar to the United Kingdom, but was also experienced in some measure by Belgium, France, Germany, and the United States (see Fig. 1). The most likely causes will be those which could have operated in all these countries. When, therefore, we consider the reasons given for the United Kingdom's falling behind other countries at this time, we must ask whether they mark factors common to the other countries but operative with greater intensity in the United Kingdom, or factors peculiar to the United Kingdom but working there to the same effect as different factors in the other countries.

**9.** To contemporaries these reasons seemed important: it was alleged that both management and labour were less efficient in Britain than they had been.

Criticism was directed against British management by comparison with other countries. Awareness of higher productivity in American industry, and dispatch of teams to find out how it is achieved, go back at least to the 1850's in Britain,[1] but perhaps the first team to contain trade unionists was that of Mr. Alfred Mosely, who in 1902 took twenty-three trade union officers to visit their own industries in the United States.[2] Their observations have a familiar ring to readers of recent reports, whose findings they anticipate in some detail. The special correspondent of *The Times* who accompanied them endorsed the main points of contrast which they drew between British and American management.[3] American managers were chosen for their competence, not their family connexions. 'The American

[1] See D. L. Burn, 'The Genesis of American Engineering Competition, 1850–70', *Economic History*, ii. 6, Jan. 1931.
[2] *Mosely Industrial Commission to the United States of America, Oct.–Dec. 1902. Reports of the Delegates* (Manchester, 1903).
[3] *The Times*, 16, 23, 25, and 26 Dec. 1902.

manufacturer realizes the supreme importance of order and system in the factory, and accordingly sees not only that every operation is simplified and sub-divided to the form in which it can be most efficiently performed, but also that each worker is always fully supplied with the kind of work which he or she can do best.' Probably the American 'has few, if any, machines that are utterly unknown in England, but he is more determined and wholesale in his use of mechanical appliances generally, and runs them for the utmost he can get out of them'. 'In America, employer and work-man seem to be closer together than they are in England, and in con-sequence the former is more able to benefit from the latter's knowledge and experience.'

In the following year, 1903, Marshall noted the loss by Britain of the industrial leadership she had had sixty years before. 'It was not inevitable', he wrote,[1] 'that she should lose as much of it as she has done. The great-ness and rapidity of her loss is partly due to that very prosperity which followed the adoption of Free Trade.' The combination of advantages which she enjoyed in those years encouraged 'the belief that an English-man could expect to obtain a much larger real income and to live much more luxuriously than anybody else, at all events in an old country ; and that if he chose to shorten his hours of work and take things easily, he could afford to do it'. Other causes of complacency lay in the distraction of competitors by civil war in America, and the wars which Germany fought in Europe ; and in the bounty conferred upon the entrepreneur by rising prices consequent upon the influx of gold. 'This combination of causes made many of the sons of manufacturers content to follow mechanic-ally the lead given by their fathers. They worked shorter hours, and they exerted themselves less to obtain new practical ideas than their fathers had done ; and thus a part of England's leadership was destroyed rapidly. In the 'nineties it became clear that in future Englishmen must take business as seriously as their grandfathers had done, and as their American and German rivals were doing.'

The relative decline of British industry was also attributed to an in-creased enforcement of restrictive practices by trade unionists. This was the contention of eleven articles by E. A. Pratt which *The Times* printed in the winter of 1901–2 under the title of 'The Crisis in British Industry'.[2] 'The "new" unionism, with its resort to violence and intimidation, has in turn been succeeded by a "newer" unionism, which, although working along much quieter lines, is doing even more serious injury'—by enforcing restrictive practices. The articles contained instances of these practices,

[1] Sec. L of *Memorandum on Fiscal Policy of International Trade*, completed Aug. 1903, published as H. of C. No. 321, Nov. 1908.
[2] 18, 21 Nov.; 3, 14, 16, 24, 26, 27, 30 Dec. 1901; 4, 16 Jan. 1902; reprinted in *Trade Unionism and British Industry*, by E. A. Pratt (1904).

but little definite evidence that they had increased of late. The Webbs
rejoined[1] that

'the complaints as to diminished quantity or energy of work, and of the tacit con-
spiracy to discourage individual exertion, occur with curiously exact iteration in
every decade of the last hundred years at least. . . . To give one instance only, we
have found exactly the same accusation of the bricklayers' limiting the number of
bricks, and precisely the same belief that they were only doing "half as much" as
they did twenty years before, in the great strikes of 1833, in those of 1853, again in
1859–60, and again in 1871.'

It is probable none the less that the rise in the strength of trade unions
between 1889 and 1901 did increase the practical effect of restrictive tendencies which had long been present. There is a distinct, and real, possibility, that wage-earners' standards of achievement were kept down, or
even lowered, through emigration taking off many of the most energetic.

Yet with trade unionists as with management, what is well-founded in
the charges does not seem enough to account for the severe check to
productivity which came about in the 1890's. The fact that great advances in British productivity have been achieved in later years, when
similar contrasts have been drawn between British and American management, and British trade unions have been stronger than ever, reminds us
that these factors, though important, are not the only ones on which
productivity depends. In accounting for the climacteric, moreover, we
have to look not for persistent conditions which kept productivity down
at all times, but for recent changes which could have halted its previously
rising trend, and what change there was at this time in the qualities of
management and labour does not seem commensurate with that effect. It
was rather that through these factors Britain was denied some energies of
industrial advance, which were active in America, and might have sustained the rise of productivity here when a pause came in other kinds of
development. British labour generally was not prepared to risk job
security and abandon bargaining weapons for the chance of higher
earnings. British industrial society had not developed the morale and
institutions which would accumulate the practical achievements of
management as a doctrine, and impart them as a discipline, so as to maintain a general level of managerial performance not far below that of the
best firms in each generation.

These seem to have been continuing deficiencies in the endowment of
British industry, rather than the active causes of the check to British
productivity in the 1890's, which are more likely to be found in factors
affecting Britain in common with the other countries which experienced
something of the same check.

[1] *The Times*, 6 Dec. 1901.

**10.** Such common factors may reasonably be sought in the declining rate of extension at this time of the techniques of power, transport, and machinery comprised beneath the names of Steam and Steel. There is a varying but usually considerable lag between the inventions which first open the way and the massive applications which alone take effect on the productivity of whole peoples. So though the heroic age of the steam-engine lay far back, in the eighteenth century, and Bessemer's invention is usually assigned to 1856, it was not till after the civil war in America, and the Franco-Prussian war in Europe, that the general benefit began to be won of steam-engines driving steel machinery, and of transport by steam-engines on steel rails and in steel ships. Our hypothesis is that the rapid and general extension of these techniques was coming to an end in the 1890's. The supersession of sail by steam at sea is a striking example.[1] In 1860, nearly half a century after the first steamships had been tried, the tonnage of British shipping under sail was still growing, and was nearly ten times as great as the tonnage in steam; in 1880 the ratio was still about 3 to 2. But steam tonnage was now growing very rapidly, and in 1883 it overtook the declining tonnage under sail; by 1895 it was more than twice as great; and in carrying capacity of course the disparity was far wider than this. The replacement of each sailing-ship by a steamship makes a big advance in the productivity of transport, but once the sailing-ships have been replaced, such rapid improvements are no longer possible: only those annual advances remain which can be brought about by gradual improvements in the performance of the steamship itself.

The example brings out another point: the inventions which affect productivity most are those which improve processes common to many industries. All industries depend on power, transport, and the basic techniques of machine-making, and an invention which improves one of these is likely to raise productivity everywhere; unlike the inventions which are specific to particular industries. Even when technical improvements are coming forward fairly steadily, the inventions of widespread application may be made and brought into general use only discontinuously. The times of greatest rise in national productivity are those in which important inventions of widespread application have reached the stage of widespread installation.

Our knowledge of industrial history agrees with this. It shows, first,[2] that in manufacturing generally, about 1850 there was still much hand-work, and outwork, the sailing ships, so to speak, of industry, giving the opportunity for a rapid rise in productivity when they were superseded

---

[1] Tables 58A and 60 in W. Page (ed.), *Commerce and Industry*, vol. ii.

[2] J. H. Clapham, *Economic History of Modern Britain*, vol. ii, chap. ii, 'The Industrial Field in 1851'.

by factory power and machinery. Second,[1] it shows that the advance of power and mechanization in the 40 years after 1850 brought about changes in industrial methods which were widespread, far-reaching, and sometimes revolutionary. Third,[2] it shows some continuing technical progress, and the opening of new possibilities, in the 20 years before the First World War, but no longer the massive application of new equipment to raise productivity throughout industries that were already large. In the previous period, steel had ousted puddled iron; working to gauge on steel had made machine parts interchangeable, and this 'reacted continuously on the older mechanised industries';[3] spinning and weaving had been mechanized in the woollen industry; steel rollers had superseded mill-stones in the steam mills—the list might be longer. But the 20 years before the First World War do not see such widespread changes. The emphasis lies on 'widespread'. Much development was beginning now, which was to bring about the rise of nearly two-thirds in output per man-hour in British industry, which Rostas[4] has found between 1907 and 1937; but it took most of its effect only in its massive application after the war.

In sum, then, our main explanation of the check to the rise of real income in the United Kingdom about the end of the nineteenth century is that the previous rise had been carried forward by the massive application of Steam and Steel, which now had not much scope for extension; while the new techniques, especially of electricity, the internal combustion engine, and the new chemical processes, did not attain massive application until during and after the First World War.

Of the countries in Fig. 1, only Sweden shows in the aggregate no sign of the check, and this agrees with our theory if in fact the general application of Steam and Steel came later there.

**11.** The reduced rate of extension of new types of equipment in the United Kingdom suggests a lower rate of capital accumulation, and the great increase in capital export after 1904 also makes this seem likely. But the new estimates of real capital per head which we report in Appendix C show a rise sustained to 1914 along a linear trend. We have used two methods, which have a common base in Stamp's estimate of the capital stock about 1912, but are quite independent in their estimates of the changes through earlier years. The first method is to estimate annual net investment, and after reducing this to £'s of constant purchasing

---

[1] Clapham, op. cit., vol. ii, chap. iii.

[2] Clapham, op. cit., vol. iii, chap. iii, in contrast with chap. iii of vol. ii.

[3] Clapham, op. cit., vol. ii, p. 80.

[4] L. Rostas, *Comparative Productivity in British and American Industry* (National Institute of Economic and Social Research, Occasional Papers, xiii, 1948), p. 49. The coverage is manufacturing, mining, building, and public utilities. In this area output per wage-earner rose by 47 per cent. between 1907 and 1937, by 37 per cent. between 1924 and 1937 (ibid., pp. 42–43).

power, use it to decumulate the stock of 1912 and arrive by difference at
the stocks of earlier years. The second method is to capitalize property
incomes either (as Stamp did) by applying the appropriate number of
years' purchase to each category of property income in the Inland Revenue
returns, or by applying an average of years' purchase to profits as a whole.
This second method has two drawbacks—the uncertainty of the right
number of years' purchase for some property incomes, and the quasi-rent

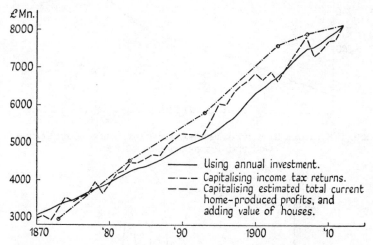

FIG. 8. TOTAL REVENUE-EARNING CAPITAL (EXCLUDING FARM CAPITAL) WITHIN U.K., IN
DEC. 1912 £s.

nature of much of the income capitalized, which causes the capital values
obtained to swing above or below the current replacement cost of the
buildings, equipment, and stocks. The first method avoids these snags of
valuation, but has drawbacks of its own: it rests on a relatively small
number of series, and involves some rough estimating; any bias in it, or
defect of coverage, will take cumulative effect on the estimates of capital
stocks. But we can use the two methods as checks on one another, and
Fig 8 shows that there is more agreement between the results than we
might expect, at least over the whole span; since two independent methods
have been used, and different price indexes, the agreement confirms the
magnitude of the movement. This magnitude is illustrated in Fig. 9,
which shows that real capital a head rose by 60 per cent. during this
period. This rise, moreover, appears to have been sustained through the
20 years before the First World War, so that the average man at work in
the United Kingdom in 1914 was working with more equipment, even
though he was not much more productive, than his counterpart in 1895.

This impression is borne out by Fig. 10, which shows total net home
investment each year, in £s whose purchasing power over investment

goods is about that of December 1912. So far from the nineties bringing a slackening in home investment, they saw a rapid rise to an average half as great again as that of the seventies and eighties, and except in 1908 a substantial increase was maintained down to the war. It has been generally

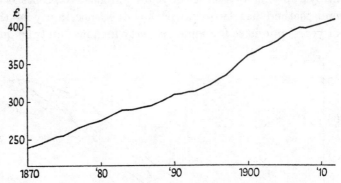

FIG. 9. U.K.: HOME REVENUE-EARNING CAPITAL (EXCLUDING FARM CAPITAL) PER OCCUPIED PERSON, IN DEC. 1912 £s.

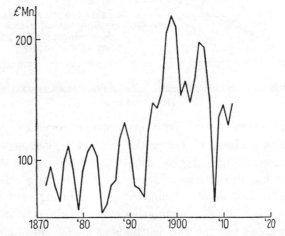

FIG. 10. U.K.: ANNUAL NET HOME INVESTMENT, IN DEC. 1912 £s.

known that a housing boom began in the nineties, but our estimates suggest that investment in industrial equipment rose then even more rapidly than housing.

The continued and indeed accelerated growth of capital a head throws doubt on an explanation of the check to productivity which otherwise would seem likely to have something in it, namely, that the decline in product wage-rates, i.e. the rise in prices of products relatively to money wage-rates in Britain after 1899, relieved firms of the pressure to introduce labour-saving equipment, to which rising product wage-rates had been submitting them throughout the preceding 40 years. Very likely there was some relaxing effect, but it does not seem to have checked the growth of equipment per occupied person.

Our findings do not conflict with the explanation of the check to productivity put forward in para. 10—the tonnage of steamships, so to speak, might continue to increase even faster than the occupied population, but adding one steamship to others would not make so much difference as substituting a steamship for a sailing-ship had done. There was no longer the innovation effect.

**12.** This working out of the innovation effect of Steam and Steel was the more serious for the British people, because they had been gaining so much from it as importers of food and raw materials.

'It has been said, and it may be with truth', wrote the signatories of Part II of the report of the Royal Commission on Gold and Silver,[1] 'that the development of machinery was as great in the fifteen or twenty years which preceded 1874, as in the subsequent years, and that steam transport had been also largely developed in the earlier period. But not only has the actual extension of railways and the cheapening of land and sea freight been greater in the subsequent years, but the effect of railways which had been previously made has been more felt. . . . Large new districts of great natural fertility, and rich in minerals, have been opened up, and consequently civilized countries have been furnished with an unprecedented quantity of raw vegetable and mineral products.'

Thus the ever-growing British population drew supplies whose rate of increase was even greater than its own, so long as Steam and Steel were opening new sources up; but when that opening up was done, though supplies continued to rise in total, their rate of increase fell, while that of population went on. The factory-worker's terms of trade with farmers and miners ceased to move in his favour.

This sort of check would have been bound to hold back the standard of living of the British people, even if it had not coincided with a reduced rate of progress in their own industrial productivity. British imports were largely of materials which we may call basic, because some quantity of them is indispensable to subsistence. Inventions and discoveries may be roughly divided into those on the one hand which open up new sources of basic materials, or increase the return to a unit of human work on the existing sources, or make transport from them easier; and those on the other hand which provide more of other materials, or increase our ability to work material up into useful and pleasing manufactures. A first rise in the standard of living above the level of subsistence requires an almost proportional rise in the intake of basic materials: it depends, that is to say, on inventions of the first class. No doubt, if the rise is maintained, and population is constant, the relative importance of the second class rises, and after some point has been passed there is no presumption that the one class is more beneficial than the other. But the population of Britain at

[1] C. 5512 of 1888; Part II, para. 26.

this time was relentlessly increasing, and if only the existing standard of living were to be maintained, supplies of basic materials had to be increased as rapidly as the number of consumers. Sooner or later the ability of an expanding economy to do this is likely to be impaired by decreasing returns at its existing sources of supply, and this obstacle cannot be avoided by however vigorous a development of inventions of the second class. The consequent set-back to real income will generally be felt most by the wage-earners, because their consumption contains a higher proportion of basic materials than does that of the better off.

The relative unimportance in such circumstances of skill in working basic materials up, compared with the availability of those materials themselves, was put with unusual emphasis by Marshall in 1903.[1]

'The progress of the arts and resources of manufacture has benefited England more than almost any other country in one important but indirect way. It has so reduced the cost of carriage by land and sea that raw materials and food can come to her, even from the centres of great continents, at a less cost than they could come from the near neighbourhood of the sea-shores and great rivers of the Continent sixty years ago; and the 300,000 miles of railways which have been built during the last sixty years in America, Asia, Africa, and Australia are rendering greater service to Englishmen than to any other people, except those in whose lands the several railways are placed.'

So far 'the progress of manufactures' as it provides inventions of our first class; now for the second.

'In almost every other respect the progress of the arts and resources of manufacture has benefited England less than any other country. For, even sixty years ago, the excess of the cost of the manufactures needed for her own consumption over that of the raw material by which they were made was small. If it could have been reduced to nothing, she would have gained by the change very much less than she has gained by the lowering of the cost of imported food and raw material for her own use.'

The changed balance between the growth of population and the supply of basic materials seemed ominous to contemporaries. On the eve of the war D. H. Robertson[2] concluded 'that the normal tendency for the ratio of exchange to alter against the manufacturing and in favour of the agricultural communities was in force in the 'seventies, was suspended in the 'eighties and 'nineties, and is now once more on the whole triumphing. This is perhaps the most significant economic fact in the world today.' We know now that those conditions were fostering their own correction, and the balance swung back after the war, so that the years 1896–1914 have fallen into their place in an historical alternation. As W. W. Rostow[3] has said, 'The three famous periods of extensive expansion, with rising

---

[1] Sec. L of his *Memorandum on Fiscal Policy of International Trade (1903)*, H. of C. No. 321, Nov. 1908.

[2] At p. 169, n. 1, of his *Study of Industrial Fluctuation* (1915). (No. 8 in the London School of Economics series of Reprints of Scarce Works on Political Economy.)

[3] 'The Historical Analysis of the Terms of Trade', *Economic History Review*, iv. 1, 1951, p. 64.

price and interest trends (roughly 1793–1815; 1848–73; 1896–1914) were part of the rough and ready process by which an appropriate balance of world production and a more or less appropriate distribution of population on the earth's land were maintained.' Even the immediate effect, moreover, though it fell specially hard upon the wage-earners, was not so very great in proportion to national income.[1] But since the Second World War we have learned again how an economy may be rapidly increasing the range and efficiency of its manufactures yet be held back by short supplies of foodstuffs, raw materials, and power.

13. In the greater scarcity of basic materials we may find a link between contemporary changes in the trends of productivity and of prices. The upturn of prices was facilitated by the increased supply of gold, but this other factor seems to have been at work to start the rise in prices and carry it on, and may well have made itself felt even without any increase in the output of gold. An initial rise in raw material prices tends to raise requirements of working capital, which in certain monetary conditions will be provided in such increased quantities as to support a general sympathetic rise of product prices and other factor prices. Consumers whose real income is reduced by scarcity of basic materials try to maintain it by getting higher money incomes; again in certain monetary conditions they will succeed, and another round of price rises follows. We have seen in recent years how in the absence of monetary constraint a price rise in one sector can spread outwards, and one set-back to real income can start a spiral of prices and money incomes. These processes, beginning with the greater scarcity of basic materials in the 1890's, may have been at work to draw out the monetary expansion and rise in prices which the increased gold supply made possible.

14. Some inferences may be drawn for the present prospects of Great Britain.

It seems that the substantial and general raising of productivity is brought about by the massive application of technical advances. The phase of massive application may follow that of pathbreaking invention only at a long remove. When it comes, it brings a high rate of advance, which falls off as the field of innovation is worked over. The progress of productivity, and the standard of living, thus appears to be very unstable. We cannot count upon the advance of productivity along a constant growth curve. Should at any time our standard of living not be much raised for 20 years, that would be only what has already happened in the lifetime of many people now living.

The raising of the standard of living generally requires increased supplies of basic materials. Improvements in our efficiency in working

[1] Para. 3 above.

materials up into products of existing types, and fertility in designing new products, can compensate only partially for inability to increase these supplies. Such an increase can be achieved by capital investment which develops new sources of supply overseas, by success in exporting, or by inventions which liberate new sources of energy and basic materials within the country. If advances of these kinds can be made, a limiting factor can be lifted which otherwise will restrict the use of all other technical advances.

IV

### 15. Summary

1. A number of investigators have detected a check to the rise of real income a head, in several countries, about the end of the nineteenth century. Estimates of real wage-rates show some adverse change of trend about this time, in differing degree, in Belgium, France, Germany, the United Kingdom, and the United States, but not Sweden. (Para. 1.)

2. The check in the United Kingdom was not due to a falling off in property income from abroad. It was increased by the cessation in 1900 of the improvement in the terms of trade which had persisted since 1882. But when allowance has been made for this, the greater part of the check remains, and its causes must be sought in productivity at home. (Paras. 2–3.)

3. Output per operative within the coverage of Hoffmann's index of British industrial output provides independent confirmation of the check shown by real income estimates, but its earlier rise had been more gradual, and its slowing down is marked from as early as 1885. The changes in output a man in coal-mining slowed down the rise of industrial productivity, but the remainder of industry still shows by itself a declining rate of advance. (Para. 4.)

4. Estimates of the course of output per operative in particular industries are hazardous, but contain evidence, which in the aggregate carries some weight, of checks to the rise of output per operative in a number of industries at different dates from the seventies to the turn of the century. (Para. 5.)

5. New industries at this time were significant for the future but still too small to make much difference to current output. (Para. 6.)

6. Output a head in British agriculture shows a similar pattern to that which predominates in industry; proximately, at least, the probable causes were distinct from those affecting industry, but there is a common factor in the changed trend of raw material prices. (Para. 7.)

7. Some shortcomings of management, and some increased enforcement of restrictive practices by labour, probably did hold back British productivity at this time. But it is unlikely that any contemporary growth of these influences was commensurate with the check to productivity, whose

main causes must be sought in conditions common to the other countries which also experienced it. (Paras. 8, 9.)

8. These conditions are probably to be found in the working out towards the end of the century of the massive application and extension of the techniques of Steam and Steel. There now began an interval between the rapid advances in productivity which this had brought, and those brought later, mostly after the First World War, by the wide application of the new techniques of electricity, the internal combustion engine, and industrial chemistry. (Para. 10.)

9. But there was no check to the accumulation of equipment, stocks, and buildings as a whole in the United Kingdom after 1890. Estimates by two independent methods agree in showing that the stock of capital, in physical terms, per head of the occupied population, rose by 60 per cent. between 1870 and 1914, and its growth was roughly linear throughout. (Para. 11.)

10. The working out of the innovation effect of Steam and Steel also affected the United Kingdom, in common with urban and factory workers elsewhere, by ending the rapid rise in supplies of food and raw materials which the railway and steamship had been effecting on their introduction. This kind of set-back was significant for the future, but not of so much immediate effect for the United Kingdom as the check to productivity at home. (Para. 12.)

11. The greater scarcity of raw materials may provide a link between the contemporary changes in the trends of productivity and prices. (Para. 13.)

12. Some inferences are suggested for the present prospects of Great Britain. (Para. 14.)

## APPENDIX A

### (*With* SHEILA V. HOPKINS)

### Product Wage-rates in Belgium, 1860–1913

A. WAGES

*a. Sources*

i. Marcel Peeters, 'L'Évolution des salaires en Belgique de 1831 à 1913', in *Bulletin de l'Institut de Recherches Économiques (Louvain)*, Aug. 1939. From this we took: 1860–92, wage-rates in cotton and linen; 1893–1913, these two with coal, zinc, iron, quarries and metal mining, glass, pottery, brewing and distilling.

ii. *British and Foreign Trade and Industry*, Cmd. 1761 of 1903. Gross annual earnings for coal, and 'average daily wages' for iron and zinc from dates before 1860 through 1900.

iii. R. R. Kuczynski: *Arbeitslohn und Arbeitszeit in Europa und Amerika, 1870–1909*, gives wage-rates for various industries in Liége, used here for 1870–1903 only.

iv. Statistique Générale de la France: *Annuaire Statistique, 1935*, gives 'average daily wage' of Belgian coal-miners, annually from 1881.

*b. Method*

Three series were compiled. (1) *1860–9*: The wage-rates given for cotton and linen in Source i, and for coal, iron, and zinc in Source ii, were each expressed in index form with 1890–9 = 100. In linen, for which Source i gives separate series for spinning and weaving, we first made a single weighted index for the industry. The five industrial indexes were combined to give a single weighted average. (2) *1870–1903*: The data used in Series 1 were now combined with additional data from Sources iii and (from 1881) iv. The series from iii are for masons, carpenters, painters, plumbers, building labourers; iron moulders, labourers, pattern-makers, fitters, smiths, fitters' helpers, smiths' helpers; smiths and their helpers in boilermaking; cabinet-makers; hand compositors; stone-cutters. The series from iv is for coal-miners. The series from ii and iii were arranged in industrial groups, and the unweighted mean of each group was taken; where rates for skilled and unskilled were given separately, they were combined with weights taken as roughly representative of relative numbers. All the industrial series were expressed as indexes with 1890–9 = 100, and were combined to give a single weighted average. (3) *1893–1913*: Source i: original series of hourly rates (except for coal, iron, metal mining, and distilling, for which only annual or daily rates were available), combined to give a single weighted average. Series 1 and 2 were taken as providing a continuous index through 1860–1903, and Series 3 was used to continue this index through 1904–13, being spliced with Series 2 through 1899–1903.

*c. Kind of Wage*

Hourly rates so far as possible; but, for miners, gross annual earnings 1860–80 and 'daily wages' 1881–1913; for iron and zinc, 1860–1903, 'daily wages'. It is not known if 'daily wages' are earnings or rates.

*d. Wage-earners*

Industrial only: see particulars in *b*.

*e. Weights*

Constant throughout, and proportionate to the numbers of workpeople occupied in each industry, according to the Census of 1890.

B. COST OF LIVING

No index of the cost of living is known, but we have used the index of retail prices in Fritz Michotte, 'L'Évolution des prix de détail en Belgique de 1830 à 1913', in *Bulletin de l'Institut des Sciences Économiques* (*Louvain*), May 1937. This takes the geometric mean of the indexes for 23 articles of food, with coal, charcoal, and 2 kinds of oil.

C. GENERAL PRICES

F. Loots, 'Les Mouvements fondamentaux des prix de gros en Belgique de 1822 à 1913', in *Bulletin de l'Institut des Sciences Économiques* (*Louvain*), Nov. 1936, gives an 'indice globale, produits industriels', which is the unweighted geometric mean of the indexes for 33 industrial and 26 chemical products. We combined this with our indexes of wage-rates and cost of living, in the proportions 20, 20, 60, respectively, to make an index of product prices.

TABLE I

*Belgium: Indexes of Money and Real Wage-rates, 1860–1913*

*1890–9 = 100*

| | Money wage-rate (1) | Retail prices (2) | Real wage-rate (1)÷(2) (3) | Product prices (4) | Product wage-rate (1)÷(4) (5) |
|---|---|---|---|---|---|
| 1860 | 78 | 121 | 65 | 109 | 72 |
| 1 | 78 | 130 | 60 | 115 | 68 |
| 2 | 77 | 133 | 58 | 117 | 66 |
| 3 | 78 | 124 | 63 | 113 | 69 |
| 4 | 81 | 118 | 69 | 110 | 74 |
| 5 | 87 | 123 | 71 | 114 | 76 |
| 6 | 91 | 128 | 71 | 118 | 77 |
| 7 | 91 | 132 | 69 | 119 | 76 |
| 8 | 88 | 127 | 69 | 116 | 76 |
| 9 | 89 | 126 | 71 | 115 | 77 |
| 1870 | 90 | 123 | 73 | 114 | 79 |
| 1 | 90 | 125 | 72 | 116 | 78 |
| 2 | 96 | 130 | 74 | 122 | 79 |
| 3 | 108 | 140 | 77 | 131 | 83 |
| 4 | 103 | 133 | 77 | 124 | 83 |
| 5 | 104 | 128 | 81 | 121 | 86 |
| 6 | 100 | 135 | 74 | 124 | 81 |
| 7 | 94 | 135 | 70 | 122 | 77 |
| 8 | 94 | 130 | 72 | 118 | 80 |
| 9 | 92 | 126 | 73 | 115 | 80 |
| 1880 | 96 | 120 | 80 | 114 | 84 |
| 1 | 97 | 120 | 81 | 116 | 84 |
| 2 | 97 | 119 | 82 | 115 | 84 |
| 3 | 99 | 120 | 83 | 115 | 86 |
| 4 | 95 | 112 | 85 | 109 | 87 |
| 5 | 91 | 109 | 84 | 105 | 87 |
| 6 | 90 | 99 | 91 | 97 | 93 |
| 7 | 91 | 105 | 87 | 101 | 90 |
| 8 | 93 | 103 | 90 | 101 | 92 |
| 9 | 96 | 105 | 91 | 103 | 93 |
| 1890 | 101 | 110 | 92 | 108 | 94 |
| 1 | 101 | 110 | 92 | 107 | 94 |
| 2 | 98 | 105 | 93 | 102 | 96 |
| 3 | 96 | 102 | 94 | 100 | 96 |
| 4 | 97 | 99 | 98 | 99 | 98 |
| 5 | 98 | 97 | 101 | 96 | 102 |
| 6 | 100 | 93 | 108 | 96 | 104 |
| 7 | 100 | 95 | 105 | 96 | 104 |
| 8 | 103 | 95 | 108 | 96 | 107 |
| 9 | 106 | 96 | 110 | 100 | 106 |
| 1900 | 115 | 109 | 106 | 111 | 104 |
| 1 | 113 | 111 | 102 | 111 | 102 |
| 2 | 109 | 109 | 100 | 109 | 100 |
| 3 | 110 | 109 | 101 | 109 | 101 |
| 4 | 111 | 95 | 117 | 102 | 109 |
| 5 | 109 | 97 | 112 | 103 | 106 |
| 6 | 116 | 106 | 109 | 112 | 104 |
| 7 | 125 | 110 | 114 | 116 | 108 |
| 8 | 123 | 111 | 111 | 115 | 107 |
| 9 | 122 | 110 | 111 | 114 | 107 |
| 1910 | 124 | 112 | 111 | 117 | 106 |
| 1 | 125 | 119 | 105 | 121 | 103 |
| 2 | 130 | 127 | 102 | 127 | 102 |
| 3 | 136 | 121 | 112 | 125 | 109 |

## APPENDIX B

### United Kingdom or Great Britain: Statistical Series and Sources

TABLE II

*U.K. or G.B.: Series of Prices, Income, Terms of Trade, Output and Productivity, 1860–1913*

1. *Index of prices of final products.* 1890–9 = 100. A weighted average of:

(a) *Cost of living.* Bowley, *Wages and Income in the U.K.*, pp. 121–2. Expenditure on the range of articles covered by the cost of living index seems to have been about 50 per cent. of national income in 1938 (using Cmd. 7649 of 1949) and about 48 per cent. in 1932 (using C. Clark, *National Income and Outlay*). For our earlier period, in which the standard of living was lower, we took 60 per cent. as our weight.

(b) *Wage-rates*, as the price of services rendered directly to consumers. Phelps Brown and Hopkins, 'Course of Wage Rates in Five Countries, 1860–1939', *Oxford Economic Papers*, June 1950, p. 276. Using the same sources as in (a) we found expenditure on services about 20 per cent. of the national income in 1938 and about 26 per cent. in 1932. For our earlier period we reduced these to a weight of 10 per cent.

(c) *Manufactured consumer goods*, to offset preponderance of food prices in wage-earners' cost of living in (a). Mean of price index of finished export goods in W. Schlote, *Entwicklung und Strukturwandlungen des englischen Außenhandels, von 1700 bis zur Gegenwart*, p. 180, and Sauerbeck's wholesale price index, taken here from Layton and Crowther, *Introduction to the Study of Prices*, p. 237. Weight assumed, 20 per cent., which is roughly the ratio of expenditure on this group to national income in 1938.

(d) *Capital goods.* Index described in Appendix C. Weight 10 per cent. based on ratio of gross home investment to gross national income through 1890–9.

2. *Total national income of U.K., in £s of 1890–9 purchasing power, per head of the occupied population.* Total national income of U.K. in current £s, from A. R. Prest, 'National Income of the U.K. 1870–1946', in *E.J.*, March 1948; this divided by index of product prices in col. 1 of the present table, and by number of occupied persons in U.K. in Table III, col. 1.

3. *Home-produced national income of U.K. in £s of 1890–9 purchasing power, per head of the occupied population.* As in 2, except that national income, in current £s, is first reduced by estimates of annual net receipt of property incomes from abroad, from C. K. Hobson, *Export of Capital*, p. 204.

4. *Home-produced national income of U.K., assuming actual imports obtained at terms of trade of 1881; in £s of 1890–9 purchasing power, per head of the occupied population.* Difference made by change in terms of trade calculated as value of actual imports, in current £s, multiplied by (reciprocal of index of terms of trade in col. 5 minus 1·0). This difference deducted from home-produced national income in current £s (see 3 above) before deflation.

5. *Terms of trade.* 1890–9 = 100. Ratio of import price index to export price index. Both indexes from Table 26 of W. Schlote, as in 1 (c) above. See also A. H. Imlah, 'The Terms of Trade of the United Kingdom', in *J. Econ. Hist.*, Nov. 1950.

6. *Hoffman index of industrial output in G.B.* Source and coverage as in notes to para. 4 of article. Here re-based on 1890–9 = 100.

# Appendix B. Table II

| | 1 | 2 | 3 | 4 | 5 | 6 | 7 | 8 | 9 | 10 | 11 | 12 | 13 | 14 | 15 | 16 | 17 | 18 | 19 | 20 | 21 | 22 | 23 | 24 |
|---|---|---|---|---|---|---|---|---|---|---|---|---|---|---|---|---|---|---|---|---|---|---|---|---|
| 1860 | 125 | .. | .. | .. | .. | 51 | 78 | 75 | | | .. | .. | .. | 58 | .. | .. | .. | 93 | .. | .. | .. | .. | .. | .. |
| 1861 | 123 | .. | .. | .. | .. | 50 | 75 | 72 | *Av.* | *Av.* | 36 | 35 | .. | 54 | .. | 57 | 65 | 93 | .. | .. | 83 | .. | .. | .. |
| 1862 | 128 | 46 | .. | .. | .. | 47 | 70 | 66 | *1861* | *1861* | 38 | 40 | .. | 54 | .. | 71 | 29 | 92 | 53 | .. | 82 | .. | .. | .. |
| 1863 | 131 | .. | .. | .. | .. | 49 | 73 | 69 | *–70 =* | *–70 =* | 46 | 41 | .. | 59 | .. | 102 | 33 | 92 | .. | .. | 88 | .. | .. | .. |
| 1864 | 139 | .. | .. | .. | .. | 51 | 74 | 70 | *319* | *108* | 51 | 43 | .. | 60 | .. | 123 | 37 | 93 | .. | .. | 94 | .. | .. | .. |
| 1865 | 132 | .. | .. | .. | .. | 54 | 79 | 74 | | | 50 | 46 | .. | 59 | .. | 118 | 48 | 95 | .. | .. | 98 | .. | .. | .. |
| 1866 | 134 | .. | .. | .. | .. | 56 | 81 | 76 | | | 49 | 49 | .. | 53 | .. | 98 | 58 | 96 | .. | .. | 103 | .. | 79 | 56 |
| 1867 | 131 | 50 | .. | .. | .. | 56 | 79 | 74 | | | 52 | 50 | .. | 54 | .. | 77 | 63 | 96 | 60 | .. | 103 | .. | 82 | 59 |
| 1868 | 129 | .. | .. | .. | .. | 59 | 82 | 78 | | | 53 | 56 | .. | 55 | .. | 92 | 65 | 95 | .. | .. | .. | .. | 90 | 65 |
| 1869 | 127 | .. | .. | .. | .. | 59 | 83 | 78 | | | 60 | 62 | .. | 59 | .. | 96 | 60 | 94 | .. | .. | 103 | .. | 87 | 64 |
| 1870 | 126 | 57 | 54 | 53 | 108 | 64 | 87 | 83 | | | 75 | 67 | .. | 63 | .. | 96 | 71 | 94 | .. | .. | 107 | 59 | 89 | 67 |
| 1871 | 128 | 59 | 56 | 54 | 104 | 68 | 92 | 87 | 371 | 113 | 86 | 68 | .. | 69 | .. | 95 | 80 | 94 | .. | .. | 115 | 49 | 88 | 67 |
| 1872 | 139 | 57 | 54 | 50 | 98 | 70 | 94 | 89 | 416 | 106 | 86 | 61 | .. | 70 | .. | 112 | 77 | 96 | 71 | .. | 118 | 54 | 85 | 65 |
| 1873 | 142 | 60 | 57 | 53 | 95 | 72 | 95 | 91 | 514 | 88 | 79 | 57 | .. | 69 | .. | 108 | 82 | 96 | .. | .. | 119 | 50 | 89 | 69 |
| 1874 | 135 | 62 | 59 | 56 | 99 | 73 | 96 | 93 | 539 | 83 | 73 | 60 | .. | 64 | .. | 157 | 83 | 96 | .. | .. | 114 | 52 | 97 | 76 |
| 1875 | 129 | 62 | 59 | 56 | 102 | 72 | 94 | 89 | 536 | 87 | 77 | 60 | .. | 67 | .. | 105 | 80 | 97 | .. | .. | 115 | 57 | 97 | 77 |
| 1876 | 127 | 62 | 60 | 58 | 109 | 73 | 94 | 90 | 515 | 92 | 80 | 60 | .. | 69 | .. | 85 | 82 | 97 | .. | .. | 114 | 57 | 90 | 72 |
| 1877 | 125 | 63 | 60 | 59 | 114 | 75 | 95 | 92 | 494 | 97 | 78 | 65 | .. | 70 | .. | 98 | 80 | 97 | 77 | .. | 112 | 60 | 84 | 68 |
| 1878 | 119 | 64 | 61 | 60 | 112 | 71 | 89 | 86 | 475 | 99 | 72 | 63 | .. | 59 | .. | 101 | 74 | 97 | .. | .. | 107 | 58 | 93 | 76 |
| 1879 | 115 | 63 | 60 | 59 | 112 | 68 | 84 | 80 | 477 | 100 | 65 | 58 | .. | 64 | .. | 85 | 74 | 98 | .. | .. | 104 | 63 | 74 | 61 |
| 1880 | 119 | 63 | 60 | 60 | 114 | 80 | 98 | 95 | 485 | 108 | 79 | 63 | .. | 82 | .. | 98 | 89 | 99 | .. | .. | 109 | 67 | 92 | 77 |
| 1881 | 117 | 66 | 63 | 63 | 117 | 81 | 98 | 94 | 496 | 111 | 76 | 56 | .. | 89 | 106 | 124 | 92 | 100 | .. | .. | 109 | 74 | 91 | 77 |
| 1882 | 115 | 69 | 66 | 66 | 117 | 86 | 103 | 100 | 504 | 111 | 82 | 61 | .. | 96 | 110 | 155 | 93 | 100 | 83 | 92 | 110 | 74 | 87 | 74 |
| 1883 | 115 | 70 | 66 | 66 | 115 | 88 | 104 | 101 | 515 | 113 | 82 | 67 | .. | 94 | 109 | 171 | 94 | 100 | .. | 88 | 111 | 75 | 94 | 81 |
| 1884 | 110 | 69 | 66 | 65 | 113 | 86 | 100 | 97 | 520 | 110 | 80 | 75 | .. | 86 | 99 | 109 | 92 | 100 | .. | 90 | 107 | 82 | 98 | 86 |
| 1885 | 104 | 71 | 67 | 66 | 112 | 83 | 95 | 92 | 521 | 109 | 80 | 80 | 96 | 83 | 97 | 77 | 83 | 100 | .. | 90 | 103 | 87 | 95 | 83 |
| 1886 | 102 | 73 | 68 | 67 | 109 | 81 | 91 | 89 | 520 | 108 | 77 | 72 | 97 | 83 | 93 | 57 | 92 | 100 | .. | 87 | 101 | 87 | 100 | 88 |
| 1887 | 100 | 76 | 70 | 70 | 110 | 85 | 94 | 92 | 526 | 110 | 76 | 75 | 96 | 94 | 104 | 64 | 92 | 99 | 85 | 89 | 102 | 87 | 93 | 84 |
| 1888 | 102 | 79 | 73 | 72 | 110 | 91 | 100 | 99 | 535 | 113 | 90 | 85 | 94 | 101 | 112 | 93 | 94 | 99 | .. | 89 | 102 | 80 | 95 | 86 |
| 1889 | 103 | 82 | 77 | 75 | 107 | 97 | 105 | 104 | 564 | 112 | 95 | 89 | 94 | 106 | 115 | 135 | 93 | 99 | .. | 90 | 104 | 74 | 99 | 91 |
| 1890 | 104 | 85 | 79 | 75 | 101 | 97 | 103 | 102 | 613 | 105 | 96 | 94 | 93 | 102 | 109 | 125 | 100 | 98 | .. | 96 | 105 | 84 | 102 | 94 |
| 1891 | 105 | 82 | 77 | 73 | 102 | 97 | 102 | 101 | 649 | 102 | 96 | 98 | 93 | 94 | 101 | 119 | 98 | 99 | .. | 99 | 105 | 92 | 103 | 96 |
| 1892 | 103 | 82 | 76 | 73 | 103 | 92 | 95 | 94 | 664 | 97 | 86 | 96 | 100 | 84 | 89 | 114 | 92 | 99 | 93 | 99 | 102 | 102 | 101 | 96 |
| 1893 | 102 | 80 | 74 | 71 | 103 | 90 | 92 | 92 | 638 | 92 | 85 | 90 | 109 | 86 | 89 | 81 | 91 | 100 | .. | 98 | 95 | 106 | 96 | 93 |
| 1894 | 97 | 86 | 80 | 76 | 99 | 96 | 96 | 95 | 705 | 95 | 95 | 94 | 111 | 91 | 92 | 91 | 99 | 100 | .. | 97 | 98 | 105 | 100 | 99 |
| 1895 | 95 | 91 | 85 | 80 | 98 | 99 | 98 | 98 | 700 | 96 | 98 | 104 | 109 | 94 | 94 | 85 | 100 | 100 | .. | 95 | 97 | 110 | 98 | 98 |
| 1896 | 96 | 91 | 85 | 80 | 99 | 104 | 102 | 103 | 693 | 100 | 107 | 113 | 108 | 108 | 106 | 98 | 101 | 101 | .. | 101 | 99 | 106 | 100 | 102 |
| 1897 | 97 | 92 | 86 | 82 | 100 | 105 | 101 | 102 | 695 | 103 | 109 | 96 | 99 | 112 | 107 | 79 | 100 | 101 | 107 | 102 | 100 | 101 | 99 | 104 |

| | 1 | 2 | 3 | 4 | 5 | 6 | 7 | 8 | 9 | 10 | 11 | 12 | 13 | 14 | 15 | 16 | 17 | 18 | 19 | 20 | 21 | 22 | 23 | 24 |
|---|---|---|---|---|---|---|---|---|---|---|---|---|---|---|---|---|---|---|---|---|---|---|---|---|
| 1898 | 100 | 93 | 87 | 83 | 100 | 108 | 103 | 105 | 707 | 102 | 113 | 115 | 89 | 110 | 104 | 101 | 108 | 102 | : | 105 | 99 | 94 | 102 | 109 |
| 1899 | 101 | 95 | 89 | 84 | 96 | 113 | 107 | 107 | 729 | 107 | 116 | 107 | 88 | 118 | 108 | 113 | 111 | 103 | : | 107 | 102 | 100 | 99 | 109 |
| 1900 | 108 | 93 | 87 | 79 | 89 | 113 | 105 | 105 | 780 | 103 | 113 | 107 | 89 | 113 | 103 | 108 | 105 | 102 | : | 108 | 102 | 94 | 98 | 110 |
| 1901 | 105 | 93 | 87 | 79 | 90 | 111 | 102 | 102 | 807 | 97 | 100 | 128 | 89 | 104 | 97 | 116 | 107 | 101 | 110 | 105 | 99 | 123 | 99 | 113 |
| 1902 | 105 | 92 | 86 | 80 | 95 | 113 | 102 | 102 | 825 | 98 | 107 | 115 | 92 | 108 | 101 | 102 | 105 | 100 | : | 107 | 100 | 128 | 104 | 117 |
| 1903 | 106 | 89 | 83 | 77 | 96 | 113 | 100 | 100 | 842 | 97 | 106 | 127 | 97 | 109 | 102 | 80 | 98 | 99 | : | 108 | 100 | 126 | 95 | 107 |
| 1904 | 106 | 90 | 84 | 78 | 96 | 112 | 97 | 97 | 848 | 97 | 104 | 123 | 94 | 106 | 103 | 93 | 98 | 100 | : | 106 | 99 | 130 | 103 | 114 |
| 1905 | 108 | 91 | 84 | 79 | 96 | 119 | 102 | 104 | 858 | 98 | 108 | 133 | 94 | 117 | 114 | 108 | 114 | 101 | : | 103 | 99 | 124 | 104 | 114 |
| 1906 | 111 | 93 | 87 | 80 | 95 | 124 | 104 | 106 | 882 | 101 | 112 | 142 | 95 | 124 | 115 | 117 | 115 | 101 | 122 | 102 | 103 | 115 | 106 | 115 |
| 1907 | 114 | 94 | 87 | 80 | 94 | 127 | 104 | 105 | 941 | 101 | 111 | 154 | 93 | 122 | 110 | 101 | 117 | 100 | : | 103 | 105 | 116 | 107 | 115 |
| 1908 | 111 | 91 | 83 | 77 | 93 | 119 | 97 | 97 | 988 | 94 | 104 | 176 | 94 | 104 | 99 | 52 | 99 | 99 | : | 103 | 102 | 132 | 109 | 116 |
| 1909 | 111 | 92 | 84 | 79 | 98 | 121 | 97 | 97 | 1,014 | 92 | 101 | 178 | 96 | 110 | 107 | 57 | 108 | 98 | : | 100 | 101 | 128 | 111 | 117 |
| 1910 | 113 | 94 | 85 | 81 | 101 | 126 | 99 | 100 | 1,049 | 90 | 101 | 189 | 97 | 115 | 112 | 60 | 94 | 99 | : | 99 | 103 | 116 | 109 | 114 |
| 1911 | 115 | 95 | 86 | 81 | 97 | 130 | 100 | 103 | 1,067 | 91 | 101 | 191 | 97 | 110 | 110 | 98 | 111 | 101 | 135 | 101 | 103 | 104 | 104 | 108 |
| 1912 | 118 | 97 | 89 | 82 | 96 | 132 | 100 | 104 | 1,089 | 85 | 88 | 200 | 99 | 106 | 106 | 96 | 120 | : | : | 105 | 100 | 78 | 103 | 106 |
| 1913 | 121 | 97 | : | : | 94 | 145 | 109 | 113 | 1,128 | 91 | 100 | 280 | : | 120 | 122 | 107 | 119 | : | : | 104 | 109 | : | 102 | 103 |
| 1914 | 120 | 93 | : | : | : | 135 | 100 | : | : | : | : | : | : | : | : | : | : | : | : | : | : | : | 107 | 108 |

7. *Index of output per operative within Hoffmann industries in G.B.* Col. 6 divided by estimates of number of persons occupied within Hoffmann coverage, obtained by linear interpolation from Table III, col. 4; rebased on 1890–9 = 100.

8. *Index of output per operative in G.B. within Hoffmann industries other than coal-mining.* Hoffmann index of output recalculated with omission of coal, and divided by numbers occupied as in Table III, col. 4, after deduction of number occupied in coal-mining, Table III, col. 5. 1890–9 = 100.

9. *Number of persons employed in coal-mines in U.K.* Differs from series 5 of Table III because it is available annually for most of the time, and gives numbers employed at all mines under the Coal Mines Regulation Act, which includes some in Ireland, whereas series 5 of Table III is confined to census years, numbers of operatives occupied, and G.B. Includes a small number of persons employed in mines of fireclay, ironstone, and shale. Sources: 1871: Reports of the Inspectors of Mines, 1871 (C. 653 of 1872). 1872: obtained by deducting annual figures for 1871 and 1873–80 from aggregate of 1871–80. Averages, 1861–70 and 1871–80, and annual outputs 1873–81: Reports of the Inspectors of Mines, 1881 (C. 3241 of 1882). 1882–3: p. 78 of *4th Abstract of Labour Statistics* (C. 8642 of 1897). 1884–98: p. 82 of *6th Abstract of Labour Statistics* (Cd. 119 of 1900). 1899–1913: p. 320 of *17th Abstract of Labour Statistics* (Cd. 7733 of 1915). Thousands.

10. *U.K.: output of coal in tons per annum per person employed in coal-mines.* Annual tonnage raised from Table 72 in vol. ii of W. Page (ed.), *Commerce and Industry*, divided by numbers in 9 above, and reduced to base 1890–9 = 100.

11. *G.B.: output of iron ore per operative in iron-mining.* Output of iron ore in whole U.K. (Irish component inconsiderable), divided by number of operatives in iron-mining in G.B., from col. 6 of Table III. Sources for output: 1860–88: Return relating to minerals (Output 1860–90), *Parly. Papers*, 1890–1, lxxviii. 1889–1913: Table 91 in vol. ii of W. Page (ed.), *Commerce and Industry*, for which the original source was *Statistical Abstracts for the British Empire*. 1890–9 = 100.

12. *G.B.: output per miner in 'other mining', viz. copper, lead, and tin.* Hoffmann's physical output series for copper, lead, and tin combined into one index and divided by numbers of miners from col. 7 of Table III. 1890–9 = 100.

13. *Output per unit of input (all factors), viz. reciprocal of G. T. Jones's index of real costs, in the Cleveland pig-iron industry.* Reciprocal of 5-year moving average of index of selling prices of Cleveland pig-iron corrected for changes in unit prices of labour, material, and other factors, at p. 278 of G. T. Jones, *Increasing Returns*. The significance of this index is discussed at ibid., p. 143. 1890–9 = 100.

14. *G.B.: output of iron and steel per operative in furnaces, rolling mills, foundries, and some manufacturing processes.* Hoffmann's series for 'iron and steel manufacture' divided by numbers of operatives, from col. 8 of Table III. This number contains some makers of products of iron or steel who cannot be separated in earlier years from those producing the pig or billet. The index is therefore partly an index of throughput as well as of output. 1890–9 = 100.

15. *G.B.: output per operative in the manufacture of iron and steel wares, machinery, and tools.* Hoffmann's series (No. 15) for output, divided by the numbers of operatives in col. 9 of Table III. These numbers cannot be followed in a consistent form back of 1881. 1890–9 = 100.

•16. *G.B.: shipbuilding tonnage per operative.* We estimated net tonnage of ships built (excluding vessels for British Navy but including war vessels for other countries) by deducting Irish output (from *Annual Statements of Navigation & Shipping*) from U.K. output (1860–1902: *Charts prepared for the St. Louis Exhibition*, Cd. 2145 of 1904, Table 20, p. 26; 1902–13: *17th Abstract of Labour Statistics*, Cd. 7733 of 1915, p. 37). But net tonnage built for foreigners in Ireland could not be separately obtained for 1872, 1883, 1893, and 1894, and therefore remains in the estimates for G.B. in those years; it is likely to have been small. We divided the resultant series for tonnage by the number of operatives, from col. 10 of Table III. The exclusion of ships built for the British Navy gives the resultant index a downward bias in the years before 1914 when the amount of such construction was rising. 1890–9 = 100.

17. *G.B.: output per operative in cotton spinning and weaving.* Index of output of Lancashire cotton industry from G. T. Jones, *Increasing Returns*, p. 275; described at pp. 111–13 of that book. This index of output is the mean of indexes of yarn produced and yarn consumed. The index of yarn produced is derived from cotton consumed. The index of yarn consumed is given by yarn produced minus yarn exported minus increase of stocks. The index of yarn consumed is a reliable index of the throughput of weaving only if there is no substantial change in the qualities of cloth and in the proportion of yarn going into lace and hosiery. We divided the index of output by an index of the numbers of operatives, from col. 11 of Table III. 1890–9 = 100.

18. *Output per unit of input (all factors), viz. reciprocal of G. T. Jones's index of real costs, in the Lancashire cotton industry.* Original index at p. 273, of G. T. Jones, *Increasing Returns*, with commentary at pp. 114–19. We give here the reciprocal of Jones's index, which itself is a 10-year moving average. 1890–9 = 100.

19. *U.K.: output per operative in wool spinning and weaving.* We constructed an index of the physical output of the wool industry, on the pattern of G. T. Jones's index for cotton (see series 17 above). Source: Report of the Balfour Committee, *Survey of Textile Industries*, 1928, pp. 275–6; the 5-year averages which this source gives have been assigned by us to the mid-year of each span. We derived our index of spinning output from the movements of: retained home output of raw wool plus retained imports, less 6 per cent. of this total for wastage, minus export of wool tops (which we assumed to be nil before 1892). The index of weaving output we derived from the movements of yarn processed, which we estimated as yarn spun (as just described) minus yarn exported. As in cotton, there is a possible source of error here through changes in the proportion of yarn going to hosiery, of which we have no record. Our index of output of the whole industry is the mean of the indexes of spinning and weaving outputs; we based it on the mean of 1892 and 1897. We divided the index of output by an index of numbers of operatives, from col. 12 of Table III. These numbers are for Great Britain alone, whereas the statistics of wool cover the whole United Kingdom. The output entries of 1862, 1867, 1872, &c., have been divided by the entries for occupied numbers in 1861, 1866, 1871, &c., respectively. Mean of 1892, 1897 = 100.

20. *G.B.: output of beer per operative in brewing. Output:* Before 1882 duty was charged on malt, not on beer. From 1882 through 1901 the *Annual Reports of the Commissioners of Inland Revenue* give the number of standard barrels charged with duty annually, including beer produced not for sale. For 1902–13 the *17th Abstract of Labour Statistics* (Cd. 7733 of 1915) gives the number of bulk barrels produced annually, exclusive of beer produced not for sale: the latter had been a steadily declining component of total output, and by 1899 amounted to only 0·08 per cent. of it. We have converted bulk barrels to standard. The *number of operatives*, from col. 13 of Table III, is the number of 'brewers and maltsters', and some maltsters may have been working for distillation of spirits. 1890–9 = 100.

21. *G.B.: Rail traffic per person occupied on the railways.* W. Page (ed.), *Commerce and Industry*, ii, Table 66, gives annual figures of the numbers of railway passengers and (from 1871) the tonnage of goods loaded on the railways. We made indexes of these and combined them with weights of 5 and 6—the approximate ratio of the gross revenue from each kind of traffic—to get a combined index of traffic. We

divided this by numbers of persons occupied on the railways (certain occupations excluded) from col. 3 of Table III. 1890–9 = 100.

22. *Real freight rates, inverted: an index of the efficiency of shipping relatively to the efficiency of all other production.* We divided the index of freight rates at p. 187 of C. K. Hobson, *The Export of Capital* (described at ibid., pp. 178–83), by the composite index of prices of final products in col. 1 of the present table; and took the reciprocal of the quotient. 1890–9 = 100.

23. *G.B.: Drescher's index of agricultural output.* From *Weltwirtschaftliches Archiv*, xli, 1935. 1890–9 = 100.

24. *G.B.: output per person occupied in agriculture.* Series 23 above divided by numbers occupied, from col. 2 of Table III. 1890–9 = 100.

TABLE III

*G.B. (except Series 1): Numbers of Occupied Persons (Series 1–3) or Operatives (Series 4–13) in Whole Economy or in Particular Industries and Groups of Industries, in Census Years, 1861–1911*

| | 1 (000's) | 2 (000's) | 3 | 4 (000's) | 5 | 6 |
|------|---------|---------|---------|-------|-----------|--------|
| 1861 | 11,678 | 1,706 | 60,449 | 2,364 | 282,549 | 31,956 |
| 1871 | 13,064 | 1,477 | 96,700 | 2,647 | 314,636 | 30,018 |
| 1881 | 14,450 | 1,327 | 157,964 | 2,961 | 435,504 | 36,591 |
| 1891 | 16,020 | 1,205 | 213,058 | 3,428 | 591,375 | 21,093 |
| 1901 | 17,740 | 979 | 310,546 | 3,916 | 751,763 | 19,432 |
| 1911 | 19,700 | 1,081 | 357,100 | 4,668 | 1,020,647 | 24,302 |

| | 7 | 8 | 9 | 10 | 11 | 12 | 13 |
|------|--------|---------|---------|---------|---------|---------|--------|
| 1861 | 51,175 | 149,882 | .. | 52,933 | 524,008 | 241,431 | 32,742 |
| 1871 | 28,878 | 216,353 | .. | 61,421 | 510,411 | 266,613 | 38,674 |
| 1881 | 28,246 | 239,741 | 423,359 | 72,572 | 526,973 | 252,278 | 36,091 |
| 1891 | 18,283 | 242,458 | 519,317 | 94,036 | 572,531 | 275,252 | 38,392 |
| 1901 | 12,304 | 264,611 | 680,165 | 121,293 | 543,936 | 234,646 | 40,908 |
| 1911 | 10,903 | 310,989 | 766,917 | 155,643 | 620,072 | 247,965 | 40,623 |

Series 1–3 contain as far as possible all occupied persons, whatever their grade or function, within the bounds stated. The remaining series 4–13 contain for the most part only operatives, as distinct from clerical, administrative, managerial, and technical employees, who are generally classified 'horizontally' by occupation rather than according to the 'vertical' divisions of industry.

Except for series 1, the coverage is of Great Britain throughout.

We have made all estimates for intercensal years by linear interpolation.

*Series 1–3*

The figures of numbers occupied are derived as follows:

1. *Total occupied population of U.K.* Bowley, *Wages and Income in the U.K.*, p. 91, gives estimates for census years 1881–1911. For 1860–80 we used the estimates described at p. 266 of Phelps Brown and Hopkins, 'Wage-Rates in Five Countries, 1860–1939', in *Oxford Economic Papers*, June 1950.

2. *Numbers occupied in agriculture.* Occupational classification of the Census of 1911, Order VII, sub-orders 117–23, 128, 129: see *Census of England and Wales*,

*1911*, vol. x, *Occupations and Industries*, Part I (Cd. 7018 of 1914), Table 26, p. 543. We excluded farmers' relatives throughout.

3. *Numbers occupied on railways, certain occupations excluded.* Occupational classification as in source of (2) above, VI, 78–83, 86, 87. Since reclassification sharply raised the recorded numbers of platelayers, gangers, and packers, and of railway labourers, in 1901, we excluded them throughout.

*Series 4–13*

In estimating the numbers of operatives, we tried to follow the occupational classification of England and Wales in 1911 as closely as possible in Scotland and in other census years. *Census of England and Wales, 1911*, vol. x, *Occupations and Industries*, Part I (Cd. 7018 of 1914), Table 26, p. 540, gives a synoptic statement of the occupational distribution in England and Wales in the censuses of 1881–1911 according to the classification of 1911; the main changes of classification in this period are discussed in Table 25 of the same volume. A main difficulty in securing continuous series is the decrease in the numbers left in general classes and not assigned to particular industries: a note to Table 26 states that 'the fact that a considerable number of persons, who in 1881 and 1891 would have been returned under the indefinite term of "Labourer", "Mechanic", &c., were in 1901 and 1911 described more precisely, affects not only the numbers under such indefinite headings but also those under some definite headings, whilst the addition to the 1911 Schedule of a column for "Industry or Service" has had the further effect of causing transfer between some of the definite headings'. We have tried to maintain a consistent grouping through a number of censuses, but there will have been changes in the actual coverage underlying our constant or equivalent descriptions. Some of these shifts will cancel each other out when the series are combined to form an aggregate for the area of Hoffmann's index, but there is also likely to be a pervasive upward bias in the totals of 1901 and 1911, relatively to those of earlier years, because in 1901 and 1911 a higher proportion of all operatives were ascribed to particular industries.

In deciding what groups to include, we have assumed that any index of production will be weighted towards basic materials and away from highly fabricated products, and in doubtful cases we have therefore generally included the jobs in which 'value added' is low relatively to material content, and excluded those in which it is high— e.g. in the manufacture of iron and steel ware we have included the makers of nails, nuts and bolts, and anchors, but excluded gunsmiths and swordsmiths and watch-makers.

All references in the following descriptions of series are to Table 26, vol x, in *Census of England and Wales, 1911*. The occupational groups cited from this source under each head have been followed as closely as possible in the tables for Scotland.

4. *No. of operatives in industries whose outputs are comprised in Hoffmann's index.* The following occupational groups are comprised: 131–3, 138, 155–6, 158, 161–4, 166–7, 168, 169, 170, 171–2, 173–4, 175–6, 177, 178, 180–3, 184–6, 187, 200, 206–9, 213–19, 220, 230–6, 266–8, 274, 275–9, 281–2, 291–8, 299–301, 303–4, 305–6, 309–12, 316, 335–41, 342, 343–8, 349–52, 353–9, 361–9, 370–3, 400–19 less dealers, 420–1, 422–3, 447. We include no numbers of operatives corresponding with the following components of Hoffmann's index: mining other than coal- and iron-mining; tin; tramcars and automobiles. In other groups the correspondence is not always exact.

5. *No. of operatives in coal-mining.* IX. 131–3. Not the same as series 9 of Table II, for the reasons stated there.

6. *No. of operatives in iron-mining.* IX. 138. There is an abrupt fall in the numbers recorded in Scotland between 1881 and 1891.

7. *No. of miners in copper, lead, and tin mines.* IX. 139, 140, 141.

8. *No. of operatives producing or working up iron and steel in furnaces, rolling mills, foundries, and some manufacturing processes.* We have had to take the following

group of operatives, which contains not a few engaged in working up metal, but is the most basic group we can follow in a consistent form through the earlier years, in which, for example, we cannot separate the bedstead makers: X. 155, pig-iron manufacture (blast furnaces); 156, puddling furnaces, iron and steel rolling mills; 157, tube manufacture; 158, steel-manufacture, smelting, pounding; 168, ironfounders; 198, stove, grate, range, fire-iron makers; 199, bedstead makers, iron or brass; 211, iron workers (undefined).

9. *No. of operatives manufacturing iron and steel goods, machinery, and tools.* The following series: X. 160, 205, tinplate manufacture, also tinplate goods; 166, patternmakers; 167, millwrights; 170, blacksmiths; 171, erectors, fitters, turners, and 172, their labourers; 175, metal machinists; 177, boilermakers; 176, 178, 179, labourers in engineering; 184, toolmakers; 185, filemakers; 186, sawmakers; 195, nail manufacture; 196, bolts, nuts, screws; 197, anchor, chain manufacture. We have not found it possible to follow a consistent classification back of 1881.

10. *No. of operatives in shipbuilding.* X. 213–19. A few ships' chandlers are included through 1891.

11. *No. of operatives in cotton mills.* XVIII. 335–41. Through 1861–91, numbers in cotton thread manufacture are given separately, and we have included them in our total.

12. *No. of operatives in woollen and worsted mills.* XVIII. 343–8. We excluded dealers, knitters, and carpetmakers.

13. *No. of operatives in brewing and malting.* XX. 422–3.


# APPENDIX C

## Capital in the U.K., 1870–1914

### 1. *Previous estimates*

Two methods of estimating the total stock of capital are surveyed in c. xi of J. C. Stamp, *British Incomes and Property*.

The first, in Giffen's words, is 'to take the income returned for assessment to the Income Tax, capitalise the different portions of that income derived from capital—land, houses, and so on,—at so many years' purchase, and then make an estimate for other property in the country where the income was not yet within the sweep of the Income Tax net' (R. Giffen, *The Growth of Capital*, 1889, p. 6). This method was first used by Newmarch (*The Economist*, 1863, pp. 1381 and 1411; *J.R.S.S.* xli, pt. ii, June 1878, 'On the Progress of the Foreign Trade of the United Kingdom'). Sir R. Giffen made estimates for 1865, 1875, 1885 (op. cit., p. 43), which were continued for 1895, 1905, and 1909 in *The Economist*, Nov. 1911, p. 1087. Estimates for about 1914 were made by E. Crammond ('The Economic Relations of the British and German Empires', *J.R.S.S.* lxxvii, 1914, p. 803) and J. C. Stamp (*British Incomes and Property*, 1920, p. 404). These estimates were reviewed and adjusted by P. H. Douglas ('An Estimate of the Growth of Capital in the U.K., 1865–1909', *Journal of Economic and Business History*, ii. 4, Aug. 1930), but Douglas was working without the Inland Revenue reports, and his results differ considerably from those we give in para. 7 below.

The second method is to take the valuation for purposes of death duties of property annually passing at death, and raise this by 'the multiplier' which gives the ratio of all property of a given kind in existence in a given year to that part of it which passes at death during the year. This method was used by B. Mallett and H. C. Strutt (B. Mallett, 'A Method of estimating Capital Wealth from the Estate Duty Statistics', *J.R.S.S.* lxxi, 1908, p. 65; B. Mallett and H. C. Strutt, 'The Multiplier and Capital Wealth, *J.R.S.S.* lxxviii, 1915, p. 555). Its difficulty is the determination of 'the multiplier'.

Estimates of the annual accumulation of capital were made by A. K. Cairncross in his unpublished Ph.D. thesis, 1936, 'British Home and Foreign Investment, 1870–1913' (Cambridge University Library). The outcome is presented, after further adjustment for maintenance, depreciation, and obsolescence, in Tables III and IV of J. H. Lenfant, 'Great Britain's Capital Formation, 1865–1914', *Economica*, xviii. 70, May 1951. We have used Cairncross's materials to attempt a somewhat broader estimate, which is adjusted to the coverage of Stamp's estimate of the stock of capital, and should therefore yield by cumulation estimates of the change in the stock of capital comparable with those implicit in the direct estimates of that stock.

## 2. *Present method*

We start from Stamp's estimate for 1914, which we believe to be the most reliable of the above estimates—he himself gives it a 'range of doubt' of $\pm 13$ per cent. We select those elements which make up the total current value of all buildings, equipment, and stocks, except farmers' capital, within the U.K. We then decumulate this total by the estimated amounts of net investment in the preceding years, when these amounts are expressed in £s of the same purchasing power over investment goods as those in which Stamp's estimate is expressed. The result is an annual series for the real stock of capital, expressed in £s of constant purchasing power.

Stamp's estimate is headed '(1914 Figures)', but it is based on the income-tax returns for the financial year ending with March 1914, and these returns are of incomes received in various periods. The Schedule D returns, which provide most of our information, are of the income of the preceding year (railways, ironworks, gasworks, waterworks, canals, and other concerns), or the average of the preceding three years (businesses not otherwise detailed, the biggest category), or the average of the preceding five years (mines). Considering these things, and the times of year to which businesses make up their accounts, Stamp concluded that 'the assessed profits for the year ending 5th April, 1909, may be taken to be the actual profits for the year to the beginning of June, 1907, in times of normal and regular increase' (*British Incomes and Property*, p. 178). We have also the Schedule A returns for Houses, and these relate to the financial year in which they are reported. The weighted average centres upon the end of August 1907. But since our estimates of annual investment are for calendar years, it is convenient to be able to treat the estimates of capital stock as belonging to the end of the year, and no great error is involved if we treat the capitalization of the 1908–9 assessments as centring on the end of December 1907; and so on. So Stamp's capitalization of '1914 Figures' will be taken to centre on the end of December 1912.

We now have to form estimates of annual net investment within our selected coverage, and deduct them successively from the estimated capital stock in December 1912. We first make estimates of annual net investment, in current £s, then apply an index of the price level of investment goods to reduce them to £s of purchasing power over investment goods as at December 1912. Then by successive subtraction we obtain estimates of the total capital stock at December 1911, December 1910, and so on, and these being expressed in £s of constant purchasing power form an index of the physical stock of capital.

**3.** *Estimate of capital in U.K. at December 1912*

We have taken the following items from Stamp, *British Incomes and Property*, p. 404.

|  | £mn. |
|---|---|
| (2) Houses, &c. . . . . . . . . . . | 3,330 |
| (6) Railways in the U.K. . . . . . . . . | 1,143 |
| (8) Coal and other mines . . . . . . . . | 179 |
| (9) Ironworks . . . . . . . . . . | 37 |
| (10) Gasworks . . . . . . . . . . | 182 |
| (11) Waterworks, canals, and other concerns (Schedule A) . . | 278 |
| (15) Businesses not otherwise detailed . . . . . . | 2,770 |
| (17) Income of non-income-tax paying classes derived from capital . | 200 |
|  | £8,119 |

We have left out (4) Farmers' capital: this ought to be included, but we have found no means of estimating the year-to-year changes in it. Stamp puts it at £mn.340, or about 4 per cent. of the total included. The other items left out are: land (1) and (3); the capitalized value of certain transfer incomes (5), and probably (14) for the most part; overseas property (7), (12), (13), (14); movable property not yielding income (furniture, &c.) (18); non-revenue yielding property of government (19).

**4.** *Construction of estimates of annual net home investment in current £s*

i. We adjusted Cairncross's estimate of total gross investment, new construction only, in 1907, to the coverage of the items taken from Stamp in para. 3 above (A. K. Cairncross, 'British Home and Foreign Investment, 1870–1913', Ph.D. thesis, 1936, in Cambridge University Library; figures reproduced in J. H. Lenfant, 'British Capital Export 1900–13', Ph.D. thesis in University of London Library). This meant removing from Cairncross's total the following elements which have no counterpart in our list:

Investment in non-revenue yielding property of Local Authorities.
Naval shipbuilding.
That part of building and contracting (construction of roads and non-revenue earning properties of government) which does not add to the income-yielding properties capitalized by Stamp.

The schedule of investment in 1907 thus adapted from Cairncross is, in current £mn.:

|  | Gross investment | New construction | Repair |
|---|---|---|---|
| 1. Houses . . . . . | 76·0 | 45·0 | 31·0 |
| 2. Other building and contracting . | 11·0 | 7·0 | 4·0 |
| 3. Local Authorities' revenue-yielding properties . . . . | 11·0 | 3·5 | 7·4 |
| 4. Public utilities . . . . | 10·4 | 3·4 | 7·1 |
| 5. Engineering, general . . . | 55·5 | 32·8 | 22·7 |
| 6. Engineering, electrical . . . | 8·0 | 7·7 | 0·3 |
| 7. Shipbuilding, mercantile . . | 27·4 | 19·0 | 8·4 |
| 8. Railways . . . . . | 35·8 | 9·8 | 26·0 |
| 9. Miscellaneous . . . . | 16·5 | 13·7 | 2·8 |
| TOTAL . . . . . | 251·6 | 141·9 | 109·7 |

ii. We obtained annual estimates for the above nine components of new construction, as follows:

1. *Houses*. Cairncross's series for 'value of new building'.

2. *Other building and contracting*: we assumed this to bear the same ratio to 'value of new building' throughout as in 1907, viz. 7:45 (see above schedule).

3. *Local Authorities' revenue-yielding properties*. We calculated the ratio in 1907 of Local Authorities' expenditure out of loans on gasworks, electric lighting, harbours, docks, &c., tramways and light railways, and waterworks, to their total loans raised. We applied this ratio to the annual total of loans raised, given in the *Statistical Abstract*, so as to get a series for gross investment. We applied to this the ratio of new construction to gross investment in 1907, viz. 3·5:11 (see above schedule), so as to get a series for new construction.

4. *Public utilities* we included, for lack of separate evidence, under 9, *Miscellaneous*.

5. *Engineering, general*. Cairncross's annual 'value of home consumption of machinery', multiplied by the ratio of new construction to gross investment in 1907, viz. 32·8:55·5 (see above schedule).

6. *Engineering, electrical*. In 1907 new construction here was about 24 per cent. of that in general engineering (see above schedule). We have assumed that the corresponding percentage began as 1 per cent. in 1884 and rose by annual steps of one percentage point to the 24 per cent. of 1907, continuing by the same steps to 31 per cent. in 1914. (The gross output of electrical engineering, which was less than one-sixth of that of general engineering in the Census of 1907, had become nearly one-half of it in the Census of 1924.)

7. *Shipbuilding, mercantile*. Cairncross's 'value of new mercantile construction' annually.

8. *Railways*. Cairncross's 'estimated capital expenditure of all British railway companies' annually.

9. *Miscellaneous*, with which we combine 4, *Public utilities*. In 1907 these two together made up £mn.17·1 against £mn.124·8 as the sum of the other items. We applied this ratio throughout.

iii. The above procedure gave us annual estimates of total new construction, and to reduce these to net investment we deducted depreciation (as an item to be set off against new construction, and not made good by the repair work which is separately accounted for in the Schedule in (i)). We have three estimates of depreciation in 1907. In the 1907 Census of Production Flux estimated depreciation and maintenance of 'plant' at £mn.175; the repairs actually reported in the Census account for £mn.125 of this, and leave £mn.50 for depreciation. Colin Clark, in his *National Income and Outlay*, put depreciation and maintenance at £mn.139 for a smaller coverage in 1907, and if raised proportionally this gives £mn.157 to compare with Flux's £mn.175, and leaves £mn.32 for depreciation alone. Cairncross takes the Schedule D allowance of £mn.20 for depreciation of machinery, plant, and ships, adds £mn.9 for houses (reckoned at ½ per cent. of capital value) and £mn.2 for public buildings, hospitals, &c.—a total of £mn.31, which he thinks may be £mn.10 too small, for the Schedule D allowances were 'very moderate'. But Stamp (op. cit., pp. 196–8) points out that any inadequacy of annual allowances under Schedule D was made up in a lump allowance when equipment was actually replaced, so that in a large aggregate of equipment the total allowed each year would be accurate enough. The only omission would be so much residual value of scrapped equipment as could not be claimed because that equipment was not replaced, and he thinks an addition of 3 per cent. would cover this. We have therefore taken an estimate of £mn.32. To obtain corresponding estimates for years other than 1907, we have assumed that the trend of depreciation was that of national income, but that the rate of replacement year by year varied about that trend proportionally to the variations of 'new construction' about its trend. We took a 9 years' moving average of 'new construction', expressed the actual values as relatives thereto, applied these relatives to the 9 years' moving average of national income, and used the resultant series as an index-number to extrapolate the £mn.32 of 1907.

iv. We have to add changes in stocks. We assumed that the value of stocks lies around 40 per cent. of national income (Keynes, *Treatise on Money*, ii, p. 108, suggests 40 to 50 per cent.; C. Clark's estimates for 1931–4, in *National Income and Outlay*, p. 296, imply 35 to 42 per cent.; A. P. Zentler's estimate, in *Economica*, xvii. 68, Nov. 1950, implies 45 per cent. in 1948). Deviations from a given relation will occur because (a) stocks are kept down when prices are falling, and conversely; (b) stocks rise or fall inadvertently when a change in prices sets in. Some allowance is made for movements under (a) if we take not the value of the physical change in stocks but the change in the value of stocks; and for movements under (b), if we put in a lag, e.g. enter as the change in stocks during a calendar year the change which prima facie belongs to the 12 months ended with June of that year. Something of both allowances is implicit in taking as the net investment in stocks in, say, 1910, 40 per cent. of the excess of the national income of 1910, in current £s, over that of 1909, which we have done throughout, using A. R. Prest's series for national income (*E.J.*, Mar. 1948).

5. *Conversion of annual net home investment from current £s to December 1912 £s.*

We used an index of the prices of investment goods, constructed from the following price series, whose weights we chose as roughly proportional to the corresponding components of investment, on the average of the period.

(a) Index of prices of finished export goods (as an index of the prices of finished goods generally), from W. Schlote, *Entwicklung und Strukturwandlungen des englischen Außenhandels von 1700 bis zup Gegenwart*, p. 180, col. 7. Weight 3.

(b) Sauerbeck's index of raw material prices (taken from Layton and Crowther, *Introduction to the Study of Prices* (1938), pp. 238–9). Weight 3.

(c) G. T. Jones's index of building costs, in *Increasing Returns*, 1933, p. 268. Weight 3.

(d) Index of prices of iron and steel exports, in T. H. Burnham and G. O. Hoskins, *Iron and Steel in Britain, 1870–1930*, p. 276. Weight 1.

The resultant annual series of net investment in £s of 1912 purchasing power is illustrated in Fig. 8 of the main text.

6. *Estimates of the stock of capital in the U.K., annually, in December 1912 £s.*

We obtained these by successive subtraction of the annual investment series, converted as in para. 5, from the estimates of the total stock of capital in December 1912, drawn from Stamp in para. 3. The result is given in Table IV, together with the same series expressed per head of the occupied population of the U.K.

TABLE IV

*Estimates of Investment and its Components, and of Capital (except Land and Farmers' Capital) in the U.K. annually, 1870–1914*

Col.

1. Index of price-level of capital goods, av. 1912/13 (taken as equivalent to December 1912) = 100.

2. New construction of houses, in current £s.

3. Change in stocks, in current £s.

4. New construction of equipment other than houses, in current £s.

5. Depreciation, to be offset against new construction to leave net investment, in current £s.

6. Total net investment, including houses, in current £s (sum of cols. 2, 3, 4, less col. 5).

7. Total net investment, excluding houses, in current £s (sum of cols. 3, 4, less that part of col. 5 which does not relate to col. 2).
8. Total net investment, including houses, in 1912/13 £s (col. 6 adjusted by col. 1).
9. Total net investment, excluding houses, in 1912/13 £s (col. 7 adjusted by col. 1).
10. Total capital stock, including houses, in 1912/13 £s (total of £mn.8,119 in December 1912 decumulated by col. 8).
11. Total capital stock, excluding houses, in 1912/13 £s (total of £mn.4,789 in December 1912 decumulated by col. 9).
12. Capital stock, including houses, per head of the occupied population, in 1912/13 £s (col. 10 divided by occupied population).
13. Capital stock, excluding houses, per head of the occupied population, in 1912/13 £s (col. 11 divided by occupied population).
14. Capital stock, including houses, obtained by capitalizing estimated current profits and adding value of houses, in 1912/13 £s.

| | 1 | 2 £mn. | 3 £mn. | 4 £mn. | 5 £mn. | 6 £mn. | 7 £mn. | 8 £mn. | 9 £mn. | 10 £mn. | 11 £mn. | 12 £ | 13 £ | 14 £mn. |
|---|---|---|---|---|---|---|---|---|---|---|---|---|---|---|
| Dec. | | | | | | | | | | | | | | |
| 1870 | 104 | 28 | .. | 42 | 17 | .. | .. | .. | .. | 3,082 | 1,692 | 239 | 131 | 2,984 |
| 1871 | 105 | 25 | +23 | 53 | 18 | 83 | 58 | 79 | 55 | 3,161 | 1,747 | 242 | 134 | 3,026 |
| 1872 | 115 | 30 | +22 | 58 | 19 | 91 | 66 | 79 | 58 | 3,240 | 1,805 | 245 | 137 | 2,916 |
| 1873 | 120 | 35 | +37 | 61 | 20 | 113 | 83 | 94 | 70 | 3,334 | 1,874 | 250 | 141 | 3,239 |
| 1874 | 112 | 40 | .. | 68 | 20 | 87 | 53 | 78 | 47 | 3,411 | 1,922 | 253 | 143 | 3,509 |
| 1875 | 106 | 47 | −19 | 61 | 20 | 69 | 27 | 65 | 26 | 3,476 | 1,947 | 255 | 143 | 3,425 |
| 1876 | 102 | 58 | +1 | 63 | 22 | 100 | 48 | 98 | 47 | 3,574 | 1,994 | 260 | 145 | 3,555 |
| 1877 | 99 | 66 | +2 | 66 | 24 | 111 | 51 | 112 | 51 | 3,686 | 2,046 | 265 | 147 | 3,606 |
| 1878 | 95 | 56 | −9 | 59 | 21 | 86 | 35 | 91 | 37 | 3,776 | 2,083 | 269 | 148 | 3,928 |
| 1879 | 91 | 42 | −20 | 48 | 16 | 53 | 16 | 58 | 17 | 3,834 | 2,100 | 271 | 148 | 3,646 |
| 1880 | 95 | 48 | +1 | 56 | 19 | 86 | 44 | 91 | 46 | 3,925 | 2,146 | 274 | 150 | 3,924 |
| 1881 | 91 | 41 | +16 | 60 | 20 | 98 | 62 | 107 | 68 | 4,032 | 2,214 | 279 | 153 | 4,185 |
| 1882 | 91 | 42 | +17 | 66 | 23 | 103 | 67 | 113 | 74 | 4,145 | 2,288 | 284 | 157 | 4,264 |
| 1883 | 88 | 42 | +11 | 61 | 23 | 92 | 56 | 104 | 64 | 4,249 | 2,352 | 288 | 159 | 4,495 |
| 1884 | 86 | 37 | −19 | 50 | 20 | 48 | 17 | 56 | 20 | 4,305 | 2,372 | 289 | 159 | 4,466 |
| 1885 | 84 | 36 | −7 | 43 | 19 | 53 | 23 | 63 | 27 | 4,368 | 2,399 | 290 | 159 | 4,559 |
| 1886 | 79 | 36 | +7 | 37 | 18 | 62 | 31 | 79 | 40 | 4,447 | 2,438 | 292 | 160 | 4,695 |
| 1887 | 79 | 35 | +12 | 36 | 18 | 65 | 35 | 83 | 44 | 4,529 | 2,483 | 294 | 161 | 4,667 |
| 1888 | 80 | 36 | +33 | 46 | 21 | 94 | 64 | 118 | 80 | 4,647 | 2,562 | 299 | 165 | 4,945 |
| 1889 | 82 | 40 | +35 | 59 | 26 | 108 | 75 | 131 | 92 | 4,778 | 2,654 | 304 | 169 | 5,106 |
| 1890 | 85 | 38 | +26 | 59 | 26 | 98 | 67 | 115 | 79 | 4,893 | 2,733 | 309 | 172 | 5,277 |
| 1891 | 84 | 39 | −5 | 57 | 25 | 66 | 34 | 78 | 40 | 4,972 | 2,773 | 310 | 173 | 5,246 |
| 1892 | 80 | 35 | −10 | 59 | 24 | 60 | 32 | 76 | 41 | 5,047 | 2,814 | 312 | 174 | 5,206 |
| 1893 | 78 | 36 | −12 | 52 | 22 | 54 | 24 | 69 | 31 | 5,116 | 2,845 | 313 | 174 | 5,120 |
| 1894 | 75 | 38 | +19 | 59 | 23 | 93 | 61 | 124 | 81 | 5,240 | 2,926 | 317 | 177 | 5,650 |
| 1895 | 74 | 46 | +26 | 60 | 24 | 109 | 69 | 147 | 93 | 5,387 | 3,019 | 322 | 181 | 6,081 |
| 1896 | 75 | 55 | +11 | 66 | 25 | 107 | 59 | 143 | 79 | 5,530 | 3,098 | 328 | 184 | 6,020 |
| 1897 | 75 | 47 | +20 | 75 | 24 | 117 | 77 | 156 | 102 | 5,685 | 3,200 | 333 | 188 | 6,339 |
| 1898 | 76 | 63 | +33 | 89 | 29 | 156 | 101 | 205 | 133 | 5,890 | 3,333 | 342 | 194 | 6,533 |
| 1899 | 81 | 78 | +28 | 107 | 35 | 178 | 110 | 220 | 136 | 6,110 | 3,469 | 351 | 199 | 6,662 |
| 1900 | 90 | 72 | +34 | 120 | 35 | 190 | 128 | 211 | 142 | 6,321 | 3,611 | 360 | 206 | 6,860 |
| 1901 | 88 | 68 | −13 | 112 | 32 | 135 | 76 | 153 | 86 | 6,475 | 3,698 | 365 | 209 | 6,698 |
| 1902 | 86 | 59 | +6 | 107 | 30 | 142 | 92 | 165 | 107 | 6,640 | 3,804 | 370 | 212 | 6,884 |
| 1903 | 87 | 63 | −10 | 106 | 31 | 128 | 74 | 147 | 85 | 6,787 | 3,889 | 374 | 215 | 6,642 |
| 1904 | 89 | 71 | +8 | 103 | 34 | 149 | 87 | 167 | 98 | 6,954 | 3,987 | 379 | 218 | 6,923 |
| 1905 | 90 | 81 | +30 | 105 | 38 | 179 | 109 | 198 | 121 | 7,152 | 4,107 | 386 | 222 | 7,221 |
| 1906 | 93 | 63 | +48 | 105 | 36 | 181 | 128 | 194 | 137 | 7,346 | 4,245 | 392 | 227 | 7,555 |
| 1907 | 97 | 52 | +38 | 90 | 32 | 149 | 105 | 153 | 109 | 7,500 | 4,353 | 397 | 230 | 7,824 |
| 1908 | 93 | 59 | −44 | 77 | 33 | 60 | 10 | 65 | 11 | 7,564 | 4,364 | 396 | 228 | 7,334 |
| 1909 | 92 | 54 | +19 | 87 | 35 | 124 | 81 | 135 | 88 | 7,699 | 4,452 | 399 | 231 | 7,491 |
| 1910 | 93 | 46 | +36 | 87 | 35 | 135 | 99 | 145 | 106 | 7,844 | 4,558 | 402 | 234 | 7,706 |
| 1911 | 95 | 34 | +31 | 96 | 38 | 122 | 99 | 128 | 104 | 7,972 | 4,662 | 405 | 237 | 7,749 |
| 1912 | 98 | 31 | +51 | 103 | 41 | 144 | 125 | 147 | 127 | 8,119 | 4,789 | 408 | 241 | 8,119 |
| 1913 | .. | 36 | +40 | 131 | 42 | 165 | 140 | .. | .. | .. | .. | .. | .. | .. |
| 1914 | .. | 42 | −41 | 118 | 41 | 79 | 48 | .. | .. | .. | .. | .. | .. |

### 7. *Comparison with estimates made by capitalizing incomes*

The three main sources of capitalization estimates listed in para. 1 above—Giffen, *The Economist*, and Stamp—differ in some matters of procedure. A first step is to obtain estimates by the same procedure throughout, and we have adopted Stamp's. The results are shown in Table V, the notes to which describe the working. The same table records the original estimates for comparison; the main difference between these and our adjusted estimates lies in the assumptions on which the profits of 'Businesses not otherwise detailed' are capitalized—a big component, and a very uncertain one. Throughout our period the time-lag in the reporting of income was as we have described it in para. 2 above, so that the estimate which *The Economist* gave for 1895, for example, really centres upon December 1893; but in the headings of Table V we have retained the same dates as in the original estimates.

TABLE V

*Estimates of Total Capital, in Certain Categories, within the United Kingdom, made from the Original Income-Tax Returns, in the Common Form of Stamp's Estimate from the 1914 Figures*

£mn. throughout

| Nominal year . . . . . | 1875 | 1885 | 1895 | 1905 | 1909 | 1914 |
|---|---|---|---|---|---|---|
| 1. Houses, &c. . . . . | 1,378 | 1,870 | 2,208 | 2,935 | 3,155 | 3,330 |
| 2. Railways in the U.K. . . . | 655 | 832 | 859 | 1,030 | 1,084 | 1,143 |
| 3. Coal and other mines . . . | 129 | 69 | 116 | 194 | 152 | 179 |
| 4. Ironworks . . . . . | 65 | 20 | 17 | 28 | 46 | 37 |
| 5. Gasworks . . . . . | 53 | 101 | 102 | 152 | 157 | 182 |
| 6. Waterworks, canals, and other concerns . . . . . | 97 | 179 | 178 | 242 | 263 | 278 |
| 7. Businesses not otherwise detailed . | 956 | 1,070 | 1,256 | 2,028 | 2,410 | 2,770 |
| 8. Income of non-income-tax paying class derived from capital. . | 90 | 95 | 100 | 160 | 175 | 200 |
| 9. TOTAL . . . . . | 3,423 | 4,236 | 4,836 | 6,769 | 7,442 | 8,119 |
| 10. Corresponding estimates from Giffen (1875, 85), *The Economist* (1895–1909), Stamp (1914) . | 3,505 | 4,760 | 5,585 | 7,520 | 8,086 | 8,119 |

*Notes to Table V*

1. *Houses, &c.* Stamp took the mean of two figures—14 years' purchase of an adjusted gross annual value, and 17·4 years' purchase of the net annual value. His resultant estimate is equivalent to 14·56 years' purchase of the unadjusted gross value, and we have applied this multiplier to the gross values throughout.
2. *Railways in the U.K.* 25 years' purchase of Schedule D gross assessments.
3. *Coal and other mines.* Stamp took 9½ years' purchase after deducting wear and tear allowance; this is equivalent to 9·13 years' purchase of the gross assessment, which has been adopted here in the absence of knowledge of the relevant allowances.
4. *Ironworks.* 9 years' purchase of gross assessment.
5. *Gasworks.* 20 years' purchase of gross assessment.
6. *Waterworks, canals, and other concerns.* 20 years' purchase of gross assessment.
7. *Businesses not otherwise detailed.* These are made up of 'public companies' and 'local authorities' on the one hand, and 'trades and professions' or 'persons and firms' on the other. Stamp took the mean of the results of Giffen's method and Chiozza Money's method. *Giffen's method* was: profits of 'public companies' at 15 years' purchase (20 in 1885); profits of 'trades and professions', one-fifth of total income, at 15 years' purchase. *Money's method* was: all profits together, gross profits minus 'employments', 'wear and tear', and 'overcharges' plus allowance for evasion: one-half at 10 years' purchase. The two methods give very similar results for earlier years, but Giffen's total rises much more than Money's as a greater proportion of profits comes to appear under 'public companies'. Stamp concluded, 'On the whole I am of opinion that the truth is certainly between the two extremes or methods' (*British Incomes and Property*, p. 395), and he split the difference. We have done the same throughout.

8. *Income of non-income-tax paying class derived from capital.* Stamp's estimate of £mn.200, assumed to vary in rough proportion to total income in our included categories under Schedule D.

The totals obtained in Table V are in current £s—in £s of capitalized current income flows. To reduce them to terms of constant purchasing power we should use a general price index, rather than an index of the prices of capital goods, because such an index is more appropriate to the flow of money incomes from which they are derived. We have therefore applied our index of prices of final products, from Table II, col. 1, expressed as a relative to the base December 1912 (taken as given by the mean of 1912 and 1913). The result is shown in row 2 of Table VI for comparison with our estimates by decumulation (row 1).

TABLE VI

*Estimates of Total Capital, in Certain Categories, within the United Kingdom; in £s of the Purchasing Power of 1912/13*

| Estimate centred on 31 December | 1873 | 1883 | 1893 | 1903 | 1907 | 1912 |
|---|---|---|---|---|---|---|
| 1. Using annual investment | 3,334 | 4,249 | 5,116 | 6,787 | 7,500 | 8,119 |
| 2. Capitalizing income-tax returns | 2,956 | 4,506 | 5,799 | 7,597 | 7,934 | 8,119 |
| 3. Capitalizing estimated total current home-produced profits and adding value of houses. | 3,239 | 4,495 | 5,120 | 6,642 | 7,824 | 8,119 |

Row 3, Table VI, shows another check, though this, like row 2, is based ultimately on the income-tax returns. In the appendix to their paper 'The Share of Wages in National Income' (*Economic Journal*, June 1952), Phelps Brown and Hart have used A. R. Prest's 'unscrambling' of the profit returns to make estimates of current home-produced profits, exclusive of rents. The estimate for 1912 was £mn.692, and the estimate from Stamp, centred on December 1912, was of a capital stock, excluding houses, of £mn.4,789. This represents 6·92 years' purchase in the aggregate of the £mn.692 profits. We have applied this multiplier to the whole run of estimated current home-produced profits. To the resulting capitalizations we have added annual estimates of the capital values of houses, made by capitalizing at 14·56 years' purchase (see note to Table V, row 1) the annual values of houses under Schedule A (Stamp, *British Incomes and Property*, p. 50) after smoothing out the effects of reassessment by Stamp's graphical method (ibid., p. 36a). We have then reduced the totals to terms of constant purchasing power by applying as before our index of prices of final products, based on 1912/13. The resultant series is given in Table IV, col. 14.

This series, together with our estimates from annual investment, and the estimates by capitalization in row 2 of Table VI, are shown in Fig. 8 in the main text.

# 8

# Economic Growth and the Price Level

1.0. THE object of this paper is to account for the alternating phases, of twenty to thirty years in length, apparent in the course of economic growth, and particularly to offer an explanation of the associated movements of prices, as these things have presented themselves in the United Kingdom. In 1930 Kuznets [1] named them "secondary secular movements," and summarised earlier discussion. Since then, they have been further studied by Arthur Burns,[2] Kuznets himself,[3] Rostow [4] and Brinley Thomas.[5] In the United Kingdom they present the following pattern.

1.1. Their best-known manifestation is the rise and fall of *the wholesale price level* (Fig. 1(*a*)) by whose turning-points, indeed, the successive phases are usually marked off.[6]

1.2. *The long-term rate of interest*, as shown by the yield of Consols (Fig. 1(*a*)), has moved in strikingly close sympathy with the wholesale price level. This has become known as the Gibson paradox.[7]

1.3. The movements of *the terms of trade* (Fig. 1(*b*)) suggest that the rise and fall of wholesale prices were not simply part of a general movement of all prices, but were connected with shifts in the barter rates of exchange at which primary products were available. In one sense, such rates are displayed by the net barter terms of trade.[8] But since these were so

[1] S. S. Kuznets, *Secular Movements in Production and Prices.*

[2] A. F. Burns, *Production Trends in the U.S. since 1870*, Ch. V.

[3] S. S. Kuznets, *National Income, a Summary of Findings*, II, 5.

[4] W. W. Rostow, *British Economy of the Nineteenth Century*, I, 1; *The Process of Economic Growth*, I, 6. Gayer, Rostow and Schwartz: *The Growth and Fluctuation of the British Economy*, Vol. II, Pt. I, Chs. IV, V.

[5] Brinley Thomas, "Migration and the Rhythm of Economic Growth, 1830–1913," *The Manchester School*, September 1951; *Migration and Economic Growth* (National Institute of Economic and Social Research, 1954).

[6] Rostow (*The Process of Economic Growth*, I, 6), gives the phases of the price level as 1793–1815, rising; 1815–48, falling; 1848–73, rising; 1873–96, falling; 1896–1920, rising; 1920–35, falling; 1935 to the present, rising. But all four series in our present Fig. 1 give reason to believe that the downward trend of 1873–96 actually set in from the end of the American Civil War, the boom following the war of 1870 being only an interruption of a process already well under way; cf. Pedersen and Petersen, *An Analysis of Price Behaviour during the period 1855–1913*, p. 136.

[7] *The Banker's Magazine*, A. H. Gibson, January 1923; E. G. Peake, May 1928. Appendices to the *Report of the Committee on National Debt and Taxation*, 1927: W. H. Coates, Appendix XI, paras. 55, 56. J. M. Keynes, *A Treatise on Money*, Vol. II, Ch. 30 (viii).

[8] W. Schlote, *British Overseas Trade from 1700 to the 1930's*, Table 26; A. H. Imlah, *Journal of Economic History*, X, 2, November 1950; Debenham's estimates, corrected for import contents of exports, at Table 44 of A. K. Cairncross, *Home and Foreign Investment, 1870–1913*.

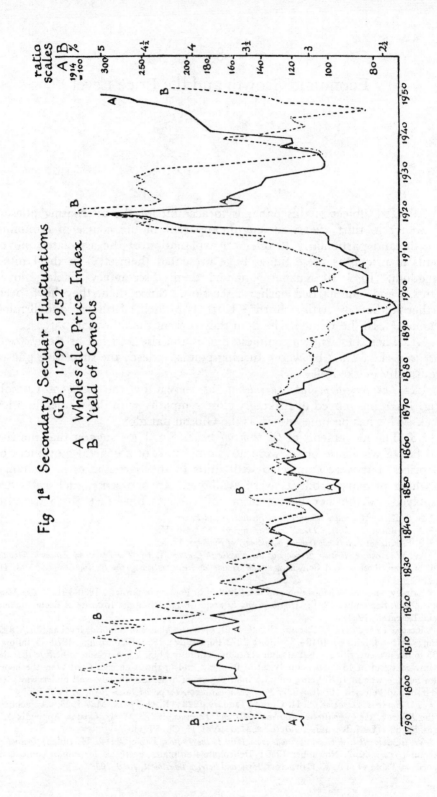

Fig 1ᵃ  Secondary Secular Fluctuations
G.B. 1790 - 1952

A  Wholesale Price Index
B  Yield of Consols

ratio
scales
A   B
1914 %
=100

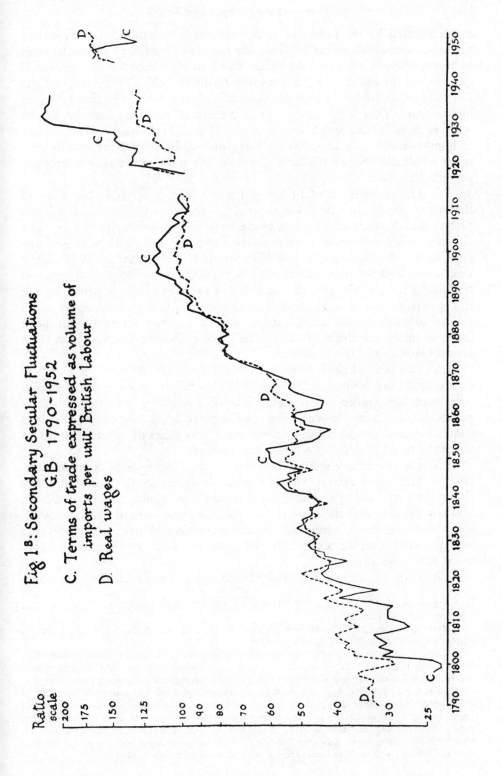

Fig. 1B: Secondary Secular Fluctuations
G.B 1790-1952

C. Terms of trade expressed as volume of
   imports per unit British labour

D. Real wages

much affected by the industrial improvements which raised the amount of manufactures which could be given for the unit of primary products, even at times when this unit could be obtained in exchange for less industrial effort, they do not directly display the terms on which primary products were available to the industrial population. We have therefore taken as our measure of the terms of trade here the rate of exchange between British wage-earners' labour and British imports. Fig. 1(*b*) shows that the quantity of imports obtainable in exchange for a unit of British labour usually rose when wholesale prices were falling, and fell when they were rising, throughout our 150 years.

1.4. The movements of British *real wages* (Fig. 1(*b*)) resemble those of the last series, in that they are generally in phase with those of wholesale prices, usually rising faster when prices were falling, and conversely.[1] The closeness of agreement between our terms of trade and real wages is in one sense only to be expected, in that both are derived from the index of money wage-rates, and the index of import prices which we use to get our terms of trade is highly correlated with the index of the cost of living which we use to get real wages. But in another sense the facts that the cost of living depended so much on the cost of imports, and that money wages did not move so as to offset the drifts of change in those costs, are findings about the actual behaviour of the economy.

1.5. The active British foreign investment of 1878–90 came in a time of markedly falling wholesale prices, and in general the movements of foreign investment were more intermittent than those of prices, and their turning-points did not coincide with those of the price level. None the less, it is significant that British foreign investment[2] was generally highest at times when the trend of wholesale prices was upwards.

1.6. The secondary secular movements are long enough to cover two, three or four trade cycles; but no systematic difference has been found between the cycles that fell within the different movements. In particular, it was not the case that the upward phase of the cycle was stronger, or investment more vigorous, when the secular movement of prices was upward; nor that expansion was cut off by any shortage of money when that movement was downward.[3]

1.7. Thus, in sum, we recognise the existence of secondary secular move-

---

[1] See also A. H. Hansen, " Factors Affecting the Trend of Real Wages," *A.E.R.*, March 1925, with note at p. 294, June 1925.

[2] Rostow, first and third works cited under para. (1.0) above; A. K. Cairncross, *Home and Foreign Investment, 1870–1913*, Table 40, p. 180.

[3] Gayer, Rostow and Schwartz, *The Growth and Fluctuation of the British Economy 1790–1850*, Vol. II, Part I, Ch. II, para. 9, and Ch. IV, para. 5. Between 1850 and 1914, both the trade-union unemployment rate and Beveridge's index of construction and instruments (Beveridge, *Full Employment in a Free Society*, Appendix A) suggest a rather higher level of activity in the phase of rising prices down to 1873 than in the twenty years of generally falling prices which followed, but reveal practically no difference between these twenty years and the next phase of rising prices, here taken as running from 1894 to 1914. Burns and Mitchell, in *Measuring Business Cycles*, Ch. 11, look for differences between American business cycles according to their positions within the long waves of activity, as these have been variously defined, and find hardly any.

ments mainly because four important variables show alternating periods of change lasting twenty to thirty years, and these periods are roughly in phase in all four series. They are the wholesale price level, the long-term rate of interest, the terms of trade and real wages. In one phase wholesale prices will be rising, the long-term rate of interest rising, the terms of trade moving less favourably to the British worker, and real wages improving less rapidly; in the next phase the reverse, in all four respects. We noticed also that though British foreign investment was not regularly aligned with price changes, most of its more active years fell within periods of rising prices.

How can we account for these associated movements?

2.0. The traditional explanation of the movements of the price level was expressed by Marshall when he wrote, in his " Remedies for Fluctuations of General Prices," [1] that " long-period fluctuations . . . are chiefly caused by changes in the amounts of the precious metals relatively to the business which has to be transacted by them, allowance being of course made for changes in the extent to which the precious metals are able at any time to delegate their functions to bank-notes, cheques, bills of exchange, and other substitutes." The movement of the price level, that is to say, depends on the rates of growth not only of (*a*) the quantity of specie, but also of (*b*) the business to be transacted, as measured by the flow of payments reckoned at constant prices, and (*c*) the specie-economising practices. Cassel and Kitchen [2] set out a striking simplification of this explanation. They calculated the constant rate of growth which would have produced the end-to-end change actually recorded in (*a*) over a span of years. They then showed a high correlation between the divergences of the actual growth of (*a*) from this constant rate, and the contemporary movements of the price level, which they treated as uniquely dependent on those divergences; though this could be so only on the implicit assumption that meanwhile all divergences of (*b*) from the same constant rate of growth were exactly offset by changes in (*c*). This procedure has been dealt with thoroughly by Phinney,[3] and can now be regarded only as a statistical curiosity. But the more complex Marshallian formulation holds the field. For our present purpose its essential assumption is that the stock of gold acts on the price level but is not adjustable to it: hence Marshall's inference, in the paper just quoted, that long-period fluctuations in prices " would certainly be much mitigated if each decade's supply of the metallic basis of our currency could be made uniform —*i.e.*, to grow proportionately to our commercial wants." We believe that this view is mistaken. We do not, of course, deny that a change in the metallic basis or in any other form of the medium of exchange could, and sometimes in the short run did, cause a movement of prices in the same direction; but the evidence obliges us to conclude that in the secondary secular movements of prices the quantity of money played a passive part,

---

[1] Reprinted in A. C. Pigou, *Memorials of Alfred Marshall.*

[2] Interim Report of the Gold Delegation of the Financial Committee, Annexes X and XI (*League of Nations, II Economic and Financial*, 1930, II, 26).

[3] J. T. Phinney, " Gold Production and the Price Level," *Q.J.E.*, XLVII, 4, August 1933.

adapting itself to the requirements of changes in turnover which were independently initiated.   The influence of the quantity of money on the price level, on this view, has for the most part been only secondary, and has been exerted only through the readiness or reluctance with which that quantity adapts itself to changes in turnover; and even here the evidence suggests that its effect was in fact small, that a greater stock of gold would have done little to check a secular fall in the price level, or a smaller to check a rise. The evidence is as follows.

2.1. The world's monetary stock of gold was only a part of the whole stock; in the first half of the nineteenth century it seems to have been about a third, by 1909 it had become a half.[1]   Much of the non-monetary stock could have been buried deep, while leaving a substantial amount which could be induced to move from one use to the other; and the new output of each year could be and was divided between the two uses in proportions which varied from time to time.

2.2. The connection between the monetary stock of gold and the quantity of means of exchange in actual use was both indirect and flexible: it was liable to change, and was in fact changed, at many points within the inverted pyramid of the banking system.   " Such data as are available show that little or no relation existed between the rate of growth of the gold supply and the rate of growth of either bank reserves or bank notes and deposits. . . . This absence of correlation is especially striking in the period from about 1875 to 1913, when so many of the statistics examined show a relatively constant rate of growth of bank reserves and of bank currency, quite unaffected by variations in gold production or by trends in prices." [2] Even, moreover, when we reach the quantity of the actual means of exchange, we find that only some of them were at any time held under the transactions motive; the rest, which were probably the greater part,[3] were held under the precautionary and speculative motives, and were available to reinforce the circulating balances.   It is, to say the least, very hard to believe that in these circumstances a change in the monetary stock of gold would have enforced a change in the flow of spending which would not have come about otherwise.

2.3. The belief that changes in the supply of gold took effect on the movements of the price level can appeal to the coincidence between each of the two big rises in gold output and a turning point in the trend of prices: the first coinciding with the end, about 1848, of the thirty years' fall in prices since Waterloo, and the second with the upturn of prices in the mid-1890s.   There is no doubt that these spurts of gold output seemed very important to contemporaries, and that they made an immediate difference to the monetary ease of the City of London.   But it is not clear that, even in

---

[1] Table A of Annex X, *League of Nations, II Economic and Financial*, 1930, II, 26.

[2] J. T. Phinney, " Gold Production and the Price Level," *Q.J.E.*, XLVII, 4, August 1933.

[3] " In practice they (idle balances) are probably many times larger than those being used in income transactions."   F. W. Paish, " Open and Repressed Inflation," ECONOMIC JOURNAL, September 1953, p. 536.

the short run, it was the change in the monetary stock of gold which caused the upturn of prices, rather than the increase in the demand for British exports: it was on this last that Newmarch [1] laid emphasis in 1857, in his Keynesian analysis of the expansion of " effective demand " (his own term) for the products of the whole world, which spread out from gold-digging as a form of investment.

Yet after the initial outburst of investment in the gold-fields had ended, the effect on prices persisted: uncertainly in the 1850s and 1860s, when we do not know how far some underlying tendency of wholesale prices to fall back was overpowered by the many wars, but clearly in the fifteen or twenty years down to 1914; and it is natural to ask whether this was not caused by the rise at these times in the world's monetary stock of gold, which doubled in the ten years after 1848, and again in the twenty years after 1890. But if it was these accumulating reserves that raised prices by way of easy money, why in each of these periods did the rate of interest rise? This is a vital point, to which we recur below. Nor is it necessary to suppose that the gold was brought to passive bankers, whose reaction to it was mechanical and according to fixed reserve ratios. We have noticed already the lack of a regular relation between the growth of gold reserves and of money held by the public; and we have Keynes's observation [2] that Central Banks " are all natural gold-hoarders, and are always keen to increase their stocks of it whenever they find themselves in a position to do so without inconveniencing the business world."

2.4. A change in prices brought about from the side of money must be expected to raise most product and factor prices, at any rate those which can be re-negotiated, in much the same degree, save only for such shifts in relative values as are always going on; but in fact the British terms of trade (para. (1.3) above) suggest strongly that the movements of wholesale prices were systematically connected with changes in the terms on which primary products were available to the industrial worker.

2.5. The secondary secular movements of wholesale prices persisted through two, three or four trade cycles, so that cyclical phases of tight money and falling prices occur in periods of rising price trends, and conversely. If in fact these price trends were themselves also due to changes in the supply of money, it is hard to see how they could exert themselves except, so to speak, by tilting the trade cycle, by making the phases of monetary ease and expansion rather longer or further-reaching when the price trend was rising than when it was falling, and correspondingly adjusting the phases of recession. But the evidence summarised in (1.6) above shows that there was no such systematic difference in the British trade cycles of 1790–1914.

2.6. If the price trends were caused by changes in the supply of money, we should expect rising prices to go with easy money and low interest rates, and falling prices with the contrary. In fact, the record shows it was the

---

[1] Tooke and Newmarch, *A History of Prices*, Vol. VI, Part VII, Sec. 11, p. 212, and Sec. 14, p. 226.
[2] *Treatise on Money*, Bk. VI, Ch. 30, p. 205.

exact opposite that happened: the rate of interest rose and fell with wholesale prices, not against them. This is " the Gibson paradox," but it is no
paradox if we give up the assumption that the supply of money was exerting
pressure on the flow of payments, and suppose it was the other way round.[1]
When the movements of wholesale prices and the long-term rate of interest
are compared in Fig. 1(a), the two post-war phases which we may call the
Cunliffe and Dalton phases stand out as exceptional: in both (though in
opposite directions) the initiative came from the supply of money, in both
the price level and the rate of interest moved in contrary senses. This
strengthens the inference that when they moved in the same sense, as they
generally did elsewhere, the initiative came not from the supply of money
but from the demand for it.

2.7. Thus there are three reasons which permit us, and three which
induce us, to believe that the secular movements of prices were not due to
changes in the supply of gold. The monetary stock of gold was not physically
limited but was never more than half the whole stock; there seems to have
been no systematic connection between changes in monetary stocks of gold
and in the quantity of money in the hands of the public; an alternative
explanation can be given of the coincidence between the two spurts of gold
output and the changed direction of price movements. More than this, the
price movements were not those of a *numéraire* but were regularly bound up
with movements of the terms of trade; there was no systematic difference
between the trade cycles in the different phases of price movement; and the
long-term rate of interest moved not in the contrary direction to the price
level but in the same.

If, then, the origin of the secular movements of prices does not lie in
gold, where does it lie?

3.0. From his study of the annals of the British economy since 1790,
Rostow has developed an explanation built on changes in the rate of growth
of the output of final products,[2] or, latterly, of primary products,[3] relatively
to that of effective demand, the periods of rising prices being broadly those
of a reduced rate of growth in the flow of products into the market, and
conversely. Any explanation of this kind is exposed to the objection that
what records we have of the growth of the outputs of primary products do
not show the changes it supposes. These records, whose sources are described in the Appendix to this article, are illustrated in Fig. 2. What is
required is a general check to rates of growth at the time of the great upturn
of wholesale prices in the mid-nineties, and a generally higher rate of growth
to accompany the weakness and decline of those prices in the inter-war
years. But we do not find such changes. Of the ten products in Fig. 2,

---

[1] Cf. para. 9 of Phelps Brown and Weber, " Accumulation, Productivity and Distribution in
the British Economy, 1870–1938," ECONOMIC JOURNAL, June 1953, with the acknowledgment there
to Dr. A. W. H. Phillips.

[2] W. W. Rostow, *British Economy of the Nineteenth Century*, Chs. I, III, IV, VII. A. D. Gayer,
W. W. Rostow and A. J. Schwartz, *The Growth and Fluctuation of the British Economy, 1790–1850*,
Vol. II, Part I, Chs. IV, V.

[3] W. W. Rostow, *The Process of Economic Growth*, Ch. 6.

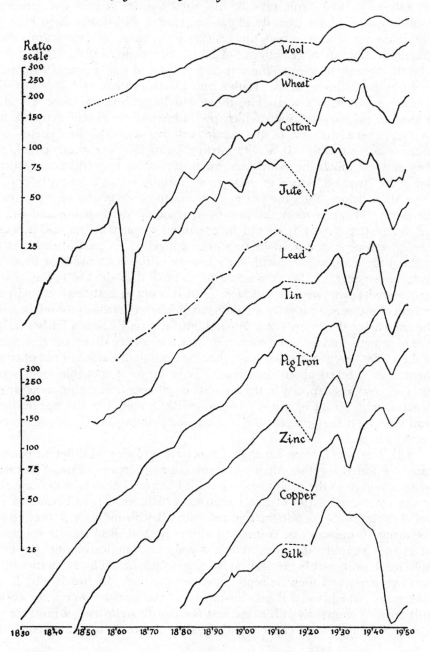

Fig.2: Total Output of some Primary Products.
[3-yr. av. of cyclically-cleared series]

only wool, and to a less extent jute, move conformably. The others are remarkably alike in showing no check to the rate of growth through the nineties and on to 1914; and, save for silk, their outputs in 1930 were all lower than they would have been if the pre-war rate of growth had been kept up. The inference is strong that the general movements of prices arose from changes in the rate of growth not of supply but of demand.

4.0. We can picture changes in the growth of real demand as coming about in the following way. With a given barter rate of exchange at which primary products are available, there will be at any one time a certain volume of primary products which the industrial world will demand, and another which the rest of the world will supply. As time passes both volumes are growing. If at our starting point they are about equal, and they grow at much the same pace, then the barter rate will change little; but if the demand begins to grow more rapidly while the supply rises no faster than before, then the barter rate will move in favour of the primary producer. What governs the rate of increase of the demand, and can we see, for instance, why it should have caused a spurt in the mid-nineties? The governing factor must be industrial capacity: in part directly, as the demand for leather grows with the capacity of the boot-and-shoe industry; and, more generally, because what the industrial world has to buy with is ultimately its own power to produce. But it is not at first apparent why the growth of industrial capacity should have quickened in the mid-nineties. On the contrary: the records of industrial output usually show a fairly constant rate of growth, and for some countries there is evidence that " the climacteric of the 1890s " went the other way, that the growth of output, if not of equipment, was checked about this time.[1] It is, however, possible for constant rates of growth of capacity in the separate economies to compose an aggregate demand whose rate of growth varies greatly; and it is this aggregate or world demand that governs the markets for primary products, and so concerns us here.

4.1. The explanation [2] is that if two series growing at different constant rates are added together, their sum grows at an increasing rate. This holds without regard to their relative sizes at the outset. Let us take the capacities of the cotton industries of two countries, which we will call America (*A*), and Britain (*B*). At our starting point the British industry has a capacity requiring 10 units of raw cotton (*C*) annually, and this capacity is growing at 2% per annum; the capacity of the younger American industry is as yet only for 1 unit, but is growing at 10% per annum. The capacities of the two industries will then be represented by the lines *AA*, *BB* in Fig. 3, and their sum (which we will take to represent the world demand for cotton) will grow as shown by *WW*. At first the British industry accounts for ten-elevenths of the world capacity, whose rate of growth is consequently close

---

[1] Phelps Brown and Handfield-Jones, " The Climacteric of the 1890s," *Oxford Economic Papers*, October 1952.

[2] I claim the privilege of a senior partner to state that the argument of this paragraph is due wholly to S. A. Ozga. E.H.P.B.

to the British 2%; but as time passes the American industry forms an ever-greater part of the whole, whose rate of growth therefore comes nearer to the American 10%. Suppose that the supply of raw cotton was at the outset just the 11 units which the world industry required, and that this supply rose at 5% per annum: its movements are shown by *CC*. At first the supply rises faster than capacity, but after about twenty-five years the two rates are the same, and thereafter world capacity is overtaking the growth of supply.

But clearly the actual course of events could never be such as Fig. 3

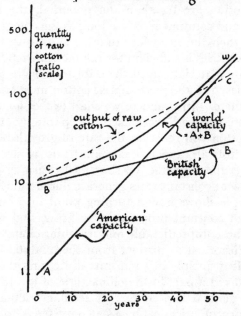

Fig 3: Illustration of changing effect on price of constant potential rates of growth

shows: the disparity of demand and supply would soon set up too much pressure. The rates of growth which the lines *AA*, *BB*, *CC* show are those potential rates which may be expected as part of the organic growth of the whole economy in population, capital and technique, but the actual growth can be speeded up or slowed down by changes in the rate of return to the particular activities concerned, and in this way potentially disparate rates of growth can be adjusted to one another. Suppose first, always for the sake of exposition, that the task of adjustment is borne wholly by supply. Then the output of raw cotton will have to follow not *CC* but *WW*. The tendency to grow along *CC* will have to be held back for some time by prices which must become successively lower as the extent of the divergence to be enforced increases. But then we reach a stage in which the slope of *WW* is as great as that of *CC*, the world capacity is rising as fast as the potential rate of growth of supply, and the price of raw cotton need no longer fall;

and after that capacity begins to grow faster than supply, and the price of raw cotton must rise progressively.  So after a period of pressure to slow down the growth of the output of raw material, by falling prices, we have one of pressure to speed it up, by rising prices; and this without any increase in the potential rates of growth of industrial capacity, or check to that of raw material output.  The same effect appears if, alternatively, we suppose that the task of adjustment is borne wholly by industrial capacity.  The actual output of raw cotton now follows $CC$, and the two industrial capacities must follow curves which rise more steeply than $AA$ and $BB$ at first, but are concave downwards, and after a time turn back to $AA$ and $BB$: for such are the curves which (if the adjustment is divided between the two industries proportionally to their sizes) will sum to the line $CC$.  To stimulate a rate of industrial expansion greater than the potential, the price of the raw material must fall, and continue to fall so long as the extent of the divergence must widen; but then the need for stimulus ends, and the potential rate of growth of the industries is sufficient for the moment to absorb the increase in the output of raw materials, until the industries begin to try to grow too fast for their supplies, and the price of raw cotton must rise progressively to put the brake on them.  In practice, we shall expect a combination of the two kinds of adjustment we have looked at separately: the movements of the price of raw cotton will react on the rate of growth both of raw cotton output and of industrial capacity, checking one while it stimulates the other.  But however the adjustment is shared, the turning point will appear. Propensities to grow at constant rates generate fluctuations of prices.

4.2. This example shows how a turning point in economic history can be generated out of constant propensities to grow, and without the intervention of any of those unpredictable and irregular changes which are commonly called the historical as distinct from the analytic factors in an economic problem.  In principle it is not unrealistic, and the relations it illustrates may have played a part in the climacteric of the 1890s.  But it is far from providing a general explanation of secular fluctuations.  It cannot generate a downturn of prices.  Once capacity tends to grow faster than raw material output, prices rise without limit; if raw-material output grows faster than even the fastest component of capacity, they fall without limit.  But, in the actual world, downturns of prices have occurred, and price trends have not risen or fallen without limit.  The evident explanation is that the potential rates of growth, both of raw material output and of industrial capacity, are changed from time to time by the march of events. The first has been checked by the exhaustion of resources, and raised by the opening of new regions and by technical advances in transport, cultivation and extraction.  The second has been checked by upheavals during and after wars, and raised when nations have bestirred themselves and entered upon a new course of industrialisation.

4.3. Can we then provide any indication of the tendencies of growth of industrial capacity, relatively to those of primary products?  Some indication is available if we can assume that in the long run the production of pig iron is roughly proportional to the size of industrial capacity, while its fluctuations in the short run indicate (though not proportionally) the extent to which that capacity is utilised. A comparison of this production with that of a composite index of some outputs of primary products will then suggest the extent to which these outputs were keeping pace with the demand: not of course that the *trend* of the ratio through any period is significant, because this is bound to be affected by divergences between pig-iron production and industrial capacity, and between this capacity as a whole and that part which uses the particular raw materials which our index covers; but that any marked *change* in the trend will suggest a corresponding change in the scarcity of primary products. The results of such a comparison, using the world output of pig iron less Russia, are shown in Fig. 4. We notice the successive contrasts between 1872–94, 1894–1912, 1921–39 and

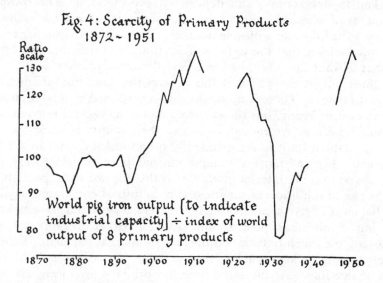

Fig. 4: Scarcity of Primary Products 1872–1951

World pig iron output [to indicate industrial capacity] ÷ index of world output of 8 primary products

1946–51. These are not inconsistent with our account of the origin of the movements of the wholesale price level.

5.0. We can now offer our own explanation of the secondary secular movements.

5.1. The relation between the rates of growth of world industrial capacity and the output of primary products has passed since 1815 through alternating phases of some twenty or thirty years in length. When industrial capacity tends to grow more quickly than the output of primary products, a shortage of these products is felt, and their prices rise, in terms of money, and also relatively to the price of industrial effort. When industrial capacity tends to grow more slowly than the output of primary products, the opposite effects follow. We can at present regard the observed length of these phases only as a fact of their epoch of history, and not as a property of the processes of growth which is likely to persist as long as growth continues.

5.2. When a phase of shortage of primary products sets in, the industrial economies experience a rise in wholesale prices. This spreads through the economy: rises in the cost of raw materials raise the prices fixed for final products; the rise in the cost of living moves wage-earners to press for rises in money wages; with more or less lag, other money incomes are raised to maintain customary differentials, and this causes further rises in costs and prices. Where sellers fix their prices, their decisions are affected not only directly, through the rise in prime costs, but also indirectly, through a change in their valuation of the risk they take when they put a price up. At a time when prices of raw materials, and wages, are known to be generally rising, and when consequently such changes in price as other sellers announce are usually upward, the risk appears smaller that to raise one's own price will leave one isolated and exposed, out of line with one's competitors and with the expectations of one's customers. Decisions in this region of price-making are taken in uncertainty, and depend on expectations. The conspicuous movements of wholesale prices are a magnet which draws the expectations of many men into line with one another. A market environment [1] forms: each now believes that the trend is if anything upwards, because he thinks that that is what the others believe; and the belief justifies itself.

It must not be thought that this process is necessarily inhibited by the supply of money. There is no doubt that a restricted supply of money can stop prices from rising, but the evidence shows that actual restrictions have not usually been severe enough to do so: the quantity of money in circulation has adapted itself to independently originated increases in the flow of payments. The resistance to adaptation has been sufficient only to raise the long-term rate of interest gradually as the upward trend goes on.

The rise in the prices of the imports of industrial communities will make their balances of payments more adverse than they would have been otherwise, but Paish [2] has pointed out that for Great Britain at least this did not impose much restraint on the flow of internal payments, because the primary producers kept much of their accruals in sterling, and did not hold much of this idle. At the same time the primary producers' banks, with higher reserves and more prosperous customers, expanded credit. So for the community of the industrial economy and the primary producers together, a rise in wholesale prices did not merely transfer money income from one sector to the other, but raised the sum of income in the two; and similarly a fall of wholesale prices lowered it. "When ' customer ' countries are enjoying favourable balances of payments, incomes in the world as a whole tend to rise, while when their balances are unfavourable world incomes tend to fall."

All these reactions to a rise in wholesale prices appear in the opposite direction when wholesale prices fall.

---

[1] Phelps Brown and Hart, " The Share of Wages in National Income," ECONOMIC JOURNAL, June 1952, para. 17.

[2] F. W. Paish, " Open and Repressed Inflation," ECONOMIC JOURNAL, September, 1953, p. 543. The point was made previously in Section VI of the same author's " Banking Policy and the Balance of International Payments," *Economica*, November 1936; reprinted in his *The Post-war Financial Problem* (1950).

5.3. The argument has already suggested the connection between the secondary secular movements in wholesale prices, the terms of trade and the rate of interest; it remains to bring in those in the real wages of the industrial economy. When a phase of shortage of primary products sets in, the rise of real income must be checked, most of all for the wage-earners, whose " basketful " contains the highest proportion of primary products. Rises in money wages might reduce this impact, and bring about some redistribution of income from other sectors, were it not that, in the soft market environment which is now developing, rises in money wages only raise costs and prices throughout the system, and there is no squeeze of other shares, save for some transfer from those whose money incomes lag. An insufficient rate of growth of raw-material supplies must check the growth of processing equipment: to entrepreneurs this check appears as a rise in costs keeping pace with rising prices, and it may be reinforced, as the rate of interest rises, by a worsening of the terms on which capital can be raised. Some home investment may none the less be diverted to house building, but investment in primary production will become attractive, and a larger part of the accumulation of the industrial economy will take place beyond its own bounds. Thus a period which superficially is one of prosperity, with ever-rising money totals of turnover and income, and a comfortable sense of the ability to bear some extra costs without embarrassment, is really one of comparative stagnation, because a community such as ours cannot raise its standard of living much faster than its intake of the basic materials.

When primary products become abundant, these features of the phase of shortage are all reversed: a time of downward pressure on prices, of a hard market environment and talk of depression is actually one of more rapid advance in the standard of living, in the wage-earners' standard most of all.

6.0. In sum, it appears that monetary changes have done little to cause or control the movements of prices. The long-period falls of prices were not due to shortage of money, and when the trend set the other way, our monetary institutions provided the needed means of payment. This was so before ever a moral obligation to maintain employment was accepted, and we cannot expect greater ruthlessness in the future. It remains true that a big enough change in the quantity of money can push the system over into inflation or deflation. It is also true that publicised changes in monetary policy, so long as the reactions to them continue to follow conventional lines, will influence expectations; and that changes in the rate of interest will affect some investment decisions. But the prospects of controlling price movements flexibly by monetary policy appear much poorer than would be inferred from the view which ascribes causal primacy to changes in the quantity of money; though not poorer, perhaps, than is really assumed in practice to-day, when " the struggle against inflation " would be needless if all that had to be done was to regulate the quantity of money.

This conclusion is of much importance to the United Kingdom, which not only shares in any general contemporary tendency to a wage–price spiral, but is specially exposed to that spiral being set off by a rise in the cost of its imports. It appears that we cannot rely on central controls to do just so much as is necessary to restrain such tendencies, because the source of these lies not in a monetary equation but in the consensus of opinion of thousands of free agents. In these conditions the possibility of control is bound to depend on the understanding and responsibility shown by business-men and trade unionists generally. Given this, we are not solely at the mercy of the terms of trade, but have two ways in which to meet an adverse movement. First, the terms of trade which matter are not the net barter terms, but the quantity of imports which can be gained per unit of British effort, and each rise in productivity which increases our output of goods per man hour makes it easier for us to meet a demand from the world market for more British goods per unit of our imports. Second, it can become generally recognised, and an axiom of the public interest, that a rise in the prices of our imports, with the consequent rises in the cost of raw materials and the cost of living, must be regarded for the purpose of price-fixing and wage-fixing decisions as distinct in kind from other rises in costs, and as constituting a burden to be fairly shouldered rather than a charge to be automatically passed on.

## APPENDIX

### Statistical Sources and Methods

Fig. 1(a): Wholesale Price Level.—1790–1850: Gayer, Rostow and Schwartz, *The Growth and Fluctuation of the British Economy*, 1790–1850, Vol. I, Pt. III, Ch. I, Table 39. 1850–1924: Jevons's index 1850–60, Sauerbeck's 1860 onwards, as given in Appendix A, Table II, in Layton and Crowther, *Introduction to the Study of Prices*. 1924–53: *Board of Trade Index*, old series, all items.

Yield of Consols.—1790–1830: T. S. Ashton, "Some Statistics of the Industrial Revolution in Great Britain," Table I, in *The Manchester School*, XVI, 2, May 1948; supplemented by Gayer, Rostow and Schwartz, *op. cit.*, Vol. I, pp. 47, 54, 221. 1830–50: Gayer, Rostow and Schwartz, *op. cit.*, Vol. I, pp. 221, 259, 289, 320. 1851–59: W. Page (ed.), *Commerce and Industry*, Table 120. 1860–1939: Phelps Brown and Hopkins, "The Course of Wage-rates in Five Countries, 1860–1939," Tables Id, IId, in *Oxford Economic Papers*, June 1950. 1939–present: *Annual Abstract of Statistics*.

Fig. 1(b): Volume of Imports Obtainable per Unit of British Labour. —(a) Index of money wage-rates (earnings from 1939), divided by (b) index of prices of British imports. (a) 1790–1850: Index made from following series, gaps in which were filled by rough estimate to complete annual entries; series combined with following weights, chosen in light of weights proportional to numbers of employees given by Bowley for 1840 in Table II of Appendix to his *Wages in the 19th Century*: Total 20; Agricultural 7, Industrial 13; the Industrial divided, 1790–1805, into Building 5, Engineering 6, Printing 2; 1806–50, Building 3, Engineering 4, Printing 1, Cotton 5. *Agriculture.*—Bowley, *J.R.S.S.*, September 1899, Table at p. 562; weighted av. of England and Wales (6) and Scotland (1). *Building.*—Bowley, *J.R.S.S.*, March 1901, p. 112, index for Great Britain 1830–50, carried back on basis of series for London only at p. 107. *Engineering and Shipbuilding.*—Bowley and Wood, *J.R.S.S.*, March 1906, p. 190; unreliable before 1824. *Printing, compositors.*—Bowley and Wood, *J.R.S.S.*, December 1899, p. 708, Table I. *Cotton, factory operatives.*—G. H. Wood, *J.R.S.S.*, June 1910, Table 41. 1850–60: G. H. Wood, index for workman of unchanged grade, *J.R.S.S.*, March 1909, p. 102. 1860–1939: Phelps Brown and Hopkins, *loc. cit.* 1939–53: Ministry of Labour six-monthly wage census, average weekly earnings, all workers (*Ministry of Labour Gazette*). (*b*) From 1801: Table 26 of W. Schlote, *British Overseas Trade from 1700 to the 1930s*; carried back to 1798 by splicing with import price index given by A. H. Imlah, *Journ. Econ. Hist.*, November 1950.

REAL WAGES.—(*a*) above, divided by (*c*), index of cost of living. This index obtained, 1790–1860, by calculating linear regression of Bowley's cost of living index (*Wages and Income in the U.K.*, Table VII, p. 30) through 1880–1913 on the Jevons–Sauerbeck index of wholesale prices (Layton and Crowther, *Introduction to the Study of Prices*, Appendix A, Table II), and applying this regression to the index of wholesale prices obtained as above. 1860–1939: Phelps Brown and Hopkins, *loc. cit.* 1939–53: R. G. D. Allen, *Bulletin of London and Cambridge Economic Service*, February 1949, and tables in later Bulletins.

FIG. 2.—General source for 1937–52, *Commodity Year Books (CYB)*, published by the Commodity Research Bureau, N.Y. Outputs are those of the whole world, so far as recorded, except where stated below. We removed cyclical fluctuations down to 1937 from those series in which they were evident, viz., copper, jute, pig iron, silk, by the following method. Each specific cycle was divided into nine equal periods, and where the boundary between two of these periods fell within a year the output of that year was distributed between them, so that a total output within each period could be estimated. The cyclical movement shown in the successive nine-period groups was then removed as if it were a season fluctuation. The corrected period entries were then regrouped by years. We smoothed the cyclically cleared series, and the other six series (except when they were five-yearly only), by taking a three-year moving average.

Sources for particular materials:

(1) COPPER.—1879–1930: E. L. Knight, *Secular and Cyclical Movements in the Production and Price of Copper*, University of Pennsylvania Press, 1936, p. 147. 1931–51: *CYB*, 1942, p. 57; 1950, p. 81; 1952, p. 94; 1953, p. 103.

(2) COTTON.—Output that of the United States alone through 1901; spliced at 1902 with index of world output. 1830–1902: *Historical Statistics of the U.S.A. 1789–1945* (Bureau of the Census, 1949), p. 108. 1902–32: J. A. Todd, *The Marketing of Cotton* (1934), p. 235. 1932–37: Imperial Economic Committee, *Industrial Fibres* (1939). 1937–51: *CYB*, 1950, p. 86; 1953, p. 118.

(3) JUTE.—From 1873 Indian exports only, spliced at 1892 with Indian crop, which in turn is spliced at 1922 with world output. 1873–92: *Review of the Trade of India* (Government of India, yearly). 1892–1922: *Area and Yield of Certain Principal Crops* (Government of India). 1922–37: *International Yearbook of Agriculture* (International Institute of Agriculture). 1937–51: *CYB*, 1950, p. 44; 1953, p. 58.

(4) LEAD.—1860–1935 (five-yearly only): Berg, Friedensberg and Sommerlatte, *Blei und Zink* (Stuttgart, 1950), pp. 78–9. 1935–52: *CYB*, 1950, p. 174; 1952, p. 196; 1953, p. 199.

(5) PIG IRON.—1830–1913: Sum of outputs in five countries: (a) the United Kingdom.—*Commerce and Industry* (ed. W. Page, 1919), p. 180. (b) the United States.—*Historical Statistics of the U.S.A. 1789–1945* (Bureau of the Census, 1949), p. 4. (c) Belgium. S. S. Kuznets, *Secular Movements in Production and Prices* (N.Y., 1930), p. 450. (d) France. Kuznets, *op. cit.*, p. 501. (e) Germany. H. Marchand, *Säkularstatistik der deutschen Eisenindustrie* (Essen, 1939), pp. 115–19. 1913–37: *Statistical Yearbook* (League of Nations)—World, excl. U.S.S.R. 1937–51: *CYB*, 1950, p. 161; 1952, p. 184; 1953, p. 188.

(6) SILK.—World output of exportable silk, through 1936; thereafter total world output. 1873–83 (five-yearly): E. Flügge, *Rohseide* (Leipzig, 1936), p. 109. 1885–1937: Chabrier, Morel et Cie, *Silk Report* (Lyons). 1937–51: *Commonwealth Economic Committee Reports,* 1948, p. 68; 1953, p. 65.

(7) TIN.—1851–1937: International Tin Research Bureau, *Statistical Yearbook* (The Hague, 1939), p. 15. 1937–52: *CYB*, 1950, p. 272; 1952, p. 231; 1953, p. 319.

(8) WHEAT.—1885–1932: M. K. Bennett, " World Wheat Crops 1885–1932 ", *Stanford Wheat Studies*, Vol. IX, pp. 239–74. 1932–37: *League of Nations Statistical Yearbook*. 1937–51: *CYB*, 1950, p. 288; 1953, p. 339.

(9) WOOL.—1850, 1860–99: W. Senkel, *Wollproduktion und Wollhandel im 19n. Jahrhundert* (Tübingen, 1901), p. 25. 1899–1900 (for link only): G. Blau, " Wool in the World Economy," *J.R.S.S.*, 1946, p. 228. 1900–36: T. A. Hamilton, *A Statistical Study of Wool Prices* (Texas, 1938), p. 56. 1936–37: Imperial Economic Committee, *Industrial Fibres* (1939), p. 41. 1937–52: *CYB*, 1950, p. 304; 1952, p. 359; 1953, p. 357.

(10) ZINC.—1845–1913: sum of outputs in Belgium, France, Germany and the United States, in S. S. Kuznets, *Secular Movements in Production and Prices* (N.Y., 1930), pp. 458, 509, 479, 382. 1913–37: *Yearbook of the American Bureau of Metal Statistics* (N.Y.). 1937–52: *CYB*, 1950, p. 311; 1953, p. 362.

FIG. 4.—(1) Output of pig iron, as under Fig. 2, cyclical pattern removed down to 1937, and smoothed by three-year moving average. This divided by (2) combined index (with equal weights) of outputs of some primary products, viz., all series of Fig. 2 except pig iron and lead; wheat included only from 1885.

# 9
# The Economic Consequences of Collective
# Bargaining

# I. THE INFLUENCE OF COLLECTIVE BARGAINING ON THE MOVEMENTS OF THE GENERAL LEVEL OF PAY

1. To assess the consequences of collective bargaining with certainty we should have to be able to compare what happens in its presence with what happens when some other method of regulating pay is used in societies otherwise the same. The actual course of events gives us little chance to do this. There are differences in plenty, it is true, between the ways in which pay has been regulated in different countries, periods or industries, but much else has been different at the same time. Nor can we very well make the needed comparison by way of what the physicist calls an "ideal experiment", and ask what we can see happening, in the mind's eye, when a given society changes its ways of regulating pay. The trouble is that these ways are an organic part of the society. Their working depends on attitudes and traditions which they in turn help to mould : even in imagination we cannot lift them out and install others in their place as we might change the carburettor in a car.

2. None the less, if we are to reach any verdict on proposals for improving them we are bound to base it on some judgment of the effect they take, of what would come about differently if they were different. Ultimately this judgment must be intuitive, but it can also be informed. Comparisons are possible which, though far from controlled experiments, do throw light on the probability of different judgments. In a number of western economies, for instance, we can compare the movements of rates of pay before and after the extension of collective bargaining. Where collective bargaining is established, we can compare the movements of rates of pay in different phases of the economy. Within any one country, again, we can sometimes compare different industries, or different regions of the same industry, some of which bargain collectively while others as yet do not ; or we can compare the course of events in one industry before and after it adopts collective bargaining. None of these comparisons is rigorous: other things always vary at the same time. But we can often judge how far it is to these other things that any differences in the movements of pay are likely to have been due ; and then we are left with an estimate of the consequences specific to collective bargaining. We can also ask whether such estimates agree with the expectations created by an analysis of bargaining power.

3. It is the purpose of this note to give an account of these materials and the conclusions to which they lead. For the sake of brevity the account will be summary, and the conclusions will be stated baldly. In a fuller account there would be more qualifications, but also more marshalling of evidence.

4. The United Kingdom is one of a number of western countries in which we can follow the movements of pay and other incomes over the last hundred years. Fig. 1 shows the course of the average earnings in money of manual workers, mainly in industry, in France, Germany, Sweden, the UK, and the USA, since 1860. Only in the UK was collective bargaining of much account in the earlier years of this period, and even here it was less extensive than trade unionism, and was effective only for a small minoritiy of the country's wage-earners. Between 1890 and the first world war, however, there was a remarkable growth of trade unionism in all five countries, and this brought with it a substantial though inter-mittent development of collective bargaining. The number of trade union members per 10,000 of the occupied population in industry rose as follows :

|            |     |     | France | Germany | Sweden | U.K. | U.S.A. |
|------------|-----|-----|--------|---------|--------|------|--------|
| About 1890 | ... | ... | 220    | 400     | 210    | 810  | 510    |
| About 1913 | ... | ... | 1,440  | 2,520   | 3,300[1] | 2,690 | 1,830 |

We thus have an opportunity to see how money wages behaved in some western economies in the comparative absence of collective bargaining, and also to ask whether the early development of collective bargaining seems to have made a difference.

5. The salient feature of the general level of money wages in all five countries, before ever collective bargaining could have taken much effect, is that it rose cumulatively. Earlier records show that, even excluding years of war, this tendency

---

[1] This was in 1907, a high point reached after membership had more than doubled since 1904; through 1910–12 membership averaged nearly 20 per cent. less.

had been present from the early years of industrialism. How did it arise? Except in France, most of the rise—indeed, more than all the net rise—came about within only about half the total number of years. A cycle ran through the business activity of all these countries, with a period on the average of about eight years. It was in the four years or so in which activity was rising or near its crest that money wages rose. The other four years in which activity was falling or near its trough brought no change in money wages or some cuts. These cuts, however, were smaller than the immediately preceding rises, so that on balance each cycle raised money wages. So far it looks as though the source of the cumulative rise of money wages lay in the cycle. If, moreover, the size of the rise in each prosperous phase depended on its intensity, the differences between the rates at which money wages rose in various periods and countries might be due simply to the different intensities of their cycles. But though some systematic dependence of this kind appears in Germany, the UK and the USA, there is too much variation about it for us to take it as a sufficient explanation of the rate at which money wages rose from time to time. From the mid-90s onwards, for instance, money wages rose a good deal faster in Germany, Sweden and the USA than they had done through the twenty years before, but there was no corresponding intensification of the cycles in those countries. What explanation, then, can we offer? One account which is not incompatible with the evidence runs as follows.

6. We think of the labour market as a gravitational field, in which the force of gravity has been a pressure exerted from the side of labour towards wage rises and against wage cuts. This force has been present at all times, though in varying strength. Its action has not depended on labour being unionised, though union militancy intensified it.

7. The balance of supply and demand in the labour market operated in some times and places to reinforce what we have called the force of gravity, in others to counteract it. In the successive phases of the trade cycle the demand for labour rose now faster and now slower than the supply. This supply itself rose at a rate which, especially through the changing numbers of migrants, varied significantly from time to time. When it was the demand for labour that was extending the more rapidly, in some occupations and places an absolute excess of vacancies over applicants would appear, and if competition between employers for labour did not actively bid wages up, at least the pressure to raise them from the side of labour would now be reinforced by the scarcity. When the demand for labour lagged behind the supply, the competition of workers for jobs might only exceptionally be allowed to underbid the going rate, but the pressure from the side of labour to keep that rate up would now be counteracted by redundancy.

8. Thus two factors bore on rates of pay within the labour market itself—a persistent pressure from the side of labour, and the varying balance of supply and demand. Within the employer's business their joint influence came into contact with that of two other factors, the methods of production and the state of the market for the product.

9. The methods of production bore on rates of pay most directly according as they determined productivity, that is, output per man. The unit wage cost (wage cost per physical unit of output) is given by the wage per man divided by the output per man. To the extent that this output rose, the wage per man could rise without any rise in unit wage costs and, with unchanged selling price, any change in the profit margin ; and any tendency arising in the labour market to raise the wage per man would meet with correspondingly less resistance. When productivity failed to rise the wage per man could be raised only to the extent that the selling price of the product was raised or the profit margin reduced. That productivity did in fact rise at different rates in different periods and countries is shown by Fig. 2, which presents estimates of the course of the real product per occupied person within the industrial sectors of the five economies whose wage movements we have already surveyed. We find also, by comparison with Fig. 1, that where productivity rose more the general level of money wages usually rose faster. This implies that the course of unit wage costs varied less than that of wages. Fig. 3 illustrates this. The case of the UK between the 1890s and 1914 is particularly striking. Money wages rose through this period more slowly in the UK than in Germany, Sweden and the USA ; industrial productivity also rose less at this time in the UK than in those other countries—indeed, in the UK it hardly rose at all, while in the others it rose rapidly : so that unit wage costs by no means rose less in British

# FIG. 1 AVERAGE ANNUAL WAGE EARNINGS (MAINLY INDUSTRIAL) IN FIVE COUNTRIES, 1860–1960.

IN £s AT GOLD STANDARD PAR OF EXCHANGE

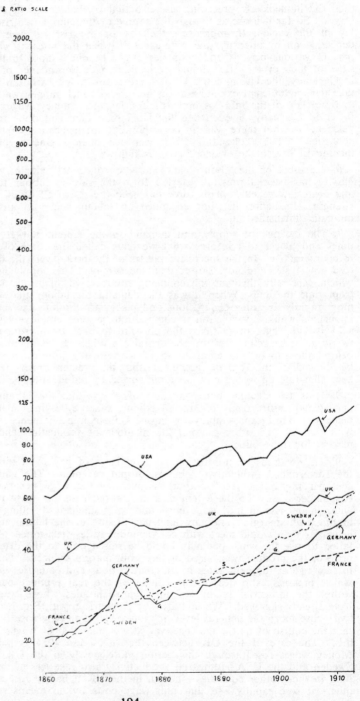

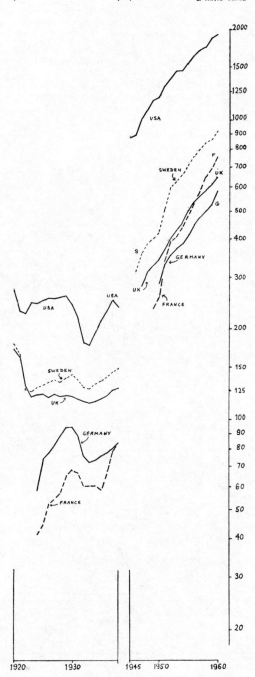

# FIG. 2. PRODUCTIVITY (PHYSICAL OUTPUT PER OCCUPIED PERSON EXPRESSED IN £s OF 1905 PURCHASING POWER) IN THE INDUSTRIAL SECTOR IN FIVE COUNTRIES 1870–1964.

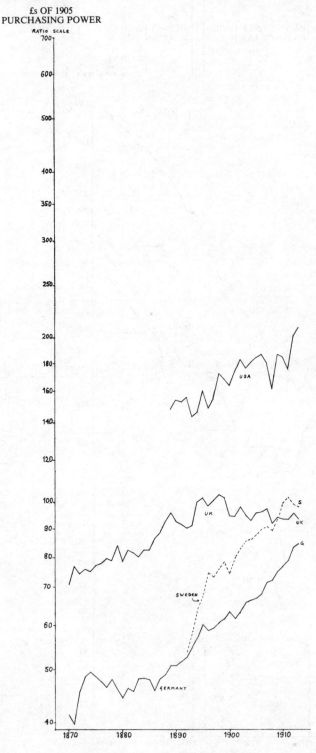

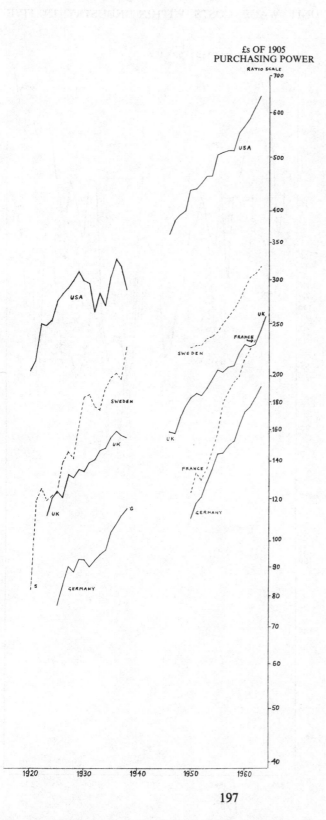

£s OF 1905
PURCHASING POWER

197

# FIG. 3. INDEXES OF UNIT WAGE COSTS WITHIN INDUSTRY IN FIVE COUNTRIES 1870–1964.

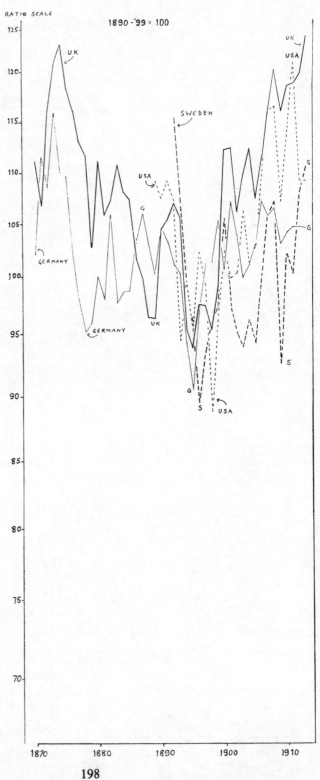

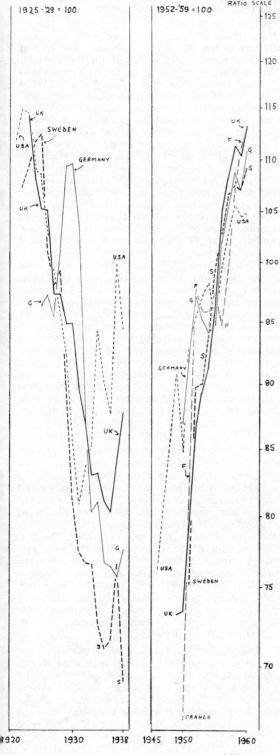

industry than among its competitors. We may suppose that international competition would have prevented any trading country from letting its unit wage costs rise much more than its competitors', or from failing to reduce its own costs if they were reducing theirs.

10. On the other hand, all countries could let their unit wage costs rise, and cover them by higher prices, if all moved together. Here appears the second influence we noted on business decisions—the state of the market for the product. For any one firm at any one time, the possibility of raising its selling price would depend upon what its competitors at home and abroad were tending to do. What each did depended on what it expected the others to do : a common course will have been shaped by a consensus of expectations. When the common course of product prices was downwards, any one seller who raised his price ran an evident risk of isolating himself and damaging his business : a rise in his unit wage cost would therefore mean a lower profit margin for him, and he would be correspondingly concerned to resist it. He might indeed be instigated to lower the wage per man as a means of reducing his unit wage cost in the same proportion as he felt obliged to reduce his selling price. But in the opposite permissive state of the market environment those who raised their prices would find that they had not worsened their competitive position, and as such experiences accumulated they would have ever less reason to involve themselves in conflict to prevent a rise in their unit wage costs. Thus whether the forces of the labour market could raise wages more than productivity depended upon whether the market environment was hard or soft.

11. The product market did in fact evince a tendency for prices to move now upwards, now downwards, in either case for twenty or twenty-five years at a time. Between 1873 and 1896 the trend was downwards : in the U.K., we know, manufacturers felt themselves under a powerful and much resented competitive pressure to keep their costs down, pare their margins, and reduce their prices. During the 1890s, however, the tide turned ; price rises, small but cumulative, became prevalent ; a rise in unit wage costs could now more easily be covered by higher prices, and in cycles of no greater intensity than before money wages per man generally rose more. But in the inter-war years the market environment became hard again. The violent deflation that followed the first world war brought prices down not merely absolutely but relatively to unit wage costs ; and even outside the great depression that began in 1929, few manufacturers could expect that a rise in their own prices would not lose them business. In this period accordingly unit wage costs in industry were not allowed to rise ; and the considerable rise of productivity that came about at the same time was used more to reduce prices than to raise wages.

12. But since the second world war the market environment has been entirely different. Though old apprehensions about the bad effects of higher costs may have persisted at first, experience began to show that prices and real output could rise together year after year, and profits increase in the same proportion as wages and salaries. The soft market environment *par excellence* now developed. It was conditioned not merely by the experience of the opening years, but by knowledge of governments' commitments to full employment—if employers made wage settlements that raised unit wage costs, governments would not in the event deny them the flow of monetary demand needed to keep their capacity fully occupied at the new level of costs. In such a setting, resistance by any one group of employers to a wage settlement of the prevailing size came to be seen as equally futile and needless. Differences between countries in the rate of rise of unit wage costs still, it is true, took their effect on international trade, and in any one country the rise of money wages would tend to be checked in so far as productivity did not advance enough to keep the rise in costs down to something like the international trend. But this trend still rose more steeply and persistently than ever before.

13. If this was the system of forces bearing on the general level of money wages, what difference should we expect collective bargaining to make, and what if any do we find? In the first place, we might expect collective bargaining to give more effect to the persistent pressure to raise wages and resist cuts. In 1892 Alfred Marshall[1] noted the claim of the trade unions " to receive an earlier rise, a greater rise, and a more prolonged rise than they could get without combination. . . . When the time has come for the trade to reap the harvest for which it has been

[1] *Elements of Economics of Industry*, VI, XIII, 5.

waiting, the employers will be very unwilling to let it slip ; and even if an agreement to resist the demands of the men is made, it will not easily be maintained. . . . Unions further hold that the threat of a strike, though less powerful when the tide of prosperity is falling than when it is rising, may yet avail for the comparatively easy task of slackening the fall in the high wages they have gained." The stress here is on greater gains in prosperity. On the other hand it has been held that when a boom goes far enough to set up a competitive scramble for labour among employers, an accepted procedure for regulating wages collectively will slow down their rate of rise. Other observers have held that collective bargaining has taken most effect in depression. The historian of the rise of Swedish trade unions,[1] discussing the strikes of 1880-85 in which unions played an effective part for the first time, observed that " rises in wages won by unorganised strikes were easily taken away from the workers in times of depression . . . if they could not offer an organised resistance. The unorganised strike was a way of gaining momentary improvements in specially favourable circumstances. But only through organisation could these improvements be made lasting." In similar terms the historians of British trade unions from 1889 to 1910[2] have written : " Unorganised or weakly organized workers frequently strike in years of good trade, but they lack the resources to sustain a defensive struggle during depression."

14. To see how far if at all these possibilities were realised we must ask whether, as collective bargaining extended, money wages departed from the course they are likely to have followed under the influence of the trade cycle and the market environment alone. In a number of ways they do seem to have done so, ways moreover that collective bargaining will account for. That the swing of money wages both up and down was generally narrower in later cycles that it had been in those of the 1860s and 1870s, without a corresponding difference in the cycles' own amplitude, supports the view that collective bargaining exerted some steadying influence on wages in boom as well as slump. The much smaller cut in wages in the 'inionized sector than in the rest of the US economy in 1929-32 also suggests that :ollective bargaining reduced the movement of wages under cyclical pressure. In a number of instances a phase of exceptional trade union vigour was associated with a bigger rise or smaller fall in wages than we should have expected from the level of business activity of the time. In the UK, for instance, rises in wages even greater than were to be expected from the rising phase of the cycle at the time were associated with the New Unionism of 1889, the release of the unions in 1906 from the constraint of Taff Vale judgment, and the growth of union membership and militancy in 1911-12. In the USA the fall of wages was exceptionally small during the depression of 1884-85 when the Knights of Labor were in their heyday ; and in France wages actually rose during the depression of 1909, when trade union membership had increased by more than half over the six preceding years, and the number of strikes had nearly doubled. There are instances also that suggest the effect of trade union weakness—in the UK, the smallness of the rise of wages during the increasing business activity of 1880-83, after what the Webbs[3] called " a general rout of the Trade Union forces " in 1879, and the bigness of the wage cuts in 1901–02, when the cyclical recession was mild but the unions lay under the shadow of Taff Vale ; in the USA, the smallness of the wage rises of 1905-08, when union membership that had increased perhaps fourfold between 1898 and 1904 suddenly ceased to grow, and the unions came under organised attack by the employers and were increasingly subjected to court injunctions.

15. These instances all indicate some difference made by collective bargaining to wage movements, and a positive association between those movements and the strength of trade unionism. But there are also negative indications. In two instances money wages rose exceptionally fast at a time of exceptional weakness of the trade unions—in France, in 1874–79, when every sort of workers' organisation lay crushed beneath a régime of surveillance and repression ; and in Sweden, when after the defeat of the unions in the general strike of 1909 their membership fell by nearly a half, yet within three years the average earnings of men in industry rose by more

---

[1] T. Lindblom, *Den Svenska Fackföreningsrorelsens Uppkomst* (1938), p. 73.

[2] H. A. Clegg, A. Fox and A. F. Thompson, *A History of British Trade Unions since* 1889, Vol. I, p. 362.

[3] S. & B. Webb, *The History of Trade Unionism* (1920 edn.), p. 345.

than 12 per cent. But more remarkable than these particular indications is the general and prevailing absence before the second world war of any marked and systematic change in the course of money wages that could be cited as an effect of the extension of collective bargaining. It is true that in the 1890s, when trade unionism in a number of countries began to grow to its present proportions, the trend of money wages in Germany, Sweden and the USA turned upwards; but there was so such turning-point in France and the UK; nor did the much wider extension of collective bargaining from the end of the first world war bring any upward trend at all. Whether we look into the changes in wages year by year in the course of business fluctuations, or stand back and survey the trends over the longer run down to 1939 we see no discontinuity in any country that would imply the entry on the scene of some new factor in wage determination.

16. So far we have been concerned with the effects of collective bargaining as those may appear on the surface of the movements of money wages. We may look below to see whether any effects appear on the rise of productivity. Such effects might conceivably be various. On the one hand, the extension of trade union membership could give more effect to wage-earners' existing understandings about stints and norms of output, their dislike of changes in working practices, and especially their resistance to labour-saving innovations. On the other hand, the enforcement of the union rate throughout a district would prevent inefficient managements from surviving by paying low wages; and in a hard market environment that did not allow of higher unit wage costs being simply covered by higher selling prices, a stronger drive for wage rises and resistance to wage cuts would put management under greater pressure to realise economies. In point of fact, the record of Fig. 2 shows many differences in the rate at which productivity rose in various periods or economies, but none that suggests a systematic relation with the extension of collective bargaining. It is true that in the UK this extension at the end of the 19th century was accompanied by the virtual cessation of the rise of productivity, a change that was soon seized on by contemporaries and, under the title of "the crisis in British industry", laid at the door of the New Unionism. But in Germany, Sweden and the USA the no less rapid extension of unionism at this time went with an accelerated rise of productivity. In the UK itself the rise was resumed and maintained through the interwar years, when the coverage of collective bargaining was far wider than it had been in the years of stagnation before the war. The years since the Second World War, in which the coverage of collective bargaining and the strength of the unions have been greater than ever, have seen an advance of productivity no less rapid than in any earlier period, in Germany, the UK and the USA. Any effect that collective bargaining may have taken on the rate of that advance must be small in comparison with that of other factors.

17. We may also ask whether collective bargaining seems to have taken any effect on the trends of money incomes and product prices that characterise different market environments. It might have done so because in a number of ways it induced a greater concertation of decisions affecting costs and prices. It gave wider publicity to particular claims and settlements. Though the unions engaged in bargaining still did little to concert their actions formally, the timing as well as the vigour of the moves each made to seize its own opportunities would be strengthened by the sight of others on the move. Employers for their part, aware that the claims confronting them were part of a general movement, would have less reason to fear that a settlement which raised their costs would worsen their relative position. Especially within any one industry, or at least within the district that bargaining covered, each firm would know that any pressure it was being put under to raise its prices was being exerted at the same time on its competitors. To bring wages and prices under collective control together was indeed the explicit aim of the "Birmingham alliances" in the 1890s, and the Royal Commission on Trade Unions was led to consider the possibility of collective bargaining becoming generally linked with price controls in this way. There is thus some reason to expect that the extension of collective bargaining would tend to raise the trend of money incomes and product prices. The course of that trend from its turning point in the 1890s down to the first world war does not conflict with that expectation. But then come the interwar years, with more collective bargaining than before, but a hard market environment and a downward trend of prices. Evidently more factors went to make the market environment than collective bargaining alone: this could function as a price cartel only if those

other factors permitted. But after the second world war they did permit. Though the course of money incomes and product prices through these last twenty years has been unprecedented, we do not have to suppose that any new mechanism has been at work, only that a constraint on the mechanism has been removed. Proximately, this constraint was the expectation of employers that wage settlements which raised their unit costs would get them into trouble ; ultimately, it was the absence of public policy to ensure that total monetary demand would not lag behind unit costs. Once public policy stood committed to ensure this, employers generally could reckon on being able to cover higher costs by higher prices without loss of business. It then became the function of collective bargaining to determine the movement of prices as well as of pay.

18. One way in which collective bargaining might make a difference to wage movements remains to be examined. With a given level of productivity, and a price for the product that cannot be put up to cover a higher unit cost, the wage can still be raised if the profit margin is narrowed. It has been an aim of trade unionism to gain for the worker a larger share in the product. How has that share in fact behaved? There has been much discussion of the share of wages in the whole national product, but this share is too much of an amalgam to tell us much. In a labour-intensive industry like coalmining the share of wages is naturally higher than in a capital-intensive industry like electricity supply, and the national aggregate of all such shares will vary with the relative sizes of different industries. What we need to follow is the division of the product per man between pay and profits in each industry by itself, and even here the amount of capital per worker will be increasing over time. The evidence at this level is complex, and does not allow of a broad comparative presentation. It tends, however, towards three general conclusions. First, the share of pay in the product fluctuated widely in the course of the trade cycle because of the inverse fluctuation of profits. But, second, the level around which these fluctuations occurred showed no sustained trend upwards or downwards. In some instances the level may have been displaced through one or both of the two Great Wars, but otherwise what is remarkable is the absence of permanent change in the ratio between two quantities which themselves changed so much. Third, the share of pay has been able to follow a level trend through periods which have brought a progressive increase in the amount of capital per worker and therefore in the amount due for the remuneration of capital, because in practice the output per worker has risen in the same proportion as the capital per worker.

19. This third finding is worth developing in more detail because it brings together the main elements of the distributive system on which collective bargaining has impinged. Let us take as typical the manufacture of a given product in two periods, I and II, in the second of which the amount of capital per worker was twice as great as in the first. We suppose for simplicity that the £ has the same purchasing power throughout. How the situations have in fact tended to compare is indicated by Table 1.

## TABLE 1

Typical changes in output, and in incomes of labour and capital, that have in practice been associated with an increase in capital per worker.

|  | *Period I* | *Period II* |
|---|---|---|
| 1. Capital per worker ... ... ... ... ... | £300 | £600 |
| 2. Net physical product per worker ... ... ... | 50 tons | 100 tons |
| 3. Net value product per worker at price of £2 a ton... | £100 | £200 |
| 4. Annual earnings per worker ... ... ... | £79 | £158 |
| 5. Profit at 7 per cent. on (1) ... ... ... ... | £21 | £42 |
| 6. Unit wage cost, (4) ÷ (2) ... ... ... ... | £1·58 | £1·58 |

While capital per worker has doubled (row 1) output per worker has also doubled (row 2). The shares in the product have remained the same, so that the annual earnings per worker (row 4) and the total profit (row 5) have both doubled ; but the rate of profit (row 5) and the unit wage cost (row 6) have remained the same. With constant purchasing power of money the doubling of earnings in money represents a doubling of real earnings, and these have risen in the same proportion as the physical product per worker.

20. In this system there are three relations, constancy in any two of which implies constancy in the third[1]: the ratio of capital to output (in our example, 3 to 1); the division of the product between earnings and profits (79 and 21 per cent); and the rate of profit (7 per cent). We need not ask which have been the governing relations or why any of them should be stable. For our present purpose the essential is that the available estimates of the relevant magnitudes in the course of the development of some western economies indicate that predominantly these relations have in fact been stable. The most significant of them for us here is the division of the product. If earnings per worker have tended to be a constant proportion of the product per worker, real earnings must have risen in proportion to productivity.

21. That this relation has held through periods in which there have been many and various changes in the course of money rates of pay and product prices implies a running adjustment between them. In fact this seems to have been made through the linking of product prices and unit wage costs. If in a given period money wages rose at 5 per cent a year, but productivity at only 3 per cent, and real wages correspondingly rose at only 3 per cent, prices must have risen at the rate of 2 per cent a year: but this they would have done if they were kept at a constant mark-up over unit wage costs, which themselves must have been rising by 2 per cent a year, the excess of the rise in money wages over that in productivity. Alternatively, if with productivity rising at 3 per cent money wages did not rise at all (as they did not, for instance, in the UK as between 1874 and 1889, or 1923 and 1937) real wages would still rise at the same rate as productivity if prices fell at 3 per cent a year, as they would do if they keep a constant ratio to unit labour costs.

22. In a system that behaves like this, power to raise the general level of money wages has not been power to raise real wages. If collective bargaining makes the general level of money wages rise more than it would otherwise have done, it will raise real wages only where prices cannot be adjusted so as to retain their previous relation to unit wage costs. But usually the circumstances in which money wages are most readily raised are those in which prices are most readily raised too ; and at other times, when the price level is pinned down, rises in money wages in excess of the current rise in productivity are hard to wrest from employers. Generally, a difference made to the rate at which the general level of money wages rises affects the rate of rise of prices but not that of real wages. Much more enters into the welfare and status of the wage-earner than the size of the basketful of goods that his wage will buy, and there are many benefits not included in this basket that collective bargaining has gained for him. But the basketful itself remains a principal component of his material welfare, and a comparative study of different periods and countries strongly suggests that only occasionally has collective bargaining taken much effect upon its growth. This has been governed by the rise of productivity.

## II.  THE INFLUENCE OF COLLECTIVE BARGAINING ON THE STRUCTURE OF WAGES AND SALARIES

23. So far we have been concerned with the general level of rates of pay: now we turn to the differences between one rate and another. Since the general level is only an average of particular rates, any effect that collective bargaining takes on these is liable to affect the general level and might therefore seem to have been taken into account already. But one rate may be raised at the cost of lowering others, and some observers have held that this is what has actually happened. There are also grounds to believe, as we shall see, that collective bargaining can raise the pay of one group of workers relatively to others at its

---

[1] They form the identity:
Share of earnings $= 1 -$ (rate of profit) $\times$ (Capital/output ratio),
or here,
$$0 \cdot 79 = 1 - (0 \cdot 07 \times 3)$$

introduction without widening the difference in the course of time: in this case it may raise the general level somewhat by its impact, but will take no effect on the later movements of that level. In general, the influence of collective bargaining on those movements depends on considerations different from those that determine its ability to raise one rate of pay relatively to the rest and so change the pay structure.

24. The effect that collective bargaining is capable of taking on any one relative rate of pay can be seen by comparing the workings of the labour market before it arose. Here the worker lay under two disabilities. One was that he might find himself only one of a number of applicants from whom the employer could fill a job, while he himself had no corresponding access to a number of alternative employers. In such a case the employer could simply announce the rate for the job unilaterally provided it was high enough to retain at least one suitable applicant; or, in effect, put the job out to tender, and give it to the man who would do it for the lowest pay. Many employers, it is true, would not have done this, but would have thought it fair and right, as well as the best policy in the long run, to observe a customary rate; but that left the worker dependent on the goodwill of an employer with whom he was in no position to argue. It is true again in the history of the labour market that periods of the excess of applicants over vacancies have alternated with others when it was the applicants that were scarce, and the competition of employers raised the pay they offered. But competition for jobs has recurred sufficiently often to burn itself in on the mind of the worker as a risk against which he—and his son after him—needs insurance. This insurance can be provided by an agreement among the applicants that whoever gets the job shall take it only at "the union rate". Formally, this is to counter one monopoly by forming another. But even when this has been done, the workers may still be at a disadvantage. If there is bargaining now about the rate for the job, it will be effectively between only one party on each side, but suppose the parties cannot agree on the rate—how much will each suffer from failure to fill the job? In general, the employer will lose only part of his profit, but the worker must go without his whole earnings; and in any case his reserves are likely to be lower. Herein lies the second disability to which the worker was liable who made his own bargain. Bargaining power is the power to change offered terms by withholding consent. Either party has that power to the extent that leaving the job unfilled will put the other party under greater pressure of loss or suffering than it does him. Under collective bargaining the worker is less likely to be under the greater pressure than when he bargains alone, partly because his union supports him through the stoppage, but even more because failure to agree now means for the employer not one vacant place merely but the stoppage of his whole works.

25. The two disabilities we have just examined both arise in the absence of effective competition in the labour market. Such competition would ensure that each worker had the benefit of the best offer that any employer would make for him, that a single rate would rule in the market at any one time for each type of labour, and that this was the highest at which all applicants could be employed. Collective bargaining would remedy the two disabilities if it arrived at that sort of rate. But can it not do more for the worker? Will there not generally be at least some groups of workers who by threat of strike can win a higher rate than the most active competition among employers would assure them if they bargained singly?

26. It has been generally held that indeed there will be some groups in that position. Of the various possibilities envisaged, two seem of the most practical importance. One arises where certain workers are indispensable and irreplaceable, but the sum of their pay is a small part of the total costs of the employer. Examples would be airline pilots, and newspaper press operators. Their position is the stronger if, as in these examples, an interruption of production is specially damaging to the employer. Even where this is not so, the cost of a big rise in the pay of this group alone will involve a proportionate rise in his total costs so small that he may well reckon it less than the cost of a stoppage. This will be so, however, only on one further condition, that his other employees will allow this group to raise its own pay, without being instigated—indeed, feeling themselves morally obliged—to insist upon equivalent advances for themselves. In the absence

of this condition, no one group can push forward on its own, and the employer must in practice deal with all his employees together, even if negotiations are separate. But this very comprehensiveness opens up a second possibility: let all the employees of all the firms that market a certain product bargain with those firms together, and they may be able to get a rise in pay although it will raise the cost of the product, because all the firms will bear it, and their competitive relations with one another will remain as before if each covers it by a higher price for his product. True, if this higher price resulted in a sharp fall in the quantity sold, jobs and profits would both suffer. It is a condition, therefore, of this possibility, that the demand for the product should be inelastic. But this condition is quite often satisfied, especially for industries that do not have to contend with foreign competition in their markets at home or abroad. In such cases, industry-wide collective bargaining can function as a price cartel.

27. These possibilities do not include the creation of scarcity—the raising of the pay an occupation commands by restricting entry to it. This device may be used by a party to collective bargaining, but is quite distinct from the bargaining, and has indeed been used by bodies that do not bargain at all. We are concerned only with the consequences that flow from bargaining collectively instead of singly, in a given state of supply and demand in the labour market. But it is true that if these consequences include a raising of the rate of pay and this induces employers to engage fewer workers, much the same effect comes about as when the supply of labour is restricted in the first place.

28. If the consequences of collective bargaining have been looked for only in rates of pay that are higher, not lower, than would obtain when workers bargain singly, that is because competition between workers for jobs is taken to be usually keener than competition between employers for workers. The single employer, it is said, has always been a monopoly in himself, and when a trade union is formed to bargain with him, that does but match one monopoly with another. But there have been many phases in which the employer, far from having any monopoly in the labour market, has been in active competition for labour. In such a situation collective bargaining may actually check the rise of pay. If a number of competing employers associate for a collective bargain, their competition may, it is true, be resumed after the settlement has been reached, and take effect as wage drift; but it is also possible that it will become less active in practice as well as in profession. In that case the rate of pay may rise less under collective bargaining than it would do if workers and employers bargained singly. It is even possible that the associated employers should enjoy a counterpart to the power of the union to raise the rate of pay when the rise is imposed on all firms selling in a given product market: when this common rate is fixed for all workers with qualifications which only the associated employers require, they have formally as much possibility of pushing it down as the union has of pushing it up. The monopoly is bilateral, and may work in either direction. But in each direction there are resistances that become stronger as time goes on and monopoly power is eroded. The power of the union to run the industry as a price cartel will be reduced as the buyers of the product learn to use substitutes, or new suppliers enter the field. The power of the employers to keep down the pay of a captive labour force will be reduced as its members find ways out of captivity and young entrants avoid it.

29. But these considerations remind us by their starkness of an essential factor that has been left out of the argument so far. In considering how the outcome of collective bargaining might differ from that of an effectively competitive market. we have relied on a calculus of coercion. But those who take part in collective bargaining do not use the language of that calculus. No doubt this is sometimes a matter of diplomacy, of public relations and the velvet glove; but generally it goes deeper. Collective bargaining is usually conducted on the assumption of common standards of what is fair and reasonable, standards common to the two sides and to the public whose opinion in the last resort may be decisive. A group whose bargaining power might enable it to drive its own rate of pay up will not generally try to exploit that power to the full, partly because that would seem barefaced exploitation, partly because what is seen as an unfair demand may be resisted on principle even though giving in to it would cost less. Employers generally accept the view that pay should wherever possible be raised, and are concerned in collective bargaining not so much to seize advantages as to transmit to their workers some of the pressures that the market puts on them. In the days

of the single bargain, custom was strong, and no doubt what was customary was thought equitable. Collective bargaining, no less, must be seen in its setting of prevailing notions about what is fair and reasonable.

30. This discussion suggests that we should look for the effects of collective bargaining in two features of the wage structure. One is the dispersion of rates paid to labour of a given grade in different employments: we should expect collective bargaining to reduce this dispersion, at least by enforcing a minimum that extinguishes the exceptionally low rates. But we should expect it not only to establish more of a common level in this way, but to raise that level, so that the workers who bargain collectively will be found to be earning more, grade for grade, than those who do not. The second feature of the wage structure in which we should look for the effects of collective bargaining is therefore the relative average earnings of groups of organised and unorganised workers in employments otherwise similar.

31. We can estimate the actual effects of collective bargaining at particular points only if we can compare what happens where it is established with what happens where it is absent but much the same kinds of labour are being engaged in much the same sort of economy. An unusual opportunity to do this has been afforded by the USA, where the coverage of collective bargaining has for long been more partial than in other countries of similar industrial development. The findings we shall set out are based on the many studies made by American economists of the comparisons so afforded. They have been able to compare the scatter of rates within local labour markets in the presence and absence of collective bargaining. They have also compared the levels of wages at a given time in sectors of the same industry where collective bargaining does and does not prevail; the relative wages in an industry before and after collective bargaining is established in it; and the movement of wages in the course of time under collective bargaining and elsewhere. They have further been able to compare the apparent effects of collective bargaining according as the workers concerned are less or more strongly organised. None of these comparisons is straightforward, in the sense that the presence or absence of collective bargaining is the sole difference between the two situations, but ways can be found of taking some of the other differences into account. Where two sectors of the same industry are being compared, for instance, they will commonly be in different regions which have their own prevailing differences in wage levels: what is done then is to compare not simply the levels of wages in the two sectors of the given industry, but the ratios which those levels bear to the wage of some grade of labour found in both sectors and not regulated by collective bargaining in either. Even after these precautions, no one of these studies by itself can reach conclusions rigorously; but taken together their findings show enough agreement to lend them probability. There seems no reason to believe that they do not apply to the British economy.

32. They suggest that collective bargaining has taken a marked effect in the first of the two ways we noticed, by substituting "the rate for the job" for a scatter of rates. The extent of variation found even within a local labour market in the absence of collective bargaining is remarkable: it is evidently possible for two firms in the same town, even in the same street, to go on paying very different rates to the same grade of labour, and not all of the difference is offset by other conditions of employment or by the level of exertion expected. Beyond this are wide regional variations. So far as these are common to most employments in a region, they may arise in the same way as differences between the levels of pay in different countries, but for any one occupation or grade of labour they often go beyond that. At any rate the coming of collective bargaining has been associated with a marked reduction in them. In all, the effect of collective bargaining has been to reduce greatly the differences between the rates of pay for the same kind of work that arise in practice from the inability of particular workers or groups of workers to deal with different employers.

33. It has not necessarily done this by bringing the rate for the job up to the level being paid already by the "best employers". On the contrary, the rates set by collective bargaining are generally thought to be limited by the capacity to pay of the weaker part of the industry. But this does not mean that their enforcement has not raised the wages of many workers, some of them substantially. In this respect it has acted like a statutory minimum wage. In the United Kingdom, indeed,

a kind of collective bargaining was instituted by statute to fulfil just this purpose. The " sweated " workers whom the Trade Boards were set up to help were such because they were tied to a particular employment, without effective access to alternative employers ; nor in their case did the cheapness of their work bring an extension of the demand for it through growing sales of the product.  The Trade Board was needed to do what more competition in the labour market could have done—raise the wages of particular groups of workers to the level generally prevailing for workers of their grade who had some effective choice of employers.

34. So far we have seen the effect of collective bargaining in a reduction of the disparities due to the imperfections of an actual labour market.  Has it done more than this?  Has it not only brought the lower rates up towards the higher, but raised these too?  The answer is certainly yes.  Most conspicuously that holds for certain groups that have been able to take advantage of their being indispensable yet accounting for only a small part of total costs.  The most notable case (already mentioned) is that of the commercial airline pilots, whose earnings (after allowance for length of working life) have been estimated to have stood in 1956 at from 21 to 34 per cent above those generally obtained by men of equivalent professional qualifications.  It has been remarked that one permissive condition here is the agreement of the public, as passengers, that their pilot had better be a highly paid type.  In a lesser degree the craft unions in building have been found to have exploited a similar situation—equipment that can be substituted for the craftsman's skill has been developed for particular operations but not for his functions as a whole.

35. But such cases as these, even in the aggregate, are not of great extent. Much more significant is the finding that even where the bargain covers a great part or the whole of the labour force and therefore takes a major effect on costs, unionization and the collective bargaining it brings with it have been associated with a substantial raising of the relative wage.  Gregg Lewis's survey and reworking of twenty recent studies has led him to estimate that in recent years the average wage of American workers who were union members was 10 to 15 per cent higher, relatively to that of other workers, than it would have been but for their unionism.[1]  This is in an economy where only about a quarter of the whole labour force is unionized.  In an economy like the United Kingdom in which collective bargain extends more widely some corresponding differential effect might still be expected between bargaining areas according as the unions concerned were less or more cohesive and militant.  But otherwise the advantage gained by one group of workers as it begins to bargain collectively will have been progressively reduced as others do the same.  The grounds for this conclusion are twofold.

36. First, the studies we have drawn on are agreed in finding that the raising of relative pay by collective bargaining is an impact and not a progressive effect. When a group begins to bargain collectively it is lifted in the league table, but after that it tends to hold its place, or change it only under the influence of market forces.  There is no evidence of any progressive divergence.  As successive groups establish collective bargaining, therefore, the old order of the league table will tend to be restored.

37. But this, it will be said, is still at a higher level all round ; if not a relative, at least an absolute advantage remains.  The reasons for doubting this provide the second ground for the conclusion that the gains brought by collective bargaining to any one group of workers diminish as more groups begin to bargain.  For such gains do not seem to have been made at the expense of profits.  Though we lack detailed studies of the impact of collective bargaining on profits, there is strong negative evidence in the absence of any complaint or discussion of the lower profitability of industries under collective bargaining.  We know that its coming has put some inefficient firms out of business, and that on others it has had a shock effect, forcing reorganisation and re-equipping, but there has been no cause to allege that profits have generally ruled lower in the sector of collective bargaining than elsewhere.  Where, then, did the impact effect come from?  American observers, used to an only partially unionised labour force, have laid stress on the lowering of the relative wages of unorganised labour: in so far as the two groups have a common employer, his ability to pay the unorganised has been

---

[1] H. Gregg Lewis: *Unionism and Relative Wages in the United States:  an empirical inquiry* (University of Chicago Press, 1963), pp. 4–5.

reduced by the gains of the organised, and in so far as their employers are different, the rise in the relative pay of the organised will check the growth of employment in that sector and cause more workers to compete for jobs in the other. Under the wider extension of organisation in the United Kingdom this effect is less likely. There remains the possibility already discussed, that collective bargaining becomes a way of adjusting not only pay but prices. In so far as the impact effect on wages is not offset by the shock effect on efficiency it will raise unit costs, and so long as the price of the product remains unchanged the profit margin will be reduced. But all firms will want to restore it, and know that their competitors want this too, and are more likely to follow another firm's rise than try to undersell it. Opportunity will then be taken to raise selling prices relatively to unit cost, it may be by an immediate rise, it may be only by retaining the benefit of reductions in unit cost that would otherwise have been passed on in lower prices. In any one industry the outcome will be the division of the net product in the same proportions as before, but a price to the buyer that is higher either absolutely or at least relatively. If one industry moves alone, that can raise its total proceeds ; but when all move together, they will all be raising their prices to one another. A compact instance is provided by " l-expérience Blum ". In the nine months following the return of the Popular Front in the summer of 1936, hourly wage-rates in French industry were raised by some 60 per cent. The effect was that the prices of industrial products generally rose in the same proportion. Only in so far as the prices of farm products lagged was there a gain in real wages.

38. There is thus reason to believe that the relative advantage conferred by the impact effect of collecting bargaining is unlikely to be maintained as the coverage of collective bargaining extends. We return to our findings on the general level of real incomes. Some redistribution of real income may persist between groups the demands for whose products are of differing elasticity—the sheltered or home market industries may gain, for instance, at the expense of the unsheltered and internationally competitive. But what effect of this kind there may be is in any case likely to be reduced as the economy approaches full employment. The studies of the differential effect of collective bargaining suggest that this has been at its greatest in times of generally slack demand and lack of competition between employers for labour. At a high level of demand the apparent effect has been much lower: in one way or another the demand for labour in the unorganised sector brings it near parity with the organised. A similar effect may be felt by an economy in which collective bargaining prevails in all sectors but has raised pay by more in some than in others.

39. The main effects of collective bargaining on the structure of wages and salaries may now be summarised as follows. Collective bargaining reduces the wide disparities between rates of pay for the same grade in different employments that in practice prevail in its absence. In doing this it substantially raises the pay of pockets of labour that have lacked the protection of access to alternative employment ; it provides a continuing protection against that disability, and enables the employee who remains in post to gain the rise for which he might otherwise have to seek alternative employment. For particular groups it may do more than this. A few groups, under special conditions of inelastic demand and permissive attitudes of other workers or the public, have been able to raise their relative pay greatly. More generally the coming of collective bargaining has been associated with a rise in relative pay of from 10 to 15 per cent. But it seems that this has been possible largely because collective bargaining functions as a price cartel ; and the relative gain of any one group is reduced as other groups adopt collective bargaining and raise their product prices too. In sum, collective bargaining distorts the structure of wages and salaries at a few points while making it more orderly and equitable at many others and leaving its main proportions unchanged.

40. It remains to be noted that collective bargaining has been the channel, and probably the indispensable channel, through which the form that advances in real wages should take has been decided—how much should be taken out in the pay packet and how much in shorter hours or fringe benefits. The institutions of collective bargaining provide for the formation of a common policy on these issues from time to time, and for the administration of changes some of which have to be made collectively if they are to be made at all. As productivity and standards of living continue to rise these issues are likely to be of increasing importance in shaping the whole way of life of the working community.

### III. THE ORGANISATION OF COLLECTIVE BARGAINING: BARGAINING AREAS

41. The preceding discussion may have served to delimit the consequences of collective bargaining. On the one hand, this bargaining does not seem to have much affected either the rise of the general level of real earnings or the main internal proportions of the pay structure. On the other hand, by protecting the worker from disabilities to which he is exposed if he bargains alone it has made a big difference to the pay of particular workers, and by reducing disparities between persons, firms and regions it has changed the pay structure considerably. Its influence in the course of the general level of money as distinct from real earnings, if only conjecturally or intermittently apparent in earlier years, has been unmistakable under full employment. It stands in any case as the accepted procedure through which changes in the general level and structure of pay, whether these changes are ultimately due to impersonal forces or lie within the discretion of the parties to the bargain, are in practice brought about. We can usefully examine its organisation in that light. Its basic function, we may say, is to provide for the administration of rates of pay by procedures that reconcile the interests and independence of the individual as far as possible with the forces of the market and the common interest. Its organisation may be well or ill adapted to the performance of that function in the circumstances of its day. We shall ask what forces have shaped the present organisation, and in the light of our findings consider what developments are practicable that would help it to meet the needs of our time.

42. Our study of the forces that have shaped the present organisation of collective bargaining can be usefully concentrated upon the bargaining area. This may be defined as comprising all workers whose rates of pay are adjusted in common. As such it may be both wider and narrower than the coverage of a negotiation. It will be wider, when a number of nominally distinct negotiations are in practice closely connected—when, for instance, one trade union negotiates separately with a number of different firms, but having made a key bargain with one of them obtains substantially similar agreements from the others. It will be narrower, when negotiation proceeds in two tiers, and the lower and broader tier only provides for very general changes, the actual rates of pay job by job depending on numerous negotiations in the upper tier. But for brevity we may treat the bargaining area here as if it coincided with the coverage of a single negotiation.

43. From the earliest days of collective bargaining down to its most recent developments, the bargaining area has been shaped by the interplay of a number of often conflicting forces. One of these has been the tendency for a given grade or occupation to receive the same rate throughout all firms and industries. This tendency arises in part from the individual's sense of justice: it seems plainly discriminatory to him that another man should be paid more than he for doing the same work, and if that does happen, it gives him a claim in equity for a rise that will re-establish " the rate for the job ". But the tendency also arises in part from the working of the market. Changes in the demand for a particular kind of work may take their first effect by differentiating the rate that is paid for it, but the function of such differentiation in a market economy is to extinguish itself by drawing labour away from the employments where the rate is lower to those where it is higher: the labour will be deployed most efficiently when it commands the same rate of pay in all employments. If this tendency to level out the rate of pay for a given occupation had the field to itself, bargaining areas would be coterminous with occupations. All the members of each occupation would bargain with all their employers. Both sides would come together from all industries in which they might be found. Members of other occupations would not take part, although they worked for the same employers. The craft unions with which British trade unionism began aimed in this way at fixing and holding a common rate for all their members in whatever employment, at least within each region, even though they sometimes announced the rate rather than negotiated it. To this day unions with distinctive occupational qualifications—the draughtsmen, for instance—work along the same lines. But the formation of the single occupational bargaining area has been restricted by a second force.

44. This is the close watch that most occupations and grades keep on differentials. They do so for more than one reason. The resentment that the craftsman often feels when the labourer's rate goes up relatively to his own is not just the

attitude of the dog in the manger. It arises in part from the difficulty of distinguishing between rises that are meant to change the wage structure and those that are part of a general rise: if the rise in the labourer's rate is seen in the latter light, it will appear as discriminatory. But more than this: the craftsman may regard his own rate as the Commonwealth Commission in Australia would see it—as made up of a basic rate for general labour and a margin for his own special skill. To raise the basic component without raising the total is actually to reduce the margin for the craftsman's distinctive asset. Insistence on the maintenance of customary differentials arises, therefore, partly out of the determination not to get left behind when there are general rises going, and partly out of concern with the differential, as the specific rate for the qualifications of a given grade or the requirements of a given job. Where this insistence is present any one occupation is unlikely to be able to bargain separately. It may wish to do so, and have reason to think it would gain if it did; but the employers will learn that whatever they grant to it will forthwith be demanded by the others, and go no farther with it than they are prepared to go with them. The tendency of the close watch on differentials is to bring all the grades it covers into the same bargaining area.

45. So far we have been concerned with forces that make for a single occupational or multi-occupational bargaining area. Whichever of these forms the area takes, it can cover one employer or many. The force that makes for the single employer area is the desire to make the most of each employer's capacity to pay; or, on the employer's side, to limit what he pays by that capacity. If the firms that are making bigger profits will generally agree to higher rates, a union will maximise the aggregate gains of its members, at least in the short run, if it bargains with each firm separately. It may also hope to get the best of both worlds, by bringing the initially lower-paying firms up towards the others, or striking a pattern bargain first where it expects to do best and then pressing other firms to follow the pattern. But employers equally may prefer to bargain separately, in so far as they regard their profitability as setting a limit on what they should concede, and believe they can ensure that it will do so. A big American corporation may on this account wish even to see a separate bargain for each of the " profit centers " between which its operations are divided.

46. But though the single employer area offers advantages in this way to both sides, it puts either side in an exposed position when on the defensive. A union in the old days trying to stave off a wage cut in a slump would be very conscious of its flanks. It could not hope to maintain the rate with one employer if his competitors could cut it and undersell him. To hold the line it must extend it across all employers who competed in the same product market. Employers recognising this would sometimes instigate the union to organise their competitors and " put a floor under competition " throughout the trade. For their own part, when resisting a claim for a rise, employers would find an advantage in negotiating together, for though one employer might be able to stave the rise off for his own part, if his competitors gave it he would have to follow suit or find himself placed in a difficult moral position and threatened with the loss of good workmen to his competitors. The advantages of multi-employer bargaining, however, were not so great for employers in the boom as they were for the union in the slump: particularly when a grade of labour became scarce, an employer would not mind taking the lead in raising the rate for it. In the slump, moreover, the employers often shared the interest of the union in holding the line throughout the product market, for if the rate was cut they would not expect a relief to their profit margins so much as a further cutting of the price of the product. Thus the multi-employer bargaining area was adopted as best suited for maintaining a minimum wage-rate against downward pressure.

47. But it also revealed its advantages as a means of raising the rate. Advances were easier to get when they would take effect all along the line. Any one employer, invited to settle for terms that would raise his unit labour costs, had to consider what would happen to his sales if he maintained his profit margin by raising the price of his product, and any adverse effect would be smaller if his competitors were having to raise their prices too. We have seen already how when the wage-bargain extends across all firms who sell in the same product market it may operate indirectly as a price cartel, and realise the benefit of any monopoly power the industry may possess when its price policy is co-ordinated. Though it has not

generally been possible to exploit this monopolistic potential of industry-wide bargaining overtly, the greater ease with which wage rises can be born when all competitors bear them alike has made for the adoption of the industry-wide area.

48. Thus there have been forces making respectively for the single occupational and the multi-occupational, for the single employer and the multi-employer bargaining area. Of the four possible types formed by the combination of these alternatives, one has come to predominate in practice in the western countries with developed systems of collective bargaining—the multi-occupational, multi-employer area. That it has done so implies the strength of the considerations of defensive strategy and of the reduction of price-competition in the product market. But these considerations have not been of overwhelming force: the bargaining area to which they lead shares the field with others and is itself subject to division and supplementation. The predominance of single-employer bargaining in the manufacturing industries of the USA, moreover, reminds us of how much in the formation of actual bargaining areas has depended upon accidents of history. Collective bargaining in American manufacturing grew up under legislation of which one branch promoted the representation of all the manual workers in a plant by a single union, and another deterred its management from entering into understandings with competitors even though these were lawful if for the purpose of collective bargaining. The firms is any one industry, moreover, were commonly scattered over great distances ; and a competitive and self-reliant spirit was regarded as an essential attribute of management. In British manufacturing, collective bargaining grew up more gradually, in earlier years, under different laws, in a country with greater regional concentration and a different culture of management. Its trade union structure, too, was different. In its effects upon the bargaining area, this structure may be regarded as another accident of history, for it had itself been shaped by more considerations than the aim of covering the best bargaining area alone ; it had also commonly taken shape first. Thus in various ways the present organisation of collective bargaining in each western country can be regarded only as the outcome of history, for this alone explains why different countries operate different organisations in circumstances themselves not so evidently different.

49. In one way this prompts caution: we are dealing with a product of evolution that has had to prove itself viable in its environment, and we cannot simply design a new shape for it on paper. But on the other hand there seems to have been nothing inevitable about the evolution. The conflicting forces that have borne upon it have made for different outcomes, of which one has predominated here and another there: in any one country it seems likely that arrangements different from its present ones could well have been arrived at and be working acceptably now. At least in the matter of bargaining areas, therefore, we can envisage substantial changes without leaving the practicable for the visionary. The actual course of evolution, moreover, has been adapted to the needs for defence and betterment of those who take part in bargaining, and has not necessarily served the common purpose of the economy. There seem to be two such purposes that the British organisation for collective bargaining now fails to serve.

50. One of these is the administration of the pay structure, that is the adjustment of the relative rates of pay of different occupations and grades. Our present organisation fails to provide adequately for this, for a number of reasons. Traditionally the function of collective bargaining has been to enforce *minimum* rates only, and to make *general changes* in these from time to time: the actual rates to be paid at any one time, save only such as were at the minimum, were not an object of bargaining. Nor could they very well be so in industry-wide bargaining. This will usually have taken over a great variety of rates that differed from firm to firm and from region to region. A common structure for the industry could have been bargained over only if one had been worked out, but the task of doing that was formidable. When different occupational unions associated for the purposes of a single bargain in one industry, moreover, they could best present a united front if they left customary differentials undisturbed: the unavoidable question whether their joint claim should be for a flat rate or a percentage rise all round might be sufficiently troublesome in itself.

51. None the less, the economy needs a way of working out agreed changes in the pay structure. Until recently, it is on the need to promote changes in the deployment of the labour force by adjusting relative earnings in different industries that stress has been laid ; but the experience of a number of countries

has shown that big changes in the deployment of the labour force between different industries have been brought about without any associated change in their relative earnings.[1] The relative pay of different occupations, however, is another matter. Ultimately, the only basis and justification of differences in the prevailing rates of pay of different occupations is that, at the numbers now demanded, the supply price of labour to them differs: the rate of pay required to attract and retain the number demanded is higher in one occupation that another. In the short run this principle of the supply price has made itself felt sharply when the pay of one occupation, such as the police or the nurses, has lagged behind that of others open to labour of similar qualifications. We know little of the effect on supply in the longer run of changes in pay common to all occupations at the same level of qualification. But if market forces make themselves felt here, they need to be accommodated: that is, it should be possible to change differentials, to raise the pay of one occupation without setting up a claim for an equal rise for others. To the extent, moreover, that the relative pay of different occupations and grades is fixed by market forces only within broad limits, there is room for social policy. The community may wish, for instance, to raise women's pay relatively to men's, or more generally to narrow the spread between the higher and lower paid occupations. On this account also it is desirable that the internal proportions of the pay structure should be brought under the administration of collective bargain-ing.

52. If a change in the differential between the pay of two occupations is to be agreed through bargaining, how should the bargaining be organised? When the occupations are at some remove from one another, and the members of each do not judge the fairness of their own pay by comparison with that of the other, no problem arises. But often the two occupations are related as different grades in a common employment. If then they bargain in different areas, there is nothing to stop a rise agreed for the one setting up a claim as of right for an equal rise for the other. This can be avoided only if the watch commonly kept on differentials is recognised as a factor that must be brought into the bargaining: that is, the parties to the differential must both take part in the negotiation, and the differential itself must be an object of negotiation. In general, negotiation of the pay structure requires a multi-occupational bargaining area, as in most present British bargaining ; but the narrowing of the former gap between the terms and conditions of the staff and manual grades implies that employees of all occupations should now be brought within the one negotiation. But the structure can be the subject of negotiation only if it has first been formulated. To do this for the first time is an immense task, but the examples of the coal industry in Britain and the steel industry in the USA show the possibility of assigning a multitude of jobs to a limited number of grades, each of which carries its common rate of pay or bracket of rates. Save in an industry whose processes are much alike firm by firm, however, an industry-wide structure is likely to need supplementation by job classifications drawn up and negotiated in the circumstances of particular firms.

53. The second need of the economy that is not met by our present organisation for collective bargaining has been set up by full employment—or, more exactly, by the expansive conditions of monetary demand under which full employment has been maintained. Our present bargaining areas were worked out in a world where changes in rates of pay within those areas were rare except as negotiated, and the settlement reached in each area depended mainly on its own position and prospects. Both of those conditions have now been removed. Many rates of pay are changed by agreements formal or informal at the place of work, or on the initiative of employers: the effective rate of pay has often come to stand well above the rate nominally applicable to the job, and the general level of pay continues to rise between the settlements reached for the bargaining area. These settlements, meanwhile, have effectively ceased to be limited by the particular circumstances of each area: the spontaneous development of the institution of the "annual round" has made it possible for each area to raise its pay at a rate limited only by the rate at which the others are concurrently raising theirs. Thus changes in pay are being brought about in two regions outside the control of the

---

[1] *Wages and Labour Mobility:* a study of the relation between changes in wage differentials and the pattern of employment (OECD 1965).

negotiators in our established bargaining areas—at the place of work; and by concertation at the national level.

54. If the movement at the place of work is to be brought under the control of negotiators, the present largely industry-wide bargaining areas need to be complemented by an accepted procedure for negotiation between the single employer and his employees. The object of the negotiation would be to agree a detailed schedule of job rates and working practices to be observed until a fixed date of expiry, when it would come up for renegotiation. The agreement should cover all employees, without distinction of staff and manual. The procedure would complement, not supersede, existing industry-wide negotiations, and the schedule should not conflict with any pay structure adopted in them. A firm could, however, negotiate a general supplement to industry-wide rates, as a payment for special contributions made by its workpeople to its profitability, or as a form of profit-sharing by negotiation, but a distinction would be maintained between this supplement and the rates for the jobs. "Productivity bargaining" is a particular operation that might be carried out under this procedure, but is no part of its main purpose, and is not to be identified with it; the extra pay arising from such an operation should in any case be treated as a supplement obtained by profit-sharing and not as a change in the schedule of rates. The distinction could be maintained more firmly if the schedule were based on a job evaluation.

55. Proposals for the recognition and establishment of single-employer bargaining have hitherto been opposed in this country on the ground that they would expose firms one at a time to the full bargaining power of national unions, and would result in whipsawing or leapfrogging. American experience of the "plant contract", however suggests that it is the unions rather than the employers who feel themselves constrained by the narrowness of the bargaining area. The unions generally try to widen the area, and establish a common rate throughout a number of competing firms; the management of any one firm clings to the limitation of its own settlement by its own capacity to pay. This limitation is real because the employees in negotiating their contract know that the management will take a strike rather than agree to terms that will put the firm out of business, and because their own job security is at stake. Where local pressures have been exercised in Britain unofficially and on one point at a time, this element of responsibility has been lacking; in an established procedure it is inescapable. But in any case the forces that bear on both employers and unions to shape bargaining areas will seldom allow the single-employer area to operate in isolation. The procedure in American manufacturing may be regarded as single-employer bargaining co-ordinated by industry-wide union policy: what is suggested here for Britain is industry-wide bargaining complemented by single-employer agreements. In their grievance procedure some British industries have already provided for a linking of the two bargaining areas, when failure to agree between management and employees leads on to works conference and district conference, and brings in officers of employers' associations and national unions. A similar procedure might prove applicable to the negotiation of single-employer agreements.

56. The second region in which recent changes in pay have been determined outside the control of our established procedures, that of the "annual round", constitutes a bargaining area none the less real for its being unintended and amorphous. In an economy maintaining full employment, market forces cannot determine the general rate of rise of pay, which is bound to remain discretionary. Hitherto this discretion has been exercised by spontaneous concertation, by a falling into step without conscious choice of what the step shall be. Since the choice is inescapable we need a procedure for taking it deliberately. Such a procedure is provided by a central framework agreement between the national centres of employers' associations and trade unions, which will lay down for an ensuing period limits within which negotiations in the smaller bargaining areas can proceed. These limits will not necessarily be uniform guidelines, but may provide for some diversity of change. A central agreement of this kind is possible only after a strenuous process of co-ordination of purposes and mutual adjustment of claims within each of the two sides, and implies a high level of internal communications as the means to the community of outlook which alone allows of such adjustment. The recent development of its early warning system by the Trades' Union Congress is to be regarded accordingly as a landmark.